The Carolingians

THE MIDDLE AGES SERIES

Ruth Mazo Karras, General Editor
Edward Peters, Founding Editor

A complete list of books in the series
is available from the publisher.

The Carolingians

A FAMILY WHO FORGED EUROPE

PIERRE RICHÉ
Translated from the French by
MICHAEL IDOMIR ALLEN

PENN

UNIVERSITY OF PENNSYLVANIA PRESS

Philadelphia

This work was translated with assistance
from the French Ministry of Culture

10 9 8 7

Published by
University of Pennsylvania Press
Philadelphia, Pennsylvania 19104-4011

Les Carolingiens: une famille qui fit l'Europe by Pierre Riché
copyright © 1983 by Hachette

Library of Congress Cataloging-in-Publication Data
Riché, Pierre
    [Carolingiens. English]
    The Carolingians : a family who forged Europe / Pierre Riché ; translated from the
French by Michael Idomir Allen.
        p.   cm. — (Middle Ages series)
    Includes bibliographical references and index.
    ISBN 0-8122-3062-0 (cloth). ISBN 0-8122-1342-4 (paper)
    1. Carolingians. 2. France—History—To 987. 3. Europe—
History—476—1492. 4. France—Kings and rulers. 5. Middle Ages—
History 6. Civilization, Medieval. I. Title. II. Series.
DC70.R5313   1993
944'.01—dc20   91-303532
                                                                                     CIP

For my children and grandchildren, European citizens of the third millennium

Contents

Translator's Note

In *The Carolingians*, Pierre Riché seeks to trace how one family, its off-spring, and its allies helped to bring about a new reality between the seventh and tenth centuries A.D. It is a sketch of the spatial, cultural and spiritual integration of Europe in terms of the families and individuals who first achieved it. Thus the story that Professor Riché recounts is at once straightforward and complex. Its themes develop and coalesce, but they hover over a wash of names and places that might risk distracting or deterring the reader were they less deftly presented.

The text draws on a large body of historical research and offers an introductory synthesis in palatable form. In the English translation, I have sought to ensure that the book would remain what Professor Riché intended. This has often required me to expand on geographic and other details likely to be unfamiliar to North Americans, though I suspect that many readers will still find a historical atlas helpful. Wherever primary sources are quoted, I have sought to base my translation on the Latin originals to insure clarity and accuracy.

After some reflection, I concluded that most readers would find an English-language list of "Suggested Works for Further Reading" more valuable than the largely French and German bibliography of the original edition. Quite brief, my own list includes a selection of classic treatments, translated sources, and recent publications in English that build on the French and German scholarship noted by Professor Riché in the original bibliography. As a measure of economy, I chose not to reproduce the "Chronological Table of Events" found in the French edition, trusting the text to speak for itself. At the request of the publisher, I have reduced the number of maps and genealogical tables.

A chief merit of *The Carolingians* is to remind us that the achievements of the Carolingian period were wrought by a great nexus of families and individuals. Both a place and an idea, Europe was forged by men and women.

Preface

Europe has lately become an object of reflection, debate, and hope. Whoever speaks of Europe also inevitably seeks to trace its origins in the distant past, to lay hold of its roots.

For some, the point of departure is the Roman conquest. Rome unified a portion of the western world stretching from Africa to Great Britain, created towns and highways to link them, and erected physical monuments whose vestiges remain today. Yet the Roman world left a durable mark only among the thoroughly romanized lands of the south. Few inroads were made east of the Rhine or north of the Danube, while the western lands of the Empire succumbed to the barbarian invasions of the fifth century.

At this point, there arose a Europe at once Roman and barbarian, where various new peoples—Franks, Anglo-Saxons, Burgundians, and Lombards—settled and renamed the lands they occupied. These peoples introduced their own social forms, and they established language boundaries that still exist today. Compared with the Empire that remained in the east, this barbarian Europe was little more than an assemblage of rival petty kingdoms that a veneer of rudimentary Christianity could do little to unify.

Yet must we await the twelfth or thirteenth century to witness the awakening of Europe and its first flowering? Did Europe only become conscious of itself when its crusaders embarked on the conquest of the east, when urban centers and national monarchies took on clearly recognizable forms?

This is not my view. For this reason, I wished to trace the emergence of Europe in the period that spans the seventh to the early eleventh century, the period that witnessed the formation of the Carolingian Empire and its aftermath. In this interval, we can discern the first European unity, the first contours of a broad new civilization from which medieval Europe would emerge. In the seventh century, Europe was as yet only a geographic term. Thus, it sufficed for Isidore of Seville (d. 636) to echo the definition of the ancient geographers in his *Etymologies*: across from Asia and Africa, Europe was the space that extended from the river Don to Spain and the Atlantic Ocean. By the ninth century things had changed. Europe had gradually acquired a collective being vested with what we might call a "corporate identity." The political, cultural, and spiritual activity of laymen and churchmen had fostered the creation of a common European fold stretching from the Atlantic to the Vistula and the plains of the middle Danube.

This transformation resulted in large part from the activities of a single noble family and of the families related and allied to it. The Carolingians, their relatives and their followers became masters first of Gaul and then of much of the west. By tracing the destiny of this family, I shall examine the parallel history of Europe. I shall stress the role of outstanding personalities who, profiting from favorable social and political circumstances, imposed themselves by force, diplomacy, and culture. For this period at least, it seems impossible to discount the personal role of kings, princes, conquerors, missionaries, and even artists, whose creative powers influenced peoples of diverse origins and backgrounds.

The work wrought by the Carolingians and their successors has often been misjudged by historians who speak of Carolingian "illusions" and "smoke screens," or of the "missed start" or even "misstart" of Europe. It is no mystery that Charlemagne's empire failed to endure as he would have hoped. Yet this empire survived him by a century, to be revived by the self-styled "new Charlemagne," Otto the Great, whom it also long outlived. Within it arose the principalities which over centuries nurtured Europe's nations and institutions. The activity of Charlemagne himself captivates our attention. Personally, he enjoyed an exceptional destiny, and by the length of his reign, by his conquests, legislation and legendary stature, he also profoundly marked the history of western Europe. Too often, however, his achievements have been allowed to overshadow those of his predecessors, especially those of Pippin, his father, as well as those of his successors, in particular Charles the Bald. It is equally important not to overlook the activity of the many nobles related to the Carolingian house, and likewise the achievements of the kings and emperors of the tenth century who equally "forged Europe."

In order to understand how Carolingian Europe emerged, it is necessary to review political, social, and religious events from the time when the ancestors of the Carolingians first laid the foundations of their power up to the end of the first millennium. The history of this period is often obscure, especially in the tenth century, but I have attempted to present its outlines as clearly as possible. First, I trace the development of the Carolingian family from its beginnings in Austrasia in the seventh century to its first successes in the mid-eighth. I then consider the importance of the reigns of Pippin and Charlemagne. Following this, I examine the transformation of the Carolingian Empire in the ninth century and, in a later section, the organization of regional principalities and the rebirth of the empire. I conclude with a general portrait of European civilization emphasizing the varied activities of princes in the domains of politics, religion, economy, and culture.

It is my hope that this book will be of service to all who are interested in the ages that were once called "dark." An acquaintance with them is indispensable to understanding the emergence of European civilization.

Introduction: Western Europe in the Seventh Century

The seventh century has long suffered from a bad reputation. Whereas in the sixth the west is thought to have basked in the last rays of Roman civilization, it supposedly plunged thereafter into a profound darkness that overtook everything—government, culture, and social institutions. The west was seemingly devoured by unremitting tumult, brutality, and anarchy until the Carolingians took control of matters.

I take a rather different view of the seventh century. For it also laid the groundwork of the western cultural and political community that contemporaries began to call Europe. During the seventh century, an array of social, political, religious, and economic structures emerged that combined to reshape the west's inner fabric and outer appearance.

THE DECLINE OF BYZANTINE POWER

At the death of the Emperor Justinian in 565, the Mediterranean was still the heartland of the civilized world. Having reconquered Africa, Italy and southern Spain from the Vandals and the Goths, Justinian could entertain the illusion of having taken back the western empire that his predecessors "had lost by their indolence." Yet only three years after his death, the Lombards invaded an Italy that the twenty-year-long reconquest had bled to exhaustion. They firmly established their domination in the north—to be known henceforth as Lombardy—and founded the duchies of Spoleto and Benevento, whereby they sought to cut links between Rome and Ravenna, the Byzantine administrative center on the Adriatic coast. The power of Byzantium was too distant, and from this time on Italy was largely left to fend for itself. The Roman institutions and civilization which the Ostrogothic King Theodoric (d. 526) had protected slowly disappeared. Pope Gregory the Great (590–604) viewed with horror the ruin of what had still been the greatness of Rome in the sixth century:

> What has become of Rome, who seemed formerly to be the mistress of the world? Where is the Senate? Where are the people? Where are all those who

used to relish in her glory? Where are their attendants, their pride? The prophet's words are fulfilled in Rome: "Enlarge thy baldness as the eagle" (Micah 1:9). Human baldness is limited to the head. The eagle, however, becomes completely bald when it ages, losing its plumage entirely.

Gregory was painfully witnessing not the end of the world, but rather the end of *a* world.

In the seventh century, Byzantium lost control of many of its Italian lands and also of the southern coast of the Mediterranean. Over several decades Muslim Arab forces conquered the Levant, Egypt, and finally North Africa. In 698 Carthage slipped permanently from Byzantine hands, and by the beginning of the eighth century Arab commanders led Berber forces against Spain. Although the Visigoths had built up one of the strongest barbarian states, their kingdom collapsed in a matter of weeks. With it perished a brilliant civilization whose classical culture was vividly exemplified by Isidore of Seville (d. 636). The Visigothic leaders who remained took refuge in the north of the Iberian peninsula, in what would become the Kingdom of the Asturias. Their ties with Byzantium and the Mediterranean world were broken. However ancient, these ties had also made for weakness; they had opened the way to invasion.

Thus, a considerable portion of the Mediterranean coastline passed into Arab hands. Even though—contrary to the view of Henri Pirenne*— links between east and west were not completely broken, the Byzantine emperors, who faced their own struggles against Islam, the Persians, the Slavs, and internal disorder, progressively lost interest in the west. Slavic inroads into the Balkans also produced a partition of sorts between the two halves of the old Roman Empire. After the Mediterranean ceased to be the center of gravity in the west, we can discern to the north, amid the coastal regions of the English Channel and the North Sea, the outlines of a new inter-regional forum for products, people, and ideas.

THE CONVERSION OF ENGLAND

The Christianization of England at the beginning of the seventh century made this "northern Mediterranean" possible, and the importance of the Anglo-Saxon mission cannot be overestimated. Thanks to the initiative of

---

*The Belgian historian Henri Pirenne viewed the loss of the Mediterranean to Muslim control as more or less complete. For him it marked the opening of a great and decisive divide between east and west, which resulted in the northerly refocusing of western life and trade. His influential ideas on this subject are crystalized in Henri Pirenne, *Mohammed and Charlemagne*, trans. Bernard Miall (London: Allen and Unwin, 1939; with frequent reprints). See also Alfred F. Havighurst, ed., *The Pirenne Thesis: Analysis, Criticism, and Revision*, 3d ed. (Lexington, Mass.: Heath, 1976).—*Trans.*

Gregory the Great, a pope of Roman culture but a man able to look beyond the horizons of the old Mediterranean, a new world was converted to Christianity. The Angles, Jutes, and Saxons had progressively overrun the land that would become known in the seventh century as England. The indigenous Celtic peoples had been forced to submit or flee to the western hinterland of Wales, Cornwall, and Cumberland. The Celts, like the Irish, had been Christians, yet, isolated from the Mediterranean world by invasions on the continent, they had lived apart and adopted religious rites and practices that differed from those current in Rome. The Celts avoided all contact with their Anglo-Saxon conquerors and refused to work for their conversion to Christianity so as not "to find them again in Paradise." Thus Rome moved to convert the Anglo-Saxons. The first mission sent to Kent by Gregory the Great succeeded in baptizing the king and his war band, but the complete conversion of England required over a century. Rome attended to the needs of the newborn church by sending monks, priests, and manuscript books. In 653, the Anglo-Saxon Wilfrid left to study religion in Rome rather than among the Irish as was the common practice. Then, in 669, a second mission led by Theodore and Hadrian was sent from Rome, and the English church was firmly and definitively established. Throughout its long history, the Church of England has had to recall—with feelings of pride or regret—that its birth was wrought by monks and the papacy.

After 630 Roman monks and their disciples often found themselves in the company of the Irish who began to evangelize the lands of northern England. After much contention, some of these Irish, or Scots, as they were called, accepted Roman liturgical and disciplinary observances at the Synod of Whitby in 664, an event that further enhanced the influence of the papacy in this part of the west. Some Irish monks also went beyond the confines of England to Gaul, where they established new links between the British Isles and the continent.

Along with religious exchanges, this period also witnessed new developments in the domains of trade and coinage. Continental ports on the English Channel and the North Sea—Rouen, Quentovic, and Dorestad—received pilgrims and merchants from Britain. The Rhine, Scheldt, and Meuse rivers served as natural highways into the interior, where Frisian traders and pirates plied the waters as intermediaries between formerly separate worlds. After 650, these Frisians minted and used a silver coin, the *sceatta*, which gradually replaced the gold coinage of antiquity. The dawn of northern trade and the advent of silver coinage—destined to predominate until the thirteenth century—marked the beginning of a new era.

ECONOMIC RENEWAL

Gaul, and more especially the part of Gaul north of the Loire, profited most from the new patterns of trade. In the sixth century Merovingian rulers had extended their realm to the Mediterranean, but increasingly they looked to the Germanic lands, as though to anticipate and prepare the footings of Carolingian Europe. In 536 the Franks gained control of the lands of Alemannia, bounded by the Neckar, Rhine, Danube, and Iller rivers. Dagobert I (d. 639) probably established dukes over the territory and commissioned for the Alemans the earliest written code to regulate their legal dealings, the *Pactus alemanorum*. Likewise, the Bavarians—who first settled along the upper Danube and later across the region bounded by the Alps and the Danube, Iller, and Enns rivers—were administered by several noble families, the most eminent of which were the Agilolfings. Yet the prologue of the first Bavarian law code of about 630 also recalls how "these dukes must be confirmed by the Frankish king." Thuringia, another region, lay between the Main, Werra, Unstrut, and Saale rivers, and was subject to the Franks after 531. Of Frankish origin, the dukes of Thuringia were bound to protect Austrasia from eastern menaces posed first by the Saxons and then by the Slavs.

In the course of the sixth century, Slavs migrated upstream along the Danube and across the great plains to the north, occupying lands that the Germanic peoples had abandoned. Their progress was hastened by pressures applied from behind by a new Asiatic people, the Avars, who settled in the Danube basin, much like the Huns of the fifth century. About 625, Slavic tributaries revolted against the Avars and banded together under the leadership of a Frankish merchant, Samo, a trader in slaves and furs. Samo's dominion ranged over Bohemia, Moravia, Lower Austria, and Carinthia, that is, from Thuringia to Friuli. In 631 Dagobert sought unsuccessfully to subdue Samo, probably in order to protect other merchants who followed the Danube trade route, but the "empire" persisted until 660, when it abruptly disappeared after Samo's death. Dagobert could not, or would not, push further east to attack the Avars, and they remained fixed in central Europe until the destruction of their Ring by Charlemagne.

GAUL UNDER DAGOBERT

The eastward advance of the Merovingians benefited from the relative political stability of the first half of the seventh century. Clovis had established the Merovingian dynasty within a unified kingdom, but his sons and grandsons proceeded to break up the realm like any other inherited property. Each prince thus governed a fraction of the kingdom (*Teilreich*) and often wrangled bitterly to gain control of lands ruled by his relatives. As home of the most abiding remnants of Roman civilization, Aquitaine was especially coveted, thought the region's inhabitants struggled to gain their independence. North of the Loire, ferocious internecine wars were fought by the rulers of Neustria, or Francia proper (which lay between the Seine and the Somme), and those of Burgundy, Austrasia, and the territory of Reims with its Rhine appendages. After 613 the entire territorial patrimony—the realm (*regnum*) of the Franks—was fortunate to come under the control of a single king, first Chlotar II and later Dagobert I. The so-called "century of Dagobert," which in fact lasted 25 years, was a period of comparative stability. By means of intimidation or diplomacy, the kings were able to hold together the disparate patchwork of Gaul with limited concessions to regional particularism.

During this period, the coalescence of the various national groups began to bear fruit. Although each maintained its own customs and legal remedies, they were collectively subject to the same public law. The counts set up in each administrative center (*civitas*) represented the authority of the king. They called together public assemblies, pronounced justice, and levied taxes. All free men were bound by military service, and as such they gradually came to sense that they were members of a common fold. In the face of enemies of the kingdom, they were all "Franks." Among the nobles who were to become the leading force in Gaul, there numbered both "senators" of Gallo-Roman extraction and Frankish chieftains. Marriages linked the great families. In their desire to serve the king, nobles sent their sons to the royal court at the coming of manhood. The court itself became a sort of "business school," graduating functionaries and military officers. Thus the court of Chlotar II and his successor Dagobert included from Aquitaine, young men such as Desiderius of Albi, future bishop of Cahors, and Eligius of Limoges; from Neustria, the likes of Dado, better known as Audoen, bishop of Rouen; and from Austrasia, men like Paul, future bishop of Verdun. These men all proved themselves as servants in the royal administration, directing such services as the royal treasury. They became counts and later bishops.

EPISCOPAL POWER

The alliance between the royal house and the church buttressed the power of the Merovingian monarchy. Their partnership dated from the fifth century. In an age when other barbarian princes in the west adhered to heretical Arian beliefs, the pagan Clovis opted for catholic Christianity. He did not suspect that his choice would have weighty consequences for the history of his lineage and kingdom. Long before the Carolingians chose to assert the title authoritatively, the Merovingian king called himself the "elect of God" and considered the bishops as his foremost supporters.

Established in his town, the bishop collaborated with the count in the proper administration of the locale and often rose in defense of the inhabitants against the tyranny of public officials. But too often these former officials maintained their own past habits and favored their administrative over their spiritual duties. Thanks to the monks who came from the British Isles and their followers, a part of the clergy rediscovered its spiritual call.

MONASTICISM

The groundswell of interest in monasticism is the great hallmark of the seventh century in both Gaul and the west as a whole. Whereas important monastic centers in the sixth century were chiefly situated in Provence, Burgundy, and Aquitaine, northern and eastern Gaul now welcomed numerous new houses of monks and nuns. This change was in large measure a result of the arrival of Irish monks and their prodigious success. Their example drew followers attracted by their severe austerity, nonconformism, and spiritual independence. Although the ritual practices and customs that they brought from Ireland offended some Merovingian bishops, they also fascinated many lay men and women. Kings, bishops, and nobles established monks on their lands and gave them protection. The primitive huts first used to house the new bands of monks and nuns were replaced by large permanent buildings. Soon, monastic houses looked much like any other large domain. They attracted peasant laborers, possessed dependents or slaves, and obtained royal charters of privilege and immunity. In a word, they became forces to be reckoned with.

This success did not diminish the religious zeal of the monks. In the northern and eastern lands of Gaul, they were the most active agents of Christian conversion. They soon adopted a mixed monastic observance that combined Irish elements with the milder Rule of Saint Benedict, which at that time was known only in Italy and England. This practice lent greater stability to their monastic institutions. The brilliant success of the Irish and Frankish monks of Gaul and their Anglo-Saxon counterparts brought considerable prestige and influence to the papacy in the west.

THE PAPACY

After the death of Gregory the Great in 604, there followed a succession of 22 seventh-century popes, of whom only three reigned for more than seven years. They were obliged to defend their city against the Lombards and to struggle against the Byzantine emperors, who sought to impose on them novel theological views. Yet the popes slowly managed to consolidate their position. The final conversion of the Lombards to Catholic Christianity in about 680 gave cause to hope for peace in Italy. Whereas Martin I was deported on imperial orders in 653, the people of Italy guarded Sergius I (687–701) from the same fate. In the course of the seventh century, the pope's Lateran Basilica rounded out a liturgy that would later become a model for the whole west. While the bishops of the barbarian kingdoms were united behind their kings, they also upheld the primacy of the bishop of Rome, the vicar of Christ. Pilgrimages to Rome and the tombs of the apostles greatly increased. Throughout the west, churches dedicated to Saint Peter and Saint Paul multiplied, and monasteries such as Bobbio and Jarrow placed themselves under direct papal protection. Well before the papacy and the Carolingians sealed their alliance, the pope represented the highest moral authority of the west, or of Europe. Saint Columbanus seems to have sensed this when he called Pope Boniface IV (d. 615) "the head of all the churches of all Europe."

This portrait has traced the principal contours of the west in the seventh century. It is meant to set the stage for understanding how one Austrasian noble family would gradually distinguish itself from the rest, first imposing its authority in Gaul and then over the greater part of Europe.

Part I

The Rise of the Carolingians (from the Early Seventh to the Mid-Eighth Century)

The history of Carolingian Europe began with the rise of a noble family whose existence was first noted by chroniclers of the early seventh century. This family profited from disruptions in Merovingian Gaul in order to impose itself first in Austrasia and then across the entire Frankish kingdom. Its rise to political dominance proceeded by fits and starts and often with real difficulty, but in the course of a century and a half the Carolingians persisted against every obstacle. They came to occupy the first place in the kingdom, and by the mid-eighth century they were the masters of the Frankish royal family.

1. The Beginnings of the Carolingian Dynasty

AUSTRASIA

The good fortune of the early Carolingians began with two noble families settled in an area of the Frankish realm known since the close of the sixth century as Austrasia. One of three kingdoms in Merovingian Gaul, Austrasia stretched from Reims in the west to the upper valley of the Weser River in the east, and from the mouths of the Meuse and the Rhine in the north down to the headwaters of the Meuse and the Mosel, at the plateau of Langres. Thus Austrasia was traversed by the Meuse, the Mosel, and the middle Rhine with its tributaries. It covered the former Roman provinces of *Belgica Prima*, *Germania Prima*, *Germania Secunda*, and the eastern part of *Belgica Secunda*, whose respective capitals had been at Trier, Mainz, Cologne, and Reims. In addition, the kings of Austrasia had extended their realm across the Rhine into the valley of the Main and up to the frontiers of Thuringia, Alemannia, and Bavaria—a small duchy controlled from without by Frankish influence. This continued contact with Germanic lands made Austrasia the most germanized of the kingdoms. Traces of Roman civilization remained in a few towns in the form of more or less ruinous ancient monuments and pockets of romanized inhabitants. In the course of the sixth century, the Franks restored former Roman episcopal sees along the Rhine at Mainz, Speyer, and Worms, on the Meuse at Verdun and Maastricht, and on the Mosel at Trier and Metz. But the decline of Trier had opened the way for Metz to serve as capital of Austrasia.

NOBLE FAMILIES

Yet if towns were home to episcopal centers and county seats, the realities of life lay outside them, on the great domains of the nobility. By the end of the sixth century this nobility of Roman and Germanic extraction had become the dominant force in Austrasia as in other parts of the west. Initially, the noble had been a comrade at arms and companion in peace of a chieftain, and thereby had acquired grants of land or taken them for himself. He then continued to serve his leader, now a king, and his lineage distinguished him from other people. His family descended from a note-worthy forebear, whose name passed down from one generation to the next. He was marked as well by his way of life, his dress, and his arms. Above all, the noble was a soldier, and in death he was buried with his horses and his arms. The nobility possessed vast, diffuse domains, com-prising thousands of hectares scattered in patches across different regions. The group maintained itself by exploiting these domains, by hunting in the forests and farming the arable land with free peasants or bonded la-borers. Slavery did not disappear with the advance of Christianity. War-fare, in fact, had the contrary effect of boosting the trade in slaves, from which some great merchants grew rich. These slaves labored in the work-shops attached to the house of their master or on the outlying fields. The great proprietors increasingly opted to establish their slaves on individual plots. The result was a mixing of bonded laborers with the free peasantry, which itself came increasingly under noble control. Thus emerged the out-lines of the great medieval domain, the *villa*. It included the demesne, or land of the lord, as well as the individual peasant allotments.

Established in a fortified house, the noble ruled freely over the people who served him, and over his landed possessions, which he sought to expand by purchase or marriage. His aim was to increase the wealth that made for material strength, friendships, and political allegiance; these in turn opened the way to political advancement. Every noble harbored the dream of ruling the lands in which he lived, either as the king's servant or, should the royalty grow weak, as the king's rival.

From the middle of the sixth century, the Austrasian nobility profited from recurrent wars between the kings of Neustria and Austrasia. At the death of Chlotar I in 561, the kingdom of Austrasia passed to Sigebert I while his brother Chilperic I inherited Neustria. The two brothers pro-ceeded to make war on each other. After the notorious Fredegund, wife of Chilperic, arranged for the murder of Sigebert, his widow, the Visigoth Brunhild, ruled Austrasia in the name of her son Childebert II and then on behalf of her grandsons Theudebert and Theuderic. When in turn these two brothers raised arms against each other, Chlotar II of Neustria, the son of Chilperic, sought to intervene and subdue Austrasia on his own account. Brunhild's authoritarian manner had disaffected the Austrasian nobility, and in 613 they rallied behind Chlotar II. Among the leading men who worked for the defeat and death of Brunhild figured two ancestors of the Carolingians, Arnulf and Pippin.

ARNULF AND PIPPIN I

In the eighth and ninth centuries, the story of Arnulf underwent mythical retouching as part of an effort to exalt the achievements of this glorious forebear of the Carolingians. Fabricated legends connected him with the nobility of Aquitaine and even went so far as to make him a scion of the Merovingian family, a fantasy to be sure. On this account, it is best to follow Arnulf's biography as written in the mid-seventh century by an anonymous contemporary.

Arnulf was born about 580, to a family that possessed vast domains in the Woëvre plain (an expanse lying between the Mosel and Meuse rivers) as well as in the vicinity of Worms. In his youth, Arnulf learned to read and write under a tutor; such was the tradition among noble families who wished to outfit their children with the rudiments of learning and a religious upbringing. With the coming of adolescence, he moved on to the royal court, as did many well-born sons of the time, where he was placed in the care of Gundulf, the mayor of the palace and a landowner near Metz who seems to have stemmed from the family of Gregory of Tours. Arnulf distinguished himself by his military skills and entered the service of King Theudebert II, son of Childebert II. He became a manager of royal domains and was also entrusted with administrative duties in the counties. Despite his success, Arnulf probably began to dream with his friends Romaric and Bertulf of leaving the world and joining the Irish monks settled since 590 near the Vosges highlands. Although Columbanus had been obliged to flee to exile in Italy, he had left disciples whose brand of ascetic life appealed to youthful Austrasian nobles. Nevertheless, under pressure from his parents, who sought to transmit and augment the family patrimony by marriage, Arnulf agreed to wed a young woman of illustrious birth. The marriage produced many children, and to two of the sons, Chlodulf and Ansegisel, we shall have occasion to return. A leading figure at the court, Arnulf cast his lot against Brunhild, as noted above, and rallied behind Chlotar II. In doing so, he linked his interests to those of Pippin, a fellow nobleman. The marriage of Ansegisel, son of Arnulf, with the daughter of Pippin would strengthen this tie (see Table 2).

Known since the thirteenth century as Pippin of Landen (from the name of one of his domains), but better termed Pippin the Elder or Pippin I, this noble also came from an immensely wealthy landed family. The domains of this clan lay, however, in a different area of Austrasia, in Brabant, Hesbaye, and the vicinity of Namur—in the basin of the lower Meuse, the river highway that, as noted above, became a major axis of

economic life in northern Europe. Pippin had married Itta, sister of Mo-
doald, the future bishop of Trier. She was a wealthy heiress and celebrated,
as one text reports, "on account of her virtues, the extent of her lands and
the number of her slaves." The territories near Metz on the one hand
and those along the lower Meuse on the other constituted together the
material underpinnings of the early Carolingians.

When Chlotar II became conqueror and master of the entire Frankish
realm in 613, he rewarded the two noble families that had supported him.
Around 614, Chlotar offered the vacant bishopric of Metz to Arnulf,
whose administrative and religious merits the king appreciated. The duties
of bishop of Metz were important ones owing to the town's role as capital
of the Austrasian kingdom. Within the town of 70 hectares walled with
Roman fortifications, the cathedral of Saint Stephen, the baptistery, and
other churches formed a special quarter; in the southern section lay basilicas and monasteries, of which the famous St. Pierre-aux-Nonnains remains to this day. A Merovingian bishop was more than the leader of his
clergy; he was the watchful administrator who supervised the working of
his town and assisted the king in political matters. Arnulf wielded an ac-
cumulation of administrative and religious duties, since, as his *vita*, or
"saint's life," reports, he continued to hold his former duties as *domesticus*
and *palatinus* (steward and courtier). Moreover, when Chlotar II chose to
accommodate Austrasian particularism by establishing his ten-year-old son
Dagobert at Metz, the king entrusted Arnulf with the upbringing of the
young prince and the government of the realm. To share this heavy responsibility, Chlotar II named Pippin as mayor of the palace of Austrasia.

The duty of mayor of the palace was an ancient one. In the sixth
century, the *maior palatii* was attached to the person of the king or queen,
and he oversaw the managers of the royal domains. This important responsibility vested great power in the mayor, who subsequently became
the king's principal collaborator and sometimes his rival. When Pippin I
was named mayor of the palace of Austrasia, he in fact ruled the kingdom
together with Arnulf. Soon he ruled it alone.

Now about forty years of age, Arnulf returned to the resolve of his
youth and took up monastic life. He resided increasingly at hermitages
situated on his domains around Metz and along the fringe of the Vosges
highlands. His friend Romaric had left the court around 613. After spending several years at Luxeuil, Romaric founded the monastery of Habendum
on his own properties, which later came to be known as Remiremont.
Arnulf hoped to join him and relinquish his episcopal responsibilities, but

Chlotar II refused permission. Only after the death of the king in 629 did Arnulf succeed. He retired to a place near Habendum in the company of a few monks and lepers whom he served in humility. There he died between 643 and 647. Buried at Remiremont, he immediately gained a reputation as a saint. This renown would serve the future prestige of his family.

RIVAL FAMILIES

Pippin now governed alone as mayor of the palace. The chronicler known as Pseudo-Fredegar favored the Pippinids, or progeny of Pippin, and he presented the mayor himself as "the wisest of all," a well-informed and faithful counselor who loved justice, and so on. Other sources reveal that Pippin was hard pressed to restrain other noble Austrasian families who likewise sought to play an active role in religion and politics. The Pippinids and the Arnulfings—in the person of Arnulf's sons, the *domestici* (royal retainers) Ansegisel and Chlodulf—were two great, closely allied families, but they also had to contend with other ambitious clans whose wealth and power were considerable.

Chrodoald was precisely such a rival. About 624, this wealthy ancestor of the Agilolfings—later a leading family in Bavaria—had sought to harm the interests of Arnulf and Pippin. The bishop and the mayor complained to King Dagobert, who temporized, but finally ordered Chrodoald's murder. Here we have one example of the rivalries afoot among leading individuals, or rather among their families, since vendettas and mutual hatred were inevitably a family affair.

The Gonduins were another rival clan established in the vicinity of Toul and along the borders of Burgundy. They contributed significantly to the expansion of Columbanian monasticism. In 614, Gonduin received the abbot of Luxeuil, Eustasius, into his domain near the source of the Meuse. At the prompting of Waldebert of Luxeuil, Gonduin's daughter Salaberga founded the monastery of St. Mary at Laon. His son Bodo Leduinus became bishop of Toul, and his granddaughter Teutberga became abbess of Bonmoutier, near Lunéville. Gonduin himself became duke of Alsace. Subsequently, he made a grant of land to the abbot of Luxeuil in order to set up another noble from Trier, Germain de Granval, who founded the monastery of Moutier-Granval near Bern.

Thanks to an extant will, we can appreciate the impressive fortune of still another family, that of Grimo Adalgesil. His testament from the year 634 is a remarkable documentary source for evaluating noble wealth in land, vineyards, and lay and ecclesiastical buildings. It also sheds light on the geographical distribution of landed properties, which are recorded in the Woëvre plain, Hunsrück, the Ardennes, and the vicinity of Trier and in the valleys of the Chiers, Meuse, and Ourthe rivers. Moreover, Grimo's family was to inherit almost nothing; the will survives as a witness to the soon widespread practice of leaving worldly goods to ecclesiastical establishments. Grimo was the uncle of duke Bobo, who governed Auvergne; he was also a relative of another Adalgesil who, after 633, replaced Pippin at the head of the Austrasian kingdom.

The Policies of Dagobert

During the personal reign of Dagobert from 629 to 639, Pippin I held no official post in Austrasia, a fact that is remarkable and revealing. Formerly his pupil, Dagobert now summoned Pippin to Neustria, where he established the political center of the realm. At the beginning of his rule, Dagobert had hoped to keep Austrasia under his direct control, but, as Pseudo-Fredegar records, the Austrasians manifested their discontent. When Dagobert organized his campaign against Samo, the Austrasians fought with little fervor and lost. Increasingly, Austrasia was threatened by the Slavs. They had invaded Thuringia, and despite a treaty concluded by Dagobert, Saxon allies alone could not effectively protect the frontier. The wiser course was to charge the Austrasians with keeping watch over the movements of these new barbarians.

Dagobert was obliged to follow the example of his father and make a concession to Austrasian particularism. He gave the land a king in the person of his eldest son, Sigebert, the three-year-old child of an Austrasian concubine. He did not, however, appoint Pippin to manage the kingdom, but looked to other families who were rivals of the Pippinids. Dagobert turned to Adalgesil and Cunibert, archbishop of Cologne. This city was the capital of the emerging duchy of Ripuaria, and these men were the leading figures of the region. As tutor to Sigebert, Dagobert chose Otto, the son of a manager of his domains. He came from a Wissembourg family allied, it seems, with that of Gonduin, the duke of Alsace; the Gonduins too were no friends of the Pippinid clan. Finally, Dagobert established another Austrasian noble, Radulf, in Thuringia, a principality that lay under Frankish control. Radulf was likewise connected to the family of Gonduin. With Arnulf in his hermitage and Pippin in Paris, the political ambitions of the two families seemed for a time compromised.

The death of Dagobert in 639 allowed Pippin to recoup his position

in Metz. If we can believe the chronicle of Pseudo-Fredegar, Pippin proceeded to make an arrangement with Archbishop Cunibert, who was to
encourage the Austrasians to recognize Sigebert III, now aged 10, as king.
According to the chronicler, Pippin "governed the great vassals of Austrasia with prudence and attached them to himself by ties of friendship,"
which is to say, he enhanced the influence of his own party. Dagobert
himself had appointed that the Frankish realm should be divided in two,
restoring Austrasia as a distinct kingdom, while Neustria and Burgundy
passed jointly to his younger son, Clovis II. The royal treasury remained,
however, in the hands of the queen mother. One of Pippin's first political
acts was to recover and bring to Metz part of this treasury, where it was
turned over and inventoried. Yet in 640 death came unexpectedly, just as
Pippin moved to repossess his office of mayor of the palace.

2. The Obstacles to Power

The Ambitions of Grimoald

HIS POSITION

The children left behind by Pippin I included Begga, the wife of Ansegisel; Gertrude, who withdrew to the monastery of Nivelles with her mother, Itta, its foundress; and Grimoald, then 25 years old. As head of the Pippinid family, Grimoald was an enterprising and, according to Pseudo-Fredegar, a popular figure. He sought to take the office of mayor of the palace, which was held by Otto, the tutor of the young Sigebert III. There were several rivals pitched against him, including Radulf, duke of Thuringia, who had taken advantage of the death of Dagobert to shake off Frankish control. He was supported by Fara, the son of the Agilolfing Chrodoald, whom Dagobert had murdered at the request of the Arnulfings. The revolt of Radulf was not a national uprising, but rather an attempt by the duke to loose himself from the authority of the young Merovingian prince.

Grimoald accompanied Duke Adalgesil and King Sigebert III on their expedition against Radulf. The Austrasians were crushed, and the king owed his very survival to Grimoald's intervention. Hereafter, Grimoald gained the king's friendship. He contrived to remove Otto by inducing an Aleman to assassinate him and then took his place as mayor of the palace. "He held all Austrasia firmly in his grasp," according to Pseudo-Fredegar, and he well deserved the title "ruler of the realm" (*rector regni*) applied to him by Desiderius of Cahors in a letter of about 643.

Grimoald controlled immense domains from Frisia down to the region between the Meuse and the Rhine. His possessions were located at Utrecht and Nijmegen, at Tongeren and Maastricht in the valley of the Meuse, and near Reims. His landed wealth would allow him to found monasteries where he set up relatives and friends. Thus, Grimoald embarked on a political course followed by all Carolingians: to possess abbeys and monks who prayed for the family and who supported it in its undertakings.

Monastic Foundations

The time was right for this endeavor thanks to the expansion of Columbanian monasticism across Austrasia, both in the Vosges highlands and in the basins of the Scheldt and the Meuse. Two especially distinguished monks, Amandus and Remaclus, established abiding ties with Grimoald and his family. An Aquitainian convert to Columbanian spirituality, Amandus was consecrated bishop after a pilgrimage to Rome, but according to the Irish practice, he did not receive a fixed episcopal see. With the support of Dagobert, he preached in northern Gaul from his monastery at Elnone, later called St. Amand. In 640, he persuaded the widow of Pippin, Itta, to establish a monastery on her lands at Nivelles, with three small churches, whose remains were excavated between 1941 and 1953. One of these was dedicated to Saint Peter, the first bishop of Rome, whose cult was beginning to develop in northern Gaul. Through Amandus, Grimoald's mother entered into spiritual contact with the papacy and the Roman shrines of the apostles. Itta came to Nivelles with her fourteen-year-old daughter Gertrude. The young woman, whom the son of an Austrasian duke had tried forcibly to marry, devoted herself to divine service. In 652, on the death of her mother, she became abbess of Nivelles. Her first biographer, writing about 670, recorded that the abbess was very learned in religious matters and that she had sent to Rome and Ireland to obtain books. She ruled a double monastery of men and women, according to the Columbanian rule. Her hagiographer asserts that her reputation had spread beyond the confines of Austrasia across "all Europe." Gertrude died aged 33 in 659. The daughter of Grimoald, Wulfetrude, succeeded her as abbess until her own death in 669. For his part, Amandus continued his missionary travels, living for three years in the diocese of Tongeren, which is better called the diocese of Maastricht because the bishops more often resided at the latter *villa* on the Meuse. In 650, no doubt with the accord of Grimoald, Amandus arranged for the election of his follower Remaclus as bishop.

Remaclus was also an Aquitainian. He had been the first abbot of Solignac, a monastery founded by Saint Eligius in 632, and then chose to join Amandus in northern Gaul. In 643, his name appeared in a charter that the king of Austrasia, Sigebert III, addressed to "illustrious Grimoald, mayor of the palace." The king, after taking counsel with his bishops and leading men, had decided to found a monastery in honor of Saints Peter, Paul, and John, at Cugnon on the Semois River. This project seems, however, to have been abandoned, since Remaclus's name appears again shortly thereafter in another charter of Sigebert III, which entrusted him with the two monasteries of Stavelot and Malmédy situated in the Ardennes forest, "a place of horror and solitary isolation which abounds with wild beasts." The king made a grant of forest land, and Grimoald was charged with furnishing money to build two monasteries, one on the Amblève River and the other, Malmédy, a few kilometers to the east. Even as bishop of Maastricht, Remaclus continued to direct his two communities, which formed a double monastery after the Irish fashion and followed the Columbanian rule. While he continued to foster these foundations at Stavelot and Malmédy with personal gifts or means derived from the king, Grimoald also received monks from Ireland who arrived by way of Neustria. Fursy, the founder of the monasteries of Lagny and Péronne, had a brother, Fuilan, who had been expelled by the Neustrian mayor of the palace, Erchinoald. Itta and Gertrude of Nivelles received the Irish, and Grimoald gave them a domain 40 kilometers south of Nivelles at Brebona (later Fosses-la-Ville), near Namur. This foundation was still known as the "Scots' monastery" (*monasterium scottorum*) in the ninth century, and it served as a base for the missionary monks who traversed northern Gaul. While Grimoald did not go so far as to establish proprietary monasteries, as would his successors, he did assure himself of the support of most dynamic element of the church, and he saw to it that the special powers of local holy men and women reinforced his position.

Metz

As mayor of the palace in Austrasia, Grimoald lived in Metz. The town had lately been enriched by the relics of Arnulf, who was already considered a saint. The translation of his body from Remiremont to Metz took place during the episcopacy of Goeric, Arnulf's successor. The remains were placed in the church of the Holy Apostles within the cemetery precinct south of the town. Once Saint Arnulf had returned, it was natural that his son Chlodulf, a cleric, should be chosen bishop about 656, no doubt at the prompting of Grimoald.

Chlodulf was in close contact with the monastery at Nivelles and with Remaclus of Stavelot, who sent a young noble from Hesbaye, Trudo, to be educated in Metz. Trudo later founded a monastery on his domain at Sarchinum (today St. Trond) between Landen and Tongeren, and he bequeathed all his worldly goods to the church of Metz. This example demonstrates the ties that existed between Metz, the homeland of the Arnulfings, and the most northerly region of Austrasia, the homeland of the Pippinids.

In 656, the young Sigebert III died at age 26. His saintly reputation earned him a local cult, but as king he had reigned under the absolute control of the mayor of the palace. Thus Grimoald now felt himself strong enough for what has been called the first Carolingian coup d'état. He installed his own son on the throne of Austrasia.

The Coup d'État of Grimoald and Its Failure

Favorable to the Pippinids, the Pseudo-Fredegar chronicler does not mention Grimoald's failed usurpation. The event was recounted at the beginning of the eighth century by a Neustrian monk of St. Denis in the *Liber historiae Francorum*. By comparing this account with other contemporary sources, we can sketch out the failed plans of the son of Pippin I.

CHILDEBERT THE ADOPTED
Sigebert III despaired of having a male heir. He accepted a proposal to adopt Grimoald's son and gave him the typically Merovingian name of Childebert. The Austrasian queen then produced a son, named Dagobert after his grandfather, and Sigebert changed his arrangements and entrusted Grimoald with Dagobert's education. When Sigebert died his own son was to succeed him as Dagobert II. But as the Neustrian chronicler reports, Grimoald had the infant tonsured and gave him to Dido, bishop of Poitiers, who took him to Ireland. Grimoald put his own son, known as Childebert the Adopted, on the throne of Austrasia.

The story of these events has prompted many commentaries. Some historians have used other sources to establish that Dagobert II reigned for several years under the authority of Grimoald, since he is said to have decided to leave of his own accord at the counsel of the mayor of the palace. Grimoald would then have replaced him with Childebert the Adopted. Yet it is difficult to believe that Dagobert II would have accepted the tonsure voluntarily or out of piety and then departed for Ireland for religious reasons, even though Ireland was at that time the most renowned place for spiritual training. Grimoald gave Dagobert to Dido in order to exile him to the outermost fringes of the western world, in the hope of perpetually excluding him from secular affairs.

THE NEUSTRIAN REACTION
A further problem is raised by the attitude of the Neustrians to these events. Since the death of Dagobert I, Clovis II had reigned in Neustria

under the tutelage of his relative, the mayor of the palace, Erchinoald. The mayor even obliged him to marry one of his Anglo-Saxon slaves, Bathild, who bore him several sons. In 656, when Sigebert III, the brother of Clovis II, died, it lay perhaps in the interest of the Neustrians to acquiesce to the exile of the dead king's son by Grimoald and thereby secure a re-unification of the Frankish realm under their king. They did in fact allow Dido and Dagobert II to embark for Ireland. But Grimoald's next step went contrary to their plans. According to the chronicler of St. Denis, they lured the mayor and his son into Neustria and put them to death at dates that remain uncertain. Grimoald's wife came into the hands of the Austrasian Frodebert, who subsequently became bishop of Tours and thus unable to marry her, at which point he confined her to a monastery. Grimoald's daughter, Wulfetrude, the abbess of Nivelles, was also perse-cuted. The Neustrians were unable to force her out of her abbacy, so they ravaged her monastery's possessions.

An enterprising man, Grimoald succeeded temporarily at making his son the first Carolingian king, but his daring move ended tragically. His failure proved that the hour was not yet ripe for a change of dynasty. The Pippinids were dislodged from power for a time, but later and with far greater prudence, they would wait for their moment to act.

The Pippinids Await Their Moment

After the death of Clovis II in 657, his wife Bathild reigned in Neustria in the name of her son Chlotar III. She had undeniable political skills and profited from the removal of Grimoald and Childebert the Adopted in order to install her second son, Childeric II, as king of Austrasia. This very young prince was placed in the care of the widow of Sigebert III, Himne-child, and the Austrasian Wulfoald, who was named mayor of the palace. Wulfoald, whose name appears in several documents, was immensely rich in landed property and was probably allied with the Gonduins, the rivals of the Pippinids. Dogged by the hostile Ebroin, the new mayor of the palace in Neustria, Bathild withdrew to the monastery of Chelles, which she had founded in 664. A period of confusion ensued, which saw the nobles of each realm, whether favorable or hostile to the mayors, making and unmaking kings. They looked out for their own various interests, and the royal persons were their puppets.

THE REIGN OF CHILDERIC II

The only prince in this troubled interval to merit the name of king was Childeric II of Austrasia, the last for many years to reign over the entire Frankish realm. At the death of Chlotar III, the nobles of Neustria and Burgundy—under the influence of Dido of Poitiers—asked Childeric II to govern them. For two years, 673 to 675, the Kingdom of the Franks was reunified. Childeric had agreed to "accord each of the three realms its own laws and customs."

Childeric II was assassinated, perhaps at the behest of supporters of Ebroin. The Austrasians—that is, Wulfoald and probably Adalric of Alsace, progenitor of the illustrious Etichonids—managed to locate Dagobert II and secured his return. Ebroin as well as factions within the Austrasian nobility plotted against Dagobert, and in 679, in the Woëvre Forest, he too was assassinated "traitorously through the trickery of the dukes and with the consent of the bishops." About the same time the Austrasian mayor of the palace, Wulfoald, also disappeared.

Among the dukes in question there surely numbered some who had remained faithful to Grimoald, to his heirs, and to his relatives. After the death of Grimoald and his son, the former mayor's nephew Pippin II, "the Middle," a son of Begga and Ansegisel, represented the family. Ansegisel had been assassinated as part of the vendetta against his clan, and his widow Begga had retired to one of her domains on the Sambre River and founded the monastery of Andenne. Pippin II and his brother Martin could not come to terms with Ebroin, who dreamed of unifying Gaul under his own control. At an engagement in 680 at Lucofao, near Rethel in the Ardennes, the Pippinids met with disaster. Pippin II reached safety, but his brother Martin took refuge at Laon and was treacherously executed on the orders of Ebroin.

PIPPIN'S VICTORY AT TERTRY

The tyranny of Ebroin was also destined to end tragically. An officer of the royal fisc murdered him and fled to Pippin in Austrasia. A new mayor, Waratto, and then his son Gislemar, continued to rule Neustria in the name of the Merovingian Theuderic III. Pippin remained on bad terms with the father, and when war erupted, he was again routed near Namur. Berchar, Waratto's son-in-law, later became mayor of the palace, but his attempts to restore the harsh policies of Ebroin led to discontent in Neustria. Certain of the great nobles, among them Bishop Reolus of Reims, hoped to maintain their privileges and perhaps above all to put an end to the civil wars, and they turned to the duke of Austrasia for help. Pippin prepared his attack with care. He levied troops from his own domains along the Meuse and advanced along the ancient Roman highway that passed through Tongeren, Bavay, and Cambrai. He defeated the Neustrians in 687 at the battle of Tertry, near Saint-Quentin, and his victory was decisive. The Pippinids had avenged Grimoald. Now master of Theuderic III and the royal treasury, Pippin moved to assure himself of the respect of all the nobles of the realm.

3. The Principate of Pippin II (687–714)

Pippin's Political Program

Pippin II, first called Pippin of Herstal in the thirteenth century, was master of the whole Kingdom of the Franks—that is, of Austrasia, Neustria, and Burgundy. By political skill, he came to terms with the various factions of the Frankish nobility. His son Drogo married Anstrude, the daughter of the former mayor Waratto and widow of his successor, Berchar. Pippin chose to maintain the office of Neustrian mayor of the palace, but he appointed one of his own followers, Norbert, count of Paris. Longtime partisans of Pippin, such as Ermenfred, the assassin of Ebroin, now peopled the Neustrian court, along with other nobles of Roman or Germanic origins.

Pippin II ruled in the name of the Merovingian Theuderic III, whose signature is preserved on a number of royal charters. When Theuderic died in 691, Pippin installed the infant Clovis IV, who reigned for four years. Clovis IV was succeeded by his brother Childebert III (695–711), whose son Dagobert III followed as king until 715 (see Table 1). These Merovingians resided at their Neustrian palaces, at Compiègne, Valenciennes, Noisy, and Montmacq-sur-Oise among others, but the Austrasian mayor kept in regular contact. Writing to glorify Pippin in the ninth century, the compiler of the *Annals of Metz* reported:

> Each year at the beginning of March, the mayor of the palace, Pippin II, convened a general assembly with all the Franks according to ancient custom. On account of the reverence due to the royal title, he had the king preside until he had received the yearly gifts offered by all the leading men among the Franks; made a plea for peace and for the protection of the churches of God, and of orphans and widows; forbidden the raping of women and the crime of arson; and ordered the army to be ready for departure on the appointed day. Then Pippin sent the king away to his royal *villa* at Montmacq to be guarded with honor and veneration, while Pippin himself governed the Frankish kingdom.

This kingdom comprised three sections, Austrasia, Neustria, and Burgundy, each with its own special features. Pippin lived in Austrasia, and from there, he drew his power, that is, his followers. By his marriage with Plectrude, he had allied himself with a great family that possessed lands in the regions of Cologne and Trier. His father-in-law, Hugobert, called count of the palace, had married Irmina, who became second abbess of Oeren near Trier after her husband's death. In addition to Plectrude, this marriage had produced other daughters who were among the progenitors of the great families of Austrasia. Pippin II could reckon with the support of the nobles of the duchy of Ripuaria, whose center was Cologne. In addition, despite initial hesitations, the dukes of Alsace had rallied to his cause. Adalric, also called Eticho—whence the family name of the Etichonids—was a brutal man, but he proved dependable whenever the Alemans attacked the kingdom.

In Neustria Pippin II installed his followers as bishops and abbots. At the death of Bishop Reolus of Reims in 690, he named the Ripuarian noble Rigobert as successor. Likewise Bishop Angebert of Rouen, also abbot of Fontanelle, was sent into exile in the diocese of Cambrai and replaced by a certain Grifo, who seems to have been a scion of the Pippinid clan. The abbey of St. Wandrille at Fontanelle was given to Hildebert, an Austrasian, and then to Bishop Bainus of Thérouanne. Pippin also opted to secularize some ecclesiastical properties, a practice that his son Charles Martel would generalize. After 700, Pippin replaced the Neustrian mayor of the palace, Norbert, with his own son Grimoald. The two offices of mayor were thus in the hands of father and son.

Pippin transferred northern Burgundy to the control of his eldest son, Drogo, who received the title of duke of Champagne, or perhaps, as another text records, "duke of the Burgundians." When Drogo died in 708, his brother Grimoald inherited his charge. In southern Burgundy, there appeared another duke of the Burgundians; he remains obscure, although he seems to have been at odds with Bishop Godwin of Lyon. Significantly, many bishops of the day sought to organize their own episcopal princedoms after the example set a few decades earlier by Saint Leodegar of Autun, yet for the moment Pippin himself remained unconcerned about this. In Provence, on the southern fringe of Burgundy, the nobleman Antenor, formerly at the Neustrian court, represented the mayor of the palace and eventually sought to rule on his own.

There were no great problems within the Frankish kingdom, but considerable dangers menaced it from without. As the compiler of the *Annals of Metz* recalled:

> At that time war threatened the undefeated prince, not so much to contest his leadership of the Franks as to pry away the various peoples who had formerly been obedient to the Franks: the Saxons, Frisians, Alemans, Bavarians, Aquitainians, Gascons, and Bretons.

Nothing is known of the relations between Pippin and the Bretons, but he did for a time concern himself with happenings in Aquitaine. In the sixth and seventh centuries, Aquitaine was more or less a dependency of the north, divided between the princes of Neustria and Austrasia. A rich and still highly Romanized region, it had never accepted the authority of the Merovingians, and the men whom the Franks called "Romans" had frequently revolted. But their attempts to secure autonomy failed. The Aquitainians seemed to accept the ties that bound their destiny to that of the Franks. They contributed to the civilizing of the north with their artists, missionaries, and learned men. The links of Metz and Trier with Aquitaine were still quite close in the seventh century, so much so that legends from a later time would speak of familial alliances between the "senators" of the south and the Arnulfings.

By the close of the seventh century, the fierce Gascon mountain warriors, the Basques, had advanced toward the Garonne River and now posed a serious threat. In face of the onslaught of these fearsome horsemen, new local leaders appeared who sought with the support of the nobility and the church to conduct themselves independently. Victorious over the Basques, Duke Lupus exploited the struggles between Ebroin and the Austrasians to carve out a new princedom for himself south of the Garonne. When Pippin II became master of the Frankish realm, he was obliged to occupy himself with Aquitaine because churches in Austrasia had possessions south of the Loire and because monks from the south like Amandus and Remaclus had founded monasteries in the north with the help of the Pippinids. In Auvergne Bishop Avitus II of Clermont and later his brother and successor Bonitus, the former governor of Provence, presided over a small princedom, but remained on good terms with Pippin. After the retirement of Bonitus in 701, a certain Norbert succeeded him; he was either a relation of the count of Paris and former mayor of the palace, or the count himself. Pippin, however, followed the events in Aquitaine with greater concern. After the disappearance of Duke Lupus around

700, Odo took his place and termed himself "prince." According to the *Miracles of Saint Austregisilus*, Pippin at one time engaged Odo militarily somewhere in the vicinity of Bourges. He thus inaugurated the Aquitainian policy that would be followed energetically by his successor.

The Advance into Germanic Lands

Pippin was surely more absorbed by the threats posed to the north and to the east by the Frisians and the Alemans. Settled along the Rhine delta, the Frisians sought to extend their dominion toward the Scheldt. They were both pirates and merchants. They possessed a considerable fleet, and from their base at Dorestad, they traded widely with England and Scandinavia, as is attested by scattered finds of the silver *sceattae* that they minted.

At the request of Archbishop Cunibert of Cologne, Dagobert had established a fortress (*castellum*) at Utrecht to keep watch over the progress of the Frisians and no doubt also to begin the work of their conversion. About 678, the Anglo-Saxon missionaries Wilfrid of York and Wigbert took advantage of the good will of Aldgisl, the Frisian king, and began to preach the Gospel. Their work was continued by Willibrord, a monk of the Northumbrian abbey at Ripon who settled in Frisia about 690. Willibrord was in contact not only with the Frisians but also with Pippin. The meeting of the missionary and the Frankish prince was of capital importance for the future of both Frisia and the Pippinid dynasty.

Pippin had decided to halt the encroachments of the Frisians. After several expeditions, he defeated the pagan chieftain Radbod. He took back Utrecht and Vechten, the ancient Roman *Fectio*, and extended his authority up to the former Roman frontier on the Old Rhine. The region was thoroughly colonized by Austrasian nobles who sliced out vast new domains. Pippin hoped that Radbod would accept baptism, but he refused. The *Life of Saint Wulfram* recounts how, when told that he would not find his parents in heaven, Radbod replied that he would prefer to be damned with his ancestors than be saved with a few others. But he did allow the baptism of his daughter, who became one of the wives of Pippin's son Grimoald. A wave of new churches and the creation of the diocese of Utrecht followed the Frankish conquest. Pippin considered Willibrord to be the most fit to lead the new church and so appointed him with the accord of the papacy. This move was decisive for subsequent relations between the Pippinids and Rome.

We have already noted the close ties between the Anglo-Saxon church and the papacy. It was thus normal for Willibrord to make a pilgrimage to Rome about 692 and to request the blessing of Pope Sergius I for the Frisian mission. After his victory over Radbod, Pippin invited Willibrord to return to Rome to be consecrated bishop by Sergius, who not only assented, but also conferred on Willibrord the title "archbishop of the Frisians," thereby creating a new ecclesiastical province. The cathedral at Utrecht was dedicated to the Holy Savior, recalling the dedication of the Lateran Basilica in Rome. Two further bishops were consecrated, and an indigenous group of clergy developed. Willibrord received gifts of land from the nobility, including Pippin's own domain at Echternach, which was to become a center for educating missionaries.

Fortified by their successes in Frisia, Willibrord's disciples pushed on even further. Swidbert left to evangelize the Frankish tribe of the Boructuari, who were settled between the Lippe and Ruhr rivers. When the Saxons took back the southern part of Westphalia, Pippin set up Swidbert on an island in the Rhine near Dusseldorf, which soon became the monastery of Kaiserswerth. Two other Anglo-Saxons, Hewald the White and Hewald the Black, were martyred as they attempted to convert the Saxons. Pippin brought their bodies back to the church of St. Cunibert in Cologne. More to the east, the Thuringian dukes Theobald and Heden (d. 717) fostered Christianity and made grants of land to Willibrord in the area of Kitzingen.

To the southeast of Austrasia, the Alemanian and Bavarian dukes no longer wished to recognize the authority of the distant Merovingian king. As one source reports:

> At that time, the duke of the Alemans, Gottfried, and the other dukes refused to obey the Frankish dukes, since they could no longer serve the Merovingian king as they had been wont to do formerly. They therefore kept away.

For the moment, Pippin tolerated this situation. But after the death of Gottfried in 709 he led several expeditions against his successor and forced the princedom back into the sphere of royal influence, without, however, annexing it.

In Bavaria, the dukes of the Agilolfing family dreamed of ruling independently. Because of their geographic position, they looked as much toward Italy as to Austrasia, the land of their origin. Theodo was the first

Bavarian duke to be fully conscious of his power and to seek to make a great princedom of his duchy. Good relations existed between Bavaria and the Lombard kingdom of Liutprand, who ruled after 712. Like Liutprand, Theodo wanted to organize a national church within his realm. To this end, he summoned the retired bishop of Worms, the monk Chrodebert, better known as Rupert, and set him up in Salzburg, the former Roman town of Iuvavum. At the same time, he received the monks Emmeram, an Aquitainian, at Regensburg and Corbinian at Freising. Yet Theodo also hoped to create bishoprics at Regensburg, Salzburg, Freising, and Passau. During a pilgrimage to Rome in 716, he requested bishops for his duchy from Pope Gregory II. Increasing preoccupied with converting the Germanic lands, the papacy could only respond favorably. A Roman mission was dispatched to Bavaria. The untimely death of Theodo in 724, however, and the subsequent partition of the duchy among his sons made the creation of the bishoprics impossible. For his part Pippin was content to remain in close contact with Bavaria through the marriage alliances between his family and the Agilolfings.

Monasteries and Palaces

Thanks to his political acumen, Pippin II gained the respect of various national dukes and brought about a period of peace in Europe. He was "prince of the Franks," but he remained above all duke of Austrasia, the land of his ancestors. Like his uncle, Grimoald, he knew that the growth of his power would depend on the support of the churches and monasteries that came increasingly under familial proprietary control. His mother, Begga, had founded the monastery of Andenne on one of her domains. At Lobbes, Pippin established Ursmar (d. 713) as abbot and bishop; he was succeeded by Abbot Ermin. Along the Meuse north of Maastricht, three new monasteries were founded: Odilienberg, whose abbot came according to tradition from Pippin's clerical entourage; Susteren, given by the mayor and his wife to Willibrord; and nearby Aldeneyck, where the noblewomen Herlind and Renild became nuns between 705 and 710. In the bishopric of Trier, the Pippinid supporter and future bishop of the locale, Liutwin, established the abbey of Mettlach; it was dedicated to Saint Dionysius, whose cult was expanding into Austrasia about the time that Paris and the nearby abbey of St. Denis came under Pippin's control. Likewise, Pippin's sister-in-law, Adela, set up a religious community at a former Roman *villa* along the Mosel that took the name Pfalzel, "little palace." Finally, the Pippinids had a veritable family monastery at Echternach. Irmina, Pippin's mother-in-law, gave land to Willibrord for a first foundation. On 13 May 706, Pippin and Plectrude increased the monastic domains and stipulated that the abbot and his successors were to remain under the patronage of Pippinids: "When Willibrord passes from this life, his brothers will freely chose an abbot. This man should show himself faithful in all things to us, to our son Grimoald, to his son, and to the sons of Drogo, our grandsons."

Pippin II resided most often among his domains in the Meuse region, at Herstal, Jupille, and Chèvremont, a fortified bastion overlooking the Vesdre River. The Meuse was by this date a great commercial highway, and the settlements at Namur, Huy, and Maastricht possessed active mints. Liège had long been a *villa* belonging to the bishop of Maastricht (-Tongeren). It now became an episcopal residence. Bishop Lambert, whom Pippin II had reinstated, was assassinated at Liège in 705. His disciple and successor Hubert, perhaps Pippin's brother-in-law, returned Lambert's remains to Liège in 718, and himself settled in the hamlet, which lay near the Pippinid heartland.

As he grew older and ever more prone to illness, Pippin was forced to consider the question of his succession. His eldest son, Drogo, had already died and been buried in the church at Metz known by 708 as St. Arnulf's. Drogo had four sons. Of these, we can name Hugo, who was destined for the church and made bishop of Rouen in 720, and Arnulf, who remains otherwise a mystery. Pippin's younger legitimate son, Grimoald II, was murdered on the road to Jupille as he returned from venerating the relics of Bishop Lambert. Two further male offspring had been born to Pippin by the concubine Alpais: Charles and Childebrand. Pippin chose neither of these sons as his successor, but not out of consideration of their "illegitimate" status, since polygamy was and long remained an accepted practice among the great Germanic families. Pippin II preferred a bastard son of Grimoald, six-year-old Theudoald, and he obliged the nobles to recognize him as the future mayor of the palace. This choice was probably dictated to him by his wife, Plectrude, who hoped by this means to displace the sons of the concubine and herself direct the affairs of the kingdom. Worn down by age and sickness, Pippin accepted this solution. He died on 16 December 714.

4. The "Reign" of Charles Martel (714–741)

Difficult Beginnings

Pippin II had maintained control of the Frankish kingdom thanks to his own strong personality. Of their own, his political achievements proved fragile. Following Pippin's death, effective authority crumbled in the hands of his widow. The interests formerly subdued and checked by Pippin himself promptly rebelled against Plectrude. The Neustrian nobility had accepted Austrasian ascendancy only reluctantly, and they now moved "against Theudoald and those who had been the great vassals of Pippin and Grimoald," as the Continuator of Pseudo-Fredegar reports. They defeated the Austrasians in the forest of Compiègne, and taking advantage of the death of Dagobert III (d. 715), the Neustrians fished up a monk named Daniel—a real or supposed son of Childeric II—and made him their new king as Chilperic II.

AN INDEPENDENT NEUSTRIAN MAYOR
Ragenfred became the new mayor of the palace and effective leader of Neustria. He acted quickly to remove the followers of Pippin II from positions of power. Thus, Abbot Benignus of Fontanelle was replaced by Wando, and at Corbie, Abbot Grimo was forced out by a certain Sebastian (mentioned in a charter of 716). Ragenfred now went on the military offensive against Austrasia, helped by the Frisian chieftain Radbod, the grandfather of the boy-mayor Theudoald, and by the Saxons, who staged separate attacks from the north and the east. Ragenfred himself crossed the frontier into Austrasia and advanced on the road leading from Reims to Cologne. Plectrude had withdrawn to Cologne, the capital of Ripuaria, and when he arrived there, Ragenfred seized part of the fortune amassed by Pippin II.

CHARLES, VICTOR OVER THE NEUSTRIANS
At this point Charles, the bastard son of Pippin II, intervened. Named Karl, or Charles, by his father, he was the first of his family to bear this

name, and to him we owe the dynastic label of the "Carolingians." Until 714 he had lived with his father, and now aged 30 he was in his prime. We know little of his character, but his actions reveal his energy and political skill. After Pippin's death, a suspicious Plectrude had imprisoned Charles. He had managed to escape and assembled a group of fighters in an attempt to defeat the marauding Frisians, but he had retired in defeat to his domains in the Ardennes. Now, in 716, he tracked the army of Neustrians as it returned from Cologne and inflicted heavy losses on it at Amblève. Charles then recaptured several towns, including Verdun, which was held by Wulfoald, the grandson of the similarly named mayor of the palace of Dagobert II and a devoted adherent of the Merovingians. Bishop Peppo of Verdun contributed to Charles's victory and received several domains in return. But peace with the Neustrians proved evasive, and Reims itself remained in the hands of the recalcitrant Bishop Rigobert. Finally, Charles successfully attacked and routed the enemy on 21 March 717 at Vinchy, some eight kilometers from Cambrai. He then drove the Neustrians back to Paris.

Despite his success, Charles did not feel strong enough to finish off his adversaries. He lacked both money and a royal figurehead in whose name he could rule. He therefore chose to return to Austrasia and forced Plectrude to relinquish what remained of Pippin's treasury. Charles then made himself Austrasian mayor of the palace and had a Merovingian prince, perhaps the son of Theuderic III, proclaimed king as Chlotar IV. Plectrude lived out her life in Cologne and was buried there at the monastery of Notre Dame, which she had founded. Charles then secured the frontiers of his "kingdom." He pushed the Saxons back to the Weser, and he easily obtained the withdrawal of the Frisians after the death of Radbod in 719.

ODO OF AQUITAINE

Unlike his ancestors, Charles was not to content himself with reigning in Austrasia alone. He hoped to subdue the Neustrians, and against him, the Neustrians in turn sought and found an ally in Aquitaine. There, as we have noted, Duke Odo had carved out a princedom and nurtured his own kingly ambitions. With an army of Basques—the fiercest warriors to be found in Aquitaine—Odo marched north to Paris to assist the Neustrians. Charles responded without delay, and Odo was obliged to flee, taking with him both the royal treasury and King Chilperic II. Whereas Ragenfred managed to retire to Angers and set up a local dominion, Odo recognized his need to negotiate. In 719, he made peace with Charles and returned the king and the treasury. After the death of Chlotar IV in 719, Chilperic II became king of both Neustria and Austrasia until his own death in 720. He was followed by the son of Dagobert III, Theuderic IV. Throughout these changes, Charles maintained control of the kingdom, for he was now mayor of the palace in both Austrasia and Neustria. He appeared ever more the prince (*princeps*), the true son of his father.

Yet his situation remained precarious. Charles had to reckon with the potentates whom Einhard would later call "tyrants." These were laymen and ecclesiastics who had set up autonomous princedoms across the north of the Frankish realm. Thus Ragenfred ruled at Angers until his death in 731, and Bishop Godwin of Lyon governed a territory of his own. Similarly, Bishop Savaric of Auxerre and (by force of arms) of Orléans controlled nearly all of the *ducatus* (duchy) of Burgundy. Savaric's heirs, Ainmar of Auxerre and his nephew Eucher of Orléans, sought to perpetuate his legacy. On the periphery of the Frankish realm, Bavaria and Alemannia also evaded control by the Carolingian prince, and to the north, the Frisians were ever ready to move against him. Charles had to face these challenges and still work to consolidate his recent victory over the Neustrians.

Charles and His Methods of Action

The New Regime

In order to assure his domination in Neustria, Charles appointed his relatives and supporters everywhere he could. Following his father's example, he seized control of the important posts in the ecclesiastical province of Rouen. To Maastricht he exiled Wando, Ragenfred's abbot of Fontanelle, and replaced him with his own nephew Hugo (d. 730), who also became abbot of Jumièges and bishop of Rouen, Bayeux, and even Paris. At Le Mans, an important crossroads between the rivers Seine and Loire, Bishop Erlemund was replaced by a lay follower of Charles, one Carivius, the son of Rotgar, the local count; Carivius was later succeeded by his brother Gauziolen, an unlearned cleric of the sort common among bishops of the time. At Nantes Count Agatheus also held the offices of bishop and abbot of Redon. To the east Abbot Celestine of Ghent was deposed and ended his days in Rome. At Corbie the monk Grimo became abbot; he renewed the monastery and was later to journey to Rome as an emissary of Charles Martel to the papacy. For his refusal to surrender, Archbishop Rigobert of Reims was exiled to one of his domains. The see of Reims was bestowed additionally on Milo, archbishop of Trier, a scion of the powerful Widonid clan whose father and episcopal predecessor Liutwin had founded the abbey of Mettlach. Milo was a trusty of Charles and probably fought with him at the battle of Vinchy. He would retain Reims until 744 and grow infamous for his brutality and immorality, yet in his powerful positions, he was one of the most valued supporters of Carolingian policy. Many abbeys and bishoprics likewise became trophies for Charles's cronies. Although religion suffered from such appointments, they were politically effective.

Vassalage

For our purpose, the origins of vassalage are of less interest than its actual manifestations. Yet we must remember that after the sixth century men actively sought to overcome hardship by placing themselves in the service of their betters and supporting them. An early eighth-century text from the *Formulary of Tours* spells out the generic causes and terms of this common arrangement:

> *No. 43. Who places himself under the authority of another.*
>
> To the magnificent lord so-and-so, I, so-and-so: As it is evident to all that I have no means to feed or clothe myself, I have appealed to your piety and you have willingly agreed that I should deliver or commend myself to your protection. This I do under the following conditions: You must help and support me with food and clothing, according to the degree that I serve you and merit from you. And for as long as I live, I must provide you service and honor according to my free rank, and at no point in my lifetime shall I have the power of releasing myself from your power and protection. Rather, I must remain under your power and protection all the days of my life. Accordingly, it has been agreed that should one of us wish to withdraw from these stipulations, he shall pay so many *solidi* to another of equal station [to take his place], and the agreement shall remain in force. It has also been agreed concerning this undertaking that two charters identical in wording shall be drafted and confirmed by the parties. This they have done.

At first a private undertaking, such acts of commendation came to embrace society as a whole because the lone, unaided individual was virtually condemned. There was no choice but to enter the service of a magnate and thereby gain his protection. Society thus witnessed a vast proliferation of "dependent free men," as one text calls them. As long as the Merovingian kings were strong, it was normal to seek their protection, but later the weak or needful turned to the mayor of the palace. Hence in the *Formulary of Marculf*, compiled between 650 and the early eighth century, we find a model charter of protection granted by the king, but effective by the power and authority of the mayor of the palace:

> No. 24. Charter of royal and princely protection.
>
> It is right that royal power should accord its protection to those whose need is proven. Therefore, Your Greatness and Favor should know that we have publicly received, at his request [and] on account of unlawful acts of aggression by evil men, into the promise of our protection Bishop so-and-so, *or* the worthy so-and-so, *or* so-and-so of such-and-such monastery established in honor of Saint so-and-so, with all his goods, vassals, retainers, friends, and lawful dependents wherever they may be, in order that he may abide in peace under the oversight and protection of the illustrious so-and-so, mayor of our palace, with all the goods of the aforesaid church, *or* monastery.

Whoever commended himself to a master (*dominus*) or lord (*senior*, "elder" in Latin, hence *seigneur* in French) became his "man." To designate this dependent person, a new term appeared in the laws of the Alemans and the Bavarians at the beginning of the eighth century: *vassus*, or "vassal." After this date one can speak properly of vassalage.

As much as it obliged the lord to protect his man, commendation also required the vassal to give aid to his protector. In a world where men ruled by force, this aid was above all military. Individual nobles assembled an armed entourage that was prepared to defend their interests. Whoever collected the largest following naturally held sway over the others. The mayor of the palace and his friends gathered a household of warriors around themselves who had both a taste for military adventure and the expectation of financial gain.

SECULARIZATION OF CHURCH PROPERTY

It went without saying that all services rendered called for some recompense. To ensure the support of their followers, nobles made them gifts of both gold and land, the latter being the prime source of wealth. In this regard, the Merovingian kings had been very generous. They had distributed parts of their own royal domain, or fisc, as it was called, so much so that their landed fortune was gradually dissipated. Thus, the kings themselves could no longer attract clients. The Pippinids, however, possessed vast domains, as we have seen. They made use of them to provide for monastic foundations, but they were careful to maintain their family fortune while they garnered supporters. Thus Charles Martel possessed the resources needed to execute the "stroke of genius that lay behind the growth of Carolingian power," to echo the view of Jan Dhondt. Nevertheless, many writers, above all churchmen, were to condemn Charles relentlessly for having secularized ecclesiastical goods, although other leaders before and after him engaged in this practice without meriting the same opprobrium that has shrouded his memory. On the whole, Charles appears to have been a pious prince, well disposed toward the abbots and bishops who supported his cause, but he also profited from circumstances to fortify his power and assure his success.

Many modern writers have associated the secularization of church property with the rise of cavalry forces, which the Franks possessed in numbers long ahead of their rivals. Yet the Franks were above all foot-soldiers who fought with axes, projectiles, spears, short-swords, and massive double-edged swords (as long as 90 cm). They protected themselves with heavy leather shirts covered in metal plates, cone-shaped helmets, and large wooden shields. In the late sixth century, Gregory of Tours noted that some Frankish warriors were mounted. They, however, constituted an exception. Outfitting a horse represented a considerable outlay of resources: more than 40 *solidi* according to the Ripuarian law code, the equivalent in price of 20 cattle; and this does not include the costs of fodder and maintaining the horseman's attendants. It was only in the seventh century that the Avars introduced the Franks to the stirrup, which allowed a mounted fighter to use a lance effectively and hold a sword with both hands. But the stirrup did not immediately transform the Franks from an army of foot soldiers to a great squadron of cavalry. It is quite possible that the enrichment of warriors and the use of horsemen spawned new tactics that in turn favored the victories of Charles Martel, but centuries of development would pass before cavalry became the dominant force of medieval warfare.

Charles and the Periphery of the Frankish Realm

Just as he obliged the north of the Frankish realm to respect him, Charles Martel also reestablished his presence in neighboring princedoms with the help of his warriors and missionaries. The Anglo-Saxon Boniface came to play a key role in this process, and in the view of Christopher Dawson his influence on the history of Europe was "greater than any other exercised by an Englishman."

BONIFACE IN GERMANY

In Frisia, the death of King Radbod in 719 was greeted by all as the end of a nightmare. Willibrord continued to preach the Gospel to the Frisians from his bases at Antwerp and Utrecht. In 716 and again in 719, he welcomed the help of his compatriot Winfrith, later called Boniface, whom he hoped to make his successor. Yet as we shall see, Boniface was to find a different niche in the vast missionary effort. In 734, a Frisian revolt led by Duke Bubo briefly halted the progress of Christianity. Charles Martel moved to crush the Frisians for good by launching a novel land and sea attack with ships penetrating northern Frisia beyond the Zuider Zee. He killed the treacherous Bubo, sacked the region, and destroyed its pagan temples. The disciples of Willibrord recommenced their work under the protection of Charles and his soldiers. Boniface was not among them because by now he had received the special task from Pope Gregory II of converting Germany.

In 719, Boniface went to Rome as a pilgrim, where he met Gregory II. This pope, like his predecessor Gregory the Great, was keen to convert barbarian peoples to Christianity and realized the role that his Anglo-Saxon visitor could play in the effort. He dispatched Boniface to Germany with a letter explaining his mission: to preach Christianity to the pagans according to their needs, to maintain the liturgical rites of Rome, and to remain in contact with the papacy.

Boniface began his work in Thuringia and Hesse. Although these regions had been annexed by the Franks, they knew little of Christianity and were constantly threatened by Saxon raids. Against the Saxons, Charles Martel could do little more than was dictated by longstanding Merovingian policy. He organized several punitive expeditions, hoping thereby to shield the peoples of Hesse and Thuringia. The mayor of the palace also repaired local roads and erected a few strongholds, as witnessed by the remains of the Kestenberg fortress (found in a locale today known as Christianberg, north of Marburg). Protected by Frankish forces, Boniface established a first monastery at Amöneburg and then, after destroying the sacred Donar Oak at Geismar, a second in nearby Fritzlar, in 723. These initial successes prompted Gregory II to recall Boniface to Rome in order to consecrate him bishop. He also provided him with papal letters of introduction to powerful men in the kingdom, to nobles in Thuringia, and above all to Charles Martel. In 723, Charles ordered his own chancery to draft a letter addressed to the bishops, dukes, counts, and other royal agents proclaiming his official protection of Boniface. This step was necessary because several followers of Charles, in particular Archbishop Gerold of Mainz, did not welcome the activities of the Anglo-Saxon newcomer. When Gerold died fighting the Saxons, his son and successor Gewilib remained a staunch adversary of Boniface.

Despite these difficulties, Boniface received help in shoring up his work from other newly arrived Anglo-Saxon missionaries and from a number of Frankish nobles, including Gregory, the grandson of Adela of Pfalzel. He founded the monastery of Ohrdruf, near Gotha, on the domain of a Thuringian noble, and later in the Main basin, the abbeys of Tauberbischofsheim, Kitzingen, and Ochsenfurt, the last of which he entrusted to the Anglo-Saxon nuns Lioba and Thecla. Despite the opposition of the Austrasian bishops, he also established new sees in Würzburg, Büraburg, and Erfurt, which were to form a new ecclesiastical province. In 732, the new Pope Gregory III, pursuing the goals of his predecessor, sent Boniface the pallium. This garment symbolized the missionary's privileged spiritual authority, set Boniface above other bishops in dignity, and reinforced the ties between him and the papacy. But Rome was far away, and the moral and religious influence of the pope could not replace the practical aid of the mayor of the palace. Boniface recognized this in a letter to his mentor, Bishop Daniel of Winchester:

> Without the patronage of the prince of the Franks, I could neither govern the faithful nor defend the priests, clerics, monks, and nuns. Without an order from him and the fear it inspires, I could scarcely hinder the pagan rites and the practice of idolatry.

Boniface needed powerful secular help to achieve his goals. For his part, Charles Martel fully appreciated that Boniface's work strengthened Frankish power in Hesse and Thuringia. He followed the same policy in other outlying regions when he supported the missionary work of Pirmin.

PIRMIN IN ALEMANNIA

Further to the south, Charles encouraged the work of Pirmin, the "apostle of Alemannia." From 710 to 725, Lantfrid of Alemannia had ruled as an independent prince, as witnessed by his legislative activity in the *Recensio lantfrida* of the Alemanian law code. In 725, Charles moved militarily to reimpose Frankish authority. After the death of Lantfrid in 730, the rights of his brother and successor Theudebald were severely curtailed, and his ducal authority limited to the Neckar valley with the eastern slopes of the Black Forest. Several years earlier, Charles had granted his protection to Pirmin, an itinerant bishop who may have come from Visigothic Spain; the mayor of the palace hoped to find in him a new Boniface for Alemannia. In 724 he lent his support to a monastic settlement by Pirmin on the island of Reichenau in Lake Constance. Unfortunately, Duke Lantfrid perceived the newcomer as an agent of Charles Martel and chased him from Reichenau only three years later.

Pirmin withdrew to Alsace, where he was well received by the local Etichonid clan. This illustrious family had rallied to the cause of the Pippinids, and they now possessed more than 70 domains stemming from gifts and conquest, situated in the Alsatian plain and near Porrentruy and Délémont in modern Switzerland. On an island in the Rhine north of Strasbourg, Adalbert, the son of Eticho, founded the monastery of Honau in 722 and there set up a group of Irish missionary monks. In turn, his eldest son, Liutfrid, richly endowed the monastery of Wissembourg, which had been founded between 630 and 680 by the Gonduin clan of the Mosel region. His second son, Eberhard, founded Murbach in 727 and entrusted it to Pirmin. Eberhard later retired to Remiremont and left to Murbach a large part of his landed wealth. Likewise, his sister Odilia is supposed to have withdrawn as abbess to Hohenburg, later called Mont-Sainte-Odile; a tenth-century *vita* would earn her wide renown as the patron saint of Alsace. Upon the death of Duke Liutfrid about 740, Charles Martel took control of the duchy of Alsace and divided it into two bishoprics: Basel to the south, including the abbey of Murbach and the eastern Jura highlands, and Strasbourg to the north (corresponding to the modern French *département* of Bas-Rhin). Bishop Hedo of Strasbourg, a disciple of Pirmin, used monks as missionaries in his diocese.

Pirmin himself was called on by Bishop Sigebald of Metz (716–741), a follower of Charles Martel, to help restore the seventh-century monastic foundation at Marmoutier. Together they also brought monks to Hilariacum, later known as St. Avold. Pirmin then settled down at Hornbach in Rheinland-Pfalz, a monastery founded by Count Warnarius of the Widonid clan. From there he extended his influence over the whole region up to Wissembourg. Thanks to Pirmin, his disciples, and their noble sponsors, Charles Martel gained a firm hold on the eastern provinces of the realm. The abbeys richly endowed by eminent local families later came into the control of the Carolingians.

CHARLES MARTEL IN BAVARIA

Still further east in Bavaria, success was more limited because the Agilolf-ings, the most powerful family in the region, clung tenaciously to their autonomy. But after the death of Duke Theodo in 724, Charles exploited squabbling over the succession to launch two raids. He forced Duke Hug-bert to concede territory that would later form the bishopric of Eichstätt. At this point, the laws of the Bavarians were revised and repromulgated in the name of the Merovingian King Theuderic IV. Charles hoped to maintain his influence in Bavaria by means of Boniface. As it happened, Duke Hugbert and after 739 his successor Odilo pursued the plan for a Bavarian church first espoused by Theodo, and they asked local mission-aries to set it up. Boniface accepted the task, and in accord with Rome, he created four bishoprics: Salzburg, Freising, Regensburg, and Passau. Odilo, however, kept charge over the sees and did not permit Frankish clergy to intrude. Charles had to be content with a marriage alliance with the Bavarian dynasty. After the death of his wife Chrotrude, he married Sunnichild, a relative of Duke Odilo.

Charles in Aquitaine, Provence, and Burgundy

Charles Martel might well have been satisfied to rule directly as mayor of the palace in Neustria and Austrasia and indirectly through third persons in Thuringia, Alsace, and Alemannia. But the unforeseen Muslim invasion made it possible for him to penetrate south of the Loire and the plateau of Langres, where Pippin II and the Merovingian kings had failed to in-tervene effectively.

MUSLIM INVASION AND THE VICTORY AT POITIERS

After 711, a combined force of Berbers and Arabs controlled most of the Iberian peninsula. Visigothic princes and a few nobles had taken refuge in the mountains of the northeast and established a kingdom in the region of Oviedo. The east, however, remained open to the Muslims, and they entered Aquitaine by way of Septimania. In 721, Toulouse was saved by Duke Odo of Aquitaine, but the Muslims remained free to advance to the lower Rhône basin and proceed upstream. In 725, they came as far as Bur-gundy by this route and sacked Autun. Duke Odo was encouraged by his own success. He made an alliance with a Berber prince and did not hesitate to offer refuge in Aquitaine to enemies of Charles Martel, including the former mayor of the palace, Ragenfred, and Rigobert of Reims.

Had Odo gone further, and actually requested the help of Muslim troops against Charles Martel? This accusation was later made by Carolingian propagandists to discredit the Aquitainians and embellish Charles's exploits. But when the new governor of Muslim Spain invaded and ravaged Aquitaine by way of Gascony in 732, Odo sought help from Charles. The famous Battle of Poitiers was the result. After burning the monastery of St. Hilary in Poitiers, the Arabs advanced along the Roman road toward St. Martin's in Tours with its fabled wealth. At the culmination of seven days of skirmishing, Odo and Charles defeated the invaders, probably near Moussais, on 25 October 732.

The victory at Poitiers quickly became famous throughout the west. The Anglo-Saxon Bede the Venerable even heard of it at Jarrow in Northumbria before his death in 735, and he noted it in his *History*: "The Saracens who had devastated Gaul were punished for their perfidy." In Spain, an anonymous Christian living in Cordoba composed a poem on the battle several years after the events. He recorded how Odo called to his aide, "the mayor of the palace of Austrasia in inner France, one named Charles, a bellicose man from his youth and an expert in the art of war." He then described the battle, depicting on one side the Saracens, and on the other, the "men of Europe," who shared the booty of victory and returned home joyously. It was surely not his purpose to exalt a first "European" victory, but the poet was conscious of two opposing worlds and civilizations. On the one hand, he spoke of Muslim Arabs, and on the other, of Franks, the people of the north, the Austrasians who stood in this instance for the peoples of Europe.

The victory at Poitiers is considered by some as a military feat of secondary importance; the battle just happened to check an Arab raid. Nevertheless, the event proved decisive for the destiny of Charles Martel and the Carolingians. The battle was interpreted as a divine judgment in Charles's favor. In the ninth century, when chroniclers gave him the epithet Martellus, "the Hammer," they seem to have been consciously recalling Judas Maccabeus, "the Hammerer," of the Old Testament, whom God had similarly blessed with victory over the Syrians.

Poitiers ended the ambitions of Duke Odo. Charles took advantage of his victory, and upon the death of Odo in 735, he marched to the Garonne valley and took Bordeaux along with the fortress at Blaye. He forced the new duke, the famous Hunald of Bordeaux, to pledge his fealty.

PROVENCE

Charles used his successes in Aquitaine as grounds to intervene in the Rhône valley and Provence, where he not only defeated the Arabs but also subdued the long independent nobility. Helped by his brother Childebrand and other friends, Charles staged several attacks in the south and induced the Lombards to assault the Muslim forces from behind. He besieged Avignon, which Duke Maurontus of Provence had been unable, or unwilling, to defend, and like Joshua at Jericho—to echo the Continuator of Pseudo-Fredegar—he made himself master of the place. Charles then moved on Septimania and besieged Narbonne. Despite his victory over an Arab relief force on the Berre River, he could not take the town. But to deprive the Arabs of possible strongholds he ravaged the settlements at Agde, Nîmes, Béziers, and Maguelonne, and his devastation was not soon forgotten. In 738, Duke Maurontus of Provence crowned his insubordination with revolt and provoked another expedition by Charles. Provence was "pacified," and Charles confiscated the lands of the rebel and gave them to his own followers. One beneficiary of this move was Count Abbo. He founded the monastery of Novalese at the foot of Mount Cenis, from which he commanded the valleys and roads that linked Gaul with Lombard Italy.

It required many years of struggle for the Carolingians to become masters south of the Alps and in Provence. The regions they came to control had been devastated, and the local population considered them strangers. But it was important for the future that the Franks had retaken the Mediterranean coast.

BURGUNDY

In order to consummate his hold on the entire Frankish realm, Charles needed to occupy Burgundy, which had fallen into the control of its own local magnates. The first step in this process was to oust the successors of Savaric of Auxerre. Savaric's monk nephew Eucher, the bishop of Orléans, was exiled to St. Trond under the guard of Duke Chrodebert, and his son Ainmar, the bishop of Auxerre, was exiled to Bastogne in the Ardennes. In 737, Charles led a second armed force to Lyon, where he forced local magnates to recognize his authority. He positioned his sons Pippin and Remigius in Burgundy and distributed domains and abbeys to a new establishment of nobles who came from Bavaria. In addition, he counted on other relatives and friends in the region, such as the Hugobertian Count Theuderic of Autun and Mâcon and Count Adalhard of Chalon, as well as on abbeys like Flavigny, which later became a great Carolingian monastic center. The roads that led through the Jura highlands to Valais and to Italy beyond now lay firmly in Carolingian hands.

The Call of Rome

After a reign of 16 shadowy years, King Theuderic IV died in 737. Charles Martel did not replace him with another Merovingian, but neither did he dare take his place or appoint one of his own sons. He was no doubt mindful of the tragic end of his great-uncle Grimoald. Charles continued to direct the affairs of the kingdom. He issued charters in the name of the deceased king, granted lands and abbeys to his followers, appointed and exiled bishops, and named counts and vassals to administer the lands he had subdued. Without the royal title, Charles Martel was still in effect king, or more exactly a substitute king (*vice regulus*). Pope Gregory III used this title to address Charles when he wrote to solicit his aid in 739. This call from Rome was itself a new and important element in the history of the Carolingians and of Europe. We must briefly consider its cause and its circumstances.

THE SITUATION OF THE PAPACY
Since the reconquest of Italy in the sixth century by Justinian, Rome had been part of the empire of Byzantium. The bishop of Rome, as successor to the Apostle Peter, had long been accorded a leading role in the church. Nevertheless, rivalries between the pope in the west and the patriarch of Constantinople in the east often created sizable geographically based tensions, which imperial attempts to impose religious compromise often dramatically heightened. In 653, Pope Martin I was even arrested and deported east on orders from Constans II in the hope of settling the dispute over Monothelitism. Happily, the Third Council of Constantinople managed to overcome this tragedy and the entire controversy in 681. Shortly thereafter Pope Leo II lauded Emperor Constantine IV as a "son of the church and new David." This phrase would later distinguish other emperors in the west.

Agreement between east and west was, however, not to last. Between 726 and 729, Emperor Leo III (717–741) launched the lengthy and violent Iconoclastic Controversy with a series of edicts against religious pictures. Pope Gregory II (715–731) refused to accept the legislation and the persecutions it unleashed against monastic piety. Although fiercely threatened by the emperor, the pope enjoyed popular local support within the duchy of Rome. As the compiler of the *Liber pontificalis*, or "Book of the Popes," reports:

> Both leading men and commoners joined together in a sacred vow never to allow the pope, the guardian of the true faith and defender of the church, to be attacked or forcibly taken away, and all were ready to die with joy to save his life.

More importantly, Gregory II felt that he had the support of the west—an ever greater body of Christians thanks to the missionaries who worked in cooperation with Rome. In a letter lately proved authentic after long uncertainty, Gregory II went so far as to address Leo III in these terms:

> It saddens us to see that while savage and barbarian peoples have joined the civilized world, you who are civilized return to savagery and violence. The entire west bears the fruits of its faith to the holy chief of the Apostles, and you send men to smash the image of Saint Peter. We have lately received an invitation from the far reaches of the west. They desire that for the love of God we should go there to give them Holy Baptism. To avoid that any should take us to task for our negligence or our lack of zeal, we are making ready to go.

This text bears striking witness to the evolving status of the papacy and to a novel consciousness of its power and prestige.

At this very time, the popes nevertheless found themselves threatened in the west by the web of Lombard expansion. Although the Lombard kings had turned from Arianism to catholic Christianity at the end of the seventh century, they hoped to control all of Italy, including the duchy of Rome. In 712, the new and energetic King Liutprand approached this task by consolidating his own authority. He complemented the legislation of his predecessors, improved administrative methods in the Lombard capital at Pavia, and shored up his links to local dukes and their followers. After 726, Liutprand moved against the hitherto independent duchies of Spoleto and Benevento, and perhaps following the example of Charles Martel, he sought to unify Italy and subject its nobles to himself. Liutprand exploited the outbreak of religious crisis and revolt against the exarch of Ravenna, the Italian representative of Emperor Leo III.

As a mark of his opposition to imperial iconoclastic policies, Gregory II might also have exploited the "Italian revolt." He chose not to do so, because he realized that a definitive break with Byzantium would leave him at the mercy of the Lombards. Rome would become a subject bishopric. Thus, Gregory II hoped paradoxically to restore the exarch of Ravenna, and he sought to gain time by negotiating with the Lombards. Liutprand however had already conquered many Byzantine possessions in Italy and even encroached on Rome. In 728, Gregory II obtained from the king a promise to "restore unto Peter and Paul" the lands of Sutri. This curious expression would later bear on the history of the Carolingians.

POPE GREGORY III

As papal successor in 731, Gregory III also sought to pursue the difficult objectives of restoring the exarch of Ravenna and negotiating with the Lombard king. But in 738, he disastrously misjudged circumstances when he gave refuge to the lately defeated duke of Spoleto. Liutprand responded decisively by moving on Rome and seizing four strategic strongholds in the vicinity. To whom could Gregory III turn for help? Byzantium was far away, and its relations with the pope had worsened further. In reprisal for the papal stance on iconoclasm, Leo III had confiscated the "patrimonies of Saint Peter" in Calabria and Sicily, and then transferred the pope's religious jurisdiction over southern Italy and the old Balkan prefecture of Illyricum to the patriarch of Constantinople. The pope had no choice but to turn to the Franks.

Close relations had developed between Charles and the papacy after Gregory II commissioned Boniface to evangelize Germany. The pope had addressed a letter to his son, the "patrician" Charles, in 724. Since then, Boniface had been able to inform Gregory II and his successor, Gregory III, about the situation inside the Frankish kingdom. Rome knew of Charles Martel and his successes, especially his victory at Poitiers. Moreover, Charles appeared to be the prince best able to help the leader of Christendom. In three letters copied and preserved in Carolingian archives, the pope besought the *subregulus*, the "king's first helper," to intervene in his favor. Charles was to send men to witness the dangers that encircled the papacy and come himself as a devoted son of the prince of the Apostles, Gregory III. To underscore the sentiments expressed, the pope sent rich presents to Charles, in particular the keys and chains of Saint Peter, or rather a reliquary containing flakes of the chains incorporated in a key. Gregory III perhaps sought to emphasize that Peter was the gatekeeper who admitted to Paradise those who upheld his cause, in the hope of appealing to his "barbarian" world view.

The papal letters and presents had no effect. In 734, Charles had sent his son Pippin to Pavia, where he had been adopted by Liutprand, and thereafter Charles continued on good terms with the Lombards. He needed their help in his struggle against the Muslims. He therefore received the pope's messengers with honor, but limited his response to an embassy to Rome in 740 led by Grimo of Corbie and Sigebert, a hermit at St. Denis. They bore fair words to the pope and gifts for St. Peter's. Although Gregory III met with no success, his plan at least illustrates the prestige enjoyed by the Carolingian leader. If nothing else, the event suggested an avenue of appeal for the future.

The End of the Reign of Charles Martel

Charles Martel was ruler of the entire Frankish kingdom. Unlike his father, he most often resided in Neustria, at Vinchy, where some remains of a palace have been unearthed, and at Quierzy, Laon, and Verberie. In Austrasia, he spent time at Amblève, Bastogne, and Herstal, the last of which was first mentioned as a palace in 722. Wherever he temporarily settled, Charles was accompanied by the clerics of his "chapel" (*capella*), a group whose name derived from the fragment of the cloak (*capa*) of Saint Martin left in their charge. The mayor of the palace entrusted court administrative duties to one of his cousins, the referendary Chrodegang, who later moved on to renown as bishop of Metz.

CHARLES MARTEL AND ST. DENIS

As a friend of the abbey of St. Denis, Charles confided the education of his son Pippin to its monks, and in doing so, he broke with the Merovingian tradition of princely tutors and governors in favor the Anglo-Saxon practice of having royal sons educated in monastic centers. The young Pippin was at St. Denis about the time one of its inmates composed the *Liber historiae Francorum*, a work of history that began as an endorsement of the Neustrian cause, but whose end could be, and was, viewed as an apologia for Charles Martel. On the Carolingian side, the mayor's brother Childebrand sponsored an unofficial chronicle that continues the work of Pseudo-Fredegar, a text Wilhelm Levison called the "family chronicle of the Carolingian house." In the circle of Charles Martel and his brother sprang up the legend asserting the Trojan origins of the Frankish people; history became a means of associating the Franks with the civilized world.

THE SUCCESSION

As he neared his sixtieth year, Charles sensed the approach of death and prepared his succession. Although he had a number of legitimate and illegitimate children, he desired above all to keep the offices of mayor of the palace within his family, and he provided accordingly. His first wife had borne him two sons, Carloman and Pippin, and his Bavarian spouse had produced one more, Grifo. To Carloman, the eldest, Charles assigned Austrasia, Alemannia, and Thuringia, while Pippin received Burgundy, Neustria, and Provence along with the "Mosel duchy" (*ducatus mosellanis*) including both Metz and Trier. It was necessary for each future mayor to have a share of the Austrasian patrimonies from which the family drew its wealth. Finally, shortly before the death of his father, Grifo was given a number of lands scattered across the kingdom. The quasi-royal partition concluded by Charles was ratified by the leading nobles, who themselves had an interest in assuring that the mayors of the palace remained Carolingian.

Charles sought to ward off the inevitable by multiplying his gifts to St. Denis, but death came for him in his palace at Quierzy on 22 October 741. His remains were taken to St. Denis for burial among the Merovingian kings. At Echternach, the successor of Abbot Willibrord (d. 739) made a note in the official calendar, where such events were often remembered: "October 741, death of King Charles."

It was in fact the end of a great reign of more than a quarter century. By his military skill and political talent, Charles Martel had triumphed over a period of uncertainty. Europe had begun the eighth century moving toward a fragmented political order of autonomous princedoms under the thumb of local dukes. Charles Martel had arrested this process and assembled under a central power nearly every region in the west. In no small measure, his success was due to the warrior followers whom he set up in the subdued regions and enriched with land, abbeys, and bishoprics. Charles had also supported missionaries like Boniface and Pirmin. He no doubt understood that their work not only brought Christianity to Germanic peoples but also drew converts into the sphere of the Frankish community.

Despite his immense accomplishments, Charles Martel is too often only remembered for two circumstances of his reign: the victory at Poitiers and the secularizations of ecclesiastical property.

5. Pippin and Carloman, Mayors of the Palace (741–751)

The death of Charles Martel inevitably triggered a crisis within the Frankish kingdom. Local magnates in Germany and Aquitaine exploited the seeming vacuum of authority to revolt; the Frankish nobility focused on its own interests; and partisans of the Merovingian family grew restive. For six years, Carloman and Pippin struggled to maintain and consolidate the work of their father.

Local Revolts and the Consolidation of Power

Carloman and Pippin found their first adversaries within the family. Their half-brother Grifo, the son of the Bavarian Sunnichild, reckoned on playing the part of an equal heir, as witnessed by a letter to him from Boniface. He wanted to take possession of his due, but neither Pippin nor Carloman accepted this, and they imprisoned him in the bastion at Chèvremont, near Liège, while his mother was consigned to the guard of the nuns of Chelles. In another quarter, Chiltrude, the elder sister of the mayors of the palace, had secretly fled the kingdom with the help of friends and married Odilo, duke of Bavaria. This new relative of the Carolingian family hoped to play some political role; he enjoyed papal support and had also lately concluded a pact with Duke Hunald of Aquitaine. Upon the death of Charles Martel, Hunald had of course revolted against the heirs. Finally, Theutbald of Alemannia, the brother of the Lantfrid subdued by Charles Martel, made a new grab for autonomy and a restored duchy. Carloman and Pippin would thus be occupied for several years to the south and east of the kingdom.

They began by attacking Aquitaine and crushing the "Romans," to use the term of the Continuator of Pseudo-Fredegar. They took Bourges, leveled the fortress at Loches, and victoriously divided the plunder of the duchy near Poitiers. In 745 there followed another revolt by Hunald and another expedition by the mayors. This time, Hunald was forced to deliver hostages and pledge a second oath of fealty. Soon thereafter he retired to a monastery on the Isle of Ré and left the task of continuing resistance to his son Waifer. In his quarter, Hunald's Bavarian ally, Odilo, also could not prevent the mayors of the palace from reaching the Inn River, despite the ready help of the Saxons against the Franks. Nevertheless, Carloman did not dare deprive Odilo of the duchy; he was satisfied to demand the surrender of the Nordgau region. Pippin also dispatched the Irishman Virgil (Fergal) to Salzburg. The learned cleric had spent two years with the Frankish court and had deeply impressed Pippin by his sacred as well as secular learning. With his help, Pippin hoped to keep watch on Bavarian activities, and after a number of years as administrator of the see, Virgil was consecrated as regular bishop of Salzburg. Further to the west in Alemannia, resistance to the Carolingian brothers was tenacious. Several expeditions were required to quell the rebels, and Carloman had to impose himself by terror, executing a part of the Alemanian nobility. Alemannia was then divided into two counties entrusted to the Franks Warin and Ruthard. The latter was a forebear of the region's celebrated Welf clan. With the help of nobles and the monastic disciples of Pirmin, new monasteries were founded in the Black Forest, while the existing foundations at Reichenau and St. Gall came under Frankish authority. To the south, the Carolingians also controlled the alpine episcopal territory of Chur and thereby held a further route to northern Italy.

Reestablishment of the Merovingian Dynasty

These rebellions made Pippin and Carloman painfully aware that their power remained unsure. So in 743 they moved to reinforce their position by placing a Merovingian king on the throne. They took a young man from the monastery of St. Bertin who was thought to be a Merovingian and set him up as king with the name Childeric III.

It is surprising that the old Frankish dynasty still enjoyed the prestige suggested by this event, all the more so because Carolingian propagandists had worked hard to discredit the figures who have been known since the sixteenth century as the "do-nothing kings" (*rois fainéants*). Writing in the ninth century with the help of eighth-century sources, Einhard recounted how the last Merovingian king had "only the satisfaction of sitting on his throne with his long hair and his flowing beard"; he had to be content to hold audiences for ambassadors from various lands and possessed a single, rather poor domain with a house and a few servants. "When he had to travel, he got into an ox-drawn cart led by a drover in the rustic manner. In this turn-out, he journeyed to the palace, went to the yearly public assembly of his people to discuss the affairs of the kingdom, and then returned home."

However picturesque, this portrait did not correspond with reality. The "flowing beard" has nothing to do with a young man, and at the time in question an "ox-drawn cart" was an ordinary means of transportation. But more important, Childeric III, like his predecessor Theuderic IV, certainly possessed more then one domain, as is amply proved by the locales named in the subscriptions to royal charters. Both kings were able to make gifts of land belonging to their fisc. They also received petitions from nobles and granted charters, and their signature guaranteed the validity of documents they issued. No doubt, they legislated with the advice of the mayors of the palace, yet apart from the short interregnum presided over by Charles Martel, the Merovingians retained their role as sovereign kings. In addition, they still represented a moral force in the eyes of the leaders of outlying princedoms. If the dukes of Bavaria and Alemannia revolted after 741, it was because the royal throne was empty and they considered themselves the equals of the Carolingians. Moreover, like other Anglo-Saxon and Lombard kings, the Merovingians represented a family that had ruled for centuries and whose origins were hallowed in powerful myths. At a time when paganism had not yet disappeared, claims of ancestral connection with some divinity was important. Finally, according to Germanic notions of royalty, the king was the bearer of salvation for his people. He guaranteed harmony and peace in the world, and as such he was necessary.

When they took back Childeric III, the mayors of the palace made a concession to the superstitious opinions of his royal subjects. In a charter, Childeric III declared himself "happy to have been reestablished on the throne." He contentedly allowed the mayors to rule "their" kingdom with the help of their lay and ecclesiastical followers.

The Reform of the Frankish Church

The mayors of the palace reached a further decision that was of capital importance for the history of the kingdom and of the west. They undertook to reform the Frankish church.

THE CRISIS OF THE CHURCH

The initiative came as much from the Carolingian princes—former students of monks—as from Boniface, the bishop who had worked as a missionary to Germany since the early eighth century. In a letter to the newly elected Pope Zacharias, Boniface wrote:

> Your Paternity will know that Carloman, duke of the Franks, has summoned me to him and has asked me to convoke a synod in the lands under his control. He has promised to reform and rectify the discipline of church, which has been trampled and shattered for at least 60 or 70 years.

There followed an ecclesiastical portrait of the realm:

> The Franks have not convened a synod in more than 80 years; they have no archbishops; they have nowhere established or restored the statutory rules governing episcopal sees; and in most cases, the bishoprics have been handed over to greedy laymen, or to adulterous, undedicated clerical carousers who profit from them in a worldly way.

Further in his letter, Boniface expatiates on bishops who protest that they are not fornicators or adulterers, while in reality they are negligent drunkards, aficionados of hunting, and still worse:

> They do battle with the army, and bearing weapons they shed human blood with their own hands, of both pagans and Christians.
> As for the so-called deacons, they wallow from their adolescence in debauchery and adultery, with four, five, or more concubines in their bed each night, and they do not blush to read the Gospel and move on to the priestly order, and then to the episcopacy.

We, however, should ask how these mostly ignorant men could read at all. The ecclesiastical schools that some Merovingian bishops had managed to organize lay in shambles, and rarely did anyone actually know the Latin language of the liturgy and written communication. Thus, Boniface also had occasion to denounce a Bavarian priest who had baptized "in the name of the fatherland and the daughter" (*in nomine patria et filia*).

It is easy to understand how under these conditions even those populations which had been converted in the fifth and sixth centuries reverted to pagan observances. A document of the period, the *Indiculus superstitionum*, gives a long list of disquieting happenings: banquets near churches and tombs; sacrifices in the forests near springs and boulders; the renewal of the cults of Mercury and Jupiter; magical incantations and various sorts of divination. In another text, we learn how Charles Martel ordered heavy fines against those who perpetuated superstition, but the rites nevertheless survived. Moreover, settlements also occasionally fell prey to charlatans masquerading as priests or bishops. In Neustria, the pseudo-bishop Adalbert gathered people outdoors around crosses that he set up near springs, and then—invoking both his connections with angels and a letter he had received from Christ—he distributed relics of his own fingernails and hair, inveighing against the clergy and declaring their sacraments useless. Another "bishop," an Irishman named Clement, and a band of wandering monks from the British Isles propagated heretical doctrines of a similar sort.

THE REFORM COUNCILS

There was a pressing need to act. Boniface devoted his every effort to the reform. Always in close contact with Rome, he asked Pope Zacharias for instructions:

> If then I am to undertake this matter and guide it at the request of the duke and at your order, I wish to have in hand a command and a decision from the Apostolic See based on the canons of the church.

The pope could only respond favorably and sent his recommendations to both Boniface and Carloman.

A gathering known as the Germanic Council opened on 21 April 742. Carloman, who presided, addressed the assembly, as we learn from the written proceedings of the event:

> On the advice of servants of God and of his leading followers, [Carloman] convened the bishops and priests of his realm to consult them about restoring the laws of God and of the church corrupted in the time of previous leaders, so that Christian people might ensure thereby the salvation of their souls and not be led astray by false ministers.

Carloman likewise resolved to establish new missionary bishops in Austrasia and to place them under Archbishop Boniface, the emissary of Saint Peter. From the outset of the synod, Carloman and Boniface made it clear that the reform in Austrasia would be wrought in close cooperation with the papacy. A number of reforming decrees were issued. In accord with the decision to convene a synod annually, Carloman met again with his bishops and counts in 743, at his *villa* at Estinnes, situated south of Nivelles along the road from Liège to Bavay. As mayor in Neustria, Pippin followed his elder brother's example. In 744, he gathered 23 bishops at Soissons from the provinces of Sens, Rouen, and Reims. The first act of his assembly was to condemn the heresies propounded by the pseudo-bishop Adalbert. Then, the Neustrian bishops promulgated canons broadly based on those agreed upon in Austrasia.

The broad lines of the reform can be readily traced without entering into exhaustive detail. First and foremost, the movement aimed at obliging clerics to lead a life worthy of their function. Unfaithful priests and licentious deacons and lesser clerics were deprived of their status. In the future, men of the church were no longer to bear arms, to do battle, or to accompany the army except to serve the prince as military chaplains. Clerics were forbidden to keep pack hounds and to hunt. They were to avoid living in the house of a woman, and they were to wear clothes that distinguished them from the laity, including a *casula*, a simple outer garment similar to one worn by monks. Nor were monastic religious forgotten. It was decided that monks who fornicated would henceforth be imprisoned and unworthy nuns would have their heads shaved. The Rule of Saint Benedict was assigned pride of place as a guide to monastic life. Second after such matters of personal behavior came the canons that restored the authority of bishops over the clergy. Too many itinerant priests and religious traipsed across the land; henceforth, they were to be attached to the jurisdiction of a bishop. To mitigate, if not eliminate, the abuses prevalent among the numerous "proprietary churches," founded and controlled by individual nobles on their domains, parish priests were obliged to meet with their bishop at least once a year. In the third place, Carloman and Pippin condemned popular superstitions and pagan rituals: the wearing of amulets, augury, incantations, animal sacrifices. Carloman demanded that the counts who embodied public authority at the local level intervene against acts of paganism. This was the first step of the relentless Carolingian policy of extirpating, by force if necessary, everything that deflected people from the path of eternal salvation.

The reform movement initiated in the Frankish realm gained adherents in other parts of the west. In Bavaria, the bishops gathered at an undetermined date and passed resolutions concerning liturgy and moral discipline. The Anglo-Saxon correspondents of Boniface also undertook reform. In 747, Archbishop Cuthbert of Canterbury convened a synod at Cloveshoe that reissued several canons lately formulated at continental assemblies. In Rome, even Pope Zacharias, the man consulted at the inception of the Frankish process, was impelled to follow the northern example. In 743, he convoked a synod at the Lateran to condemn clerical immorality; it demanded that clerics wear distinctive garb, and it also sought to uproot superstitious rites, like the celebrations practiced in Rome at the calends of January. In 745, Zacharias gave detailed consideration to the case of the two heretics Clement and Adalbert before the bishops and priests of Rome. On this occasion, the two men affirmed that only the archangels Michael, Gabriel, and Raphael had the right to veneration by the faithful. The following year Pippin with his bishops and abbots forwarded Zacharias a twenty-seven-point questionnaire. The letter sent by the pope in response provided the elements of new, hitherto lacking canonical legislation.

UNRESOLVED QUESTIONS

The reforming synods in Austrasia and Neustria had touched on two further critical problems for the Frankish church: the question of restitution of secularized property and the reestablishment of true metropolitan bishops. In these matters, the Carolingian princes showed greater hesitation.

During the first synod in 742, Carloman probably had decided to return confiscated wealth to its rightful ecclesiastical owners. But the following year at Estinnes, he determined that "because of wars that threatened and attacks by other neighboring peoples, he would retain for a while, with God's indulgence, a part of the church's wealth to aid his army." In fact, it was impossible for him to dispossess nobles who had received church lands without risking the loss of their fealty. A compromise was reached by introducing "precarial" tenure. This system, which had existed for centuries, was based on a request for tenure over a fixed term (*precaria*) made to the property owner by a private person. Precarial tenure thus resembled the lifetime tenure of a benefice granted to a vassal by his lord. As confirmation of the property rights of the church, the laymen who held the land paid an annual quit-rent of twelve *denarii* for each church or monastic holding. Carloman promised to protect host churches from impoverishment in order to reassure his abbots and bishops, but this all too convenient solution simply opened the door to further, legalized confiscations. If Pippin did not use the word "precarial" at Soissons in 744, he too envisaged that a quit-rent would be paid to monasteries as compensation for lands they had lost. By this means, the Carolingian princes could make use of church wealth to satisfy their military needs.

The second unresolved problem concerned the nomination of new bishops and the reestablishment of hierarchical authority in the church. In this domain, the reforming ideas of Boniface did not correspond with political expediency. The mayors could ill afford to antagonize the noble families who were firmly ensconced in many episcopal sees, but limited change occurred. Despite his appeal to Rome, Gewilib of Mainz was successfully deposed for an act of murder, and officially at least, the tenacious Milo of Trier lost his second post as bishop of Reims to Abel, a successor elected in 844. Many other bishoprics, however, simply remained vacant, notably in southern locales such as Lyon, Bordeaux, Chalon, Arles, and Aix.

The Carolingian princes had also promised to reestablish the metropolitan system whereby archbishops regulated bishops in their respective provinces. At the request of Boniface, Pope Zacharias conferred the pallium, the symbolic garment associated with the special dignity and authority of metropolitans, on three new archbishops: Grimo of Rouen, Ardobert of Sens, and Abel of Reims. But resistance from the clergy and the nobility—led by Milo of Trier—scuttled the implementation of the intended reform. Boniface himself fell victim to mistrust and infighting. Despite a pledge in 745 to establish him as archbishop of Cologne—with its excellent local connections to Frisia, Hesse, and Saxony—he was barred from taking office, as he wrote to the pope: "The Franks have not brought to pass what they promised." Three years later, Boniface received the archbishopric of Mainz, but this concession merely underscored the decline of his influence, for his authority was limited to one area of the eastern region of the kingdom. No bishop in the ecclesiastical province of Trier maintained links with him, and despite the loss of Reims, Milo was absolute master in Trier. Boniface despaired to see "Milo and men like him remain and cause harm to God's churches." Even the clergy and monks established by Pirmin in Alsace and Alemannia kept their distance from Boniface, the "apostle of Germany." Likewise, his prestige in Bavaria ebbed so much that Duke Odilo asked Rome to dispatch a new representative.

Nearly 60 years old, Boniface knew that his hour had passed. Younger men like Fulrad of St. Denis and Chrodegang of Metz had gained the confidence of Pippin. Yet Boniface could continue to count on Carloman, and indeed, the prince gave him land in 744 to found the abbey of Fulda. When he wrote to thank Pope Zacharias for taking the new foundation under his protection, Boniface recalled:

I have obtained this place thanks to the piety of religious and God-fearing men, above all of Carloman, prince of the Franks. I have dedicated it to the Holy Saviour, and in it, I have resolved, with the leave of Your Piety, to accord my body, wearied by old age, some time of repose, and I propose to go there to sleep after my death. The four peoples to whom, by God's grace, I brought the Word of the Gospel live in the vicinity. I can still be of service to them for as long as I live, with the help of your prayers.

THE ABDICATION OF CARLOMAN

In 747, Boniface lost his protector, Carloman, the mayor of the palace in Austrasia. After giving a portion of his domains on both sides of the Meuse to the abbey of Malmédy, Carloman withdrew from the world. He resigned his office and departed for Rome. There he received the tonsure from Pope Zacharias and retired to a monastery on nearby Mount Soracte. Several chroniclers took special care to note that Carloman's decision was "spontaneous," as if to disarm suspicions that Pippin had forced his decision. Yet Pippin certainly rejoiced at his brother's departure, for he now became sole master of the kingdom.

But the abdication also provoked trouble among the family. Carloman's eldest son, Drogo, demanded a share of the family patrimony, but was quickly neutralized. More difficult for Pippin were the consequences of having set free his half-brother Grifo, who fled to the Saxons and then to Bavaria. After the death of Duke Odilo in 748, the Bavarians moved to reaffirm their independence. Pippin, however, reacted swiftly to these challenges. He inflicted military defeat on the Saxons and imposed a new yearly tribute of 500 cattle. He then forced the Bavarians to surrender Grifo and to recognize Tassilo III as their duke; the child then reigned under the regency of Chiltrude, Pippin's sister, with close control by several Frankish counts. For his part, Grifo was pardoned by Pippin and set over several counties in the Maine region to keep watch on the Bretons.

After his triumphal return from Bavaria, Pippin could attend to affairs unchallenged. The Continuator of Pseudo-Fredegar remarked that "the land rested from war for two years." Pippin would use this time to prepare the execution of a well-ripened plan: to have himself proclaimed king of the Franks.

Part II

Pippin III and Charlemagne, Founders of Carolingian Europe (751–814)

Historians often approach the achievements of Pippin III, the first Carolingian king, as though they represent little more than a prelude to the reign of Charlemagne, his son. Although Charles acquired greater prestige than his father, the two kings deserve to be considered together because policies inaugurated by Pippin continued to shape events in Europe for a half-century after his death. His political program included such diverse elements as the consolidation and expansion of Frankish power, an alliance with the papacy, intervention in Italy, royal anointing, liturgical and monetary reform, and the renewal of relations with the east. Thus the reign of Pippin was not a mere "prefiguration"; rather, Charlemagne continued to pursue a course of action originally set by his father. Both men helped equally to forge Carolingian Europe.

1. The Reign of Pippin the Great

The Accession of the Carolingian Dynasty

THE SOURCES OF PIPPIN'S POWER

Before considering the circumstances of the coup d'état of 751, we should remember that Pippin drew immense power from his possession of vast domains in Austrasia and Neustria. As mayor of the palace he also enjoyed the support of numerous lay and clerical vassals established on ecclesiastical properties, and he could equally reckon with the help of his family, including the Austrasian nobles allied to his clan by marriage. In 744, Pippin himself had married the Hugobertian Bertrada. Her father was Count Heribert of Laon, a nephew of Pippin's step-grandmother, Plectrude (see Table 2). The wealthy Hugobertian clan owned lands in the Eifel region, and they had established monasteries at Oeren and Pfalzel and also contributed to the foundation of Echternach. One sister of Plectrude, Adela of Pfalzel, was grandmother of Gregory, the disciple of Boniface and future bishop of Utrecht, while Count Theuderic of Mâcon—an ancestor of the Wilhelmine clan—descended from yet another sister, named Chrodelind.

Pippin's most powerful ecclesiastical counselors, Chrodegang of Metz and Fulrad of St. Denis, were also close family allies. Chrodegang stemmed from an eminent noble line based in Hesbaye. His mother Landrada was a relation—perhaps the sister—of Duke Chrodebert, who had served Charles Martel and lay buried at the abbey of St. Trond. Chrodegang was a cousin of Cancor, the founder of Lorsch; of another Chrodebert, better known as Rupert of Salzburg; and finally, of Bishop Chrodegang of Sées. After his upbringing at St. Trond and a period of service as referendary at the court of Charles Martel, Chrodegang was named bishop of Metz by Pippin in 742. This appointment was a mark of special favor, since the see was that of Pippin's revered ancestor, Saint Arnulf. In 748, Pippin also helped Chrodegang to found the nearby abbey of Gorze, where the bishop probably set up disciples of Pirmin. As a close associate of Pippin,

Chrodegang worked to reform the Frankish church, yet he did not attend the Germanic Council of 743 or share in the Anglo-Roman reform program espoused by Boniface. Chrodegang was and remained a servant of Pippin.

The roots of Fulrad of St. Denis are more difficult to trace because his lands lay in various parts of Austrasia. Thanks to his will, we possess an invaluable overview of his immense landed wealth. Fulrad owned ten domains spread across Alsace: some near Strasbourg, Sélestat, Hagenau, and Colmar; several more in the Seille valley and near Château-Salins, Nancy, Sarrebourg and Dieuze; and finally, six others in Saarland, near Sarreguemines, and in the Blies valley. In 749 Pippin entrusted this great landowner with the abbey of St. Denis. Fulrad was not, however, the first Austrasian to rule the abbey, since Charles Martel had previously installed as abbot Godobald, a great noble from Avroy, near Liège. During the latter's abbacy, the monks of St. Denis had brought up Pippin and buried Charles Martel. St. Denis was the most prestigious abbey to come into Carolingian hands, but the mayors of the palace had also wrested many other abbeys from the bishops, making them over to themselves or to their vassals.

THE PREPARATIONS FOR THE COUP D'ÉTAT

Sure of the support of his followers and of the clerics and monks bound to his cause, Pippin sensed that the hour had come to replace the Merovingian king. Yet both history and personal experience made it clear to him that it was no easy task to oust a Merovingian prince, even one who was his puppet. Carolingian propagandists sought to prepare the terrain carefully by emphasizing the notion that a king who did nothing was not worthy to reign. It was not enough for the king to stem from an ancient and venerable family. A king needed to embody political and moral qualities actively, as implied by the definition of Isidore of Seville (d. 636) in his *Etymologies: rex a regendo*, "the name of king comes from the act of ruling." Moreover, it was no secret that several unfit kings had been deposed in Visigothic Spain. A literary work with the title *De duodecim abusivis saeculi* ("On the Twelve Vices of the World") conveniently appeared about this time from the British Isles, and it too underscored the obligation of kings to act rightly and effectively. This view invited a natural extension which the *Law of the Alemans* expressed with poignant concision: "The leader (*dux*) who is unable to go on campaign or to ride or to bear arms can be deposed."

Carolingian propaganda was disseminated from St. Denis and from other family circles. Childebrand, Pippin's uncle, followed by his son Nibelung, sponsored the Continuator of Pseudo-Fredegar. The resulting work constituted a semi-official chronicle, and it aimed at extolling the virtues of Carolingian ancestors like Grimoald and Pippin II, as well as the God-given victories of Charles Martel. At St. Amand, Jerome, a half-brother of Pippin III, piously copied the *Life of Saint Arnulf*, while at other centers care was lavished on the cult of Gertrude and other abbesses associated with the Carolingian clan. Such efforts made it seem natural that a family so rich in victorious warriors and saints should also rule. Forgers were perhaps already at work on spurious genealogies linking Saint Arnulf to the Merovingians.

At length, Pippin chose to question the pope concerning kingship. Although this move may seem a surprising confusion of religious and secular affairs, it was, in fact, an ingenious extension of the common practice of seeking opinions from Pope Zacharias on disciplinary questions. To learn his views on kingship, Pippin dispatched Abbot Fulrad of St. Denis and Bishop Burchard of Würzburg. Their question surely provoked discussions in Rome, but no papal document speaks of the incident.

Pope Zacharias (741–752) was an able diplomat. He had successfully negotiated the withdrawal of the Lombards from Rome, and at Terni he secured a twenty-year truce, which King Ratchis renewed after the death of Liutprand in 744. Ratchis, however, decided to become a monk in 749, first at St. Peter's and later at Monte Cassino, where he joined Carloman, who had retired there from Mount Soracte. If Zacharias rejoiced at the abdication of Ratchis, the pope shortly had ample cause for disquiet. Aistulf, the new Lombard king, renewed the aggressive policies of Liutprand and moved to complete the conquest of the Exarchate of Ravenna. In these circumstances, Zacharias probably received Fulrad's embassy favorably. The pope considered the possibility of Pippin's intervention in Italy.

Fulrad and Burchard questioned Zacharias "concering the kings in Francia, whether it was good or not that they then had no royal power." Harking back to Saint Augustine's concept of social order, the pope replied that "it was better to call him king who had royal power rather him who did not." It is likely that Zacharias gave the envoys a letter in which "he ordained by his apostolic authority that Pippin should be made king." Unfortunately, this document was not preserved in the palace archives.

When Pippin learned of the happy issue of the mission and of the pope's support for his cause, he assembled the leading men of the kingdom at Soissons in November 751. There he had himself elected king of the Franks. The young Childeric III was tonsured and sent to the monastery of St. Bertin, where he died in 755. His son Theuderic was brought up within the confines of the monastery at Fontanelle. Thus, the kings of the first dynasty were replaced by those of the second.

If the coup d'état had repercussions elsewhere in the Frankish realm, no official sources mention them. The biographer of Boniface does, however, allude to rumblings. Several texts also recount that Pippin had to dislodge a dissident from one of his strongholds near Verdun, at the site of the future monastery of St. Mihiel. The occupier was a certain Count Wulfoald, no doubt a descendant of the mayor of the palace of Dagobert II, an earlier adversary of the Pippinids.

ROYAL UNCTION

As a hedge against possible opposition by partisans of the Merovingians, Pippin followed his election with a gesture that proved immensely influential for the future. He had himself anointed by the bishops of his entourage, and perhaps even by Boniface who represented the pope in France.

This novel act merits brief explanation. Pippin's counselors did not actually invent the ceremony; they could in fact call on precedents from the near and distant past. They could refer to a canon law collection known as the *Hispana*, which had been introduced to Gaul by Visigothic refugees. From it, they would learn how the Visigoth Wamba had reacted to threats from the nobility in 672 by asking the metropolitan of Toledo to anoint him, thereby sealing the close alliance between the monarchy and the church. It is also quite likely that the practice of anointing kings was known from the Celtic regions in Britain. In this case, Anglo-Saxons would have imported an insular rite into Gaul. But the most important inspiration for Frankish clerics probably came from reading the Old Testament and noting the significant role of royal unction in the Book of Kings and its textual commentary. The Prophet Samuel had anointed Saul and later David with holy oil; he thereby affirmed for all to see that they were filled with divine grace. Gregory the Great, who was much read in the Anglo-Saxon world, wrote in his *Commentary on the Book of Kings*: "He who is elevated to the summit of power receives the sacrament of unction. . . . The head of the king should be anointed because the soul of the master must be filled with the spiritual grace." By royal unction, a Carolingian king would thus be elevated to the level of the biblical kings.

Charles Martel and his son Pippin had already been compared to Joshua leading the people of Israel to victory, and the texts of the Mass "For the prince" in the *Bobbio Missal* evoked the great leaders of the Old Testament. By such powerful associations the king became more than a general or a head of state; he became a person of sacred power, and thus inviolable. Pippin's predecessors could claim that their power came from God according to Christian tradition, but Pippin himself surpassed them by becoming the elect of God. This is what he would recall in his official documents: "divine Providence having anointed us to the royal throne"; "with the help of the Lord who placed us on the throne"; "our elevation to the throne having been wrought wholly through the Lord's help."

Yet it was not enough for Pippin to be anointed; he wanted this signal grace to encompass his entire family. In 754 Pope Stephen II came to Gaul where he not only reanointed Pippin in a unique historical repetition but also applied holy oil to his two sons Carloman II and Charles. A monk of St. Denis recorded the significance of this ceremony in a contemporary note, the *Clausula de unctione Pippini*:

> The pious and most flourishing lord Pippin was elevated to the royal throne three years earlier by the authority and order of the lord Pope Zacharias of holy memory, by the unction of holy chrism received from the hands of the blessed bishops of Gaul, and by the election of all the Franks. Then he was anointed and blessed anew as king and patrician, together with his sons Charles and Carloman, by the hands of Pope Stephen in the church of the martyrs Denis, Rusticus, and Eleutherius, the residence of the venerable abbot and archpriest Fulrad. . . . [Stephen] forbade all, under the threat of interdict and excommunication, to dare ever to choose a king from a line other than that of these princes; these whom divine piety had deigned to exalt and confirm by the intercession of the holy apostles and consecrate by the hand of the blessed pontiff, their vicar.

This time it was not a bishop acting on behalf of the pope, but rather the pope, or "Saint Peter" himself, who anointed the king. Likewise it was not one man who was chosen by God to reign over the Frankish people, but a family. Whoever had remained faithful to the elective tradition of Germanic kingship or upheld the rights of the Merovingian family now became incapable of action. A century after the failed coup d'état of Grimoald, the Austrasian family of the Carolingians had obtained royal dignity thanks to the Roman church. The Carolingians would retain this dignity for the next two centuries.

The Birth of the Papal State

THE APPEAL FROM STEPHEN II

Pippin, king of the Franks "by apostolic authority," soon had to answer the pope's request for help. In 739 Gregory III had unsuccessfully sought the aid of Charles Martel. Fourteen years later circumstances had changed on both sides of the Alps.

Zacharias's greatest fears were realized when Aistulf seized Ravenna without the least resistance and thereby brought an end to Byzantine rule in northern Italy. The king now prepared to unify the peninsula by capturing Rome. His scheme would have reduced the papacy to the rank of a Lombard bishopric, a prospect that the pope could scarcely accept. The bishops of Rome had administered the duchy of Rome for decades, and Zacharias recoiled at the thought of submitting to Lombards, who, though Catholic, remained very much barbarians in their non-Roman laws and customs. Thus, the pope felt a keen responsibility to maintain the integrity of the "Roman Republic" (*Respublica Romana*). The Roman church also owned considerable lands that had become all the more precious in the wake of the Byzantine confiscations in Sicily and Calabria. Moreover, to perform his supreme duties as successor of Peter, prince of the apostles and gatekeeper of heaven, the pope needed political autonomy.

When Stephen II succeeded Zacharias in 752, he immediately opened negotiations with Pippin, the new king of the Franks. He proposed to come to Gaul to discuss his situation in Rome. Popes had frequently traveled east, sometimes under constraint, but they had never dared venture into the barbarian lands of the north. Pippin accepted the plan and dispatched two envoys, his brother-in-law Autchar and Chrodegang of Metz, to organize the pope's journey. Stephen did not, however, come directly to Gaul, but traveled first to Pavia at the request of the Byzantine emperor in an effort to convince Aistulf to give back Ravenna. Constantine V retained a surprising degree of influence over the pope despite the fact that he perpetuated the iconoclastic policies of his father, Leo IV, and even then was convening a synod to condemn the cult of images. But like his predecessors, Stephen II could not simply reject the imperial request, even though it seemed unpromising from the start. With a refusal from Aistulf, the pope could make the voyage north without the least hesitation. Accompanied by his curia with its cardinals, priests, and deacons, Stephen continued on to Aosta in November 753, "braving the cold, the snow, and the overflowing streams, crossing the swiftest rivers and the most terrifying mountains, without shrinking before any peril," as he later wrote to Pippin. He arrived at St. Maurice-in-Valais before winter, but suffered the disappointment of finding two envoys there rather than Pippin himself. Fulrad of St. Denis and Duke Rothard were to guide the pope to the royal residence at Ponthion, near Vitry-le-François. Stephen II was met by Pippin's seven-year-old son Charles near Langres, and he arrived at the royal palace on 6 January 754, the Feast of the Epiphany.

What was the substance of the discussion held by Stephen II and Pippin? Frankish sources record that the pope asked that Rome and its territories be freed of the menace posed by Aistulf. The compiler of the *Liber pontificalis* noted in addition that Pippin was invited to restore to the pope the Exarchate of Ravenna. Some historians, including Louis Halphen, have wondered whether the pope also supported his request with the famous *Donation of Constantine*. According to this forgery, Constantine the Great was supposed to have ceded control of Rome, Italy, and the west to Pope Sylvester I when he left for his new capital at Constantinople in the east. Although it is nearly certain that the Lateran chancery concocted this document in the second half of the eighth century, the notions behind it probably circulated earlier. They may have been expressed orally in the discussions between Pippin and the pope, and set down afterward in writing.

Stephen II settled down to winter at St. Denis, while Pippin followed the advice of his leading nobles and negotiated with Aistulf. The Frankish king was reluctant to embark on an Italian adventure. Aistulf, however, made the mistake of sending Carloman from his retreat at Monte Cassino to plead the Lombard case. Pippin had his brother arrested at Vienne, in Burgundy, and imprisoned him in a monastery until his death. During the assembly at Quierzy in April 754 the king convinced his followers of the need for an Italian expedition, and made either written or oral promises to the pope to restore the lands usurped by the Lombards. When they had reached this agreement, Stephen II proceeded with his famous unction ceremony. He conferred a special blessing on Queen Bertrada, and as reported by the *Clausula* (see above p. 69), he declared Pippin and his sons "patricians of the Romans." It is unthinkable that the pope bestowed this dignity in the name of the emperor, as some historians have advanced. Byzantium was far away, but Stephen II perhaps already knew that the iconoclast Synod of Hiera had assembled on 10 February 754. The presence of Stephen II in Gaul marked the effective end of relations between the papacy and Byzantium. When Pippin and his sons were named patricians of the Romans, it was to signify that they bore responsibility for protecting the see of St. Peter.

PIPPIN IN ITALY

Pippin acted on his promise in the spring of 755. He entered Italy and captured Pavia, while his half-brother Jerome accompanied Stephen II to a triumphal reentry into Rome. The Frankish king forced Aistulf to promise the return of Ravenna, and with only a few hostages as a guarantee of Lombard good faith, Pippin returned to Gaul laden with treasure.

Scarcely had the Frankish army crossed the Alps when Aistulf resumed his efforts to take Rome in January 756. The pope now dispatched three letters to Pippin, one of which was composed in the voice of Saint Peter himself:

> I enjoin you, my adopted sons. . . . Come, snatch my city of Rome from the hands of my enemies along with the people that has been entrusted to me by God. Come, protect the place of my body's repose from the contact of these strangers. Come, deliver the church of God, exposed to the worst torments, the worst oppressions, from the doings of the abominable Lombards. You whom I love so greatly, . . . be sure that among all peoples the Franks are especially dear to me. Thus, I warn and admonish you, most Christian kings, Pippin, Charles, and Carloman; and you of the priestly order, bishops, abbots, priests; and you, dukes and counts; and you, the entire Frankish people—lend credence to my exhortations as though I were living and present before you. For if I am not there in flesh and bones, I am there in spirit.

After a lengthy discourse, Stephen II concluded his pleas with a stark threat: "Disobedience will merit you exile from the kingdom of God and from eternal life." Pippin could ill afford to refuse "Saint Peter," and he set about organizing another Italian expedition.

During his second siege of Pavia he received a Byzantine embassy that came to inform him that the lands he had promised to the pope belonged in fact to the emperor. According to the papal biographer, the envoys even sought to buy off the Frankish king with various gifts, but Pippin "refused to take from Saint Peter what he had previously offered to him." When Aistulf was defeated, Pippin forced him to deliver hostages and the keys of the various towns promised to the pope. Abbot Fulrad deposited these keys on the altar of St. Peter's Basilica with a charter conferring them as a perpetual gift. This document was purportedly saved in the Lateran archives and lost at a later date; the lands it affected came to be known as the "Republic of St. Peter." Apart from the Duchy of Rome, they included

22 citadels situated in Emilia, Pentopolis, and the former Exarchate of Ravenna, with the Tiber basin linking the northern and southern papal possessions.

In 756, the unexpected death of King Aistulf seemed an act of Providence. It allowed the pope to influence the royal election in Pavia in favor of Duke Desiderius of Tuscany, the candidate supported by Abbot Fulrad. As an aspiring leader, Desiderius had agreed to respect the undertakings of his predecessor and even to enlarge the Papal State. Nevertheless, Stephen II and later Paul I, who succeeded his brother as pope in 757, complained to Pippin that King Desiderius failed to respect his promises. They sent letter after letter to the Frankish king, whom they addressed as the "new Moses" and the "new David," as well as others to the royal princes Charles and Carloman, who were styled as adopted sons of the papacy. After Paul I transferred the remains of Saint Petronella, the supposed daughter of Saint Peter, to the Vatican, she was promoted as the patroness of the Carolingians. The pope also agreed to be the godfather of Pippin's daughter Gisela. A firm spiritual alliance thus developed between papal Rome and the Carolingians, but Pippin refused to intervene again against the Lombards. Although it was possible to do so, he had other pressing concerns. To the pope, Pippin recommended patience and concord with the Lombards.

Despite the trying circumstances, a new papal state emerged in Italy thanks to the alliance between the Franks and the papacy. This Republic of St. Peter was destined to play an immense role in the history of Europe until its dissolution in 1870.

The Conquest of Aquitaine

Pippin could not intervene again in Italy because of the challenge he faced in Gaul. His father had begun the task of permanently subduing Aquitaine, which he now sought to finish. But Pippin faced a tenacious and resourceful opponent in Waifer, the son of his father's adversary, Duke Hunald. Still bent on independence, the Aquitainians waged a merciless effort that stretched over ten years. The war in Aquitaine occupied more than eleven chapters in the *Continuations of Pseudo-Fredegar* sponsored by Nibelung, Pippin's cousin, and the chronicle mirrored Pippin's implacable resolve to break Aquitainian resistance.

THE PREPARATIONS

Reasons for the move against Aquitaine were not lacking. In 751, Waifer had given refuge to the king's half-brother Grifo after a second rebellion, and the duke likewise chose to confiscate lands south of the Loire owned by northern churches.

As preparation for the conquest of Aquitaine, Pippin had managed by 760 to grab Septimania from the Arabs with the help of local Visigoths, and to advance up to Vannes so as to eliminate the possibility of Breton reinforcements. Above all, Pippin had built up his own army.

In 755, the date for mustering the troops each year was delayed from March to May, thereby ensuring sufficient new grass for horse fodder. In the wake of another loss to Pippin, the Saxons agreed in 758 to pay a tribute of 300 horses instead of the former yearly deliveries of 500 cattle. These developments suggest an increased importance of heavy cavalry in the Frankish forces. Pippin also reinforced and multiplied ties of vassalage with nobles who could offer him military aid. In 757, the young Tassilo of Bavaria entered his majority and came to Compiègne to make his pledge of vassalage. This event was described in the *Royal Frankish Annals*:

> He commended himself into vassalage with his hands, and swore innumerable oaths. Touching the relics of the saints, he promised fealty to King Pippin and his sons Charles and Carloman, behaving honestly and faithfully, in accordance with the law and as a vassal should to his lords.

Tassilo led his army into Italy and then into Aquitaine, and he remained faithful until at least 763.

THE CONQUEST

After 760 and until his death in 768, Pippin led a yearly campaign against Aquitaine, advancing gradually across Auvergne, Berry, Limousin, and Quercy. He captured towns with highly developed siege machinery, and, contrary to custom, he even wintered on hostile territory to be able to resume combat as early as possible. In 768, he penetrated as far as the Garonne, and accepted the submission of the Basques. Waifer was tracked and cut down by an associate in the pay of Pippin.

Aquitaine was subdued, but ruined in the process. Lands were ravaged, towns burned, monasteries destroyed. The civilization and culture that Aquitaine had maintained despite numerous invasions now lay shattered. The landscape and its people would not soon recover from the traumas inflicted by the Carolingians. It was in vain that Pippin promulgated the "pacification capitulary" of Saintes in 768. His promise to respect the private law of the Aquitainian nobility—Roman law—could not smooth over the memory of years of warfare and atrocities.

Religious Reform

Pippin was more than a warrior prince. By virtue of his anointing and the rulership by divine right that it implied, Pippin had a responsibility to foster Christianity within his realm. It was his aim to address religious difficulties and to advance the reforms he had initiated with his brother Carloman. Yet Pippin looked to Chrodegang of Metz rather than to Boniface.

THE DEATH OF BONIFACE

Although Boniface may in fact have anointed Pippin in 751, he soon became isolated from the royal court. Through Abbot Fulrad, Boniface requested in 752 that his disciple Lull be made his successor as archbishop of Mainz. Although he had planned to retire to his monastery at Fulda, the zealous seventy-year-old was soon drawn back to Frisia, the land of his first missionary efforts. In the company of the bishop of Utrecht and other clerical followers, Boniface established himself at Dokkum, along the Saxon frontier. There he was attacked by a band of Frisian marauders and hacked to death on 5 June 754. His body was removed successively to Utrecht and Mainz, and was finally claimed by the monks of Fulda. The young abbey thereby became home to a pilgrimage dedicated to its founder, and it gradually emerged as the foremost religious center of the German lands that Boniface had evangelized.

CHRODEGANG

About the time of Boniface's death, Pope Stephen II was in residence at St. Denis. During his visit he decided to confer the pallium on Bishop Chrodegang of Metz, and this gesture established a new papal representative in France and a new advocate of the reform movement promoted by King Pippin. In 755 a synod at the palace of Ver moved to reinforce episcopal authority without, however, reinstituting metropolitan jurisdiction. At Verberie in 756 and at Compiègne in 757, the plan of holding yearly synods in the presence of the king was confirmed. About this time, Pippin also decided in favor of the payment of tithes to the clergy as a means of compensating for sequestered properties. He refused to restore land taken from churches, and he even ordered an inquiry into ecclesiastical holdings and provided for further distributions of property to his followers. At Auxerre, for instance, one hundred family plots, or manses, were reserved for the support of the bishop, while the rest of his domains were bestowed on nobles who arrived from Bavaria. A similar division was undertaken at Mâcon between the bishop and the lay nobility.

In 762 bishops from many important administrative centers (*civitates*) came together at Attigny along with bishop-abbots, who administered episcopal sees, and other abbots. For the first time in many years, there was a distinctive presence of the various territorial groupings within the church, with representatives from provinces like Cologne, Mainz, Reims, Rouen, Sens, Tours, and Trier, and also from regions such as Alsace, Alemannia, and northern Burgundy. Along with these northern leaders there were also southern ecclesiastics, such as the bishop-abbots of Agaune (St. Maurice-in-Valais) and Novalese and the bishop of Chur, all of whom presided over important alpine links between Italy and Gaul. Although the provinces of Aquitaine, Provence, Narbonne, and southern Burgundy went unrepresented, Pippin appointed a new bishop to Vienne in 767, and others were named for Bourges, Lyon, and Narbonne in 769. The structure of the Frankish church thus gradually took on new vigor and unity. Not every see was occupied, but signs of progress and improvement abounded.

ROMANIZATION OF THE LITURGY

A hallmark of Frankish ecclesiastical reform was the romanization of liturgical forms. Although systematic liturgical books like the Gregorian and Gelasian sacramentaries had become available in Gaul, most Frankish churches worshiped with a local mixture of texts drawn from various sources. Faced with this near chaos of forms, Pippin and Chrodegang took the initiative in reorganizing the liturgy on a common basis. Cyril Vogel summed up the significance of this move: "For the development of western worship, the establishment in Gaul of Roman liturgical usages is comparable to the importance ascribed to the alliance of the Franks and the papacy for the political destiny of Europe." It is likely that the course of liturgical reform was fixed during the visit of Stephen II to Gaul between 753 and 755. The pope traveled together with priests and deacons from Rome who could have trained Chrodegang and his clergy in Roman practices. Moreover, Bishop Remigius of Rouen, a brother of King Pippin, actively sponsored the work of romanization. After a trip to Rome in 760, he set up the head of the Roman *schola cantorum* in his town and commissioned him to train the local clergy in Roman chant.

Part of this movement was the introduction and copying of Roman liturgical books, such as the Gelasian Sacramentary of the Seventh Century, whose text is beautifully preserved in the famous *Gellone Sacramentary*. This Frankish adaptation of Roman liturgical prayers and formulae allowed a limited place to local customs; its acceptance was facilitated by this flexibility. The desire to unify liturgical practice according to Roman forms emerged as much from political as from religious considerations. The effort reinforced the unity of the church and of the kingdom through common forms of prayer. It was a long-term undertaking embraced by some churches rather than by all.

At Metz, Chrodegang was one of the first bishops to institute the reformed liturgy. The see of St. Arnulf had a duty to offer a good example. Chrodegang enlarged his cathedral church of St. Stephen and expanded the complex of episcopal buildings. This construction made it possible better to accommodate a stational liturgy in Lent along Roman lines. This Roman tradition entailed the celebration of rites in different churches or chapels on various days of the liturgical cycle. During the episcopacy of Chrodegang, Metz also became well known as a center of *cantilena romana*, or "Roman-style chant," and would remain so for decades.

THE RULE FOR CANONS

As important as his liturgical reforms was the effort by Chrodegang to improve the quality of clerical life. Between 754 and 756, he responded to the general state of laxity and negligence by drafting a Rule for Canons based on the Rule of Saint Benedict. He prescribed that canons should live in community with common quarters for eating and sleeping; that they should possess no personal wealth, care for the sick, and participate in a full round of daily prayers; and finally that they should read and study so as to preach well. The canon was to be a cleric living under his bishop and adhering to the rules (*canones*) meant to regulate his life. It was Chrodegang's hope that his "canonical order" should spread to all the churches of the Frankish kingdom. But most clergy sought to maintain their independence, and other churches adopted his regime only slowly and often in the face of real resistance. Nevertheless, the canonical life fostered by Chrodegang would later figure prominently in the life of European Christianity.

Chrodegang was imbued with the monastic spirit, and as a new bishop, he had warmly received the disciples of Pirmin already at work within the diocese of Metz. Between 748 and 754, he received help from Pippin to establish and amply endow the nearby abbey of Gorze. Monks from Gorze would later populate the foundation by Pirmin at Gegenbach in the Black Forest, while Pirmin himself helped Count Cancor to establish the abbey of Lorsch on the right bank of the Rhine across from Worms. Cancor, the son of Duke Chrodebert and cousin of Chrodegang, entrusted the abbey to the bishop of Metz and later to Chrodegang's brother Gundeland. Lorsch would become one of the greatest Carolingian royal abbeys.

Thanks to the untiring and manifold efforts of Chrodegang, Metz became the leading episcopal see in the Frankish kingdom. When Paul the Deacon wrote his *History of the Bishops of Metz* about 783, he lavished attention on the cathedral complex that complemented a cloister skirted with churches referred to in Chrodegang's Rule for Canons. Although nothing remains of these buildings, Chrodegang's throne of richly veined marble survives in the present cathedral of Metz. Outside the cathedral quarter lies Saint-Pierre-aux-Nonnains, a fourth-century Roman basilica that served as a monastery after the seventh century. Excavations inside this church have unearthed eleven stone panels once used as part of a partition separating the choir from the congregation. These stones seem to date from the time of Chrodegang or shortly thereafter. Their rich decoration of interlaced lilies, arcades, cross-hatching, and abstract flora and fauna betrays the influence of northern Italy and, seemingly, of Coptic models. But whatever their background, the panels bear witness to the Carolingian artistic renewal which stirred in the background of liturgical and political reform. Although spare, other similar evidence remains: for instance, the crypt paintings of Jouarre and the decorated Gospel book of the scribe Gundohinus (754). Renewal of various sorts did not await the reign of Charlemagne; it was a vivid feature of the reign of Pippin, his father.

The Prestige of Pippin III

In 766, Bishop Chrodegang died and was buried at the church of St. Arnulf in Metz, the funerary basilica of the first Carolingians and of the bishops of Metz. Two years later, Pippin III followed his trusted adviser to the grave. The former mayor of the palace died as a king of immense power and prestige.

PIPPIN AND THE WEST

The fame of Pippin III spread far beyond the limits of his influence. He was the first western leader to establish a rapport with the Muslim princes of the east. In 750, the Umayyad caliphs of Baghdad were overthrown and replaced by the Abbasid dynasty. The sole survivor of the Umayyads, Abd ar-Rahman I, fled to Spain, where he established the quasi-independent caliphate of Cordoba. In these circumstances it was natural for the caliph of Baghdad to seek good relations with Pippin, who was at war with the Arabs in Septimania and had retaken Narbonne in 759. Embassies traveled between the king and the caliph, and envoys from Baghdad even wintered at Metz in 768.

The year before, a Byzantine embassy had journeyed to the royal palace at Gentilly near Paris. Pippin had been in contact with Byzantium since his second Italian expedition in 756, when he refused to recognize Byzantine claims to territory promised to the pope. Constantine V had not, however, lost all hope of recovering Ravenna; he took advantage of the dispute that arose between the papacy and the Lombard King Desiderius, and of Pippin's refusal to intervene. Embassies were exchanged between Constantinople and the Frankish court. According to the Continuator of Pseudo-Fredegar, Pippin took the first step to "establish a tie of friendship between the two courts." Constantine V responded with envoys laden with gifts, whose bearers attended the assembly at Compiègne in 755. The Continuator remarked: "I do not know why, but these shared signs of amity did not have happy consequences." Nevertheless, the Byzantine diplomats had spoken of a marriage between Pippin's daughter Gisela and the emperor's son. In 762, papal emissaries encountered Frankish envoys in Constantinople. In 765, a Byzantine mission headed by the eunuch Sinesius arrived in Gaul with the probable aim of enlisting the support of Pippin in the Iconoclastic Controversy. The Frankish church had taken no position in the affair, but the pope feared the worst. At Easter in 767, a synod was convened at the royal palace in Gentilly, where Greek and Frankish theologians discussed problems concerning the Trinity and images of the saints. Some Frankish clergy were perhaps attracted by the Byzantine iconoclastic theses, because long debate was necessary to secure their condemnation at the Lateran synod attended by Frankish bishops in 769. The issue was not a foregone conclusion, and these events were a prelude to the debates that would follow the Second Council of Nicea in 787 and prompt the composition of the *Libri carolini*.

The presence of Byzantine emissaries at the court of Pippin also raises the question of familiarity with Greek in Europe. Since the sixth century, westerners knew little or nothing of this language except in a few privileged centers in southern Italy and at Rome. During the reign of Pippin III, Greek manuscripts were brought to Gaul and translated into Latin. Pope Paul I even sent Pippin Greek manuscripts of grammatical texts and works by Pseudo-Dionysius. These gifts have prompted many questions and comments, since it is difficult to identify the recipient actually intended by the pope. The mention of Pseudo-Dionysius makes it likely that these works at least were destined for the abbey of St. Denis. There, the monks were already convinced that Dionysius, the disciple of Paul (cf. Acts 17:34), Dionysius the bishop-martyr of Paris (ca. 250), and Dionysius the Mystic—Pseudo-Dionysius—were all one and the same person. Despite a common misconception, it is quite impossible that the books were intended for a "palace school," for none existed in Merovingian times or in the mid-eighth century. Yet the court did possess administrative services that Pippin developed and perfected.

THE ORGANIZATION OF THE COURT

When Pippin became king, he also became heir to the Merovingian organs of government. High officials continued to discharge their traditional duties. There was a seneschal who managed the king's table and saw to the provision of the palace; a cellarmaster; a chief cupbearer; a royal stable master; and a host of other royal officers. The office of mayor of the palace naturally lapsed, but the duties associated with it were taken up by a royal chamberlain (*camerarius*) who managed the royal treasury, which included such things as gifts to the king from foreign leaders as well as revenues from fines, tolls, and other forms of indirect taxation. Although he affirmed his royal right to transit and market tolls, Pippin sometimes conferred a portion of such revenues as benefices to ecclesiastical establishments. Thus at Mâcon, Pippin kept two-thirds of the tolls collected.

Minting also accounted for an additional source of revenue. The Merovingian kings had lost their monopoly on coin production by allowing individual abbots, bishops, and counts to strike their own silver *denarii*, while the royal minting of gold coinage finally lapsed around 670. In the north, Frisian *sceattae* also supplemented disparate private Frankish coinage. Faced with such monetary anarchy, Pippin finally directed:

With regard to coinage, we order that no more than twenty-two *solidi* [worth of *denarius* coins] should be made from a pound-weight [of silver] and that the minter should keep one [*solidus* of coins] and turn over twenty-one *solidi* to whoever brought the metal.

Dictated at Ver in 755, this instruction amounts to the first recorded instance of monetary regulation by a Frankish king. Pippin's coinage, of which some 150 specimens survive, was struck at places like Lyon, Angers, Paris, and Chartres, yet it uniformly bears Pippin's name as king in marked contrast to the coinage of the preceding century, which included the royal name only exceptionally. Pippin also managed to exert control over the mint at Dorestad, which had produced the Frisian *sceattae*. By these various means, he inaugurated new, royal standards of coinage.

Mechanisms responsible for generating official documents also underwent similar transformations. During his first stay in Pavia at age 21, Pippin had noted the efficient organization of Lombard government, which counted heavily on Roman traditions and the use of a well-qualified officialdom of laymen and clerics. Thus, when Pippin became mayor of the palace in 741, he entrusted administrative duties to the clerics of his chapel. In 751, he also replaced the lay referendary who had directed the Merovingian royal administration with a chancellor (*cancellarius*), one of the notaries of his now royal chapel. This move had decisive consequences. From this date until the end of the thirteenth century, laymen were largely excluded from the direction of the royal administration. Significant improvements in the formulation and presentation of royal documents also attended this change in personnel. The development is evident from any comparison of late Merovingian royal charters with their early Carolingian counterparts: the script became more regular, and the layout clearer. More important were the improvements in language. Whereas constant decline in the quality of Latin spelling and grammar distinguishes the charters drafted in the first half of the eighth century, ever increasing linguistic proficiency is the hallmark of the Carolingian royal chancery. In this regard, the king's notaries also evidenced far greater skill and education than clerks in private service. The clerks of the royal chancery surely owed this success to their access to spelling guides and grammatical texts. Chrodegang, the last lay referendary to function as such under Charles Martel and a man of prodigious Latin culture, probably had worked at improving Latin linguistic skills. Monks from St. Denis later played an active role in advancing administrative skills and methods. Along with the notaries who could draft documents in correct Latin, we should also remember the jurists who modeled new documents on examples from formularies and who even delved into handbooks of Roman law. In one of his charters, Pippin mentioned the persons who passed judgments along with the prince: the great nobles, the counts, and the other men "learned in the law" (*legis doctores*). By revitalizing law and written expression, Pippin initiated the work continued by Charlemagne.

PIPPIN AND ST. DENIS

Like the Merovingians, King Pippin III had no fixed residence. He led his court from one domain to another to live for a time from the produce of each. Thus, his charters were dated and issued at various Neustrian palaces in the Oise valley (Compiègne, Ver, Berny-Rivière, Verberie) and at Austrasian counterparts in Champagne (Corbeny, Samoussy, Ponthion) and in the Meuse valley (Herstal, Jupille, Düren, Aachen). Likewise, in his late ninth-century life of Charlemagne (the *Gesta Karoli*), Notker the Stammerer reported how Pippin triumphed over evil spirits at Aachen before building his own humble bathing station near the thermal spring. Pippin also resided at the ever more numerous royal abbeys, where he twice was anointed: first at St. Médard in Soissons, and later a second time at St. Denis.

The Merovingian Dagobert I had taken a special interest in St. Denis, and since his time the monastery had grown considerably. It became a veritable monastic township. Its abbatial church was surrounded by auxiliary churches, a cloister, a dormitory, a refectory, a scriptorium, a library, and sundry workshops and warehouses housing produce brought in from the many rural *villae* that the abbey had received since the seventh century. Each year on 9 October, the feast of Saint Denis, a fair drew merchants from across the Frankish realm and even from beyond its coasts. The monks had gained the right to collect the tolls levied on shipping and exchange. Although the count of Paris contested this privilege, Pippin confirmed it. In 753, he issued a charter in which he recalled how during his upbringing at St. Denis, "he had seen that the tolls were collected to the abbey's profit."

These resources were more necessary than ever to satisfy the needs of Abbot Fulrad's ambitious Italian-inspired rebuilding of the basilica of St. Denis. When Pope Stephen II sojourned at the abbey in 754, construction of the choir of the new church—of which some footings have been unearthed—had already begun, but the project would not be completed until 775. The great Austrasian landowner Fulrad was a close adviser to Pippin, and he played an important role during the Italian expeditions. He was entrusted with the relics of the royal *capella*, including the fragment of Saint Martin's cloak, and therefore received the title of archchaplain. In this capacity, he naturally assumed control of the royal notaries, who were drawn from the chapel clergy.

For their part, the monks of St. Denis were very much devoted to the Carolingian cause; they played a role in Pippin's coup d'état and at his royal unction. As guardians of the tombs of both Merovingians princes and early Carolingians, they favored the cause of Carolingian propaganda by linking the two families in a common hymn of praise. In 763, a monk of St. Denis composed a new prologue and epilogue for the code of Salic law (*Lex salica*) which Pippin had lately revised. His words resound like a Frankish "Marseillaise":

> The illustrious people of the Franks was established by God himself; courageous in war, steadfast in peace, serious of intention, noble of stature, brilliant white of complexion and of exceptional beauty; daring, swift, and brash. It was converted to the catholic Faith; while it was still barbarian, it was free of all heresy. It sought the key of knowledge under divine guidance, desiring justice in its behavior and cultivating piety. It was then that those who were the chiefs of this people long ago dictated the Salic law. . . .
>
> Yet thanks be to God, the king of the Franks, Clovis, impetuous and magnificent, was the first to receive catholic Baptism. . . .
>
> Long live Christ who loves the Franks! May he protect their reign; may he fill their leaders with the light of his grace; may he watch over their army; may he accord them the rampart of Faith; may he grant them the joys of peace and the happiness of those who rule over their age. For this nation is the one which, brave and valiant, shook from its shoulders the oppressive yoke of the Romans. After professing their Faith and receiving Baptism, these Franks enshrined in gold and silver the bodies of the saints and martyrs whom the Romans had burned with fire, mutilated with the sword, and delivered to the teeth of ferocious beasts.

The text extolled everything of importance: the Frankish people, the steadfast orthodoxy of their kings, and the glory of the martyrs of St. Denis. It heralded the Royal Acclamations (*Laudes regiae*) of the late eighth century, which would exalt the one glory shared by Christ, the pope, and the Frankish king.

Pippin III fell ill during the summer of 768, just as he secured final victory over his opponents in Aquitaine. He had himself taken to St. Denis, and there he died on 24 September 768 at the age of 54. Perhaps as a reflection on his height, historians would give him the epithet "the Short."

But neither his reign nor his attainments were anything less than great. Without him Charlemagne is inconceivable.

Pippin owed his success no less to circumstances than to his personal refinement and character. The nobles who had rallied around Charles Martel saw in his son Pippin the leader who could best serve their interests. The church too, both locally and in Rome, found in him a defender, and it cast its lot for centuries to come with that of a family "chosen by God." Pippin was a pious prince, but he was equally a warrior of great realism and tenacity, as the Aquitainians learned. He defended the material interests of his kingdom; he renewed and reshaped the structures that permitted him to rule effectively; he received at his court the embassies of the pope and the Byzantine emperor, as well as those of the caliphs of Baghdad. The effect was to affirm his position as a European prince.

On the eve of his death, Pippin judged his position strong enough to make a concession to Frankish custom. With the accord of his lay and ecclesiastical followers, he partitioned the kingdom between his two sons. This act was risky, but what more is shrewd politics than a series of calculated risks?

2. The Features and Circumstances of Charlemagne's Conquests

The Reign of Two Brothers

After Pippin's death and burial at St. Denis, Gaul was divided into two parts. The portion assigned to Charles, or Charlemagne (literally "Charles the Great"), stretched in a northern arc from Thuringia to Gascony. It included the family heartland in Austrasia as well as Neustria and Frisia, and it surrounded the territories left to the younger prince, Carloman: the Parisian basin, the Massif Central, modern Languedoc, Provence, Burgundy, southern Austrasia, Alsace, and Alemannia. The capitals of the two realms lay close together: Noyon for Charles and Soissons for Carloman. Yet the reasons behind this bizarre partition remain obscure. Carloman received a bloc of territory composed of disparate regions. Although Charles gained the lands richest in income and abbeys, he faced the prospect of governing a large, poorly integrated kingdom.

The various historical sources all agree that the two princes cared little for each other. Aged 21, Charles was the elder, born in 747, three years after the marriage of Pippin and Bertrada. The legend of Charles having been born a bastard in 742 is unhistorical. The prince seems to have been involved in politics from an early age. In 753, he enjoyed the signal honor of conducting Pope Stephen II to Ponthion, and later accompanied his father on his Aquitainian campaigns. Nothing is known of Charlemagne's childhood or upbringing, a fact regretted by Einhard, his first biographer. Carloman II was seventeen at his accession, and he soon demonstrated his hostility toward Charles by refusing to help put down an Aquitainian revolt. After the death of Pippin, a certain Hunald, possibly a son of Duke Waifer, rebelled against the Franks. Forces led by Charles intervened alone, but thanks to his Aquitainian experience, the king quickly became master of the situation. He established a Frankish fortress on the Dordogne River, at modern Fronsac, and pursued Hunald into Gascony, where Lupus, "duke of the Gascons," was forced to hand over the fugitive.

The brothers' constant squabbling obliged their mother, Bertrada, to intervene in politics. She hoped to enhance Frankish power by working for an alliance with Tassilo III, duke of Bavaria, and still another with the Lombard King Desiderius.

In 757, Tassilo had made a pledge of vassalage to Pippin, but six years later he renounced this undertaking. At age 21, the young duke hoped to make a powerful state of his realm, and he enjoyed the especial support of leading clerics like Bishops Virgil of Salzburg and Arbeo of Freising, and the Irish and Anglo-Saxon monks of abbeys like Mondsee, Niederalteich, and Kremsmünster. Like its Frankish counterpart, Tassilo's administration in Regensburg drew heavily on the example of Lombard methods. His court also attracted artists and men of letters. The Tassilo Chalice— engraved with the names of the duke and his wife and today preserved at Kremsmünster—is the most famous witness of this artistic activity. Thanks to Bertrada, to Sturmius, the Bavarian abbot of Fulda, and to the papacy, Tassilo came to terms with Charlemagne. Nevertheless, he fostered the traditional Bavarian ties to the Lombards by marrying Liutberga, the daughter of King Desiderius.

King of the Lombards since 757, Desiderius had not given up the hope of taking back Ravenna and the lands of Saint Peter. To this end he intrigued with Roman opponents of the feeble Pope Stephen III (768–772). At the same time, Bertrada hoped to strengthen ties between the Frankish and Lombard kingdoms through marriage alliances. Her daughter Gisela was promised to a son of Desiderius, and her son Charles was to marry Desiderata, the Lombard king's daughter. Although he already had a son by his concubine Himiltrude, Charles agreed to take Desiderata as his legitimate wife, and his mother personally fetched her from Italy.

Desiderius was now at the apogee of his power. Having ventured to Rome as a pilgrim, Desiderius managed to eliminate the pope's chief advisers, the *primicerius*, or first secretary, Christopher, and his son Sergius. The Lombard king then proceeded to pass himself off as the savior of Stephen III. The marriage of one of his daughters to the duke of Benevento gave Desiderius an additional toehold in southern Italy. But two events contrived to overturn his good fortune: the death of Carloman in December 771, followed by that of Pope Stephen III in January 772.

Carloman's widow, Gerberga, hoped to reign in the name of her two young sons, but Charlemagne had different plans. Supported by former followers of Carloman—including his cousin Adalhard, Abbot Fulrad, and Count Warin—Charlemagne annexed his dead brother's realm, while Gerberga fled with her children to the court of Desiderius. Meanwhile,

Charlemagne also broke off relations with the Lombard king, and smitten by a thirteen-year-old girl—the future queen Hildegard—he sent Desiderata back to her father. These events struck joy into the heart of the newly elected Pope Hadrian I. They also illustrate the determination of the twenty-four-year-old prince to formulate a political program of his own. The figure of Charlemagne the conqueror swiftly emerged in the foreign campaigns that followed the death of Carloman.

The Conditions of Charlemagne's Conquests

Although he was absolute master of Gaul, Charlemagne spent the greater part of his reign engaged in wars of conquest. When he died in 814, his empire spanned more than a million square kilometers, and it comprised much of the former Roman west. Einhard summed up and characterized this impressive expansion in the following terms:

> Such were the wars that this all-powerful king fought during the 47 years of his reign in various parts of the world with as much prudence as good fortune. Thus, the Frankish realm, which his father, Pippin, left to him already vast and powerful, emerged from his glorious hands almost doubled in size. Before him—excepting the dependent lands of Alemannia and Bavaria—this kingdom included only the part of Gaul situated between the Rhine, the Loire, the Ocean, the Balearic Sea, and the part of Germany inhabited by the so-called eastern Franks—that is, between Saxony, the Danube, the Rhine, and the Saale, which separates Thuringia from the land of the Sorbs. After the wars which we have described, Charlemagne added Aquitaine, Gascony, the entire range of the Pyrenees, and the lands up to the Ebro River. . . . To this he added Italy, which extends for over a million paces from Aosta to lower Calabria and the border between the Beneventans and the Greeks. He added the two Pannonian provinces, Dacia, Istria, Liburnia, Dalmatia. . . . Finally between the Rhine, the Atlantic, the Vistula and Danube, he tamed and subjected all the barbarian and savage peoples of Germany.

However vivid, this portrait fails to take account of the circumstances of the various conquests.

First, although Charlemagne was constantly moving about to lead his armies and inspect his domains, he journeyed across only a small part of the west. A map of his movements traced by German scholars speaks eloquently on this point. Apart from a sojourn in Aquitaine and four trips to Italy, Charlemagne's field of action was confined to northern France, Austrasia, and Germany. He never visited the western periphery of his realm, nor did he venture into Burgundy or stay even once at the dwelling prepared for him in Lyon by Archbishop Leidrad. His preferred residences lay in the valleys of the Meuse, the Mosel, and the Rhine, the lands of his ancestors. Before the construction of the palace complex at Aachen, Charlemagne most gladly resided at Frankfurt, Mainz, Worms, Thionville, and, above all, Herstal. The center of gravity of the kingdom shifted to these eastern localities.

Second, Charlemagne undertook his various conquests successively, without a predetermined plan. By circumstances of his own creation, he was drawn to advance ever further afield, and he was not successful in every instance. To prevail against his opponents, he resorted to diplomacy as much as to arms. He knew how to recognize his own failures and to listen to the counsel of others. He sometimes reversed overly brutal decisions, and he deftly exploited the weaknesses of his adversaries.

There were, however, certain guiding principles to which Charles always adhered. He sought first and foremost to protect the realm left to him by his father. By conquering Saxony, he put an end to centuries of raids by pagan marauders into Hesse, Thuringia, and Austrasia. But the occupation of Saxony entailed a new defensive strategy directed against Slavic incursions from the east. When Charles became master of Bavaria, he was obliged to intervene in Bohemia and the plains of the middle Danube against the Avars, who had terrorized central Europe since the seventh century. His Aquitainian policies brought him into contact with Muslim leaders in Spain, and this in turn led to the establishment of a buffer zone between his realm and theirs known as the Spanish March. Charles was, moreover, a Christian believer, and as a ruler he keenly recognized his responsibility to protect and foster Christianity. Thus, his campaigns against Muslims in Spain and pagan peoples in central Europe became as much religious as political expeditions. Before doing battle with the Avars in 791, the Frankish army prayed and fasted for three days. All its warriors except the sick, the old, and the young abstained from wine and meat, while the clergy processed barefoot singing psalms. However strange this scene on the eve of battle, it bears witness to the importance of Christianity to the Franks. Charles hoped to enlarge the dominion of Christ and to establish the City of God as an earthly reality. A patrician of the Romans like his father, Charles was bound to protect the pope, and this duty likewise prompted his intervention in Lombard Italy.

Finally, Charles was an ambitious prince and a warrior by nature, and herein perhaps lies the key to his conquests. He sought to reign alone in the west, to defeat and displace rivals like the Bavarian duke or the Lombard king. Charles enjoyed combat as much as he shunned inactivity. Each spring he called up the royal host and directed it to a theater of operation. Chroniclers commented on the exceptional year when his war machine lay idle, because warfare was a "national institution of the Franks," a means of self-enrichment and a source of wealth to be shared with faithful vassals and the church. The king's treasury was swelled by the fruits of victory, such as the hoard of Irminsul captured in 772, or the treasury of King Desiderius in 774, or the stockpiled riches of the Avars in 795. To these must be added tributes forced from other unfortunate adversaries, like the Duchy of Benevento. As long as the conquests continued, the king could be sure of his control over the nobility and of receiving its help. Charles himself stemmed from the nobility. He knew its needs, its desires, and the cupidity of the great families of his day.

Charlemagne's Army

The military successes of Charlemagne depended on the strength of his army. Much discussion has been lavished on this point, either in amazement at the king's power or to underscore the difficulties posed by his uncertain resources. In theory, every Frank—that is, every free adult male except for clerics—was bound by military service. Local counts called up the men required for service, while royal vassals, both lay and ecclesiastical, dispatched persons who lived on their domains. In 806 Charlemagne summarized the routine in a mobilization order to Abbot Fulrad of St. Quentin:

> Be it known to you that we shall hold our general assembly this year in eastern Saxony. . . . Wherefore we command you to be present there on 17 June with your men well armed and equipped. . . . You should come with whatever arms, implements, provisions, and clothing may be needed to proceed from there with the army to whichever region we shall command. Each horseman should have a shield, a spear, a long-sword and a short-sword, a bow, a quiver, and arrows. Your carts should contain implements for various purposes. . . . There should also be provisions for three months, and weapons and clothing for six. . . . Your men should proceed to the appointed place by the shortest route, commandeering nothing along the way except for grass, firewood, and water.

Refusal, delay, and desertion commonly hampered the effort to mobilize. Those guilty of such infractions were punished by a heavy royal fine (*heribannum*), or even by death in the case of desertion.

At length Charles came to realize that a general mobilization each year tended to paralyze his government and disorganize economic life. The time of campaigning was also the time of agricultural labor, and even if slaves remained at home, free men were still needed to oversee their work. For these reasons, Charles instituted an ingenious system of providers and participants. He apportioned military burdens according to landed wealth, taking account of the number of manses, or family plots, held or owned by each free man:

> Each free man who possesses four manses in full production and owns them or holds them as a benefice of some other should take up his equipment and join the host, either with his lord if he is also going, or with the count. Whoever possesses three manses will be associated with the possessor of one manse who will help him to do service for both of them. Whoever possesses only one manse will be associated with three others who possess one manse, and the one who goes to the host will be aided by the three others who will remain at home.

The organization of the army is known to us from capitularies. These are administrative ordinances dictated by the king, but their actual application and effect is difficult to assess. The calls to order and repeated threats of heavy fines prove that Charles had trouble making himself obeyed. To escape military service, many men sought to enter the ranks of the clergy. Others paid their count or abbot for the privilege of remaining at home.

It is difficult to determine the size of the army commanded by Charles, and any figure proposed represents educated guesswork at best. Some historians have thought that Charles led at most five thousand troops, which would explain the difficulties he encountered, notably in Saxony. Others have attempted to base a figure on the number of domains owned by the royal fisc along with those of the bishoprics and abbeys of the realm. In this case, the king may have been able to assemble thirty-six thousand horsemen, in addition to foot soldiers and auxiliaries who might represent a total of approximately 100,000 men. It must, however, be remembered that the strength of Charlemagne's armies depended less on their size than on their armament and their military skill. Given well-armed and proven troops, a good leader could readily succeed against a more numerous foe. A prime feature of the Carolingian war machine was the heavy cavalry, which had acquired ever greater importance since the time of Charles Martel. The richest royal vassals owned thousands of domains and could afford to equip armored horsemen and stockpile iron weaponry, provisions, and clothing. These men made up the warrior elite, and they could be used as a special band of warriors, or *scara*, to execute small, rapid missions or to occupy strongholds. Such *scarae* played a decisive role in the conquest of Saxony. Horsemen appeared as formidable "men of iron." In his biography of Charlemagne, Notker the Stammerer depicted the arrival at Pavia in near epic tones: From the summit of a tower, Desiderius and Count Autchar surveyed the arrival of the supply train, the foot soldiers, the palace guards, the bishops, abbots, and clergy of the court chapel, and finally Charles himself, clad in shining armor, bearing a spear in one hand and a drawn sword in the other. The Frankish weaponry glistened as far as the eye could see. This brilliant iron shook the strength of enemy walls; it rattled the courage of the young; and it shattered the confidence of the old. In a civilization based largely on wooden implements, the possession of iron made for dominance. Thus the swords used by the Franks were renowned for their effectiveness. Foreigners sought to possess them, and Charles had to struggle against a flow of contraband arms to Scandinavia and the Slavs. In 779 he forbade the export of the metal-clad leather cuirass whose price was the equivalent of four mares or six cows. Apart from the heavy cavalry, other horsemen carried shields, spears, and swords, while foot soldiers played an important, but humbler role.

The success of the military operations depended to a great extent on the rapid mobilization and concentration of forces. Charles called up the necessary warriors in the lands adjoining the war grounds. He had sufficient men to divide them into several armies, which then converged on the enemy and encircled it. Because such maneuvers involved large scale movements, Charles was always careful to maintain roads and the various means of crossing waterways. One of the great projects undertaken during his reign was the construction of a wooden bridge that crossed the Rhine at Mainz. Einhard celebrated this achievement, and Notker spoke of it as an important accomplishment for all of Europe. Unfortunately, the bridge was destroyed by fire in 813, and Charlemagne did not have time to realize his plan to rebuild it in stone. For the year 793, the *Royal Frankish Annals* record another remarkable though unrealized scheme: to connect the Rhine and the Danube by means of a canal between their tributaries.

Certain persons who claimed to be competent in the matter had persuaded the king that if a navigable canal were dug between the rivers Rednitz and

Altmühl, a ship could very easily journey from the Danube to the Rhine. For one of the rivers joined the Danube, while the other connected with [the Rhine by way of the Main]. He immediately went to the place with his entire retinue, and when he had assembled a great multitude of men, he spent the whole autumn on this project. A ditch two thousand paces in length and three hundred paces in width was dug between the two rivers in question, but to no avail. On account of the constant rainfall and the marshy, waterlogged quality of the ground, the work could not be stabilized. No matter how much the diggers removed during the day, as much earth slid back in at night.

Begun during the war with the Avars, the canal could not be completed. But a section of it remains near the village of Graben (south of Weissenburg, Bavaria) at a site known as the *Fossa Carolina* ("Charlemagne's Ditch").

The Stages of Charlemagne's Conquests

768–771

In the early years of his reign, between 768 and 771, Charlemagne was occupied with expeditions within the Frankish realm, notably in Aquitaine. After the death of Carloman in 772, he initiated a policy of conquest. His rejection of the Lombard alliance favored by his mother made it even easier to respond to the distress calls of Pope Hadrian I and overrun the Lombard kingdom. The expedition went smoothly, and Desiderius was captured. Charles became king of the Lombards. During his lengthy siege of Pavia, he also traveled to Rome as a pilgrim and confirmed the "donation" made to St. Peter twenty years earlier by his father, Pippin III.

772–778

The second sphere of conquest was Saxony. In 772, Charles led a highly successful raid against the Saxons and secured their submission. In 777, at his new residence in Paderborn, he received the Saxon chiefs, whom he hoped to see baptized. There he was also sought out by a Muslim petitioner who urged him to intervene in northern Spain. The resulting expedition was cut short, and on its return, the Frankish rear guard was massacred by Basque attackers at Roncevaux. Among the victims was Count Roland of the Breton March, later transformed into the epic hero of the *Song of Roland*. The disaster as it actually happened was less dramatic than the eleventh-century poem, but in 778, it added to the misfortunes of an already difficult year. The losses at Roncevaux followed a revolt by the Saxon leader Widukind, and in Italy, Duke Arichis of Benevento had moved to enlarge his territories at the expense of the papal state.

779–793

Faced with the crises of 778, Charlemagne took the initiative. He dictated a capitulary in 779 at Herstal which the Belgian historian François Louis Ganshof has considered one of the king's most important legislative programs. Reiterating a number of points laid down by his father, Charlemagne sought to reinforce royal authority by ensuring good order in the church and the state. He then moved to address foreign challenges, first of all in Italy.

A second pilgrimage to Rome in 781 afforded him the opportunity to have his son Pippin proclaimed king of Italy. Hereafter, both the former Lombard kingdom and other parts of the peninsula were subject to Carolingian legislation. Pope Hadrian gladly served as a representative of Frankish power. On the death of Arichis of Benevento in 787, his eldest son was allowed to succeed him, but Charles forced the new duke to obey Frankish administrators. Finally, Charles annexed Byzantine-controlled Istria to his own Lombard kingdom.

As these events transpired in Italy, the king also put a stop to the hedging and deception of his cousin Tassilo, duke of Bavaria. In 787, the duke renewed his pledge of fealty and then failed to keep it. His duchy was eliminated, and the administration of Bavaria was committed to Charlemagne's brother-in-law, Gerold. Similarly decisive moves were made in Saxony. The Frankish king pushed his advances as far as the Elbe, and in the hope of quashing the continuing Saxon rebellions, he enacted a variety of draconian measures. These included wholesale massacres as well as a capitulary requiring that individuals choose between submission and Baptism or death. Meanwhile, Frisia was also subdued and Christianized. To the southwest, Charlemagne seized territory beyond the Pyrenees to secure the kingdom of Aquitaine, which was ruled as a separate realm by his son Louis after 781. These frontier lands formed the nucleus of what would become the Spanish March.

The period of these decisive accomplishments ended with a series of setbacks potentially graver than those of 778. A Muslim army crossed the Pyrenees in 793 and advanced as far as the Orbieu River, near Narbonne, where it inflicted a major defeat on the Frankish forces led by Duke William of Toulouse. Young King Pippin of Italy faced a rebellion in Benevento, and in Saxony a general revolt had erupted against the brutalities of the Frankish regime. At home, there lingered stirrings from an abortive conspiracy mounted by Pippin the Hunchback, a bastard son of Charlemagne, and a group of nobles. Poor weather also caused bitter famine across the kingdom.

793–800

Now aged 46, Charles had once again to counter adverse circumstances. He took a number of important steps destined to result in his imperial coronation of 800. Much as he had done at the assembly at Herstal in 779, the king convened the Council of Frankfurt in 794 in order to address pressing organizational, theological, and disciplinary issues. Charlemagne affirmed his role as head of the Frankish church by restoring order within it and by taking sides against the heresies of Adoptionism and Iconoclasm. In the same year, he also promulgated several important monetary and economic reforms, and decided to establish his fixed residence at Aachen. Unforeseen events subsequently favored his interests and policies: notably, the accession of the comparatively weak Pope Leo III in 795 and the palace revolution of 798 in Byzantium. Circumstances propelled Charlemagne to the imperial dignity and crown, which he received from Leo III on Christmas Day 800. Before his fateful trip to Rome, the king had successfully prosecuted his military goals. In the east, Saxony was largely "pacified," and a mammoth expedition against the Avars in 796 resulted in the conquest of their Ring and the capture of countless treasure. In the west, the Spanish March was reinforced and further secured when Barcelona fell to the Franks in 801 after two years of blockade.

800–814

The final period of Charlemagne's reign was less a time of conquest than one of attempted consolidation. As he grew older at Aachen, the emperor sought to protect his realm from the attacks of hostile foreigners: the Slavs who lived beyond the Elbe and in Bohemia; the Danes who ravaged Frisia and against whom he built a defensive fleet; and the Muslim pirates who raided Corsica and other areas near the Mediterranean coast. Without always succeeding, Charlemagne also worked tirelessly to ensure order and discipline within the empire. Although François Louis Ganshof overstates the difficulties when he speaks of "decomposition," Charlemagne clearly faced enormous problems trying to regulate the administration of his vast empire. This is the lesson of repeated admonitions and warnings found in contemporary capitularies. Charlemagne extended and multiplied the assignments of his *missi dominici*, or "personal envoys of the king," whose task was to ensure the rule of law. Likewise, he labored for ecclesiastical reform, and even ordered the convocation of five synods in 813 at Mainz, Tours, Reims, Chalon, and Arles.

In 806 Charlemagne arranged for the eventual partition of his empire among his three sons according to the tradition of Frankish kings. By 811 the two elder sons, Pippin and Charles, were both dead, and therefore in 813, Louis was crowned co-emperor by his father at Aachen. On 28 January 814, Charlemagne died at the end of a reign of 47 years, the longest to be enjoyed by a Carolingian monarch.

We have briefly surveyed the stages of an effort whose effect was to shape the early contours of medieval Europe. Yet it is impossible to understand Charlemagne's role in the creation of Europe without reviewing his actions region by region.

3. The Conquests of Charlemagne

Italy

The alliance between the Franks and the papacy had saved Rome without settling the destiny of Italy. After 756, King Desiderius reigned over the northern plains, while other Lombard princes ruled the more or less independent duchies of Spoleto and Benevento. The popes had obtained some former Byzantine territory from Pippin III, but the "donation" to St. Peter remained more theory than fact. The papacy could not force the transfer of the lands pledged in 756. It could only worry as Franco-Lombard relations warmed under the encouragement of Queen Bertrada and were momentarily sealed by the marriage of Charles and Desiderata. Arichis, a son-in-law of Desiderius, governed the southern Duchy of Benevento after 758. He proved to be a remarkable ruler whose piety, personal culture, and architectural achievements would earn the praise of Paul the Deacon. He was also a wealthy, efficient administrator who maintained good relations with the great abbeys situated in his duchy at Monte Cassino and at San Vincenzo al Volturno. For its part, Byzantium still possessed a few centers on the southwestern coast of Italy, like Gaeta, Terracina, Naples, and Amalfi, and in the far south, the patrician of Sicily controlled Calabria and the Otrano region.

THE CONQUEST

Two closely spaced events triggered the remedy for papal insecurity: the death of Carloman in December 771 and the accession of Pope Hadrian I in January 772. Now master of the entire Frankish realm, Charlemagne repudiated Desiderata. He discovered how Carloman's widow Gerberga had fled to Desiderius with the help of Count Autchar and how the Lombard king had sought to arrange for the royal anointing of one of Carloman's sons. Desiderius posed a clear threat to Charlemagne. Moreover, Pope Hadrian was obliged to send an embassy to the Frankish king by sea, since the Lombards had blocked passage through the Alps. The purpose of the embassy was to remind Charles that he was the patrician of the Romans and the guardian of the papacy. The Frankish king realized that any concession to Desiderius was impossible, so he opted to attack despite those who still favored the Lombard alliance.

The conquest presented many potential difficulties because the Lombard army was formidable. Two Frankish forces were directed across the Alps, and Desiderius retired behind the walls of his capital while his son Adalgisus took refuge together with Gerberga and her children at the even more formidable Verona. The ensuing siege of Pavia lasted for nineteen months, and at its end in 774, Charlemagne captured Desiderius and his treasure. He had already caught up with Gerberga and her children, even though Adalgisus managed to escape from Verona to Constantinople.

CHARLEMAGNE IN ROME

While his army besieged Pavia, Charles went as a pilgrim to celebrate Easter in Rome. This visit was a first; never before had a Frankish king visited the city. The pilgrim-king suddenly arrived in the spring of 774 with his bishops, abbots, counts, and soldiers. Charles was probably brimming with emotion as he approached Rome, the domain of Saint Peter, the chief of the Apostles, whose cult had spread throughout the west. For his part, Pope Hadrian I was surprised and somewhat worried, since he had lately managed to establish workable political ties between the duchies of Rome and Spoleto. The pope received the king according to the ritual used for a Byzantine exarch or *patricius*, but Charles did not enter the city walls before the two men had sworn an oath of mutual protection and fidelity.

After the Easter celebrations, there remained a further matter of business. At the behest of the pope, Charles ordered a reading of the "donation" that his father Pippin had made to St. Peter twenty years before. The *Liber pontificalis* records what followed:

> The stipulations that were added to it were approved by the king and by all his officials. Then, Charles, the most Christian king of the Franks, ordered of his own free will, freely and spontaneously, that Itherius, his chaplain and notary, should draft another promise of donation just like the preceding one. In it, he offered to Blessed Peter and promised to the pope the same towns and the same adjunct territories within the same boundaries as had been mentioned in the aforesaid donation.

A new frontier separating the pontifical state from the Lombard kingdom was laid out. Starting at Luna, near La Spezia, the boundary had included

Parma, Mantua, the Exarchate of Ravenna, Venezia, and Istria. The new promise added Corsica and the duchies of Spoleto and Benevento. The generosity of the Frankish king seems remarkable, but it must be added that only papal sources mention Charlemagne's agreement to such terms. Herein perhaps lay the source of later disagreement between Hadrian and Charles. In a hurry to return to Pavia, the king may have made an ill-defined commitment in response to the pope's requests. He surely would have been impressed, even intimidated by the papal court and the grandeur of Rome, and may have spoken injudiciously. In any event, the pope no doubt obtained a confirmation of some sort. Hadrian would cling to it tenaciously because he was as much a Roman aristocrat as a successor to Saint Peter. He certainly aspired to rule over much of Italy, but it is uncertain whether Charlemagne actually agreed to this.

CHARLEMAGNE'S SUCCESSES

Two months after Charlemagne's return from Rome, the Lombards of Pavia delivered Desiderius to him and surrendered. Without hesitation, the Frankish king entered the city, occupied the royal palace, and richly rewarded his followers with proceeds from the captured Lombard treasury. On 5 June 774, Charlemagne replaced Desiderius on the throne, and assumed a new title as "king of the Franks and the Lombards." To guard against any reversal of fortune, Desiderius was dispatched to the abbey of Corbie in northern France, where he was confined as a monk. Thus, a blow being struck, the royal power that had ruled Italy for two centuries passed to a new king. Contemporaries were astonished by the ease of the victory and by the generosity of the victor: "Although he might have destroyed everything, he showed himself clement and indulgent, and he permitted the Lombards to retain their laws and pardoned those who were traitors."

Nevertheless, not all Italians agreed to accept the domination of the king or pope. The archbishop of Ravenna dreamed of carving out an ecclesiastical princedom on the model of Rome. He seized several towns as well as the duchies of Ferrara and Bobbio. Duke Rodgaud of Friuli betrayed Charlemagne's confidence; he led a revolt in the hope of claiming the Lombard crown for himself. Desiderius' son Adalgisus also made his way back from Constantinople, and variously connived with Arichis of Benevento, Hildebrand of Spoleto, and the Greeks of southern Italy. Pope Hadrian was anxious to meet again with Charlemagne in order to press for fulfillment of the promises of 774. The king, however, was satisfied to strike rapidly in the spring of 776, in Friuli, and perhaps in Istria, which had been transferred theoretically to the pope.

THE SECOND JOURNEY TO ROME

Only in 780 did Charles again travel to Rome to celebrate Easter, accompanied by his queen, Hildegard, his daughter Gisela and his sons Carloman and Louis. From the start, this trip was intended as more than a simple pilgrimage. On Easter day, Charles had his son Carloman baptized by the pope; the four-year-old was christened Pippin after his grandfather. Then, at the request of the king, Pope Hadrian anointed Pippin king of Italy and Louis king of Aquitaine. This step marked an important advance insofar as Pippin became not king of the Lombards but of Italy. The boy was installed at Pavia under the tutelage of Charlemagne's cousin Adalhard and other Frankish officials. He had his own court, administrative personnel, and diplomatic emissaries, and also promulgated his own capitularies. But in fact he remained his father's delegate and acted accordingly. Frankish counts and soldiers were established in local towns, and abbeys from across the Alps received Italian lands. The progress of these Frankish inroads into Italy have been carefully studied by Eduard Hlawitschka.

In the midst of the Italian kingdom, the papal Republic of St. Peter enjoyed much theoretical, but less practical independence. The pope protested constantly against the encroachments and interference of Frankish administrators and bitterly complained when Roman officials appealed to the Frankish king. Yet there was little he could do against the invasion of his protector. As patrician of the Romans and successor to the Lombard kings, Charlemagne wanted the advantages of an Italy unified under his own control.

SOUTHERN ITALY

This policy encouraged the king to intervene in the southern part of the peninsula, in the Duchy of Benevento. After the fall of Desiderius, duke Arichis of Benevento had arranged to be proclaimed prince of the Lombards. He represented a serious rival, bolstered by immense wealth, prestige, and an alliance with Byzantium. Charles did not move rashly, but rather exploited vagaries of Byzantine policy. After September 780, the empress, Irene, ruled the east in the name of her son Constantine VI. This intelligent and ambitious woman renounced imperial iconoclasm and sought a rapprochement with the west. She envisaged a marriage between her son and Rotrude, a daughter of Charlemagne, a plan that naturally pleased the king, who thereby hoped to ally himself with the illustrious Byzantine dynasty. Arichis could no longer depend on imperial support. When Charlemagne came again to Rome in 787, he sought in vain to block an invasion of Benevento, but Charles moved south to Monte Cassino before advancing on Capua. Arichis had no choice but to submit, and he promised to pay the king a yearly tribute of seven thousand gold *solidi*. As soon as Charles had returned to France, the duke forgot his pledges. He preferred to offer his submission to the Byzantine empress Irene, who promised him the title of patrician. The death of Arichis in August 787 prevented the realization of this project, but his widow, Adalberga, still resisted the Frankish king who had shamed her sister and dethroned her father. Faced with the difficulties of occupying distant Benevento, Charlemagne still preferred negotiation to force. Despite the woeful prophecies of Pope Hadrian, he agreed to return Grimoald, the younger son of Arichis, who became heir to the duchy while in Frankish custody as a hostage. Charles allowed Grimoald to rule Benevento on several conditions: that he include the name of the Frankish king on his charters and coinage and, more curiously, that the Lombards shave their chins in the Frankish manner as a mark of submission. The duchy did not revert to the pope as theory required, but became a buffer state between Carolingian Italy and the Byzantine world. Charles further proved that he intended to remain master of the situation by annexing Istria, where Duke John replaced the Byzantine *hypatos*.

Thus, Charles became master of a large part of Italy. After centuries of confusion, the peninsula was reunified and attached to the Frankish dominion. This was an event of great political and cultural importance for Europe.

Germany

THE ANNEXATION OF BAVARIA

When Charlemagne became king, several German regions were already integral parts of the Frankish realm. Thuringia, Hesse, Alemannia, and the Rhine valley lived in the orbit of Austrasia and had been Christianized. Indeed, the ties between the leading families of the Carolingian homeland and their scions in these regions were so intimate and multiple that Charles never stood in fear of revolt.

Tassilo of Bavaria

To the south, the situation was different. The Duchy of Bavaria roughly formed a square bounded by the Danube, Enns, and Lech rivers, and it was semi-independent. In 757, Duke Tassilo III had agreed to be a vassal of his uncle Pippin the Short, but he preferred full independence and ultimately sought to escape from Frankish tutelage. He was the heir of the glorious Agilolfings, who had built up the duchy, and could count on the help of richly endowed monastic houses. Though jealous of his own autonomy, he did not shrink from annexing Carinthia (a Slavic territory traversed by the Drava and Sava rivers) with the help of Bavarian missionaries. Under the menace from the Avars, the Slovenes also turned to Bavaria for protection. When the rupture came between Charlemagne and Desiderius, Tassilo had the good sense not to intervene on the side of his father-in-law, the Lombard king. Whatever his gratitude, Charlemagne still viewed his cousin suspiciously as a potentially dangerous rival. He may even have envied the prestige Tassilo enjoyed on account of the culture and refinement of his court at Regensburg.

Despite appearances, the position of Tassilo was less than secure. Seen from a different angle, the Frankish annexations of Friuli and Lombard Italy amounted to an encirclement of Bavaria, and they had predictable consequences. In 781, Charlemagne demanded that Tassilo renew the pledges he had made to Pippin in 757. The duke agreed to come to Worms provided that he were given hostages "who would allow him not to fear for his safety." This mistrust was inauspicious for the future. In 787, Tassilo sensed the gathering storm, and sought help from the papacy, traditionally well disposed toward Bavaria. On this occasion, Pope Hadrian sided with Charles. He replied to the envoy that "if the duke set a hardened heart against the words of the sovereign pontiff, Charles and his army would be absolved of all sin and declared innocent for the fires, murders, and various misdeeds they might commit to the detriment of Tassilo and his accomplices." Given this free hand, Charles summoned Tassilo to Worms, and responded to the duke's refusal with a military campaign. The duke could not withstand the three armies that converged on him from Tirol and along the Lech and Danube rivers. On 3 October 787, at Lechfeld near Augsburg, Tassilo renewed the fealty he had once pledged to Pippin. Nevertheless, his wife, Liutberga, a daughter of the Lombard king Desiderius, encouraged him to continue his intrigues and even to enter into negotiations with the Avars. The Bavarian faction loyal to Charlemagne notified the king. This time, Charlemagne summoned the rebel vassal to Ingelheim for judgment. Abandoned by his followers, the duke admitted his treason and conceded the charges laid against him. Although Tassilo was condemned to death in 788, Charles hesitated to execute a member of the royal family. The king remitted the sentence, but obliged him to do penance in the monastery of Jumièges. His wife and children were likewise relegated to monasteries across the Frankish kingdom.

The New Administration

Charles himself took up residence in Regensburg. He exiled the Bavarian chiefs who opposed him, eliminated the office of duke, and set up an administrative regime based on local counts. His brother-in-law, the Aleman Gerold, was set over the military government of Bavaria with the title of *praefectus*, or "governor." In 794 Charles disposed of further resistance by forcing Tassilo to abdicate in the presence of the Council of Frankfurt.

Thus the ancient duchy and its Carinthian appendage were joined to the Frankish kingdom. Charlemagne now controlled the Danube valley and additional passes through the Alps to Italy. Regensburg became one of the Carolingian capitals, and its abbey of St. Emmeram a great religious center. In 798, Bishop Arno of Salzburg was made an archbishop with authority over the sees of Freising, Passau, Regensburg, and Säben(-Brixen). The abbeys that had long supported the Bavarian dukes were conferred on Frankish bishops: Mondsee went to Hildebold of Cologne and Chiemsee to Angilramn of Metz. Although Bavaria became part of a wider kingdom, it retained its individual character. During their subsequent history, Bavarians would always remember the eighty years of autonomy enjoyed under the Agilolfings.

THE CONQUEST OF SAXONY

Beyond the fifty-kilometer-wide strip of Frankish territory east of the Rhine was the homeland of the Saxons. This region stretched eastward from the Ems River to the Elbe and the Saale, and from the North Sea southward to the Harz Mountains; it corresponded roughly to modern Lower Saxony. The ground was covered with glacial debris, sand, and peat bogs, and the landscape was dominated by rivers and forests. Its inhabitants had once plied the seas, but now depended on agriculture and the rearing of cattle and horses for their livelihood. By the beginning of the eighth century, most of the population had come to form three great peoples: the Westphalians between the Rhine and the Weser, the Angarii in the Weser basin, and the Eastphalians of the Harz district. On the plains of the Elbe delta, there were also the smaller tribes of the Wihmuodi and the Nordalbingi.

Indigenous Institutions

Without arriving at definitive conclusions, the German historian Martin Lintzel studied Saxon political organization with the help of legislative texts and later chronicles, including that of Widukind. Saxon society was composed of three groups of persons: the nobility, who possessed castles and strongholds; a mass of free men; and the *lazzi*, or semi-free slaves. Although the *Earliest Life of Saint Lebuin* suggests that the Saxons came together each year at Marklô, the supposed assembly is probably a literary invention. The people were, however, fiercely pagan, as recorded by Einhard and other Carolingians writers. Near the stronghold at Eresburg, they revered a column-like tree trunk thought to support the heavens, the Irminsul. There they buried hoards of gold and silver and practiced blood sacrifice. For such reasons, their hatred of the Franks was as much religious as political. Although the Saxons had spurred the Frankish advance into Thuringia, they themselves never consented to pay tribute or to be pushed back. They hoped rather to continue along their traditional path of advance, the *Hellweg*, which followed the Lippe toward the Rhine, and they naturally clashed with the Franks defending Hesse and Austrasia.

The First Expeditions

Charlemagne sought to quell the Saxons early in his reign. In 772, he seized the stronghold at Eresburg, and then destroyed the shrine of Irminsul along with other nearby idols, removing the hoarded treasures. The Saxons responded by ravaging Hesse in 774 during the king's absence in Italy, and they made a special point of burning down Christian churches. A new Frankish campaign followed in the summer of 775. Charlemagne now resolved not merely to defeat the "perfidious and infidel" Saxons but to convert them. He captured Syburg on the Ruhr and rebuilt the damaged outpost at Eresburg, from which he descended the Diemel River as far as the Weser. His new footholds were provided with churches, and in 776, the campaign resumed. Charlemagne wrought such terror that by autumn the threat of further attack brought capitulation. Near the headwaters of the Lippe, Saxon leaders made over hostages, and a vast multitude of their people were baptized. The Frankish king then organized a march-frontier along the Lippe for the defense of Hesse. He established his regional headquarters at Paderborn amid forests and springs, not far from the place where Arminius had destroyed the army of Augustus in 9 A.D. During the great assembly confidently held at Paderborn in 777, Charlemagne entrusted Abbot Sturmius of Fulda with the task of organizing the Saxon mission. Thus ended the first Saxon campaign.

The Assault Renewed

In 778, the Saxons exploited the Frankish foray into Spain in order to rebel. At the call of the Westphalian chieftain Widukind, much of Saxony rose up against the Franks. The rebels advanced up to the Rhine, descended into Hesse, and even plotted without success to storm the abbey of Fulda. Charlemagne reacted swiftly, and followed through with additional expeditions across Saxony in 779 and 780. He installed missionaries and counts to pacify the region. The Anglo-Saxon Willihad established Christianity along the lower Weser in Wihmuodia, while Liudger, a disciple of Gregory of Utrecht, evangelized in East Frisia. In 782, at an assembly held at Lippspringe, Charlemagne organized the administration of conquered Saxony, entrusting some Saxon nobles with the duties of counts. Meanwhile, the rebel leader Widukind lurked at his refuge among the Danes, and as soon as Charles departed, he struck. The churches founded by Willihad and Liudger were promptly destroyed, and the missionaries driven off. But graver still, a part of the Frankish host was overwhelmed by Saxon forces at the Süntel Promontories along the Weser. The losses included the royal chamberlain Adalgisus, the stable master Geilo, four counts, and twenty other distinguished nobles. Charlemagne's reaction to the disaster added to its infamy. When he had advanced to Verden, at the confluence of the Aller and Weser rivers, he ordered the decapitation of 4,500 surrendered Saxon prisoners.

The massacre serves as a convenient preface to the "terror capitulary" of 785. Force appeared to be the best means of subduing and Christianizing the Saxons, such is the purport of the royal "Ordinances Concerning Saxony" (*Capitulatio de partibus Saxoniae*):

> Whoever enters a church by violence, or forcibly removes or steals any object from it, or sets fire to the building, shall be put to death.
>
> Whoever refuses to respect the Lenten fast out of contempt for Christianity and eats meat during the season, shall be put to death.
>
> Whoever kills a bishop, a priest, or a deacon, shall be put to death.
>
> Whoever burns the body of a dead person according to pagan ritual and reduces the bones to ash, shall be put to death.
>
> Any non-baptized Saxon who seeks to hide among his compatriots and refuses to request the sacrament, shall be put to death.

> Whoever fails to abide by the fidelity owed to the king, shall be put to death. . . .

With the help of such severe legislation, Charlemagne hoped to put an end to Saxon resistance. Since 783, he had staged multiple campaigns, even wintered in the field at Eresburg in 784 together with his wife and children. Finally, in 785, Widukind submitted to the Frankish king. The Saxon chief received Baptism at Attigny with Charles as his sponsor.

The submission of Saxony was cause for general rejoicing. In early 786, Pope Hadrian sent his congratulations to the king who

> with the help of the Lord and through the intervention of Peter and Paul had bent the necks of the Saxons to his power and authority, and led their entire nation to the holy fount of Baptism.

On three separate days in the following month of June, the pontiff ordered the celebration of special litanies "across the realm and beyond the sea, wherever Christians lived." The Anglo-Saxon Alcuin likewise associated events on the continent with the interests of his correspondents at home when he wrote:

> The holy church knows peace, prospers, and grows everywhere in Europe, for the Old Saxons and all the Frisian peoples . . . have been converted.

But this rejoicing was premature. Conversion by force did not prevent baptized Saxons from reverting to their ancient pagan rites. Moreover, the priests entrusted with the mission work were too few and too poorly trained. They forced the Saxons to tithe before teaching them the rudiments of the Faith. For his part, Alcuin soon turned from hope to lament:

> Had they preached to the hardened Saxons the gentle yoke of Christ and his sweet burden with the same zeal they applied to the collection of tithes and legal fines for the most paltry lapses, perhaps they would not abhor the sacrament of Baptism. . . . Did the apostles, taught and sent forth by Christ to teach the world, levy tithes and demand gifts? We know that tithes are a good thing, but it is better to give them up than to destroy belief.

Alcuin might well excoriate the men "who were not preachers, but rather predators." After a few years under the regime of terror, the Saxons took advantage of the crises of 793 to revolt once again.

The Final Campaigns

The *Annals of Lorsch* report how the third stage of the conquest of Saxony began:

> Convinced that the Avars would take vengeance on the Christians, the Saxons bared for all to see what had long been secretly hidden in their hearts. Like the dog that returns to its own vomit [2 Peter 2:22], they returned to the paganism that they had formerly renounced and made common cause with neighboring pagan peoples. . . . They demolished or burned down all the churches in their land; they chased out the bishops and priests set over them, attacking some and murdering others; and they altogether reverted to idolatry.

From 794 to 799, warfare resumed with greater ferocity than ever before. The Franks gradually reimposed their regime by wreaking devastation and by taking increasing numbers of hostages. In 797, Charlemagne could safely winter at a newly founded Saxon outpost named Herstelle, perhaps after his residence at Herstal. There, he gathered his court, hunted, received Avar and Visigothic embassies, and prepared to break the remaining resistance. For the recalcitrant Wihmuodi and Nordalbingi, Frankish determination took the form of a brutal, but effective policy of population removal. In 804, Charlemagne ended their resistance by deporting them to Francia. He then distributed their lands to his followers and to a friendly Slavic tribe living beyond the Elbe, the Obodrites.

However expedient, Charlemagne recognized that such extreme measures would not suffice to maintain his control in Saxony. He had therefore installed trustworthy Saxons to head a new regime of local counties, and he had also replaced the repressive legislation of 785 with the *Saxon Capitulary* of 797. Thereafter, fines rather than death punished crimes of rape, arson, and other violence. Charlemagne likewise ordered the codification of Saxon legal customs in a written *Law of the Saxons*, which long remained authoritative. Although the Saxons enjoyed a legal code of their own, its genesis and form underscored the political ties that now bound Saxony to the rest of the Frankish kingdom. As Einhard optimistically declared: "United with the Franks, the Saxons came to form with them a single people."

Thus, by means of humane legislation and inhumane deportations, the first "Thirty Years' War" came to an end in 804. Some have praised it as one of the greatest glories of Charlemagne the conqueror, while others have condemned it as one of the darkest episodes of his reign. Nazi historians indicted Charlemagne for forcibly Christianizing the Saxons, and adherents of their views tend even today to regard the chieftain Widukind as an epic national hero of the Germanic past. Such controversy notwith-standing, Charlemagne succeeded where Roman armies had failed. The conquest and Christianization of Saxony prepared for the emergence of the territorial grouping that would constitute medieval Germany.

The Frankish Regime in Saxony

Meanwhile, the newest component of the Frankish kingdom witnessed an influx of civil officials, priests, and monks who settled at various fortified outposts along the roads leading east from the Ruhr to the Weser estuary and then to the middle Elbe. The first episcopal sees were established. In 789, Willihad returned to Wihmuodia as bishop of Bremen, where he re-mained until his death in 804. At Paderborn, a church dedicated to the Holy Saviour was erected, and its bishop was the Saxon Hathumar, a former hostage who had been raised in a Frankish monastery. On the Weser, Verden and Minden also became bishoprics. The incumbents of all these sees oversaw the Christian missionary effort, and they worked closely with new monastic foundations such as Werden and Helmstadt. In 815 the monks of Corbie founded a "new Corbie" in Saxony, their famous daugh-ter house at Korvei.

Likewise pacified and Christianized, the Frisians also received from Charlemagne a written code of customary law as well as a new bishopric at Münster in East Frisia. The settlement took its name from the minster founded on the site by Liudger before he become its bishop in 805.

At Charlemagne's death in 814, the Christianization of Saxony was advanced but not complete. It would be the task of his son Louis the Pious to create other bishoprics at Halberstadt, Hildesheim, and Osnabrück.

Central and Eastern Europe

The annexation of Bavaria had brought the Franks into contact with the Danube territories held by the Avars. Similarly, the conquest of Saxony pitched them against new Slavic adversaries by advancing their frontier some 400 kilometers to the east. Thus another emerging area of the future Europe came to feel Frankish power and influence.

SUPPRESSION OF THE AVAR MENACE

The Avars were an Asian people established in the Danube basin since 570. They exercised a reign of terror over most of central Europe. Called the "new Huns," they were led by chiefs who bore such titles as *khagan, jugur* and *tarkan*. Several chroniclers describe their "capital," the *Ring*, as a fortified camp defended by nine concentric ramparts situated between the Tisa and Danube rivers. Fearsome horsemen with Mongolian features, the Avars pillaged churches and exacted tributes, and amassed the extorted treasure in their great fortified retreat. Even worse, they also welcomed the Lombard and Bavarian enemies of Charlemagne.

After the Avars conspired with Tassilo of Bavaria against Charles in 788, reprisal was merely a question of time. Once in command at Regensburg, Charles prepared for the war that Einhard would call "the greatest of all the wars waged by him after the Saxon war, a war waged with more ardor and with much greater means than the others." In 791, a great campaign began with the celebration of Masses, fasts, and prayers to secure "the safety of the army, the help of the Lord Jesus Christ, and the defeat and punishment of the Avars." Charles led one army along the south bank of the Danube, while Count Theuderic and the chamberlain Meginfrid commanded another across the river; between the land forces, Gerold, governor of Bavaria, headed a flotilla carrying provisions and additional troops. From the south, Pippin of Italy also advanced against the Avars through Friuli and Carniola.

Avar fortifications in the woodlands near Vienna collapsed when faced with the massive Frankish drive, but when Charles reached the Danube-Raab confluence an outbreak of pestilence among the horses halted the campaign of 791. Again settled in at Regensburg, the king laid plans for another expedition. With an eye to the logistical needs of the Avar campaign, Charlemagne embarked in late 793 on his unsuccessful effort to link the Rhine and the Danube by digging a vast canal. His attention was then claimed by a revolt in Saxony, and Pippin of Italy finally received the task of launching a new expedition against the Avars. With the help of Duke Eric of Friuli and the Croatian chieftain Vojnomir, Pippin forced his way as far as the Ring in 795 and seized part of its treasures. In 796, he returned and destroyed the fortified "capital" of the Avars. Its fabled treasures were captured; to cart them home, the Franks needed 15 wagons, and each of them was drawn by four oxen. As Einhard later reported:

> Human memory can recall no war against the Franks which so greatly profited and enriched them. Indeed, although up to then they almost seemed to be paupers, they found so much gold and silver in the palace of the *khagan*,

such precious spoils carted off by force of arms, that we can rightly believe that the Franks justly took back from the Huns what they had formerly taken from others unjustly.

Missionaries from Salzburg had accompanied the Frankish forces, and they immediately set about the task of Christianizing the newly subdued territories. Alcuin and Paulinus of Aquileia warned against haste and recalled the failure of the methods applied in Saxony. The Avars were "a barbarian people, impervious to reason, uneducated, narrow-minded, and slow to accept the holy mysteries." Thus it was necessary to proceed by patient steps, to preach before baptizing, to refrain from exacting tithes. Despite their wisdom, these counsels fell largely on deaf ears. In 799 a revolt resulted in the death of Gerold, governor of Bavaria, and of Duke Eric of Friuli. At the start of the ninth century, Charlemagne needed to mount additional expeditions to quash the remnants of Avar resistance, but in 805 the *khagan* himself finally accepted baptism and pledged his fealty to the Frankish ruler.

Charlemagne also annexed Carinthia, which stretched between the Enns River and the woodlands around Vienna. Called the Avar March (*limes avaricus*), this region became the cradle of the future "Eastern March," or *Ostmark*, known today as Austria. Beyond the Raab and up to the shores of Lake Balaton, new Bavarian and Slavic colonists mingled with the Avar population. Frankish counts were appointed to regulate the differences that arose between these groups, and churches were established under the control of Archbishop Arno of Salzburg. A part of the Avar people also simply refused to submit. They fled to the east and settled within the Slavic kingdom organized by Krum (803–814), the *khagan* of the Bulgars.

CHARLES AND THE SLAVIC WORLD

The Slavs were not entirely alien to the Franks. Dagobert I had made war against them in 631 during their brief period of unity under the merchant-king Samo. Since the seventh century, various northern groups had encroached on Saxony, Thuringia, and Bavaria, while bands of South Slavs had carved out territories of their own in the Balkans. The Slovenes of Carinthia had also been evangelized by Bavarian missionaries.

The Slavic Peoples of the North

In the north there were roughly a dozen variously distinguishable groups. The Obodrites lived beyond the Elbe among the lakes and waterways of

Holstein and western Mecklenburg, followed to the south and east of the Warnow River by the Wilzi. Farther south there came the Linoni and Smeldingi, and near the Thuringian frontier, the Sorbs. These peoples lived as clans and tribes and possibly formed confederations. The Wilzi are even reported to have held regular assemblies at a shrine at Rethra.

These West Slavs lived primarily as fishermen, herdsmen, and farmers, but also traded along the great navigable rivers. Their lands were dotted with strongholds that served as homes for their military chiefs, each of whom kept an entourage of client followers, the *druzina*. The chronicler known as the "Bavarian geographer" (*Geographus bavarus*) called these citadels *civitates*, and there were some 50 of them among the Sorbs, 53 among Obodrites, and 95 among the Wilzi. They played an important role as havens amid the constant internecine strife that divided these Slavic peoples. The divisions among them were, however, an opportunity exploited by Charlemagne to his own advantage.

Threatened by the Wilzi, the Obodrites soon became loyal allies of the Franks. They helped Charles in his struggle against the Nordalbingi, and at the time of the Saxon deportations in the early ninth century, they received additional lands west of the Elbe. Charles organized several expeditions against the Wilzi and the Linoni. In 789 he crossed the Elbe with the help of Frisian, Saxon, Obodrite, and Sorb contingents and advanced up the Havel River toward the Baltic Sea. The desolation wrought by the Frankish invasion forced Dragovit, the chief of the Wilzi, to pledge his submission and surrender hostages. Although isolated persons had already sought Baptism as early as 780, missionaries now dreamed of a wholesale conversion of the Wilzi, but obscurity shrouds the actual effect of these intentions noted by Alcuin in a letter of 789. To counter periodic incursions by the Sorbs into southern Saxony and Thuringia, Charles had dispatched an army in 782 that was destroyed by Saxon rebels at the Süntel Promontories. In 806 new agitation by the Sorbs provoked a demand for hostages and an expedition that resulted in the death of their leader, Miliduoch. As a visible token of Frankish authority, the invading army erected and garrisoned two strongholds, one below Magdeburg on the Elbe and another at Halle on the Saale. The *limes sorabicus*, or Sorbian March, was still modest, but it expanded under Charlemagne's successors and became in the tenth century the springboard of the eastern expansionism (*Drang nach Osten*) of the Saxon kings.

The Czechs and the Croats

Still farther south in Bavaria, Charlemagne was obliged to secure the frontier against the Czechs and the South Slavs. In 805, he dispatched his son Charles to Bohemia to subdue the Czechs. Three Frankish armies combined in the valley of the Eger River, and then advanced upstream along the Elbe. The Czech leader, Lecho, was killed, and his warriors retired into the hills. A second expedition in 806 achieved little, although Einhard implies that Bohemia was swiftly brought under Frankish control. In Carinthia, the Croats were carefully watched by the duke of Friuli. This people was composed of two distinct groups: the Pannonian Croats, who lived on either bank of the Sava River; and the Dalmatian Croats, or Guduscani, who inhabited the mountainous coastal region of Liburnia. In collusion with the Avars, the latter group is thought to have ambushed and killed Duke Eric of Friuli in 799. The Lombard Aio, who succeeded him as duke of Friuli, was charged with containing these populations, who were gradually being converted to Christianity.

Europe Beyond the Frontiers

However considerable the expansion of the Frankish kingdom, its boundaries were subject to a variety of limitations. Frankish political power could do little to influence Anglo-Saxon England, Scandinavia and the Celtic lands, and outside the Spanish March, Iberia obeyed different masters. With all these regions, Charlemagne had to be content with more or less peaceful diplomatic relations.

THE CELTS

The Celts of Brittany had never been subdued by the Merovingian kings. Likewise, fortified barriers, or *guerches* (from the Germanic *werki*), blocked the waterways and obstructed Breton access to the Frankish kingdom. The Carolingians inherited this situation and established a military frontier zone, or march, to guard against Breton encroachments. In 778, Count Roland was one of the officers charged with the defense of this territory situated between Tours, Rennes, and Angers. After a long and largely ineffective campaign in 789, Charlemagne entrusted the government of the Breton March and the Atlantic coastal region to his eldest son, Charles the Younger. In 799, count Wido—a scion of the powerful Widonid clan of the Mosel region—exploited the rivalries of the Breton clan chieftains (*machtierns*) to invade and ravage their lands. One chronicler commented on the event:

> It seemed that [Brittany] was entirely subdued, and it would have been if the customary fickleness of those faithless people had not incited them to a prompt change of heart.

A further expedition in 811 failed to achieve the desired results. The Bretons remained independent. They maintained their religious customs and continued to look more to the Celtic lands of the British Isles than to the Frankish world.

Despite the wishful pronouncements of Einhard, the Celts of Cornwall, Wales and Scotland in fact knew nothing of Charlemagne. Whatever contact the Carolingians enjoyed with Ireland was due to the learned "Scots" who migrated to the Frankish court, or to the Anglo-Saxon scholar Alcuin. Thus, in 792, Alcuin addressed a missive "to the sons of the holy church who devote themselves to religious life and to the study of wisdom in Ireland." Perhaps Alcuin was aware of the work of contemporary Irish scribes and miniaturists who were creating such masterpieces as the *Book of Kells* and the *Book of Armagh*. Interestingly enough, these achievements grew out of the reforms of the Irish Culdees ("servants of God") of the mid-eighth century, the very period that witnessed parallel ecclesiastical reform in England and Gaul.

THE ANGLO-SAXONS

Alcuin was also a link between Charlemagne and the Anglo-Saxon kingdoms. Although he came to settle in Gaul, he maintained contacts with his homeland and returned there for extended visits in 786 and 790.

Among the various Anglo-Saxon kingdoms that vied for dominance in Britain, Mercia gained the upper hand thanks to Offa, who ruled there from 757 to his death in 796. The king is well remembered for the great rampart, "Offa's Dike," which he built along the Welsh border to defend against Celtic raids. He was also a notable admirer and emulator of Charlemagne. By allying himself with Wessex through marriage and annexing Kent, Sussex, and East Anglia, Offa unified southern England. He governed his extended dominion with the help of the bishops, and in concert with the papal legates of Hadrian I, he reorganized the English church. In 787 Offa raised his son to the Mercian throne as co-ruler, and to seal the act, he had his associate anointed after the fashion of the Frankish kings. His most enduring legacy was the introduction of a system of coinage modeled on the units prescribed by Charlemagne; this non-decimal tradition survived in Britain until 1971. Letters exchanged between Offa and Charlemagne mention the commercial ties that no doubt encouraged the adoption of Frankish units, especially the sale of Anglo-Saxon textiles on the continent.

The death of the self-styled "king of the entire homeland of the Angles" in 796 unleashed revolts among the tributary kingdoms. In Northumbria, turmoil struck when its king, Offa's brother-in-law, was murdered and his successor, Eardwulf, was later forced to flee to Charlemagne's court in 808. Charlemagne and the pope worked to restore the refugee to his throne in York, but no "Frankish protectorate" arose in Northumbria as some have contended. Charlemagne did, however, strive to cultivate good relations with this kingdom since it was the homeland of many of his Anglo-Saxon helpers, such as Alcuin, Lull of Mainz, Liudger of Münster, Willihad of Bremen, and Beornred of Sens. Moreover, Northumbria was a natural ally against the common menace posed by the Danes.

SCANDINAVIA

By the end of eighth century, the coastlines of both England and the Frankish kingdom had come under attack by Scandinavian raiders.

Scandinavia had been at the root of the Germanic invasions of late antiquity. In the words of Jordanes, the region was the "womb of nations." Nevertheless, the Scandinavian peoples had remained relatively isolated after the sixth century apart from intermittent contact with the Frisians and the Anglo-Saxons.

In the eighth century, the peoples of Scandinavia could be readily distinguished as three basic groups. Nearest to the west, on the Danish peninsula and the south coast of Sweden, were the Danes. This people lived as seagoing merchants and pirates. They traded with the Frisians on the Isle of Heligoland, and stockpiled booty in a camp at Haithabu first mentioned in 804. Along with rich archaeological evidence, the *Beowulf* epic sheds light on the common cultural background of the Danes and the Anglo-Saxons of England. Farther north came the second occupants of Scandinavia. The Swedes were in fact composed of two groups: the Svears, who lived around Lake Mälar, near modern Stockholm, and the more southerly Gotars. They had a trading center at Birka, and the Island of Gotland served as a Swedish stepping-stone to the shores of Kurland (along the Baltic coast of modern Latvia). Finally, there were the peoples of Norway, a land whose name literally meant "pathway of the north." These Norwegians lived along the Oslo and Trondheim rivers.

Judicious comparison of sagas written down at the close of the twelfth century and the findings of modern archaeologists help to flesh out our knowledge of the political and social organization of early Scandinavia. Popular assemblies, or *things*, periodically brought together the free men of the community under the leadership of the wealthy landed proprietors (*laendr*). The richest of these landholders became the founders of the royal dynasties noted in the sagas, and recently excavated burial mounds bear witness to the magnificence of their wealth. These same nobles were also the priests of a pagan cult very similar to that of the ancient Germans. In Sweden, the shrine at Uppsala, near Stockholm, was dedicated to Thor, Odin, and Freyr.

After a long period of isolation, the Scandinavians embarked on increasingly numerous maritime raids against Britain and the coasts of the Frankish world. The use of technologically advanced ships, equipped with central masts and square-rigged sails, favored the progress of the "Northmen," also known as Vikings, that is, "men who frequent the bays." The Norwegians had landed on English shores by 787, and soon also raided Ireland. In a well-known letter of 793, Alcuin painfully evoked the plundering of the monastery of Lindisfarne on the Northumbrian coast. For their part, the Danes pillaged Frisia and threatened the port of Dorestad. Charlemagne warily followed these adventures. His Saxon campaigns were hampered when the Danes for a while offered refuge to Widukind and again when the Danish chieftain Godofrid allied himself with the Wilzi and the Linoni to attack the friendly Obodrites. Einhard reports that

> Godofrid was so puffed up with vain hopes that he planned to rule all Germany. He considered both Frisia and Saxony as little more than provinces of his own. . . . He boasted that he would soon arrive with a great body of troops at Aachen where the royal court was located.

To protect Saxony, Charlemagne organized a series of defenses centered around Itzehoe, on the Stör River, and Schissbek, near Hamburg. This was the origin of the so-called Danish March, which became the name of Denmark. After the assassination of Godofrid in 810, Charlemagne made peace with his successors, but continued to shore up his maritime defenses. In 811, he personally inspected the flotillas assembled at Ghent and Boulogne. In the latter town, he ordered the restoration of the long-abandoned Roman lighthouse, and a contemprorary capitulary instructed local leaders to be ready to take to sea in the event of danger. A master of land warfare, Charlemagne realized somewhat late that his armies were ill equipped to defend the coastline.

SPAIN

Turning from the northern reaches of the Frankish realm to Spain in the southwest, we find a peninsula once ruled by the Romans, but that Charlemagne himself could scarcely hope to conquer. Spain was shared by two governments of unequal power: the Visigothic kings, who ruled the northerly Kingdom of the Asturias, and the Muslim emirs of Cordoba, who controlled the south.

Gothic refugees had established the much reduced Kingdom of the Asturias in the wake of the Arab conquest of 711. Under Alfonso I (739–757) and his successors, Christian forces had retaken the territories of Galicia, Cantabria, and León. The *Reconquista* had begun in earnest. Alfonso II, the Chaste (791–835), managed to retake Lisbon in 797, and thereafter undertook to repopulate the territory abandoned by the Muslims. Castile would later earn the name by which it is known from the castles that bristled across its landscape. Alfonso II had established his capital at Oviedo amid a newly built complex of grandiose churches and palaces. Like Charlemagne, he governed through episcopal aides, presided over councils, and sponsored literary learning. He dispatched several embassies to the Frankish ruler, but contrary to Einhard's assertion, he never sought to become Charlemagne's vassal.

Along with the envoys of Alfonso, Charlemagne also received officials from Muslim Spain. After revolting against the Umayyad emir Abd ar-Rahman (756–788), Sulaiman, the *wali* of Barcelona and a partisan of the Abbasids, journeyed to Paderborn in 777 to enlist Frankish support. Charlemagne took the risk of complying, no doubt in the hope of wresting Spain from the Arab forces against which his father and grandfather had struggled. The famous expedition of 778 ended in disaster. After failing to take Saragossa due to infighting among his Muslim allies, Charles headed back across the Pyrenees. In a mountain pass at Roncevaux, the Frankish rearguard was massacred. Although the eleventh-century *Song of Roland* attributes the attack to Muslim treachery, the rear guard in fact fell victim to the Basque fighters, who fiercely resisted any act of Frankish or Visigothic encroachment. The battle cost the lives of the count of the palace Anselm, the seneschal Eggihard, and Count Roland of the Breton March, who was laterly immortalized in the *Song of Roland*. This bitter misfortune was a hard blow, and it fostered additional threats of backlash across the sorely tried lands of "pacified" Aquitaine. To counter this menace and supply a durable solution to regional particularism, Charlemagne created the Kingdom of Aquitaine in 781 and entrusted it to his son Louis. A further consequence of the Frankish foray into Spain was the arrival in Septimania of Christians fleeing Muslim domination. Among these *Hispani* were the future bishops of Lyon and Orléans, Agobard and Theodulf, who both set their literary talents at the service of the Carolingian court.

Young King Louis and his counselors were charged with the duty of defending Aquitaine from Muslim attack. In 785 they followed up renewed offers by local Muslim princes and occupied the towns of Gerona and Urgel and the region of Cerdanya. The emir of Cordoba reacted with a massive raid in 793 that ended in the defeat of Duke William of Toulouse, a cousin of Charlemagne. Curiously, an epic legend also grew up around the hero of this defeat, who ended his life as a monk at the abbey of Gellone, which later took his name as St. Guillaume-du-Désert. The Franks soon regained their foothold south of the Pyrenees and established the Spanish March. In 801, Louis captured Barcelona while to the northwest Pamplona and Navarre came under Frankish control despite the persistent hostility of the Basques. Although Charlemagne did not manage to extend his conquest fully up to the Ebro River, the creation of the Spanish March was of immense importance for Spain. It was precursor of the future territory of Catalonia.

4. The Emperor Charlemagne

Prelude to the Coronation

Although some parts of Europe lay outside his control, Charlemagne was unquestionably the most powerful ruler in the west at the end of the eighth century. He ruled over an assemblage of territory that included Gaul, Germany, Italy, and the regions that adjoined them, and his vast dominion gave him the air of a king above other kings. Charles had appointed his own sons as subkings over Italy and Aquitaine; made his brother-in-law governor of Bavaria, and entrusted the marches to great nobles allied to his family by blood. He was a ruler who satisfied a definition current in his day: "He is emperor who dominates throughout the whole world; under him stand the kings of other kingdoms." Thus, when Alcuin wrote of the expansion of the Frankish kingdom in his *Life of Saint Willibrord*, he called it an "empire."

THE "NEW DAVID"

Charles was not merely a king vested with immense political power; he was also a Christian prince who placed his resources at the service of his Faith. He struggled against the pagan Saxons and the Muslims of Spain. Within his kingdom, he sought by means of various capitularies to ensure the rule of Christian law. In the preface of the *Admonitio generalis*, or General Exhortation, of 789, Charlemagne compared himself to Josiah, the biblical king who sought "to restore to God's service, by inspecting, correcting, and exhorting, the kingdom that God had committed to him." The Frankish king opposed even those heretics who lived outside his realm. Thus, he attacked Adoptionism, a heresy that had first been articulated in Toledo and was subsequently embraced in the Kingdom of the Asturias and the Pyrenees region. The grounds for such action had been laid on the day that Charles received royal unction. Like a new Moses, he was a religious lawgiver; like a new David triumphing over the foes of Israel, the Frankish king led a new chosen people to its salvation. By mak-

ing common cause with such a king and seeking his protection for the
Roman church, the popes confirmed the special destiny of both the Carolingian dynasty and the Frankish people. When Pope Hadrian appealed
for the territories promised by Charlemagne, he did not hesitate to hope
that the king would become "a new Constantine."

RELATIONS WITH BYZANTIUM

Nevertheless, there remained the Empire of Byzantium, which had been
the sole empire since 476. When the emperor, or *basileus*, Leo IV died in
780, his wife, Irene, reigned in the name of the young Constantine IV.
From the start, Charles sought an accommodation with Irene, and even
agreed to the engagement of his daughter Rotrude to Constantine in 781.
But the political course pursued by Byzantium in Italy soon undermined
relations with the Franks. Insult was added to injury when Irene moved in
787 to settle the Iconoclastic Controversy. To restore the veneration of holy
pictures, she convened the Second Council at Nicea, to which a papal
legate was invited while the Frankish leader received no notice whatsoever.
Charlemagne only learned of the event from a highly defective Latin translation of its canons and proceedings. Whereas the king and his advisers
were more and more taken with the weight of their religious mission in
the west, they were confronted by seeming heresy in these conciliar documents. Charles thus commanded Bishop Theodulf of Orléans to draft a
rebuttal of the mistranslated decisions of Nicea. The Franks accused the
Byzantines of worshiping images and of being idolaters. The brunt of the
attack was leveled at Irene: "The weakness of her sex and the fickleness of
her feminine heart do not permit a woman to exercise supreme authority
in matters of Faith and of rank."

In 794, Charles convened the Council of Frankfurt as his own response to Nicea. Not only did clergy gather from across the Frankish kingdom along with representatives of the pope, but delegations from England
also participated at the great assembly, over which the king himself presided. Decisions were taken concerning general reforms within the realm,
the heresy of Adoptionism, and finally, the Iconoclastic Controversy. It
became ever more clear that King Charles meant to rival the pretensions
of Empress Irene. He had himself called "the chief of the chosen people,"
and even adopted the style of the *basileus: rex et sacerdos*, "king and priest."
Likewise, the *Laudes regiae*, or Royal Acclamations, composed about 796
and chanted before the king at great liturgical celebrations, jointly exalted
the pope, the king, his lineage, and the entire host of the Franks. Charles

was portrayed as the leader of a "Christian empire," and this very expression appeared ever more frequently in the writings of Alcuin, his adviser.

THE ACCESSION OF POPE LEO III AND THE "NEW CONSTANTINE"

Two events hastened the germination of genuine imperial claims.

First, Pope Hadrian I died in 795 and was followed by a weak successor. Owing to his modest origins, the new Pope Leo III easily fell prey to the notorious infighting of the Roman nobility. He needed the protection of the Frankish king. Soon after his coronation, the pope sent Charlemagne the standard of the city of Rome and delegated to him the civil governance of the town. Later, he commissioned a revealing program of mosaics for the *triclinium*, or audience hall, of his Lateran palace: on one side, Christ was depicted granting keys to Saint Peter and a banner to Constantine; on the other, St. Peter was represented giving a pallium to Pope Leo and a banner to King Charles. The banner motif clearly expressed the parallelism between Charles and Constantine, the model of Christian emperors. Accordingly, Pope Leo III prodded Charlemagne along the path to empire. For his part, Charlemagne drew appropriate distinctions between the roles involved in his progress. This, at least, is the lesson of his words to the new pope in 796:

> With the help of divine clemency, it is my duty outwardly to defend the Holy Church of Christ by arms from the various attacks of the pagans and the devastation of the infidels and inwardly to fortify her by spreading knowledge of the catholic faith. It is your duty, Most Holy Father, with your hands raised to God like Moses, to help by prayer in our victory.

In another letter, Charlemagne enjoined the pope to live honorably and to observe the laws of the church. However curious, these admonitions were much to the point. Showered with accusations of "crimes and felonies," Leo III was nearly assassinated on a Roman street in 799, and he was forced to flee to Paderborn and Charlemagne's protection.

The second event that favored the imperial coronation in the west was a palace coup in Constantinople. In 797, Empress Irene had her son blinded and took power herself. Although this palace revolution had no repercussions on Franco-Byzantine relations, it permitted the view that in fact no emperor remained in the east and that *his* throne lay vacant. This was the attitude taken by Alcuin in a famous letter to Charlemagne of June 799:

Up to now three persons have been at the summit of this world. First, there is the holder of the sublime Apostolic Dignity, who is supposed to guide the see of Blessed Peter, Prince of the Apostles, as his vicar; and Your Kindness has informed me of what happened to him who was the guide of that see. Second, there is the holder of the Imperial Dignity, who exercised secular power in the Second Rome; and rumor spreads everywhere of how impiously the governor of that empire has been deposed by his own circle and citizens, rather than by foreigners. Third, there is the Royal Dignity, in which the dispensation of our Lord Jesus Christ has established you as ruler of the Christian people; in power a ruler more excellent than the aforementioned ones, in wisdom more radiant, and in grandeur more sublime. Behold, now in you alone lies the salvation of the churches of Christ. You are the avenger of crimes, the guide of those who err, the consoler of the afflicted, the uplifter of the righteous.

Soon after this letter, an anonymous court poet exalted King Charles as "head of the world and summit of Europe, the new Augustus who reigns in a New Rome," that is, at Aachen. Together, these texts witness clearly enough that the counselors of Charlemagne were expecting his coronation as emperor.

The Coronation

Charles, however, temporized as though he dreaded the impending promotion. He sent the refugee Leo back to Rome in the company of bishops and counts and commissioned an inquiry into the accusations made against the pope. During 800—a year supposed by some to herald the end of the world—Charles visited the northern coastal regions of his kingdom. He sojourned at St. Bertin, celebrated Easter at St. Riquier, and then traveled to Tours to pray at the tomb of Saint Martin and confer with Alcuin who had presided over the shrine since 796 as abbot. He hoped that Alcuin would accompany him to Italy, but his friend feared some action would be taken against the pope. He therefore invoked his poor health, and addressed instead a poem to his "dear David":

> . . .
> In spirit I follow you, as does this poem of my affection.
> . . .
> God has made you master of the realm. . . .
> Rome, head of the world, its father, and its people
> In pious love of peace await you as their guardian.

. . .

May the ruler of the church rule rightly thanks to you.
May the hand of the Almighty be your guide
That you may reign happily over the world.
May He who leads you ever prosperously
Also shield and guide your homecoming,
So joyous Francia may receive you victorious.

THE CEREMONY

When he arrived at Rome, Charles was received triumphally. On 1 December 800, he convened at St. Peter's an assembly of Frankish and local clergy along with representatives of the Roman nobility in order to resolve the questions surrounding the pope. Some persons asserted that no one had the right to judge the Apostolic See, but after three weeks of discussion Charles forced Leo III to purge himself by pronouncing a solemn oath in accord with Germanic legal custom. This ceremony, tremendously humiliating for the pope, took place on 23 December. Precisely what then followed is uncertain, since the sources differ appreciably from one another. According to the well-informed compiler of the *Annals of Lorsch*, the assembly moved on to debate the reestablishment of the empire:

> Since there was no longer an emperor in the land of the Greeks and they all were under the domination of a woman, it seemed to Pope Leo and to all the fathers who sat in the assembly, as well as to the whole Christian people, that they should give the name of emperor to the king of the Franks, to Charles, who occupied Rome, where the Caesars had customarily resided, and also Italy, Gaul, and Germany. Because Almighty God had consented to place these lands under his authority, it seemed right, according to the desire of the whole Christian people, that Charles should also bear the imperial title.

According to Robert Folz, who closely follows this witness, Charlemagne was thus proclaimed emperor on 23 December 800.

Hoping to wipe away the humiliation he had just suffered, Leo III took back the initiative. He prepared on his own the coronation ceremony that took place on Christmas Day 800, loosely following the ritual used in Byzantium. The Byzantine rite comprised three distinct parts: (1) acclamations by the populace and the army, (2) the coronation, and (3) the reverence, or *proskynesis*, of the patriarch before the new emperor. Leo III chose to invert this order. To retain the first place for himself, he began by setting the crown on Charlemagne's head and then invited the congregation to acclaim him thrice: "To Charles Augustus, crowned by God, great and pacific emperor of the Romans, life and victory!" The pope then knelt before the new emperor, a gesture he no doubt later regretted, since the *Liber pontificalis* discreetly omits it. Contrary to the papal account of events, the *Royal Frankish Annals* compiled by the clerics of the court chapel assign the prime role to the king rather than to the pope. They recall how Charles came to Rome to investigate the accusation lodged against the pope and for "other business," which may imply that Charles himself had made preparations for the coronation. Moreover, these same *Annals* mention the arrival at Rome of emissaries from the patriarch of Jerusalem, who presented the king with the keys of the Holy Sepulchre and the standard of the holy city. Like his father, Charles had enjoyed close relations with the Abbasids, who ruled Jerusalem. He was interested in the fate of the eastern Christians, particularly of those living near the Holy Sepulchre, which still remained a place of pilgrimage. The arrival of the envoys from Jerusalem seems to have been expected, as though Charles planned thereby to counter the weight of the Roman clergy with that of the venerable patriarchate of Jerusalem. Finally, according to Einhard, Charles was angered by the ceremony prepared by Leo III:

> He asserted that he would never have entered the church that day, even though it was a high feast, if he could have learned the pontiff's intentions beforehand.

INTERPRETING THE EVENT

Thus the coronation of 800 was hedged with ambiguity. For the Roman clergy, Charles became "the emperor of the Romans" by the choice of the pope. The "Donation of Constantine" justified the pope's claim to dispose of the imperial crown. During the course of the Middle Ages, the popes would frequently recall the precedent set on Christmas Day 800, affirming that one could only become emperor by coming to Rome and receiving the crown from the hands of the Roman pontiff. The Franks held a rather different conception of the empire. Charles abandoned the title of "patrician of the Romans," but refused to be "emperor of the Romans." After May 801, he chose rather to term himself "Augustus and emperor governing the Roman Empire." He ruled a Christian empire as the "New Constantine." This conviction is reflected in an inscription found on one of his bulls: *Renovatio romani imperii*, the "Renewal of the Roman Empire." The empire was thus something new, something reworked by Christian religion and quite different from the ancient Roman Empire. Moreover, Charles remained "by God's mercy king of the Franks and the Lombards," and far from becoming his capital, Rome became a city that the emperor never again visited. The seat of his government was Aachen, situated in the heart of Austrasia. Charles remembered his Frankish origins and that it was the Frankish people who had conquered the west. His notaries recalled this in titles they used in 806: "Charles, emperor and Caesar, the truly undefeated king of the Franks, ruler of the Roman Empire, pious and blessed, vanquisher and victor and likewise ever Augustus." When Charlemagne chose in 813 to associate his son Louis to the imperial throne, he himself crowned Louis at Aachen without the papal intervention. Yet there remained two conceptions of the empire, and this variance foreordained the conflicts between popes and emperors that later marked the history of medieval Europe.

THE GREEK REACTION

Byzantium reacted negatively to the events of 800. The leaders of the east rejected the usurpation wrought by the pope and the Franks; they found scandal in the very notion that a barbarian could be crowned emperor. Nevertheless, negotiations ensued, and a nearly incredible report by one Byzantine chronicler notes that some even envisaged the possibility of marriage between Charles and Irene, a widow since 799. Yet in 802 the "pious and orthodox empress" was overthrown and replaced by the energetic Nicephorus I. To oblige the new emperor to recognize him, Charles invaded Venezia, which had remained for Byzantium a prime center of commerce and a chief means of maintaining contact with the west.

After many years of haggling, a compromise was negotiated between Charlemagne and Michael I, the successor of Nicephorus. In 812, the *basileus* recognized the western emperor as his brother, relinquishing to him all Italy with the exception of Venezia and Dalmatia. The Franks viewed this peace accord as a great success, but it could not assuage the resentments felt on both sides.

By reestablishing the empire in the west, Charlemagne had further alienated the east. His success also contributed to the estrangement of the Latin and Greek churches. The still unsettled Iconoclastic Controversy was burdened with new disagreements over the *Filioque* clause added by the Franks to the Latin version of the Nicean Creed. Whereas the Council of Constantinople of 381 had proclaimed that "the Holy Spirit proceeds from the Father," the Frankish clergy absorbed a tradition from the Visigothic liturgy in the late eighth century and expanded the formula to "proceeds from the Father *and the Son*." What today seems a modest variant without prejudice to the doctrine of the Trinity provoked violent dispute, first between the Franks and Rome, and then between the west and the east. In a rare moment of firmness, Leo III rejected the novel formulation, but it remains today the official text of the Western Church.

In 800, two empires opposed each other. On one side, the old Byzantine Empire retained a foothold in Italy and despised the western barbarians. On the other, Charlemagne controlled a new empire that comprised most of the west and traced the first outline of Europe. Moreover, the movers and thinkers of the period sensed that it no longer sufficed to think of Europe as a geographical expression merely distinguishing one patch of land from Asia and Africa. For the first time, they expressed that Europe was a more potent reality in the making. A year before the imperial coronation in Rome, a court poet—the author of the so-called *Paderborn Epic*—described the first meeting of Pope Leo III and the Frankish king. He portrayed Charlemagne clearly and vividly:

> . . . the beacon of Europe shining with celestial light . . .
> Charles the King, the head of the world, the love and honor of his
>   people,
> The venerable paragon, excellent father and hero of Europe. . . .

The poet's vision was one that the historian can endorse.

5. Charlemagne: Emperor or Chieftain?

After the richly symbolic events of 25 December 800, did Charlemagne actually modify his political policies? In what sense, if at all, was his new empire a coherent construction? Did it in fact enjoy the unified and focused organization that has long been ascribed to it? Or did Charlemagne live out his life as a barbarian chieftain, faithful to local Austrasian traditions, governing through the Frankish nobility from which his family had sprung? The destiny of the Carolingian empire in the ninth century can only be understood in terms of our answers to these questions.

The Political and Administrative Structures of the Empire

The empire was governed by a ruler who possessed absolute authority over politics, justice, legislation, and military affairs. This authority derived as much from the royal *bannum* of the Frankish kings as from the tradition of the Christian emperors of late antiquity, some of whose enactments were known to Frankish jurists. Charlemagne followed in the tradition of Constantine and Theodosius when he regulated such matters as religion, education, fair pricing, and coinage.

Nevertheless, the emperor was not a tyrant; his monarchy was not authoritarian after the fashion of Byzantium. Charlemagne maintained the traditional contact between Frankish kings and their subjects. Each year before the summer campaigns, he convened the *conventus generalis*, or "general assembly," where great matters of state were discussed in common. Such gatherings, it is true, brought together only leading nobles, ecclesiastics, military men, and functionaries—in all a few hundred persons—but they were held. A prearranged agenda was proposed for debate and approval by the separate lay and cleric blocs that made up the assembly. Thus in 811, Charles asked of each group:

> Why do you refuse to help each other in the march regions and on campaign, although there is a pressing need to act in defense of the homeland? Why are

there these constant legal suits whose grounds are merely to claim whatever one sees in the possession of an equal? We should inquire rather how and where laymen are hampered by churchmen and churchmen by laymen in the fulfillment of their respective duties.

At the close of these assemblies, capitularies were drafted and issued as a series of ordinances in article form (*capitula*). To these well-known documents we owe much of our knowledge about life in the Carolingian realm, although we cannot be sure of their actual effectiveness in curbing abuse and prompting change. The general assembly was an extension of the closer circle of advisers that helped the king to govern and resided at the palace. Charlemagne lived amid friends to whom he entrusted various responsibilities. Some of these aides held offices in the royal household that survived throughout the Middle Ages: for example, the cellarmaster, cupbearer, and seneschal. Meanwhile, three high functionaries discharged important state duties. The count of the palace presided over the court tribunal in the king's absence, and after 800 his responsibilities expanded due to the increase in appeals to the emperor. The chamberlain (*camerarius*) supervised the royal treasury (*camera*) and the collection of revenues from indirect taxes, justice fees, tribute payments, war booty, and offerings made at the yearly assembly. Finally, the chancellor oversaw the drafting and validation of royal charters. This last activity gained appreciably in importance owing to the efforts of Charlemagne to encourage the use of writing as an administrative tool. The king dispatched ever more numerous letters, sent reminders, and demanded written reports from his functionaries. Since the work of the chancery depended on clerical notaries after the mid-eighth century, the office of chancellor became closely associated with that of the arch-chaplain, or head of the royal chapel, who was also the permanent ecclesiastical counselor of the king. After the death of Fulrad of St. Denis in 784, Bishop Angilramn of Metz held this important post until his passing in 791, and was then followed by Archbishop Hildebold of Cologne.

After the king pronounced a decision during an assembly or among his circle of advisers, orders were transmitted to his local agents, the counts. Across the empire, these royal officers administered roughly three hundred counties. Some counts presided over the former Roman *civitates*, or "town territories," while others controlled a smaller section of these territories, a *pagus* or *gau*. Where no Roman jurisdictions had existed, as in conquered Frisia or Saxony, counties were apportioned from scratch. As the king's representative, the count exercised broad powers. He implemented the rulings of the capitularies, maintained order, collected taxes and fines, convoked and led the free men liable for military service, and presided over the *mallus*, or public judicial assembly. In order to improve the effectiveness of these county courts, Charlemagne limited the number of sessions allowed and clarified their jurisdiction. The king also introduced a rank of legal assessors, the *scabini*, who were to help the count in discerning the law and questioning witnesses. The count and the *scabini* were henceforth charged with overseeing "high justice," whereas lower agents, the *vicarii* ("vicars") and *centenarii* ("hundredmen"), dealt with misdemeanors at the village level. Charlemagne took such steps to reform the system of justice because he was aware that the counts frequently abused their powers. The reasons were not mysterious. Apart from the portion of land a count received with his office, his only remuneration was a third portion of the royal tolls and fines he collected.

In the case of misconduct, the king could dismiss a count, but this rarely happened. Charlemagne preferred to regulate his agents with the help of personal envoys, the *missi dominici*. Although they first appear in the mid-eighth century, the *missi* became most effective and visible as an institution after 800. Charles defined a series of separate inspection zones, the *missatica*, which generally comprised six to ten counties to be scrutinized by his *missi*. The emperor usually paired a layman and an ecclesiastic to travel for a set period of time and gave them instructions before their departure. Such guidance was even passed on by the *missi* to local counts, as in a document of 806:

> We admonish and command you to settle fully, equitably, and justly the claims for justice presented by churches, widows, orphans, and all others, without fraud, undue cost, or excessive delay, whether these claims are laid before you or your subordinates. . . .
>
> Above all guard that no one, in the hope of delaying or frustrating a judgment, deceives either you or some helper into saying: "Keep quiet until the *missi* have passed through, then we shall come to an arrangement among ourselves." Take care rather to settle the matter before we arrive. . . .
>
> Read this letter often and keep it safe, so that it may serve as a witness to whether or not you have complied with its contents.

Not all subjects of the empire were subject to the administration of the counts. Under Charlemagne, the church benefited from the extension of grants of immunity, which had existed since the Merovingian period. These privileges entitled ecclesiastical rulers, especially abbots, to deal directly with the king and remain "immune" from the interference of local counts. An institution that possessed such immunity levied its own troops for the royal army, administered local justice, and collected fines and direct taxes, turning over a portion of the receipts to the king. To prevent individual abbots from becoming overwhelmed with worldly concerns and also to police their dealings, Charlemagne named a lay "advocate" (*advocatus*) to help them. The principal task of these advocates was to dispense justice within the immune territory.

Finally, Charlemagne also sought to ensure a personal bond between himself and his subjects by requiring an oath of fidelity from every free male in his realm. The leading agents of the emperor were also encouraged to become his vassals. Although the two procedures affected persons of different social stature, they were part of the same effort to ensure that personal ties linked individual subjects to the king.

In 789 and again in 792, Charles asked that the men of his kingdom promise to remain faithful to him and to his sons. After his imperial coronation in 800, he dispatched his *missi* to administer a further oath to every free man over the age of twelve:

> To our lord and most pious emperor, Charles, son of King Pippin and Queen Bertrada, I am a faithful servant, as a man lawfully ought to be to his lord, in the service of his kingdom and righteousness. This oath which I pledge, I shall keep, and I do intend to keep, to the best of my knowledge and understanding from this day forward, so help me God, who created heaven and earth and these relics of the saints.

However useful, the institution of such an oath implicitly allowed those who never swore it to consider themselves exempt from obedience, and it is likely that most of the population never saw the *missi*.

The formula prescribed by Charlemagne for the oath was closely modeled on the pledge of vassalage made by nobles. However, a vassal actually commending himself would have placed his hands between those of his lord, as had Tassilo in 757. To establish links between himself and the magnates, Charlemagne enjoined them to become his pledged supporters, or "faithful men." The chief interest of such personal ties lay in the promise of military support, since the king might call for immediate help from his vassals whereas his counts might delay in bringing contingents to the host. Moreover, the king could always count on the near presence of "faithful men" who would be ready to lend him their support, and this encouraged him to enlist all bishops, abbots, and counts as his vassals. In return, Charlemagne conferred a benefice on his vassal, generally in the form of land. In Aquitaine, Bavaria, and Italy, royal vassals often held immense domains in order to ensure an effective royal presence and authority. In turn, these royal vassals secured help from followers of their own to whom they parceled out land as a sub-benefice, thereby creating a secondary level of vassal clients. This practice of vassalage, whose origins were touched on above (see p. 37), became increasingly widespread at the end of the eighth and the beginning of the ninth century. It was the product of royal initiative. In principle, the ties that arose were strictly personal and limited to the lifetime of the individuals involved. The death of either party broke the bond and returned to the lord, or his successor, whatever benefice had been conferred. In the case of Charlemagne, royal authority was strong enough to ensure that this indeed happened, but under his successors, many vassals managed to keep for themselves and their progeny the lands conferred by the king.

Apart from his vassals, Charlemagne also relied heavily on the help of bishops to achieve his goals. He controlled admission to the ranks of the episcopacy, and in general he opted for clerics who had served in his palace chapel. Whether or not they were royal vassals, the bishops were bound to assist the counts with their local administrative tasks and, if necessary, to serve at the court and on foreign missions. Many in fact complained of not having any time left to attend to their pastoral duties. Nevertheless, Charles, the head of the Christian people, depended on the bishops to implement the essentials of his governmental program: respect for order, justice, social harmony, peace, and unity. As Louis Halphen has shown, a new idea of the state emerged, quite different from the notions of antiquity. The Carolingian ruler held his authority from God. He was a new David who was obliged to enforce the law of God, a law that superseded all existing legislation. Thus, Carolingian capitularies bore as much on religious issues as on secular concerns. The king sought to ensure such things as Sunday repose, attendance at liturgical celebrations, monastic observance, clerical education, and adequate religious instruction for the laity. Charlemagne presided over synods where he concerned himself with church business and even the dogmatic challenges posed by Adoptionism and the Iconoclastic Controversy. The bishops appreciated his effort to guide the church; in 813, they thanked Heaven:

> The church was been given a head so pious, so devoted to the service of God. He makes the spring of sacred power gush forth, and gives holy nourishment to Christ's sheep to shape them according to divine teaching. He struggles

tirelessly to increase the Christian people. He joyously honors the churches of Christ, and seeks to wrest from the jaws of the odious dragon a maximum of souls to restore them to the bosom of holy mother church and to guide them to the joys of Paradise and the heavenly kingdom. He is a head who surpasses all other kings of the earth by his holy wisdom and pious zeal.

Rarely has such a melding of the temporal and spiritual domains been achieved and accepted by laymen and clerics. A ruler whose favorite book (according to Einhard) was Augustine's *City of God*, Charlemagne dreamed of establishing God's "city" on earth, a sacral and theocratic kingdom that could assure the west both peace among men and eternal salvation.

Broadly sketched, these were the means of government available to Charlemagne and his imperial political ambitions. But such means and vision do not accurately reflect the far humbler realities. Without going so far as to speak with Ganshof of "Charlemagne's failure," we must mention the obstacles that the emperor faced and the solutions to which he made recourse.

Obstacles to the Unity of the Empire

REGIONAL DIVERSITY

Carolingian Europe spread across more than one million square kilometers of territory. It comprised many different regions that had been marshaled around a common focus of authority in a relatively short span of time; each region retained its own history, laws, culture, and outlook. Francia was the center of the empire; it harbored many palaces, great abbeys, and domains of the royal fisc. The "land of the Franks" extended from the Atlantic Ocean to beyond the Rhine, bounded in the south by the Loire River and the plateau of Langres. Francia itself was subdivided into the former territory of Neustria (now more narrowly conceived as the lands between the Seine and the Loire), western Francia (between the Seine and the Meuse), middle Francia (between the Meuse and the Rhine and including Frankish Burgundy), and eastern Francia (beyond the Rhine and comprising Hesse, Thuringia, and Alemannia, thus encompassing former Austrasia). To the northeast lay the lands of the Saxons and Frisians, and to the southeast, the former duchy of Bavaria. Although Saxony was subjugated and Christianized by terror, it retained its ancient laws and social order. The nobles of Bavaria likewise managed to foster their own traditions despite the loss of political autonomy and the influence of Italy and the Franks. South of the Loire, Aquitaine continued as a separate world that neither Pippin III nor Charlemagne managed to subjugate entirely. The Franks heaped contempt on the Aquitainians, whom they accused of fickleness and softness. Within Aquitaine there were further divisions due to the successive periods of Gothic, Muslim, and finally Carolingian domination. In Septimania, the future Catalonia gradually took on its own character, fueled by an influx of *Hispani* who enjoyed special status as refugees. Meanwhile, the Frankish forces based in Toulouse and Bordeaux had to guard Aquitaine against the raids of the pagan Basque mountain men. Along the nearby Atlantic coast, the Gascon dukes rallied behind the Carolingians, but remained distinct. When Louis, king of Aquitaine, came to Paderborn in 785, he wore Gascon dress: a rounded cape, flowing sleeves, puffy trousers, and boots with spurs.

To the east of Aquitaine, Burgundy and Provence formed a somewhat fluid mass of territory. Provence was a distant acquisition that the Carolingian rulers had not visited since its conquest by Charles Martel. At the heart of the former Burgundian kingdom, Lyon and Vienne were strategically important and notable religious and cultural centers. Although Archbishop Leidrad of Lyon transformed his episcopal town and invited Charlemagne to visit it, the king never came. Further east beyond the Saône lay yet another Burgundy—distinct from Frankish Burgundy and northern Provence—athwart the important alpine route to Italy. This region included the vast diocese of Besançon and the former Jura duchy.

For the Franks, Italy always remained a land foreign in both tongue and mentality. A visit there required a lengthy and difficult voyage and posed health risks. Although Charlemagne sought to unify the entire peninsula under his own authority, he had to take account of the diverse character of its regions. The subject Lombard kingdom, the papal territories, and the duchies of Spoleto and Benevento all presented multiple landscapes and populations.

LINGUISTIC DIVERSITY

A traveler who voyaged across the Carolingian Empire would have been sorely tried by the variety of dialects and languages. While the Bretons and the Basques each possessed unique tongues, the peoples of Aquitaine and most of Francia spoke an array of highly vulgarized Latin dialects, known collectively as *lingua romana rustica,* or "Romance." In the Germanic linguistic areas, there survived some pockets where Rheto-Romance, or Ladin, was spoken, as in Bavaria around Salzburg, in West Tirol near Chur, and in Friuli. The Germanic language referred to in our sources as *lingua teudisca* (whence the word "Deutsch") also presented considerable dialectical variations. Saxons could not, for instance, understand Bavarians. The "Frankish" spoken at the Carolingian court was variable according to region, as is demonstrated by the few surviving written examples. Thus, it was necessary for the rulers and their functionaries to be bilingual or even trilingual. Hoping to impose order on his mother tongue, Charlemagne even began work on a written Germanic grammar, which has not survived.

JURIDICAL DIVERSITY

In addition to the varied outlooks and languages of his subjects, Charlemagne also had to contend with their diverse legal traditions. He maintained the "personality" of law recognized in the west since the barbarian invasions of the fifth century. Instead of one law applying for all persons, the law applied in a given case was determined by the ethnicity of the litigants. Thus, since each people needed its own written legal code, "Charlemagne ordered that the laws of all the peoples under his power, which up to then had been transmitted by oral tradition, should be copied down in writing." Other texts amply confirm this statement of Einhard. Charles was responsible for revising the Salic, Alemanian, and Bavarian law codes, and he commissioned compilations of Saxon and Frisian law. After 802, he spurred his agents to round out existing laws. The king also reminded judges that they were to enquire for each case which national law was to be applied. This of course presupposed that the judges knew different law codes and possessed copies of them.

The Regionalization of Power

THE SUBKINGDOMS

As the area of the Carolingian realm expanded, its diversity obliged Charlemagne to resort to a system of regional princedoms akin to those known under the Merovingian rulers of the seventh and eighth centuries. He established unified territories that he entrusted to members of his family. After the disastrous expedition to Spain in 778, Charlemagne rightly feared Aquitainian opportunism, and he therefore named his son Louis, who had been born near Poitiers, subking of Aquitaine in 781. Upon the death of Pippin of Italy in 813, Pippin's bastard son Bernard inherited the kingdom. After the deposition of Duke Tassilo, Charlemagne entrusted the administration of Bavaria to his brother-in-law Gerold, a relation of the Agilol-fing clan, granting him the title of *praefectus* ("governor"). Charlemagne also had Salzburg elevated to the rank of an archbishopric whose incumbent was to oversee the entire Bavarian church. When Gerold died in 799, he was replaced by a pair of governors.

In Aquitaine and Italy, each subking had his own palace, chapel, chancery, treasury, and minting facilities. Charlemagne no doubt closely monitored the activities of his royal lieutenants. Apart from a few locales that were administered by Goths in Septimania, the counts ruling in Aquitaine were predominantly of Frankish origin. Yet as Louis of Aquitaine matured, his personal policy—especially in religious matters—tended to favor indigenous Aquitainians, such as Benedict of Aniane, who oversaw monastic reform. The Aquitainian king even went so far as to grant lands from the royal fisc to Aquitainian nobles, a practice that troubled his father. In Italy, King Pippin was assisted in Pavia by Adalhard, a cousin of Charlemagne. The king of Italy repromulgated special capitularies that introduced the ordinances of his father south of the Alps. Further south, the Duchy of Benevento recognized the authority of Charlemagne, while Spoleto was ruled by a local dynasty under the control of Frankish officers.

THE MARCHES

Apart from these kingdoms, Charles established frontier regions administered by governors, later called *marchiones*, or marquises, who held authority and military rank over local counts. To protect against raids from Brittany, Charlemagne organized the Breton March, which was directed by his nephew, Count Roland. In 790, the Maine region was made a "duchy" and placed under the control of Charles the Younger, the king's eldest son. Between 799 and 802, a member of the Widonid clan is also recorded as "governor of the Breton borderlands." In Aquitaine, Charlemagne's cousin, Duke William of Toulouse, guarded against the threats posed by Basques and the Muslims of Spain. East of Bavaria, a certain Count Werner governed the *Ostmark*. Counts vested with special powers were likewise set up in marches to protect the empire against the Danes and Slavs.

THE PARTITION OF 806

This tendency toward regionalized power is also demonstrated by Charlemagne's provisions of 806 for the partition of the empire, a measure that the *Royal Frankish Annals* called an "ordinance for keeping the peace."

Sensing the arrival of old age, Charlemagne assembled his leading followers at Thionville and set down how, after his death, the empire should be
divided among his three sons. Mindful perhaps of the struggle he had
waged with his own brother Carloman, the emperor hoped to stave off
similar conflict among the heirs who would share his legacy according to
Frankish custom:

> So as not to leave my sons a confused and unsettled matter of dispute and
> contention as regards the status of my entire kingdom, I have divided the
> whole body of the realm into three portions; the portion that each of them
> is to guard and rule, I have caused to be described and designated. I have
> done this so that each may be content with his portion in accord with my
> ruling, and so that each may strive to defend the borders of his kingdom
> which face foreign peoples and maintain peace and charity with his brothers.

These few lines illustrate Charlemagne's defensive and domestic objectives.
Along with Aquitaine, Louis was to receive the lands south of the plateau
of Langres down to the Mediterranean. To Pippin's Italian kingdom,
Charlemagne added Bavaria, Carinthia, and half of Alemannia. Charles,
the eldest son, was to inherit everything else, but were he to predecease
his brothers, Louis and Pippin were to divide his territories according to
the partition of 768 between Carloman and Charlemagne (see p. 85). Similar provisions were made for the premature death of the other two brothers, but Charlemagne hopefully added that a duly established male heir
should be accepted by the surviving uncles. He directed that his daughters
should enter monastic life or marry honorably.

A remarkable feature of the *Divisio regnorum* of 806 is the complete absence among its provisions of the imperial title. Joseph Calmette explained
this omission in terms of the Franco-Byzantine dispute that still clouded
the western claim; perhaps Charlemagne planned to wait before naming
his successor as emperor. Nevertheless, other historians have aptly pointed
out that Charlemagne seems to have considered his imperial title as a "personal apotheosis" and reckoned that it should expire after his death. According to this view, Charles would have acted as a normal head of family,
as a Frankish king, and this seems much in tune with his character.

Charlemagne, the Frankish Chief

Lifelong Habits
After his imperial coronation, Charlemagne remained an Austrasian Frank
who depended on kith and kin to govern his empire as much as on new

institutions. The events of 800 did little to alter his traditional way of life. This is the message of Einhard's portrait of Charlemagne. He was a Frank who shared in both the good qualities and the faults of his people. Impressively tall and healthy, he enjoyed physical exertion, such as riding and hunting (which also doubled as training for war), and especially excelled at swimming, an activity shared by his sons and followers in the baths at Aachen. Charlemagne also had a considerable preference for roasted meats despite the warnings of his physicians. On the other hand, he spurned foreign costumes, and generally wore Frankish clothing "that differed little from the normal dress of the people." Einhard also speaks of the literary efforts that grew out of Charlemagne's affinity for his native people:

> He had written out and preserved for posterity the ancient Germanic songs that recounted the deeds and wars of former kings. He likewise began a grammar of his mother tongue.

Like his father and grandfather and many of his compatriots, Charlemagne chose not to live in chastity. Married four times, he had numerous concubines even in old age. Alcuin warned one of his own disciples against "the crowned doves who flutter in the bedroom of the palace." Another poet praised a cousin of Charlemagne for having kept her virtue "amid the ardent loves of the palace and the comeliness of the young men."

Whether his successive nuptials are viewed as instances of *Friedelehe*—a Germanic form of lawful cohabitation—or Christian marriage, Charlemagne chose his wives with an eye to political goals as much as personal affection. Thus, Desiderata was to have sealed an alliance with the Lombard kingdom; Hildegard, the mother of eight royal children, came from Swabia; Fastrada was the daughter of a count in eastern Francia; and Liutgard, the fourth and last wife, stemmed from a Alemannian family. Charles demonstrated equal affection to both his legitimate and illegitimate offspring. The revolt in 792 of his bastard son Pippin the Hunchback especially distressed him. After condemning the nobles who had supported the rebellious prince, he committed his son to the monastery of Prüm.

Charlemagne enjoyed living with his family and overseeing the education of his sons and daughters. According to Einhard, "he never supped without them when he was at home, and never made a journey apart from them." Charlemagne's biographer went on to add:

> Since his daughters were very beautiful and he loved them most dearly, it is remarkable that he never wanted to marry any of them to one of his retinue

or to an outsider. Rather he kept them all with him at home until his death, saying that he could not get along without their company. Although he was otherwise happy, he suffered the adversity of misfortune on this account.

Indeed, Rotrude bore Louis, the future abbot of St. Denis, and other sons of her liaison with Count Rorgo of Maine. Likewise, Bertha was the mistress of Angilbert of St. Riquier, by whom she had several sons, including the historian Nithard. Nevertheless, Charlemagne preferred to live as a patriarch amidst his many relations.

THE ROYAL DOMAINS

Charlemagne moved regularly with his entire family and retinue from one *villa* or palace to another. The peripatetic character of the Frankish court continued under the empire, although it had become tempered by a decision in 794 to focus life at Aachen. This was in fact the first instance of a more of less fixed seat of Carolingian government. In the past, political necessity had obliged the ruler to make his presence felt by moving through his lands, and the economic backwardness made it impossible for his court to live for extended periods off the surpluses of a single local economy. Because Charlemagne "lived from his own," as would later be said of the Capetian kings, he had to draw on the resources of his personal possessions and the lands of the royal fisc. These lands were situated in the valleys of the Aisne and the Oise (for example, at Quierzy, Attigny, Verberie, and Compiègne), the Meuse and the Mosel (at Herstal and Thionville), along the Rhine (at Ingelheim, Frankfurt, Worms, and, further north, at Nijmegen), and finally in Saxony (at Paderborn). There remained, however, literally hundreds of other royal stopovers and *villae* that are known to us only from textual references. Apart from extant literary evidence concerning Aachen, an early ninth-century inventory taken at the royal domain at Annapes, near Lille, describes a large rural possession:

> We found on the crown estate of Annapes: a royal manor house, well built of stone with three rooms; the whole building surrounded by sun galleries, with eleven warming rooms, a cellar below, and with two porches. Inside the courtyard, 17 other houses made of wood with as many rooms, and with other outbuildings in good order: a stable, a kitchen, a bakery, two granaries, and three sheds. The courtyard was securely fortified with a palisade and a stone gate, above which there was a gallery for making distributions; inside it there was a smaller, carefully fenced-off area that was planted with various sorts of trees.

Like a gentleman squire, Charlemagne carefully oversaw the proper management of his domains. He required his stewards (*iudices*) to present written accounts of their operations and reserves. The famous *Capitulare de villis* ("Capitulary on the royal estates") gives an idea of the exacting detail with which the king wanted his domains to be managed. There were instructions about everything: building maintenance, furniture, handicrafts for women, forestry, wine making, salting food, raising farm animals, guarding against wolves. The capitulary even offers a lengthy catalog of flora for the ideal orchard and vegetable patch, including a reminder that the "gardener should have house-leeks growing on his cottage." The text speaks perhaps most eloquently on its own:

> Each year at Christmas our stewards should set down clearly under separate headings and forward to us an orderly statement of accounts so that we may know what we have and how much: the revenue of our fields worked by the oxen that our ploughmen keep; the revenue of those fields worked by tenants who owe ploughing services; the number of piglets; the amount of payments for tenancy, debts, fines, and for game taken from our forests without our permission; the revenue from other payments due, from mills, forests, fields, bridges, and boats; . . . the amount of hay, firewood, kindling, planks, or other building wood; the amount of fallow land; the amount of legumes, millet, panic-grass, wool, linen, and jute; the amount of fruits, large and small nuts, graftings on various trees, garden produce, turnips; the number of fish ponds, hides, skins, and horns; the amount of honey, wax, oil, tallow, soap, mulberry wine, boiled wine, mead, vinegar, beer, new and old wine, as well as new and old wheat; the number of chickens, eggs and geese; the number of fishermen, smiths, shield-makers, cobblers; the number of kneading troughs, bins, and boxes; the number of turners and saddlers; the number of workshops for iron and lead, the number of people paying tribute, and the number of colts and fillies.

CHARLEMAGNE AND THE FRANKISH NOBILITY

As the head of family, Charlemagne naturally conferred important offices and abbacies on his children, but he relied on a wide circle of Frankish nobility linked to his relations by blood. In doing so, he followed the example of his forebears. The nobles who had first helped to establish Carolingian power stemmed from a limited group of perhaps 30 families. These rich and ambitious landowners had also been officeholders. A school of German historians headed by Gerd Tellenbach has carefully studied the evolution of this "state aristocracy" (*Reichsaristokratie*), and these scholars have shown how Charlemagne established this suite of nobles across all of Carolingian Europe. Thus Franks could be found in Italy as counts, abbots, and bishops not only in the former Lombard kingdom but also in the Duchy of Spoleto. After a certain Warnar of the Lambertine/Widonid clan (see Table 6) became a son-in-law of the duke of Spoleto, other members of his family were established in western Francia. Wido, son of Lambert I, was referred to as governor of Brittany in 799, while his brother Warnar served King Louis of Aquitaine. The Widonid family was also allied with the Robertine clan, which reinforced its links to the royal family through the marriage in 794 of Louis of Aquitaine and Ermengard, the daughter of Count Ingram of Hesbaye (see Table 4). Although Count Autchar, the sometime partisan of Carloman II, seems to have been a relative of the Unruochings, this family also became important under the empire. Unruoch was one of the Frankish counts sent in 811 to confirm a truce with the Danes. His brother was a count in Alemannia, while his son, Duke Eberhard of Friuli, initiated the family's impressive history in Italy. From the Alsatian clan of the Etichonids stemmed Count Hugh of Tours. In 811, Hugh went to Byzantium as an ambassador of Charlemagne. He also received lands in Italy and became the father-in-law of Lothar I in 821. A further example of an Alsatian noble posted in Italy was Eric, marquis of Friuli. Other close allies of the Carolingian house were the Wilhelmines: Theuderic II was a count in Ripuaria and at Autun, while his brother William was duke of Toulouse and father of Rolinda, the wife of Charlemagne's cousin Wala of Corbie. The Gerardines present still another example of an expanding noble family. Of Count Gerard's two sons, Stephen continued as count of Paris while Leuthard became count of Fezensac in Aquitaine. Although Charlemagne chose other counts and vassals from lesser families, all these individuals came to establish new local dynasties. For instance, the Rorgonids traced their origin to Rorgo of Maine, the son of Count Gauzlin and the lover of Charlemagne's daughter Rotrude. Sent out from the heart of the empire, Frankish nobles forged ties with local families, and from such links there emerged a veritable European aristocracy that later spawned the leaders of the regional princedoms of the late ninth century.

Apart from the abortive conspiracies hatched by his illegitimate son Pippin in 792 and the Thuringian count Hardrad in 785, Charlemagne never had great cause to complain about the men to whom he entrusted lands and responsibilities. He strove to imbue them with political sense and to raise them above family quarreling, selfish interests, and the traditional brutality of their social milieu. The clergy also exalted those noble warriors, who by their courage and faith merited salvation as much as any good churchman. Alcuin addressed his pamphlet "On the Virtues and Vices" to Wido of Brittany. For Eric of Friuli, Archbishop Paulinus of Aquileia wrote a "book of exhortation" and posthumously praised the great noble as a fine leader, generous to his friends and caring toward the poor. When Charlemagne set out his plans for the eventual partitioning of his empire in 806, he also realized that his own faithful servants might pose difficulties for his heirs. Because they owned lands in Austrasia and held benefices in other parts of the empire, there was a risk that some nobles and their clients might be tempted to prefer one heir over another. Charlemagne prescribed that each royal vassal should remain attached to one prince who alone would be his lord, and that no one should attempt to move from one kingdom to another. Thus the emperor anticipated the problems that did in fact arise under his successors.

THE DEATH OF CHARLEMAGNE

The immediate danger of factionalism was averted because Charlemagne's two elder sons, Charles and Pippin, predeceased their father. Louis of Aquitaine was the lone successor. In 813, Charles was nearly 70 years old and—according to Einhard—"weighed down by sickness and age." No doubt under the influence of Wala, his cousin and principal adviser, Charlemagne decided to raise his remaining son to the imperial dignity, perhaps after the example of the *basileus* Michael I, who had named his son Theophylact as regent. Louis was thus summoned to Aachen, and on 11 September 813, after carefully explaining his new responsibilities, Charlemagne crowned him co-emperor without papal intervention. Louis was acclaimed "Emperor and Augustus" in the midst of the Frankish people. After a solemn Mass had been sung, the two emperors left the royal chapel, Charles leaning on his son's arm. Louis soon returned to Aquitaine. A few months later, on the morning of 28 January 814, Charlemagne died after a week-long illness. He was interred the same day in an ancient sarcophagus beneath the pavement of the royal chapel.

The death of Charlemagne brought bewilderment and sorrow to the empire. According to a rhythmic dirge composed by a monk of Bobbio, every part of the empire shared in a common lament:

. . .

From the rising of the sun to the sea-shores
where it sets, lamentation beats upon men's breasts.

. . .

Franks, Romans, and all believers
are tormented by lament and great distress.

. . .

Rivers of tears flow now unceasing,
for the world bewails the death of Charlemagne.

. . .

To echo the *Paderborn Epic*, Charlemagne had become the "beacon of Europe." Three decades later the historian Nithard would longingly remember how the great emperor had "left all Europe filled with every goodness."

In his own lifetime, Charlemagne had ruled a Europe whose diverse lands he had done much to unite. In tribute and in fact, he had become "father of Europe." Although his achievement would prove fragile and impermanent, it remained as a preliminary sketch of the first territorial outline of the west. Whoever later sought to unify Europe would hark back to Charlemagne, and his posthumous admirers have included figures like Napoleon no less than today's architects of European unity.

Part *III*

The Destiny of Carolingian Europe (814–877)

From the death of Charlemagne in 814 to that of his grandson Charles the Bald in 877, Carolingian Europe experienced profound changes. The immediate successor to the first Carolingian emperor, Louis the Pious, proved unable to uphold the ideal of imperial unity. Under pressure from the nobility, he and his successors reverted to more conventional Frankish policy. In 843, the Treaty of Verdun marked the end of a tortuous series of attempts to apportion the empire among Louis's sons. It established three new realms, each of which henceforth followed its own separate course. Although political division posed considerable risks for the church, the efforts of popes and other ecclesiastics could do little to salvage the unity of the empire. Crowned in 875, Charles the Bald was the last Carolingian emperor.

1. The Reign of Louis the Pious: The Goal of Imperial Unity and Its Failure (814–840)

The Beginning of a Promising Reign

The news of his father's death reached Louis the Pious at his residence at Doué-la-Fontaine in Aquitaine.

THE NEW EMPEROR

Aged 46, Louis had been married since 794 to Ermengard, the daughter of the Robertine count Ingram. He had three sons: Lothar, born in 795; Pippin, who was two years younger; and eight-year-old Louis. Apart from the expeditions undertaken at his father's behest, Louis had lived in Aquitaine as a grand seigneur. He had hunted and traveled with his court across the realm between various residences at Doué-la-Fontaine, Anjac, Chasseneuil, and Ébrueil. To assist him in government, he had several counselors: his future son-in-law Bego, of the Gerardine family; Helisachar, his chancellor; and Benedict of Aniane, a Gothic monk to whom he confided the reform of several Aquitainian monasteries. In addition to being profoundly religious, Louis showed especial interest in fostering Benedictine monasticism. Among his contemporaries he was already known as Louis "the Pious," even though French historians of the modern period have also given him the somewhat disparaging epithet *le Débonnaire* (the Good-natured). Too frequently, Louis has been depicted as an overly pliant devotee of monks and religion, a man wholly subject to his latest adviser. As he grew older, he did increasingly manifest volatile mood swings, alternating between brooding and resolve, especially after his second marriage. But regarding the beginning of his reign, both Louis's biographers—Thegan, suffragan bishop of Trier, and the anonymous "Astronomer" (so called because of his scientific learning)—present the emperor as an intelligent, refined, and energetic leader. His early deeds demonstrate that his reign, or at least its inception, deserves to be reconsidered, as suggested by François Louis Ganshof.

THE FIRST REFORMS

Like most newly established political leaders, Louis the Pious inaugurated his rule with a program of changes and reforms. In official documents, he now figured as "Louis, by order of Divine Providence, Emperor and Augustus," and dating was expressed according to the year of his reign over the empire. By dropping any reference to his role as king of the Franks and the Lombards, Louis affirmed the unity of the empire. Reacting against the moral laxity that had marked the close of Charlemagne's reign, the new emperor drove the prostitutes out of Aachen and banished his sisters to the monasteries that they had received from their father. The erstwhile counselors of Charlemagne were also removed. His cousins Adalhard and Wala had to withdraw respectively to Noirmoutier and Corbie, while their sister Gundrada went to Poitiers. Louis favored his own advisers from Aquitaine. He relied on the help of his son-in-law Bego, whom he now named count of Paris. Helisachar continued his work as chancellor, accumulating in return the abbacies of St. Maximinus of Trier, St. Riquier, St. Aubin of Angers, and Jumièges. Finally, for Benedict of Aniane the emperor erected and endowed the monastery of Inden, situated a few kilometers from Aachen.

Under Benedict's influence, Louis the Pious vigorously prosecuted the work of ecclesiastical renewal initiated by Charlemagne in 813. A series of reform synods held at Aachen between 813 and 818 legislated against the most flagrant ecclesiastical abuses and irregularities. These gatherings standardized the norms of religious observance. Monks were ordered to live according to the Rule of Saint Benedict and cathedral clergy according to Chrodegang's Rule for Canons, while the needs of female communities were addressed in a special body of statutes. This program of reform also sought to guarantee each group's means of support by regulating the ownership and use of ecclesiastical property.

In marked contrast to his father, Louis indulged papal aspirations for autonomy. After the death of Leo III in 816, his successor, Stephen IV, journeyed immediately to Francia, where he crowned Louis and Ermengard as emperor and empress in Reims. (Whatever myths later arose concerning the unction of Clovis by Archbishop Remigius, the actual history of Reims as a site of French royal coronations began with this event.) Louis subsequently granted Pope Pascal I (817–824) a privilege recognizing papal sovereignty and listing the papal territories.

Meanwhile, Louis sought to improve his own administration. He refined the system of the *missi dominici* and reconfigured the *missatica* they oversaw. He also appointed *magistri*, or "masters," to attend to the needs of merchants, Jews, and other groups. The official documents turned out by the new emperor's chancery were distinguished by improved layout and linguistic expression, and they bear witness to a wider effort to upgrade governmental effectiveness. The means chosen, as well as the effect of this renewal, are highlighted by the famous capitulary collection of Abbot Ansegisus of Fontanelle (822–832). This compendium of 26 documents reflects the importance now attached to the instruments of public power. It marks a new awareness of the normal workings of the state as distinguished from special rights and immunities conferred by royal privilege.

THE *ORDINATIO IMPERII* (817)

Three years after his accession, Louis moved to guarantee the shape of the empire and of the reforms he had wrought against the threat of his personal mortality. To ensure the unity of the empire, he conferred on his eldest son, Lothar, the dignity of co-emperor with right to succession and determined the lands that would pass to each of his sons. The immediate reasons behind the so-called *Ordinatio imperii* ("Disposition for the Empire") of 817 are not known with certainty, but Louis may have been reacting to a near brush with death when a portico collapsed around him at his Aachen palace. Perhaps he feared that his sons might fight over the division of their father's legacy required by Frankish custom. In the preamble to the *Ordinatio*, Louis recalled and reacted to this tradition:

> Although the petition [concerning the empire and our sons] has been made devotedly and faithfully, it has not seemed to us nor to any right thinking men that the unity of the empire preserved for us by God should be rent by a human act of division out of regard for our sons, lest perchance by this act there should arise scandal in the church and I myself offend Him in whose power lie the laws of all kingdoms.

Thus after three days of prayer and fasting, Louis crowned his son Lothar as co-emperor in accord with a principle of primogeniture alien to Frankish tradition. He made his other sons kings, Pippin over Aquitaine and Louis over Bavaria, but they were to remain subject to the authority of their elder brother. Should one of the younger brothers die, one of his sons was to succeed him. Should he die childless, Lothar was to inherit the vacant kingdom. In the event of Lothar's death, one of the remaining brothers was to be chosen to replace him by the "people." Every provision was made to avert the possibility of dividing the empire. Although Charlemagne had conferred the Kingdom of Italy on his grandson Bernard, it too was understood implicitly to remain subject to Lothar, while Louis the Pious's own bastard son Arnulf had to be content with the county of Sens.

To the joy of many of his followers, Louis the Pious thus appeared to have overcome the threat to imperial unity posed by the Frankish custom of partitions. But just as significantly, he had also acted to preserve the church from the plague of political division, largely in fact at the behest of clerical advisers. In the words of one contemporary, Louis was "Emperor by divine grace, Augustus and master of the church of Europe." Hence, his empire was understood as an expression of Christian unity that invited some, like Archbishop Agobard of Lyon, to dream of a fusion of peoples and an abolition of distinction according to race, law or person. Writing to the emperor about 817, Agobard envisaged a Christian realm

> . . . where there is neither gentile nor Jew, circumcision nor uncircumcision, barbarian nor Scythian, Aquitainian nor Lombard, Burgundian nor Aleman, slave nor freeman, but where Christ is all, and in all. [cf. Col. 3:11]

For the archbishop of Lyon and many others, Christianity alone could hold the empire together, and this was a desirable end.

But not all the subjects of the empire were willing to accept the *Ordinatio imperii*. Although his younger sons Pippin and Louis remained docile, Louis the Pious faced immediate opposition from his twenty-year-old nephew, King Bernard of Italy. The emperor's riposte was swift and effective. Bernard surrendered, was taken to Aachen, and there tried and condemned. Although Louis chose to commute his nephew's sentence, the revised punishment of blinding still ended in Bernard's death after two days of agony. To eliminate the risk that Charlemagne's bastard sons might likewise rebel and claim some part of the empire, Louis had his half-brothers tonsured and interned: Drogo at Luxeuil; Hugh at Charroux; and Theuderic at still a different monastery. Finally, the emperor took positive steps to reinforce his position. He convoked assemblies across Neustria and Austrasia, and there he exacted oaths from the nobles to respect his decisions of 817.

In order to conciliate as many factions as possible, Louis the Pious chose in 821 to recall Adalhard and Wala from exile. This move was part of a wider amnesty that also included people who had fallen from grace as a consequence of the rebellion of Bernard of Italy. Adalhard returned from Noirmoutier as abbot of Corbie, while Wala became a court adviser, replacing Benedict of Aniane, who had died on 11 February 821. Louis like-wise conferred the vacant see of Metz on his tonsured half-brother Drogo. In tandem with these events, the emperor married his elder sons to politi-cally valuable brides: Lothar wed Ermengard, the daughter of the Eti-chonid count Hugh of Tours, while Pippin married Ringard, the daughter of Count Theotbert.

In the hope of securing heavenly blessings for his empire, Louis took a further dramatic step the following year. At the general assembly at At-tigny, the emperor invited the lay and clerical nobles of the realm to join him in a common act of penitence. After admonishing the bishops to show compunction for their failings, Louis himself set an example by confessing his sinful part in the death of his nephew Bernard, the exile of Adalhard and Wala, and the forcible tonsuring of his half-brothers. In this bizarre act, Louis publicly humiliated himself. However well intended, his ad-mission of guilt and penitential almsgiving brought Louis closer to the risk of clerical domination. Yet all were content for the moment to cele-brate the general reconciliation. As Abbot Adalhard observed, "Never had so much been wrought for the public good." Yet two circumstances were destined to upset the harmony that had been achieved: the birth of a fourth male heir, and the growing ambition of Lothar.

The Network of Rival Factions

JUDITH

After the death of his wife Ermengard in 817, Louis the Pious had arranged to be shown the finest nubile maidens in the empire. He resolved to marry Judith, the daughter of Count Welf (see Table 5), the owner of vast do-mains in Bavaria and Alemannia. From the start, the fabled beauty and intelligence of the new empress captured the devotion of her older hus-band. Judith's influence soon became virtually all-powerful. She readily persuaded the emperor to confer offices and privilege on her relations. Her mother received the abbey of Chelles. One brother, Rudolph, was en-trusted with St. Riquier and Jumièges, while Conrad acquired the abbey of St. Gall and married Adelaide, the sister of Emperor Lothar's wife Er-mengard. In 827, Judith's sister Emma also married Louis of Bavaria, the last son of Louis the Pious by his first wife. Amid the web of marriages planned by his wife, Emperor Louis became the brother-in-law of his third son Louis, and the emperor's brother-in-law Conrad became the brother-in-law of the wife of his first son Lothar (see Table 5).

After four years of marriage and the birth of a daughter, Judith produced a son on 13 June 823, the future Charles the Bald. Between the three sons of Ermengard and their ambitious stepmother strife became inevitable.

THE REACTION OF LOTHAR

The eldest son and co-emperor Lothar felt most at risk. He was now twenty-eight years old, and aspired to play an active role in the government of the empire. For precisely this reason, Louis had become uneasy with the presence of his son and had dispatched him to Italy in 822 in the company of Wala. There Lothar demonstrated real political skills. He convoked assemblies and promulgated capitularies, and on Easter 823—aware that Judith was again pregnant—he had himself crowned emperor by Pope Pascal I. In 824 he took advantage of the accession of the new pope, Eugenius II, to reaffirm Charlemagne's policy of imperial control of the papacy by imposing a new "Roman Constitution." Although he agreed to serve as godfather for Charles the Bald, Lothar realized that the empress sought to find a place for the young prince among the heirs of Louis the Pious as Frankish custom demanded. Conscious of the issues in play, Lothar viewed the decisions of 817 as irrevocable. To defend his rights he easily garnered the support of a group of lay and ecclesiastical magnates who were anxious to defend the unity and peace of the empire and to enhance thereby their own political power.

LOTHAR'S SUPPORTERS

The "imperialist" camp included such prominent laymen as Count Matfrid of Orléans, who claimed to be an intimate of Emperor Louis, and Count Hugh of Tours, Lothar's father-in-law. Among the clerics, there figured eminent persons like Abbot Hilduin of St. Denis, arch-chaplain to Emperor Louis, and Wala, the cousin of Charlemagne who now served as Lothar's adviser. In addition, Bishop Jonas of Orléans supported the faction as a respected and influential moralist. In his *Life of Saint Hubert* of 825, he had exalted the Carolingian dynasty, but he possessed no less clear notions concerning politics, which he expressed in his "Primer for Laymen" (*De institutione laicali*), addressed to Count Matfrid, and in his "Primer for Kings" (*De institutione regia*), dedicated to Pippin of Aquitaine. Jonas would also serve as a spokesman for the episcopacy in drafting the proceedings of the Paris synod of 829, which aimed at reminding the old emperor of his duties as ruler. Like the prophets of the Old Testament, bishops were bound to advise their king. Their priestly "authority" was superior to his royal "power," and they might judge him should he act like a tyrant or neglect his "ministry," as Jonas defined it:

> The ministry of the king is to govern and direct the people of God with equity and in accordance with law; he should strive to maintain for it concord and peace.

Thus, should peace be menaced, the bishops might well be expected to intervene as a political force. For the moment such notions remained strictly theoretical. But as an advocate of peace and stability, Lothar would find many supporters among the episcopacy.

THE QUEEN'S STRATEGY

Meanwhile, Judith strove to ensure the position of her infant son, and assembled a coterie of her own partisans. First among them was the emperor's godson, Count Bernard of Barcelona. Bernard was the son of William, duke of Toulouse under Charlemagne, and a distant cousin of Louis the Pious. In 824, Bernard had married Dhuoda, the daughter of a powerful Austrasian family, in the Royal Chapel at Aachen. Like his father, Bernard was charged with the defense of southern Aquitaine against Muslim attack. Between 826 and 827, he proved his military prowess by repulsing a massive attack on Barcelona by the forces the emir of Cordoba, Abd ar-Rahman II. Although Louis the Pious had dispatched reinforcements under the command of Hugh of Tours and Matfrid of Orléans, the commanders reportedly tarried along the way and arrived only after Bernard had mastered the Muslim threat. In 828, Louis reacted by stripping Hugh and Matfrid of their offices, and but for the intercession of Wala, their late arrival might have cost them their lives. Bernard of Septimania, however, was received with accolades. He became a close adviser to Emperor Louis, and the great protector of Judith.

During the assembly held at Worms in August 829, Louis and his consort moved to recognize the dawn of their son's seventh year—thought to mark a child's passage from infancy to reason—by assigning him the lands of Alemannia. His allotment included the home territories of Judith's Welf family: Rhaetia, Alsace, and part of Burgundy. Louis then ordered Lothar to return to Italy, and consigned Wala to political exile at

Corbie. The appointment of Bernard of Septimania to the office of chamberlain followed. According to Nithard, Louis "entrusted Charles to him, and made him the second man in the empire." Wrought by the emperor himself, this palace revolution was destined to provoke a full-fledged revolt by his elder sons.

Nevertheless, Louis the Pious rode for the moment on the crest of his glory. In his *Panegyric* of the emperor, the learned Walafrid Strabo, abbot of Reichenau and tutor of Charles the Bald, could still depict his hero as "a new Moses, creator of a golden age, a leader of his people in the midst of darkness." At his sides the poet arrayed Lothar as "Joshua," Louis of Bavaria as "mild Jonathan," along with Pippin of Aquitaine, the third jewel of the crown, and finally Judith as "comely Rachel," leading her young "Benjamin" by the hand. The portrait was charming, but it woefully belied the struggles to come.

The Revolt of 830

Despite his forced withdrawal to Corbie, Wala refused to accept defeat. He rallied the partisans of imperial unity and order, and with the help of secret informants at the imperial court, he launched a campaign of slander and innuendo against Judith.

THE CAMPAIGN OF INNUENDO

According to the report, the empress and her accomplice Bernard of Septimania were guilty of adultery, sorcery, and even an attempted assassination. In his literary portrait of Wala, Pascasius Radbertus collected this tale:

> Oh what a day that brought abiding shadows of crisis, that wrenched apart the peaceful and unified empire and divided it into morsels, that despoiled fraternity, broke bonds of blood, and everywhere engendered enmity, that scattered fellows of one homeland, banished fidelity, destroyed charity, that so ravaged the church and corrupted all things. . . . Alas, a day of misfortune, a day followed by a still worse night. No day was more troubled than when that scoundrel Bernard was recalled from Spain, that wretch who abandoned every honor vested in him by his origins. He wallowed in self-conceit and gluttony. He came like an enraged boar: he overturned the palace, smashed the council, and cast down every principle of law and reason. He chased off and trampled all the clerical and secular advisers; he occupied the emperor's bed. . . . The palace became a sty where shame ruled, adultery reigned, where

felonies, sorcery, and all manner of prohibited black arts abounded. The emperor went like an innocent lamb to the slaughter. That great and clement emperor was deceived by the woman against whom Solomon warned, still more deluded by the intrigues of that immoral being who led him toward death.

It is difficult to determine what substance lay behind these accusations. The historian Nithard, a cousin of Charles the Bald, later wrote more simply:

> Instead of fortifying the state, as was his duty, Bernard totally destroyed it through his inconsiderate misuse of power.

Although Bernard was married, he had relegated his wife, Dhuoda, to Uzès. The charge of sorcery was not merely frivolous, especially in a period in which magic found growing numbers of practitioners among both the common people and the nobility.

THE REVOLT

Whatever its substance, Wala's campaign met with success. A revolt took shape that erupted in April 830 while Louis was preparing for an expedition against the Bretons. Pippin of Aquitaine, Counts Hugh and Matfrid, and finally Louis of Bavaria moved to "liberate" the emperor from the almighty influence of Judith and Bernard. The imperial chamberlain fled to Barcelona, while Judith withdrew to a monastery in Laon. Lothar quickly arrived from Italy and took charge of the situation. He reversed the decisions taken at Worms, and proceeded to rule in his father's name. Bernard's followers lost their positions; his brother Heribert was blinded; and Judith and her brothers Rudolph and Conrad were incarcerated in Aquitainian monasteries. Lothar held his father and the young Charles under house arrest at St. Denis, and the boy was supervised by monks who were "to get him used to monastic life and urge him to take it up himself."

THE REACTION

Lothar ruled, but it soon appeared doubtful that he could capably rule such a troubled realm. As Nithard later wrote: "The state of the empire grew worse from day to day, since all were driven by greed and sought only their own advantage." While Louis the Pious lived under house arrest, he received reports of the support he still enjoyed among churchmen in Germany. With the help of the monk Guntbald, Louis was able to communicate secretly with his younger sons. He promised to increase the kingdoms of both Pippin and Louis the German in exchange for their help, and their decision to comply sapped Lothar's position. In October in 830, an assembly convened at Nijmegen, near the German lands of the supporters of Louis the Pious. The old emperor regained his liberty, his authority, and his wife, although Judith was obliged to purge herself by a solemn oath. Disgraced but pardoned, Lothar returned to Italy. His various partisans were now deposed and consigned to monastic imprisonment.

A New Partition

There remained, however, the question of rewarding Pippin and Louis the German for their change of heart. At Aachen in February 831, Louis the Pious annulled his former testamentary provisions in a new *Divisio regni* ("Division of the Realm"). The emperor planned for a partition of the empire into roughly equal kingdoms under Pippin, Louis the German, and Charles the Bald, while Lothar would retain the Italian lands he already possessed. Until the death of the emperor, the kings would each owe absolute obedience to their father. Thereafter, each realm would be independent, and the kings were to remain content with defending their respective borders and protecting the church. The project outlined thus marked a return to the *Divisio regnorum* envisaged by Charlemagne in 806. The unity of the empire and the imperial title had no bearing on the revised provisions. The adherents of Frankish tradition had cause to rejoice.

The Great Rebellion of 833 and Its Failure

The New Coalition

The partition proposed at Aachen in 831 failed to address the underlying reasons for the crisis that wracked the empire. On the one hand, the partisans of imperial unity still longed to restore the *Ordinatio imperii* of 817, while on the other, Pippin and Louis the German continued to vie for greater power and influence. Still at large, Bernard of Septimania stoked the flames of turmoil by inducing Pippin to revolt, and in 833, Louis the Pious took back Pippin's kingdom and conferred it on the son of Judith. Meanwhile, Louis of Bavaria had attacked Alemannia and been put down by his father. Encouraged by these circumstances, Judith dreamed of a new partition of the empire between her son, Charles, and Lothar. Although he had been restored to grace in late 831, Lothar nevertheless continued to conspire against his father. Now, he joined his two brothers and led a massive coalition against Louis the Pious.

Pope Gregory IV was likewise induced to support the cause of imperial unity and family agreement. He took the opportunity to affirm the superiority of spiritual authority as a guarantee of unity and peace. As Gregory IV recalled:

> We must remember that the governance of souls, which pertains to the pope, is of greater importance than the temporal government that pertains to the emperor.

While historians such as Walter Ullmann have sought to view the pope's role in events as an attempt to realize theocratic aspirations, it is at least certain that Gregory intervened dramatically in the domain of secular politics.

THE FIELD OF LIES

With great dignity, Louis the Pious reminded his sons of their obligations to their father and sovereign. He accused Lothar of leading his vassals astray and spurring his brothers to rebel. Lothar responded to these reproaches point by point, and requested an interview with his father. The meeting took place near Colmar, in Alsace; the locale and the event are remembered as the "Field of Lies."

Faced by a coalition of his sons, the pope, and a part of the Frankish clergy, Louis could do little. His biographer Thegan recounted the pathetic event:

> The sons advanced toward him bringing along Pope Gregory. But their father refused to agree to anything they demanded. A few days later, the emperor and the pope met at an interview, but they did not speak with each other very long. . . . Now, several parties took counsel that they should all desert the emperor and go over to his sons. First of all those who had already insulted him on earlier occasions went, and others followed. In the course of one night, a majority abandoned him; they left behind their tents and went over to the sons. The next day the others who remained came to the emperor. He ordered them: "Go to my sons. I do not want anyone to lose life or limb on my account." They left him, but they were covered in tears.

Lothar separated his father from Judith, whom the pope took back to Italy, and then interned him at the monastery of St. Médard in Soissons. Meanwhile, Charles the Bald was sent for safekeeping to the monastery of

Prüm. Lothar now began to date his official documents according to a new system: it was "year one of his imperial reign."

What, however, was to be done with Louis the Pious? In answer to this question, a number of leading churchmen—including Agobard of Lyon, Ebbo of Reims, and Jesse of Amiens—seized on the points that had been articulated at the Synod of Paris of 829. A sovereign who failed in his duties was no longer a king, but a tyrant, and he deserved to be removed. Because Louis had violated the solemn undertakings of the *Ordinatio* of 817 and a "judgment of God" had deprived him of power at the fateful meeting in Alsace, he was made to avow his shortcomings publicly and do penance. Lothar convoked an assembly in October 833 at Compiègne, and from there Lothar and his clerical followers went to St. Médard in Soissons to admonish Louis the Pious to save his soul by a renewed act of penance. Under constraint, the emperor abased himself before all and avowed whatever was demanded: he confessed to sacrilege, homicide, spreading scandal, upsetting the peace, despoiling the goods of the church, breaking his vows to God and his fellow men, making arbitrary partitions and distributions of land. In a word, he confessed to every felony unworthy of a Christian king, and he "spontaneously" renounced his imperial dignity. The bishops then imposed on him a debilitating sentence of perpetual penance. Samuel had once again deposed Saul, or so it seemed.

THE REVERSAL OF OPINION

But the scandalous treatment of the emperor provoked a reversal of opinion. Many felt that Lothar had wrongfully exploited his demoralized father. Even Hrabanus Maurus, the abbot of Fulda who was otherwise loyal to Lothar and the imperial ideal, would address a treatise to Louis the Pious in 834 in which he affirmed that it was "inadmissible that sons should revolt against their father, and subjects against their sovereign."

Soon enough discord also erupted in the camp of the victors. In his *Histories*, Nithard concisely evoked the development of events:

> Pippin and Louis saw that Lothar intended to seize the whole empire and make them his inferiors, and they were greatly distressed. Hugh, Lambert, and Matfrid were also vying for the second place in the empire after Lothar, and they began to quarrel. Because everyone sought his own interest, public affairs were entirely neglected, and the people grew angry when they saw this. Moreover, shame and regret filled the sons for having twice deprived their

father of his dignity, and the whole people for having twice abandoned their emperor.

The civil war resumed. Bernard of Septimania prompted Pippin of Aquitaine to revolt as a means of vengeance against Lothar. Their coalition was joined by Louis of Bavaria and Louis the Pious, who regained his liberty and authority in early 834. Nevertheless, Lothar could still count on followers such as Counts Hugh and Matfrid, and Lambert II of Nantes, an ally of the Bretons, even though he himself was forced to flee to the south. Heartened by their victory against a force sent to dislodge them from western Neustria, Lothar besieged and captured Chalon, where he executed several nobles, including a brother and sister of Bernard of Septimania: Gozhelm, whom he ordered beheaded, and Gerberga, who was drowned as a witch. But faced with overwhelming odds, Lothar acknowledged defeat. His father allowed him to return to Italy in exchange for his promise to stay there.

As though under a spell, the followers of Louis the Pious had returned to him. At St. Denis, where he was liberated, the churchmen who had humiliated Louis restored his weapons. The emperor now returned to Aachen, where Judith rejoined him upon her arrival from Italian captivity. Finally in early 835, Louis traveled to Metz, the domain and resting place of his ancestors, and there his half-brother Drogo set the imperial crown upon his head before 44 bishops and other church dignitaries. There as well, the churchmen principally responsible for the Penance of St. Médard—Ebbo of Reims and Agobard of Lyon—were deposed.

The End of the Reign of Louis the Pious

THE FINAL PARTITION

At the behest of Judith, Louis the Pious moved again in 837 to create a vast and coherent kingdom for his son Charles, who had now reached the age of majority. At the assembly held at Aachen, the emperor conferred on Charles all the lands extending from Frisia to the Meuse River and Burgundy, and as a guarantee of the good behavior of the bishops, abbots, and counts who dwelt in this territory, Louis immediately obliged them to pledge their fealty to Charles. After the death of Pippin of Aquitaine in 838, the emperor proceeded to ignore the claims of Pippin's two heirs, and instead turned over the "vacant" kingdom to Charles the Bald. These sweeping decisions were a cause of bitter resentment for both the heirs of Pippin and their supporters among the Aquitainian nobility, and they spurred Louis of Bavaria to renewed acts of unsuccessful rebellion.

Nevertheless, as Nithard put it, Louis the Pious "was growing old and was nearly worn out on account of various afflictions." Judith hoped for a reconciliation between her son and Lothar, who had remained quietly in Italy since 834. After all, Lothar was Charles's godfather, and the two of them could divide the empire with the exception of the Bavarian lands held by Louis. Lothar arrived at Worms like the prodigal son who sought his father's pardon. On 30 May 839, he was apportioned the lands of the empire that lay east of the Meuse River, while Charles received what lay to the west. Each brother promised the other his aid and assistance, and although Lothar alone possessed the imperial title, both were established in their own lands on an equal footing.

With his half-brother Drogo at his side, Louis the Pious died on 20 June 840 on an island in the Rhine near Ingelheim. Drogo had the body brought back to Metz to be entombed in the church of St. Arnulf, the resting place of the great family ancestor. Thus ended a reign of twenty-seven and a half years.

ASSESSING THE REIGN

Louis the Pious had begun well, but finished with little glory. Shunted aside, reinstated, overthrown, and finally restored, he does not cut the figure of a great ruler. Neither stupid nor cowardly, he did too often become the plaything of his entourage, in particular of his wife Judith. To his father's cost, Lothar had also grown ambitious and impatient to assert the privileges associated with his title as co-emperor. Together with his ambition, other factors combined to weaken the Carolingian monarchy: fraternal jealousy, court infighting, selfish ambition among the lay nobility, and finally, a misguided sense of duty and idealism among the clergy. In the midst of this, Louis remained, moreover, a peaceable king. Unlike his father, he never sought to conquer, and seldom to crush. He therefore lacked the surplus of landed spoils needed to grant new benefices to his restive, acquisitive, and too often unchecked followers. Louis had simply aimed at securing the frontiers of his empire against mounting external threats.

EXTERNAL THREATS

To the east, groups of Slavic peoples had gradually formed menacing princedoms. Thus, Ljudevit, duke of the Pannonian Croats, revolted against the Franks in 819, and attempted to draw neighboring peoples into an independent federation—a sort of proto-Yugoslavia. Then in 827, Omortag, *khagan* of the Bulgars, occupied strategic lands lying between the Drava and Sava rivers and gained control of Pannonian Croatia. Farther north, the *Royal Frankish Annals* identified the Moravians as a distinct people in 822, and the Slavs living east of the Elbe—the Wilzi, Obodrites, Sorbs, and Linoni—continued their efforts to make inroads into Saxony. The peoples of Scandinavia also posed a mounting threat in the form of sea-borne attacks, which Louis attempted to neutralize by Christianizing the Danes. In 826, the Danish chieftain Harald came to Ingelheim with his wife and nobles, received Baptism, and became a vassal of Louis. To reinforce the missionary effort, two new bishoprics were erected in Saxony at Hildesheim and Halberstadt. Nevertheless, other Northmen, the Vikings, pillaged the coastline of the empire. In 820, the abbey of Noirmoutier at the mouth of the Loire River was attacked, and in 836, continued raiding forced the abbey's monks to abandon their home. Similar visitations plagued Frisia, where the port of Dorestad was pillaged four times between 834 and 837. Carolingian political crises were a boon for the northern pirates.

Along the Mediterranean coast, the most immediate danger stemmed from Muslim pirates, who attacked the Balearic Islands, Corsica, and Sardinia. Arabs from North Africa also began to attack the remaining Byzantine possessions in southern Italy. By 840, they had captured part of Sicily, and taken advantage of strife between the Byzantine duke of Naples and the Duchy of Benevento to attack the mainland. The common threat posed by the Arabs might in fact have led to cooperation between Byzantium and the Carolingians, and there were exchanges between the emperors. In 824, Michael II, a proponent of moderate iconoclasm, dispatched an embassy to Louis the Pious asking that he intervene with the pope. Although the synod held at Paris in 825 espoused a position not unfavorable to Michael, the pope refused all compromise. On another front, squabbling between the Frankish patriarch of Aquileia and the Byzantine patriarch of Grado (a nearby island) contributed to worsening relations between the Greek and Latin churches.

Faced with a host of challenges, Louis the Pious was ultimately unable to formulate adequate solutions.

2. The Partition of 843

Louis the Pious died in 840. Three years later his empire was divided into three independent kingdoms. The Treaty of Verdun was the first great European accord whose consequences proved durable, and its terms came as no surprise to contemporaries. The idea of partitioning the empire was not new. In accord with Frankish custom, Charlemagne had provided for the division of his legacy in 806, and Louis the Pious had done so several times. Nevertheless, the death of Louis did not ensure the implementation of the scheme he had proposed. Only after three years of warfare and negotiation did the three brothers, Lothar, Louis, and Charles, arrive at a solution of their own formulation.

Prelude and Circumstances

The death of his father prompted Lothar to forget the arrangements he had agreed to at Worms in 839. He meant to claim all, as Nithard reports:

> When Lothar heard that his father had died, he dispatched messengers everywhere, especially across all of Francia. They announced that he would take over the empire that had once been given to him. He promised that he would allow everyone to keep the benefices granted by his father, and that he desired to augment them. He ordered that persons whose loyalty was doubtful should promise their fealty. Moreover, he commanded that they should come before him as soon as possible, and that those who refused to do so should be executed.

Lothar's position appeared in fact quite strong. Louis of Bavaria had only a few troops, and faced threats of Saxon revolt and Slavic incursion. Lothar, moreover, could count on the help of his nephew Pippin II, who led a part of the Aquitainian nobility in a revolt against Charles the Bald.

Lothar Versus Charles

Now seventeen, Charles had been established by his father in Aquitaine, where his mother Judith also resided. Because he needed to ensure the allegiance of followers north of the Loire and west of the Meuse, he embarked on a trip across his realm. But no sooner had Charles moved on from a locale, than Lothar's promises and threats seduced the local nobility. Thus, according to Nithard, as Lothar approached the Seine, Abbot Hilduin of St. Denis, Count Gerard II of Paris, and Pippin, the son of Bernard of Italy, "chose like slaves to break their word and disregard their oaths rather than give up their holdings for a little while." Lothar sent envoys everywhere, including Provence and Brittany, to exact oaths from the nobility. Alternating flattery with threats, he promised Charles protection and a new partition, and meanwhile schemed to undermine his noble support with the help of repeated truces. Charles, however, also worked relentlessly to shore up his position by renewing ties with old supporters and gaining new ones. At Orléans, he received a pledge of fealty from Count Warin of Mâcon; at Bourges, he worked to win over Bernard of Septimania from Pippin II; and at Le Mans, he secured the support of Lambert III, count of Nantes. Nevertheless, the fruits of these efforts remained uncertain because Charles could not be everywhere at once. To obtain lasting success, he needed to defeat Lothar's numerically superior forces. For this, Charles would have to make common cause with his brother Louis, who had withdrawn into Bavaria after suffering similar desertions among his followers.

THE ALLIANCE OF LOUIS AND CHARLES

In the spring of 841 fortune smiled on the two brothers. Charles managed to force a crossing of the Seine, and Louis arrived in the west to meet him after defeating Adalbert, duke of Austrasia. The two princes combined forces near Auxerre. With the agreement of the bishops, they appealed for a "judgment of God," that is, a trial by battle. On 25 June 841, the army of Charles and Louis squared off against that of Lothar and Pippin II at Fontenay-en-Puisaye, near Auxerre. As lay-abbot of St. Riquier, the historian Nithard was also a participant, and he declared that "it was a great battle." The engagement was, in fact, one of the greatest and most horrific of the Carolingian period. Contemporary chroniclers speak of thousands of dead: "a massacre whose equal no one could recall ever before witnessing among the Franks." A certain Angilbert left an echo of the fratricidal slaughter in a rhythmic Latin poem:

> . . .
>
> May neither dew nor rain nor shower moisten that meadow where men most skilled in war did fall, who were lamented with tears by fathers, mothers, brothers, sisters, and friends.

. . .

From a hilltop I gazed upon the valley below where brave Lothar repulsed his enemies and beat them back in flight across the brook.

Likewise on the side of Charles and Louis, the fields are white with the linen garments of the dead, as they are wont to be with birds in autumn.

. . .

The battle deserves no praise; it should be no subject of fine song. North, south, east, and west, may they all lament those who died by such a penalty.

. . .

Whatever the assessment of Angilbert, his master Lothar was defeated and fled to Aachen. After celebrating a Mass of thanksgiving on the field of victory, Louis and Charles received a number of nobles who had waited to see the issue of the battle. Thus Bernard of Septimania arrived from his nearby camp, and committed his sixteen-year-old son William to the care of Charles the Bald. The young man became as much a hostage as a vassal, and his mother Dhuoda responded to his absence by composing for him her famous *Handbook*, wherein she outlined a program of education for a young Christian nobleman.

THE STRASBOURG OATHS (842)

Despite his defeat, Lothar continued to intrigue, making new offers to Charles in an effort to break his alliance with Louis of Bavaria. The two allies, however, were firm in the belief that God was on their side, and they sealed their pact of cooperation. On 12 February 842 they exchanged oaths to this effect at Strasbourg in the presence of each other's troops:

> For the love of God and for our Christian people's salvation and our own, from this day on inasmuch as God grants me knowledge and power I shall treat my brother with regard to aid and everything else as a man should rightfully treat his brother, on condition that he do the same for me. And I shall not enter into any dealings with Lothar which might with my consent injure my brother.

Nithard preserved the foregoing words, and he did so not once, but twice, in two similar yet decisively different forms. To make himself clear to the other's followers, each brother pronounced his oath in their language: Louis spoke in "Romance," while Charles spoke in *lingua teudisca*, or "Germanic." Thereupon their respective vassals proceeded to swear an oath in their own vernacular—also recorded by Nithard—promising to abandon their lord should he break his pledge. Thus the Strasbourg Oaths have come to mark not only a momentous diplomatic and political event, but also an important step in the linguistic history of Europe.

In order to celebrate the harmony that reigned between the allies, games were often arranged, as Nithard describes:

> They came together wherever a show could be accommodated. With a whole multitude gathered on either side, each with an equal number of Saxons, Gascons, Austrasians, and Bretons, they first rushed at full speed against one another as if they meant to attack. Then, one side would turn back, pretending to flee to their teammates under the cover of shields, but countering, they would dart back after their former pursuers. Finally, both kings and all the young men spurred forward their horses with immense clamor and lances in hand, and they gave chase by turns as the other side took flight. It was a show worth seeing thanks to the outstanding participants and good discipline. In such a vast array of different players no one dared hurt or abuse another, as often happens even when the games are small and among friends.

Lothar Submits

Finally the two brothers marched on Aachen. They occupied the palace, though Lothar had already carted away the treasury. With the accord of the bishops, they then proclaimed Lothar unworthy to govern, and they proposed to divide the empire between themselves. Twelve commissioners were appointed on each side to determine their respective shares. Thus, Lothar had to know that an indefeasible alliance now united Louis and Charles. After Fontenay, the Strasbourg Oaths and the capture of Aachen, the ambitious emperor had no choice but to yield. He abandoned his erstwhile ally, Pippin II. With great generosity, Charles and Louis agreed to resume negotiations on a new basis aimed at a tripartite division of empire, excluding Aquitaine, Bavaria, and Lombardy, since these regions were considered respectively as the home domains of Charles, Louis and Lothar.

Negotiations (Spring 842–August 843)

It was high time for the brothers to come to terms. Frankish political turmoil had dramatically emboldened foreign sea-borne raiders, who now went so far as to pillage important centers like Quentovic and even Rouen. To dislodge one group of Northmen, the monks of St. Wandrille had agreed to pay an enormous tribute, and thereby introduced an inviting precedent. A group of Danes also settled themselves, with Lothar's consent, on the Frisian island of Walcheren and some neighboring places. In Provence, Muslim raiders attacked Marseille and Arles, while other Arab forces made inroads against Benevento in southern Italy. Finally, the usual restiveness of Aquitaine, Brittany, Saxony, and the Slavs posed a host of additional challenges.

THE DIFFICULTIES

Nevertheless, the negotiations were to last for well over a year, such was the mistrust of the parties and the difficulty of the issues involved. On 15 June 842, the three brothers came together near Mâcon, and agreed to keep the peace until autumn, when a meeting of delegates was scheduled to convene on 30 September for the purpose of dividing the empire equally and fairly. This gathering was scuttled due to fears aroused by Lothar's behavior. Another meeting successfully convened on 19 October 842 at Koblenz, where the Rhine separated the camps of the two delegations, and the abbey of St. Castor served as a site for their deliberations. Although Charles and Louis had originally agreed that Lothar should choose first among the three parts of the kingdom, Lothar's envoys caviled over the terms of a "fair and equitable partition" in face of the avowed ignorance of all concerning the empire's extent and resources. Although Charles and Louis had offered him everything between the Rhine in the east and the Meuse, Saône, and Rhône in the west, Lothar wanted in addition those portions of the Carolingian heartland that lay west of the Meuse in the region of the Charbonnière Forest. In the end, the protests of Lothar's delegates over what was "fair and equitable" backfired. It was decided that no decision could be made until a survey of the empire was taken to ensure a just partition. The truce between the brothers was twice extended while commissioners worked to assess the resources of the empire. Though arduous and long, their work was furthered by inventories (*descriptiones*) listing bishoprics, religious foundations, counties, and royal properties.

CHARLES'S MARRIAGE

Meanwhile, Charles the Bald used the truce to consolidate his position. He married Ermentrude, the daughter of Count Odo of Orléans, on 14 December 842. Odo stemmed from a family based along the Middle Rhine which was probably related to that of Gerold, Charlemagne's brother-in-law. Odo himself had married Engeltrude, the sister of Count Gerard and the seneschal Adalhard, one of the most powerful lords in western Francia. Nithard wrote at length concerning Charles's choice of bride:

> Louis the Pious in his time had loved this Adalhard so much that he did whatever Adalhard wanted everywhere in the empire. Adalhard cared less for the public good than for pleasing everyone. He persuaded the emperor to distribute privileges and public property for private use, and since he arranged for whatever anyone requested, he totally ruined the government. By this means it happened that he could bend the people to do whatever he wanted.

Charles no doubt hoped to gain the favor of Adalhard through his marriage, even though his brother Gerard had joined Lothar's cause. For Nithard added: "Charles entered into this marriage above all because he thought he could attract the largest following with Adalhard."

Charles spent the rest of harsh winter of 843 with his new wife in Aquitaine, prosecuting the fight against Pippin II. Spring brought him a series of unpleasant reports: Empress Judith died on 13 April; Scandinavian raiders captured Nantes on 24 June; and an important victory was scored by the Bretons under the leadership of their duke, Nominoë. The young king required freedom to act, and this largely presupposed a resolution of the disputes surrounding the partition.

In August 843, the three brothers agreed to meet at Dugny, near Verdun, and there they concluded their momentous transaction.

The Treaty of Verdun and Its Terms

The text of their agreement has not been preserved, but the boundaries of the three kingdoms established around the kernels of Aquitaine, Lombardy, and Bavaria can be determined from indirect evidence. To Charles went everything to the west of a line that roughly followed the Scheldt, Meuse, Saône, and Rhône rivers, while Louis acquired everything east of the Rhine and north of the Alps. Retaining his imperial title, Lothar received the central strip of territories extending from the North Sea to Italy. Still, it is not enough to trace the map of the three kingdoms of the Treaty

of Verdun, we must also consider the underlying reasons for the boundaries that emerged.

THE RATIONALE OF THE PARTITION

Since the nineteenth century, historians, especially in France and Germany, have used a variety of rationales to account for the makeup of the
three kingdoms. In the heyday of the principle of nationality, the French
historians Jules Michelet and Augustin Thierry believed that the negotiators of 843 had sought above all to do justice to national sentiment and
linguistic distinctions. Hence, "France" and "Germany" were born at Verdun, while the portion assigned to Lothar was destined to break up into
pieces that later emerged as the Netherlands, Belgium, Switzerland, and
Italy. This idea proved so durable that Joseph Calmette could still remark
in his generally balanced synthesis *L'Effondrement d'un empire et la naissance d'une Europe* (Paris, 1941) that the Treaty of Verdun had "violated
nature" in establishing a no-man's-land between France and Germany. The
negotiators had cut into "the living flesh of France and Germany, and the
wounds thus made had never healed, and had even reopened at periodic
intervals." In his *Naissance de la France* (Paris, 1948), Ferdinand Lot was in
general more circumspect. Although he noted that "no concept of race or
language had ever determined the shape of Carolingian or Merovingian
partitions," he added that "having experienced the rupture of their close
ties, the future France and Germany could take stock of their individuality,
until then confused, and live henceforth independent existences." Moreover, he judged that "without the amputation of her eastern flank, France
could never have arisen: France could only live at the cost of losing
an arm."

At the time, however, there was no "France," no "Germany." Charles
the Bald ruled a kingdom composed of diverse peoples speaking very different languages. Precious little could serve to unite the Goths of the Spanish March, the Gascons, the Aquitainians, the Bretons and the peoples of
Neustria and Flanders. To the east, Louis of Bavaria could scarcely claim
greater cohesion among his subjects, despite the contrary assertions of
German historians of the nineteenth and early twentieth centuries.

To explain the grounds for the partition enacted at Verdun, we must
look beyond nationality and nationhood. Some historians have proposed
that the emphasis had lain on the economic needs of each of the future
kingdoms. In his *History of Europe*, written in 1917 and first published in
1936, Henri Pirenne stated that "the point of view espoused by the nego-

tiators was dictated by the prevailing system of economy." Each partaker in the division was to receive an area whose revenues were more or less equal. On the basis of this idea, Roger Dion noted in 1948 that each allotment divided the various economic zones of western Europe along a north-south axis: the coastal pasturelands of the north, the central cereal plains, forests, and wine regions, and finally the salt marshes and olive groves of the south. However intriguing, these hypotheses fail in their turn to account for all the facts. Moreover, the Carolingian princes had not read Aristotle and learned from him that polities should be self-sufficient.

The Belgian historian François Louis Ganshof turned to contemporary sources to penetrate the rationale of the partition of 843, and we shall follow his example. On the subject of partitions, Nithard had of course noted two significant facts: first, that "fertility or equal size of the lands apportioned was not considered so much as the fact that they were adjacent and fitted into the territory already held by each brother"; and second, that "Lothar complained about the fate of his followers, since in the share that had been offered to him he would not have enough to compensate them for what they had lost." Nithard's remarks suggest the most satisfactory explanation. The brothers were most concerned about the fate of their followers, for without their help, they could do nothing. Therefore, they had to keep the benefices of their vassals within their respective kingdoms, since it was recognized that no vassal could pay homage to several lords. To avoid the likelihood of incompatible obligations, Charlemagne had articulated a key principle in his *Divisio regnorum* of 806: "The followers of each king shall each receive their benefices inside the realm of their master." Likewise in the *Ordinatio imperii* of 817, Louis the Pious had instructed that "each vassal should hold his benefices only within the dominion of his lord, and not in that of any other." This concern explains, for instance, why the border of the western kingdom of Charles the Bald crossed the Saône and took in a part of Burgundy that included the holdings of his vassal Warin, count of Mâcon, Autun, and Chalon and abbot of Flavigny. Louis of Bavaria likewise received a section of the left bank of the Rhine including the bishoprics of Mainz, Worms, and Speyer, not on account of the local vineyards, as a later chronicler would report, but to keep the lands of powerful episcopal vassals inside his kingdom.

Hence, the problems of benefices and fealty weighed heavily in the negotiations that led to the treaty ratified at Verdun. As Fustel de Coulanges pointed out in the nineteenth century, "the partition was not undertaken for the people, but rather for the vassals." With the help of maps, we can easily see that each brother wanted to maximize the number of his abbeys, bishoprics, and fiscal domains in Francia. The heartland of the empire was home to choice benefices held by great Austrasian families, but there also lay the main state residences that each king strove to retain for his own use, enjoyment, and profit. Each of three brothers was a "king of the Franks." They reigned jointly over their respective fractions of the "Kingdom of the Franks," while they separately ruled Aquitaine, Bavaria, and Lombardy.

THE CONSEQUENCES OF THE PARTITION

Those who divided the empire could not possibly have foreseen that the borders fixed at Verdun would determine the map of medieval Europe, and furthermore that the boundary between the kingdom of Charles the Bald and the empire of Lothar was destined to survive for centuries. Throughout the Middle Ages, the Scheldt River separated the "kingdom" from the empire; the Saône divided Burgundy into two parts: the duchy to the west, and the county—later known as Franche-Comté—to the east, while further south one passed once again from the "kingdom" to the empire by crossing the Rhône. The border of the "kingdom" as fixed at Verdun is still visible today near the Argonne plateau along the line separating the modern French *départements* of Meuse and Marne. To the southeast, the Pyrenees did not represent a frontier at all, since Charles possessed Spanish lands that remained part of the "kingdom" until the reign of Saint Louis (1258). The boundaries between the realms of Lothar and Louis would later prove less stable as a consequence both of further partitions made among the emperor's heirs and of the territorial ambitions of the German kings. Yet there again we find the outline of the future Germany. To my mind, the Treaty of Verdun was the "birth certificate" of modern Europe.

For contemporaries, the momentous event marked above all the end of the great ideal of unity. Florus of Lyon reacted with bitterness:

> The mountains and hills, woods and rivers, springs,
> High cliffs and deep valleys too,
> All bemoan the Frankish people, which, after its rise to empire by
>   the gift of Christ,
> Now lies covered in ashes.
>   . . .

It has lost both the name and the glory of empire,
and the united kingdom has fallen to three lots.
For there is no longer any one recognized as emperor:
instead of a king, there is a kinglet; for a realm, but the fragments
    thereof.
  . . . .

This *Lament on the Division of the Empire* voiced the concerns of the clerical party, who had hoped to maintain imperial unity and who deeply feared that division would weaken the church. The ecclesiastical provinces and individual bishoprics were also partitioned as a result of the Treaty of Verdun. Thus, the sees of the province of Cologne were variously assigned to the separate realms of Lothar and Louis; similarly, the bishop of Strasbourg lived in Lothar's empire, while he remained a suffragan of the archbishop of Mainz, a subject of Louis. Sometimes, a single diocese was divided into areas controlled by different sovereigns, as happened with Reims, Münster, and Bremen. A host of additional problems arose from the fact that many abbeys and bishoprics owned parcels of land situated in far-off regions, and these now came under "foreign" political control.

Nevertheless, circumstances militated against the unitary ideal. Political realism dictated the creation of new dominions that could be ruled effectively by separate kings and their followers.

3. The Empire Disbanded (843–869)

After the conclusion of the Treaty of Verdun each king retired to his own realm and its pressing concerns. Yet the kings had to acknowledge that they faced common problems threatening the entire west. To address them, the brothers agreed to meet from time to time, thereby inaugurating the "rule of brotherly cooperation" (*régime de confraternité*). After the death of Lothar in 855, Europe moved from government by three to government by five separate kings whose cooperation became ever more difficult to secure. Clerical elites in Francia and at Rome sought nevertheless to foster the unity of western Christendom. Although these parties affirmed the continued survival of the empire, the separate kings increasingly faced their concrete problems without reference to the ideal of unity propounded by the church.

The Defense of the Notion of Unity

BROTHERLY COOPERATION
In the *Divisio regnorum* of 806, Charlemagne had stressed the brotherhood of his presumptive heirs. Louis the Pious had also dwelt on this notion in the *Ordinatio imperii* of 817 and in his subsequent schemes for dividing the empire. Now that the partition had come to pass, brotherly cooperation was sorely needed. The disturbances that led to the Treaty of Verdun had to be addressed by religious and moral reforms capable, it was hoped, of appeasing God's anger. For the enemies of the Christians had grown fiercer and more daring than ever. In 844 Northmen advanced on Toulouse. In 845 they pillaged Paris, likewise Bordeaux in 848 and Orléans in 853. Meanwhile, Arab raiders were ravaging Italy and had actually sacked St. Peter's in Rome and nearby St. Paul-outside-the-Walls.

The Conference of Yütz (844)
The brothers' first gathering convened at Yütz, near Thionville, in October 844, and was presided over by their uncle Drogo, bishop of Metz, whom

Pope Sergius II had lately named papal vicar in Francia. Attended by bishops from across the west, the three kings committed themselves to maintaining a "rule of brotherly cooperation and mutual charity." They also dispatched embassies to conciliate the stubborn adversaries of Charles the Bald: Pippin II of Aquitaine and the Breton duke Nominoë.

The Colloquies at Meersen

The continued attacks suffered by Europe obliged the three kings to meet again in February 847 at Meersen, near Maastricht. For two weeks, they discussed possibilities for mutual assistance, and among other points, they agreed to forbid the flight of agitators from one kingdom to another. At the end of the conference, each king made a statement, much as occurs today at all international gatherings. Lothar reiterated the general principles of brotherly cooperation; Louis reported a further dispatch of messengers to Pippin of Aquitaine; and Charles the Bald announced that another conference was scheduled to convene on the coming Feast of St. John (24 June) to deal with other as yet unresolved problems.

This announcement notwithstanding, four years elapsed before the next royal conference took place. In the meantime, however, Lothar met with Charles, Charles with Louis, and Louis with Lothar. Despite their individual complaints, the brothers endeavored to strengthen their mutual links. When they all met again at Meersen in 851, they sought to work out a plan for the continuance of the "rule of brotherhood" after their own deaths, and to provide for ecclesiastical and governmental reforms. It is noteworthy that they continued to speak of the "Kingdom of the Franks" as though Carolingian unity remained intact despite the Treaty of Verdun. Nevertheless, the main result of the conference was to reinforce the ties between Lothar and Charles, while Louis of Bavaria pursued an independent policy somewhat hostile to his brothers. Thus, Empress Judith's dream of harmony between the first-born son and her "Benjamin" was belatedly realized. These two men met annually until Lothar's death in 855 and waged a common struggle against the raids of the Northmen in the Seine basin. In 854 Louis refused their invitation to a conference at Liège, and in his absence, they concluded an alliance between themselves and their successors directed against the German king. Louis was thereby forced to abandon his intrigues and come to terms. The balance remained a delicate one until Lothar's death at the monastery of Prüm on 29 September 855.

New Partitions

The death of the eldest partner undercut the system of brotherly cooperation. Before his decease, Lothar had arranged for the partition of his territories among his three sons. The eldest, Louis, inherited the imperial title and ruled over Italy. Lothar II received the lands from Frisia to the Jura Mountains, henceforth known as Lotharingia. The third son, the sickly Charles, inherited the rest: southern Burgundy and Provence.

The Carolingian west was now divided into five realms and ruled by kings from two different generations who had little understanding of one another. To the three sons of Lothar, the principle of "brotherly cooperation" was unacceptable. From Italy Louis II advanced a claim to part of Francia, and Lothar II encroached on the lands assigned to his younger brother Charles around Lyon and in Provence. Only with the greatest difficulty were the three new Carolingian rulers able to agree in 856 to maintain the status quo at a conference at Orbe, near Lausanne. Their two uncles offered the nephews advice, but each uncle had an agenda of his own, especially concerning the lands ruled by Lothar II. The former "rule of brotherly cooperation" was replaced by a nexus of alliances between the nephews and their uncles. At a meeting in St. Quentin in March 857, Lothar II solemnly renewed his father's pact with Charles the Bald, while about the same time Louis of Bavaria met with Louis II for a similar purpose at Trent. The German king increasingly preferred the role of strong man. Hoping to profit from an assault by the Northmen and a simultaneous revolt by the Aquitainian nobility, Louis invaded western Francia in 858. Faced with this specter of renewed fraternal wars, the church moved to save the threatened unity of Christendom.

THE DEFENSE OF UNITY BY THE CHURCH

Since the time of Louis the Pious, many leading ecclesiastics had made it their task to uphold the ideal of imperial unity. In the wake of 843, the bishops worked hard to ensure the success of the "brotherly cooperation." Now, as one king invaded the realm of another, corrupted his vassals, and seized church property, the episcopacy responded by taking the political initiative.

Hincmar of Reims

In August 858 Louis crossed into the dominion of Charles the Bald. At Ponthion and later at Attigny, he received and rewarded with countships and abbacies the nobles who rallied to his cause. Among them figured Wenilo (Ganelon), archbishop of Sens, whose name would later be immortalized as that of the traitor of the *Song of Roland*. Nevertheless, many other churchmen refused to appear. To extort their support, Louis convoked the senior ecclesiastics of western Francia to a synod at Reims, perhaps with the hidden intention of having himself anointed king. Although the intruder had already expanded the dating of his official documents to include "year one of our reign in France," Archbishop Hincmar of Reims was unimpressed. Moreover, the leading churchmen of western Francia chose this same Hincmar to respond to the royal summons. He dispatched a searing letter of refusal in which he proceeded to remind the king of his duties and to expound the position of those who sought in truth to safeguard the welfare and unity of the Christian people. According to Hincmar, it was inconceivable that King Louis could ally himself with the very laymen who had pillaged the church, who had whipped up brother against brother, who had forsaken one lord for another out of self-interest, and who had thereby transformed the royal palace from a holy place into a place of sacrilege. If Louis has truly come to restore order to the lands of Charles the Bald, as he pretends, let him commence by listening to the bishops; let him recall the hellish torments reserved (according to a recent vision) for his ancestor Charles Martel in punishment of his violence against the church. Furthermore, the bishops Hincmar represented were unwilling to abandon Charles, whom they had anointed, for "whoever raises his hand against the anointed of the Lord attacks Christ himself." Louis should leave the kingdom, and then a conference would be arranged between the kings and the bishops, who "as successors to the Apostles have received from Christ the task of governing the church that is His Realm."

In this remarkable letter, Hincmar, the eminent canonist and able politician, rearticulated principles first suggested by the Synod of Paris of 829. He responded to a political crisis by applying episcopal notions about the kingship and the church in the service of peace and concord, and he met with success.

Surprised by the resistance of the episcopacy and panicked by the approach of an opposing army, Louis withdrew to the east, while his newfound supporters melted away. Lothar II, who had momentarily deserted Charles the Bald, renewed his ties and agreed to assemble a synod at Metz in his kingdom to examine the conditions under which Louis of Bavaria might be absolved by the church of his crimes. The German king was found guilty of fomenting "schism in the holy church and in Christendom," and he would have to do penance as had Louis the Pious.

Agreement Between Louis and Charles

Clearly, however, Louis the German was cut from rather different cloth. He did not accept the prospect of humiliating himself. At the synod of Savonnières, near Toul, in 859, forty-five prelates from western Francia, Lotharingia, and Provence, belonging to twelve different ecclesiastical provinces, committed themselves to restoring the unity of the Christian people:

> As prescribed by their ministry and the sacred authority vested in them, the bishops must unify themselves in order to guide and correct their kings, as must the leading men of the various kingdoms and their subordinates by offering their rulers the support of counsel.

Faced with this unanimity and after further intervention by Lothar II, Louis agreed to meet his brother in the Church of St. Castor at Koblenz. After five days of discussion, an accord was concluded that closely followed the terms of the second conference at Meersen in 851. On 7 June 860 both kings pledged a vow as at Strasbourg, but this time the procedure changed. Louis spoke in Germanic to his eastern followers, while Charles addressed his western party in Romance. They both approved the text drafted by the bishops and promised to respect the laws, rights, and security of the persons living in their respective kingdoms.

Thus the bishops led by Hincmar were able to restore the unity of Christendom. They undertook and accomplished this task by virtue of a tradition of religious authority going back to the fifth century. They were, however, especially encouraged to do so by a body of canonical texts that surfaced in Gaul in the mid-ninth century. This collection of largely forged sources circulated under the name of Isidore Mercator—the famed Pseudo-Isidore—and had lately been concocted somewhere in the ecclesiastical province of Reims. As part of a varied agenda, the so-called *Pseudo-Isidorian Decretals* aimed at exalting the power of episcopal office and provided new legal grounds for the inviolability of church property. The forger, or forgers, was not content merely to fabricate texts reinforcing the rights of bishops *against* their archiepiscopal superiors but also attributed new juridical powers to the papacy, powers that the popes had never before exercised. The collection thus highlighted a new local awareness of the papacy, and the popes themselves willingly entered the political fray as advocates of the unity of Christendom.

Papal Intervention

During the reign of Charlemagne and at the beginning of the reign of Louis the Pious, the papacy lived in the shadow of the emperors and subject to their authority. Faced with the prospect of partitions, the popes recognized the pending risks for imperial unity and made themselves heard. In 833, Gregory IV agreed at the behest of Lothar I to help restore order between Louis the Pious and his sons. He soon realized, however, that Lothar had merely used him as a tool in the revolt against his father. Although the popes do not appear to have protested the terms of the Treaty of Verdun, they affirmed their role as guarantors of the unity of the west. Hence, Pope Sergius II (844–847) wrote to the bishops of Francia in June 844:

> It is not tolerable that the fellowship of three brothers united in the Faith of the Trinity should depart from mutual affection and the common equity. Should any one of them, not content with the general peace, prefer to follow the prince of discord, we shall rightly do our best to chastise him with God's help and in accord with the canons.

Sergius's successor, Leo IV (847–855), crowned Louis II emperor in 850. Leo expressed his view even more boldly that two men ruled over the west: the pope and the emperor. The prerogatives of the metropolitan archbishops were curtailed in favor of Roman approvals. Thus, Leo IV reserved for himself the final decision concerning Hincmar's removal of a group of clerics unlawfully ordained by his deposed predecessor, Ebbo of Reims. By constructing a new bastion, the *Civitas leonina*, the pope also physically secured the Vatican against Arab raiders, while he launched a general appeal for Christians to oppose these enemies of the Faith. Without making him an exact precursor of Urban II, preacher of the First Crusade in 1095, it is interesting to note that Leo IV was the first pope to promise heavenly recompense to those who died for "the truth of the Faith, the welfare of their homeland, and the defense of Christians."

Pope Nicholas I

After the intervening pontificate of Benedict III (855–858), Nicholas I began his eventful papal "reign." The word appropriately characterizes the nine years during which this pope guided the Roman church. With mild exaggeration, some historians, including Walter Ullmann, have even viewed Nicholas as the first "theocratic" pope. In the letters drafted by his secretary, Anastasius, abbot of St. Mary's in Trastevere and later librarian at the Lateran Palace, Pope Nicholas affirmed that by the authority of Peter and Paul, the Apostolic See held the highest of all powers: that it had the right to control the life of all churches; that all synods must be convoked on papal order; that the metropolitan archbishops were subject to papal authority; that the pope might create rights concerning matters left untouched by earlier canons. Faced with this litany of novel claims, it is easy to see how disputes arose between Nicholas and Archbishop Hincmar, who was, if nothing else, a metropolitan jealous of his independence. Not content with his station in the west, Nicholas also went so far as to intervene in the east when he learned that Emperor Michael III had deposed Ignatius, the eastern patriarch, and replaced him with Photius, who was still a layman at the time of his nomination. The ensuing conflict with Photius was embittered by the pope's failure to regain control of old Illyricum and the newly Christianized Bulgaria of *khagan* Boris. Although the *khagan* of the Bulgars approached the pope in 863 for help in organizing his new church, Byzantine missionaries soon dashed papal ambitions. Nevertheless, in response to questions posed by the Bulgars, Nicholas spoke of the "expansion of Christianity" (*christianitas dilatata*), and his word choice marks how *christianitas*—"Christianity"—increasingly came to be understood in the social, even political sense of "Christendom."

As part of his program to "restore" the full powers of the Roman church, Nicholas I did not hesitate to interfere in temporal affairs. Although his vigorous language has sometimes led scholars to view him as a calculating opportunist bent on political ascendancy, Nicholas struggled to impress upon the hardheaded princes of his day the duties of their kingly office. His thinking was inspired by the fifth-century Pope Gelasius I, who had drawn a distinction between papal authority (*auctoritas*) and imperial power (*potestas*), and asserted the primacy of the former as the means of salvation. In his turn, Nicholas recognized kingly power in its proper sphere, but he believed that Christian rulers had particular responsibility to work for the good of the church and that he as pope had a duty to admonish and guide the wayward among them. Thus Nicholas interceded with Charles the Bald on behalf of his disobedient sons, Louis and Charles; he likewise strove to avert conflict between Charles the Bald and Louis the German; and above all, he opposed the efforts of Lothar II to repudiate his legitimate wife.

The Divorce of Lothar II

The saga of Lothar's abortive divorce concerns politics as much as morality, but it furnished the pope a ready opportunity to appear as "chief justice" of the west. The tortuous episode began with the political marriage of Lothar in 855 to Theutberga, the daughter of count Boso and the sister of Hubert, lay-abbot of St. Maurice-in-Valais (see Chart 7). Despite his advantageous marriage, Lothar kept his cherished mistress Waldrada, the mother of his bastard son Hugh. When his wife bore no children at all, Lothar resolved to annul the union and wed his mistress in order to legitimize his only prospective heir. In 860, Theutberga was accused of having had incestuous relations with her notorious brother Hubert. After extracting a confession to this effect from the queen, Lothar had the justice of his cause ratified by a gathering of Lotharingian bishops.

When asked to second their findings, Hincmar of Reims refused, and instead composed a pamphlet opposing the divorce. Because Charles the Bald hoped to take over neighboring Lotharingia upon his nephew's death, some historians have viewed Hincmar's attitude as a thinly veiled bid to further Charles's interests. Nevertheless, the archbishop of Reims argued his case above all in the name of Christian morality. However desirable or expedient, the repudiation of a wife was inadmissible, and for a king, the matter was graver still, owing to his position as leader and model for his subjects. The potential consequences of the divorce made it politic for both sides to appeal the matter in Rome. Lothar, however, trusted in the opinion of his own bishops, and married Waldrada in 862 before learning of the decision of Pope Nicholas.

In this matter of Christian morality, Nicholas I proved as unbending as Hincmar, and he exploited the appeal to Rome to affirm his apostolic authority and prerogatives. In 862 he dispatched two legates with instructions to convene a synod at Metz to rehear Lothar's case in the presence of the bishops of Francia, Germany, and Provence. Although Lothar managed to buy off the papal legates, Nicholas was not deceived. The pope reacted to the report of the synod's decisions by deposing the messengers. The archbishops of Trier and Cologne attempted to circumvent their summary deposition by appealing to Emperor Louis II; they also disseminated a widely copied anti-papal circular wherein they accused Nicholas of setting himself up as "emperor of the world." All this was of no avail. Nicholas held his ground, and announced a general council to be held at Rome that would examine all the questions facing Christendom, in the east as well as in the west.

The Carolingian kings were troubled by these unfamiliar papal initiatives. In February 865 Charles and Louis of Bavaria met at Tusey on the Meuse River. For the sake of the realm united by God for their ancestors, so they said, they renewed the undertakings pledged at Koblenz in 860. However diverse in its rulers and peoples, they affirmed the unity of Christendom and, by implication, their own duty to admonish Lothar to restore order to his kingdom and to his marital life. On the same occasion, they also notified Pope Nicholas that the Frankish bishops would not be permitted to attend his council in Rome. Nicholas responded by dispatching Arsenius, bishop of Orte, to meet with Charles the Bald, Louis, and Lothar II. Although Arsenius finally succeeded in separating Lothar from his mistress, the political world was now polarized into two opposing camps: Charles and Louis the German, on one side, and Lothar and Louis II, on the other.

The death of Nicholas I in 867 brought no relief to the contest of wills. In 869 Lothar journeyed to Italy in an effort to gain approval for his position from the new and supposedly more compliant Pope Hadrian II. Empress Engelberga, the wife of Louis II, arranged a meeting between the two men at Monte Cassino in July. By falsely claiming to have put off his mistress Waldrada, Lothar gained admission to Communion. His reconciliation with the pope was well under way when he died unexpectedly at Piacenza on 8 August 869 from an attack of malaria. His contemporaries viewed the event as God's judgment: "At Monte Cassino, the king had eaten and drunk his own condemnation."

Whatever their successes from 855 to 869, the Frankish bishops and the papacy had strained to mediate the differences of the Carolingian princes. As Hincmar of Reims commented in his *Treatise on the Divorce of Lothar*:

> This kingdom pried from the hands of many men had been united under the hand of the kings of our parents, and the one kingdom is the one church. But this church must on no account be divided according to the division of these men who ought to live as though they were one man and one ruler in one dominion.

The Kings in Their Kingdoms

While churchmen stood out increasingly as the guardians of Christian unity and the papacy developed into an international power, the Carolingian kings focused for the most part on narrower political objectives and on the numerous domestic problems facing their individual kingdoms. They had to deal with continual raids and invasions from without as well as revolts and sedition from within.

Louis II, the First Sovereign of Italy

The Reformer King

In 844 Lothar I entrusted his Italian domains to his son Louis II. Crowned king the same year and emperor in 850, the twenty-year-old prince was intelligent and energetic. Until the end of his reign in 875, he actively attended to the needs of his kingdom, venturing outside it on only three occasions. As witnessed by a capitulary promulgated at Pavia in 850, Italy stood, moreover, in need of his reforms and protection: brigands plagued pilgrims and merchants traveling to Rome; local magnates oppressed the poor; and neglected bridges and royal palaces were crumbling into ruin. The king acted to restore order, and his efforts are amply documented.

The Italian Nobility

Louis II relied heavily on the nobles who served him, and ties of marriage and blood guaranteed their support. By his marriage to Gisela, daughter of Louis the Pious and Judith, Eberhard of Friuli was a step-uncle of Louis II. An owner of extensive lands in Francia and Lombardy, the marquis also distinguished himself by his learning and his impressive personal library, later dispersed among his eight children. After Eberhard's death (ca. 864), the March of Friuli passed first to his eldest son, Unruoch, and then to his illustrious second son, Berengar, the future king of Italy and an ally by marriage of the Supponid clan. Louis II also chose his own bride, Engelberga, from the eminent Supponid family, whose progenitor, Suppo I, had been count of Brescia and duke of Spoleto until his death in 822. Other notable figures among Louis's vassals were Adalbert I, the scion of a Bavarian family who served as marquis of Tuscany from 847 to 884, with authority over Liguria and Corsica, and Adalbert's brother-in-law, Count Lambert IV of Spoleto, a descendent of Lambert II of Nantes who had joined Lothar I in Italy while other members of his family remained behind in the Breton March (see Table 6).

Relations with the Papacy

Already king of Italy, Louis II was crowned emperor by Pope Leo IV in 850. Leo IV worked closely with the new emperor in order to reassert the papacy politically after a long period of self-effacement. To defend against Arab attackers, he restored the Aurelian Walls surrounding Rome and erected a massive new circuit of fortifications beginning at the Castel Sant'Angelo and encompassing the Vatican basilica and palace complex. The pope financed the construction of his *Civitas leonina* with subsidies from the emperor and papal tax concessions. Inscriptions preserved on a gateway to Leo's fortified precinct still bear witness to the grandeur of the achievement:

> Roman, Frank, Lombard, or passerby who beholds this work, lend your voice to songs worthy of it. Celebrate golden Rome, the splendor, the hope of the world!

In addition, Leo IV founded a colony of Corsicans at Porto, and established a new fortified town, Leopolis (now Civitavecchia), to replace an earlier center destroyed by Muslim attackers. In accord with the terms of the Roman Constitution of 824, two imperial *missi* still resided at Rome. One of these was the prominent Roman noble Arsenius, who became bishop of Orte after a period of married life and whose sons Eleutherius and Anastasius, the future papal librarian (*Bibliothecarius*), were flush with ambition. Leo IV mistrusted Anastasius, the cardinal priest of St. Marcellus, for he was also a protégé of Louis II.

When Leo IV died in 855, the pro-Roman faction designated Benedict III as his successor, despite desperate efforts by Anastasius to have himself made pope. Louis II intervened, however, to ensure that the doings of Pope Benedict would be supervised by Arsenius and Anastasius, lately named abbot of St. Mary's in Trastevere. Upon the death of Benedict III in 858, Louis II secured the election of Nicholas I as pope, from whom he expected docile support. The emperor surrounded the new pope with counselors of his own choosing: Bishop Arsenius of Orte and Anastasius, who became the pope's secretary. Nevertheless, Nicholas soon revealed his own strong personality and clashed with Louis II on several occasions. Thus in 864, the pope reined in Archbishop John of Ravenna, a veritable despot guilty of all manner of abuse against the papal subjects living under his control. Despite the support he enjoyed from the emperor, John of Ravenna was forced to submit. The emperor likewise failed to prevail upon Nicholas to annul the marriage of his brother Lothar II.

With the election of a successor to Nicholas in 867, Louis II found a man more to his liking. The compliant Hadrian II was blind in one eye, partly crippled, and without great prestige, though he was very pious. Hadrian suffered considerably during his pontificate from turmoil in his own family. Having married before taking orders (still frequently the case in Rome), Hadrian had a daughter, and both she and her mother resided at the pope's Lateran Palace. In the middle of Lent 868, the young woman was carried off and forcibly married by Eleutherius, the son of Bishop Arsenius. This outrage was followed by one still graver when Eleutherius proceeded to murder the girl and her mother in a moment of fury. The incident brought about a temporary eclipse of Anastasius, brother of the murderer, but the Lateran librarian soon regained his position and influence. It was he, in fact, who continued to govern the Roman church in the forceful tradition of Nicholas I, while Hadrian acclaimed the unceasing efforts of Emperor Louis II to advance the Christian cause and to defend southern Italy against Muslim attack.

Southern Italy

The Arab incursions posed by far the greatest threat for the Republic of St. Peter and southern Italy. The Byzantine presence was now limited to the *theme*, or province, of Sicily, with its subject duchies of Calabria and Otrano, and the largely independent duchy of Naples, whose dukes had begun to date official documents according to their own regnal years. Moreover, within the Neapolitan duchy, centers like Amalfi were also emerging as hereditary princedoms. Apart from these Byzantine or formerly Byzantine territories, there were also Lombard princedoms, and first among them was the Duchy of Benevento. After the conquest of the Lombard kingdom by Charlemagne in 774, the rulers of Benevento assumed the title of "prince of the Lombards." Their functionaries were the *gastaldei*, who administered the vast princely estates and oversaw the collection of revenues. Beneventan coinage was, moreover, widely used as a medium of commerce across the Mediterranean world. Yet despite its survival and success, the duchy faced internal as well as external challenges. Thus in 846 Louis II had to intervene between Prince Radelgisus and his rival Siginulf, thereby fostering the emergence of Salerno as an autonomous princedom. Somewhat earlier, in 840, the independent rulers of Capua saw their ancient city destroyed by Arab raiders. Count Lando (840–863) rebuilt the town, and he and his brother, count-bishop Landulf (863–879), successfully resisted the encroachments of Benevento and Salerno.

The Muslim Threat

Nevertheless, the rivalries afoot in southern Italy favored the advance of the Muslim invaders. After capturing Bari in 841, they expanded their devastating raids as far as the wealthy abbeys of Monte Cassino and San Vincenzo al Volturno. Although Louis II responded to abbatial appeals with a campaign in 851/852, he was unable to retake Bari. Thus, to escape renewed pillaging, the abbots as well as the prince of Benevento had regularly to pay tribute to the Muslims. In 866, Louis II called upon all free men in Italy to join in his struggle against the Muslims. While the wealthy were obliged to serve in the army for a year, humbler persons were mobilized locally to garrison fortresses. The papacy was asked to support the effort by contributing part of the offerings sent by Boris, *khagan* of the Bulgars. From 866 to 871, Louis II never left southern Italy. He even sought an alliance with Byzantium in the hope of permanently expelling Arab forces from the peninsula.

Louis II and Byzantium

In Byzantium, Michael III had reigned since 842. His mother, Theodora, had succeeded in restoring religious concord, and on 11 March 843, Constantinople celebrated for the first time the annual "Feast of Orthodoxy," an event sometimes thought to mark the beginning of the Orthodox church. To his cost, Michael III permitted others to govern on his behalf: first, his uncle Bardas, and then a court favorite, Basil, who assassinated and replaced Michael in 867. Emperor Basil I ruled capably, and his Macedonian dynasty was destined to preside over the last great flowering of Byzantine power. In 869, Anastasius Bibliothecarius was dispatched to Constantinople to negotiate the marriage of Basil's son with a daughter of Louis II. Like an earlier bid by Louis II to marry a Byzantine princess, this proposal was refused. Yet the *basileus* agreed to furnish ground and naval assistance for the siege against Bari, and after the long years of struggle, Louis finally captured the town and its sultan in February 871.

Once victory had been secured, east and west came to dispute who had played the greater part in the success. The correspondence exchanged by the emperors lays bare their respective pretensions. For his part, Basil boasted of *his* success against the Muslims and aspired to restore Byzantine greatness. He addressed Louis II as "emperor of the Franks" and then remarked that as such Louis ruled over merely a fraction of former Francia. Louis retorted to these jibes by recounting whence he claimed his office of "august emperor of the Romans":

> I have received this name and dignity from the Romans, among whom the glorious sovereign rank and title first flourished. I accepted it in order to

govern by divine right their city and people and to defend and increase the Mother of all the churches of God, from which my forebear first received authority for his kingly rule and later for his imperial reign. For the leaders of the Franks were first called kings and then emperors, those at least who were anointed with holy oil for this purpose by the pope. Thanks to his great piety, my great-grandfather Charlemagne was the first of my people and family to be called the emperor and chosen of the Lord through such an anointing by the supreme pontiff. This happened even though the empire has often been taken over by persons who gained their imperial dignity not by a divine action made manifest through the bishops, but rather by a choice of the senate and people who both ignored the bishops. . . .

Moreover, should you vilify the Roman pontiff for what he did, you might as well vilify Samuel for having anointed David king.

After reasserting the worthiness of the Franks as proved by their fruitfulness in good works, Louis added: "Just as God could raise up sons of Abraham from stones [cf. Matt. 3:9], He could also raise up successors to the Roman Empire from the brambles of the Franks." Finally, Louis asserted that his imperial dignity lent him a pre-eminence over his uncles, brothers, and other relations:

In response to your contention that I do not reign over all of Francia, let me point out that I do reign as emperor over all of Francia. For there is no doubt that I retain whatever is held by those with whom I am of one flesh and one blood and one spirit in the Lord.

Louis, however, deceived himself on this point, for Hincmar of Reims also referred to him dismissively as the "emperor of Italy."

Although it seems to stem from the pen of Anastasius Bibliothecarius, this exaltation of the empire was important. As Robert Folz has shown, it was part of a movement to "papalize the notion of empire" (*romanisation de l'idée d'empire*) whereby the papacy became guardian of the imperial dignity. After a brief period of imprisonment by the rebellious Adalgisus of Benevento in late 871, Louis II returned to Rome. In May 872, Pope Hadrian II recrowned Louis and loosed him from the promise of non-interference he had sworn under duress to his treacherous ex-vassal, the prince of Benevento.

Whatever his achievements, failures, and hopes, Louis II nonetheless remained without a male heir. He died on 12 April 875 near Brescia, and his passing unleashed a contest for his lands and imperial title. Several chroniclers noted the untimely death of the first great Italian ruler as the end of an era and the beginning of a "great tribulation" for Italy.

LOTHARINGIA AND THE KINGDOM OF PROVENCE

Shortly before his death in 855, Emperor Lothar I divided his realm into three parts. Outside the Italian kingdom of Louis II, Lothar created two new territories: Lotharingia and the Kingdom of Provence.

Lotharingia

Lotharingia took its name from Lothar II, and comprised a strip of territory extending from Frisia in the north to the plateau of Langres and the Jura Mountains in the south. Much like his father after 843, Lothar II scarcely strayed from middle Francia or from his capital at Aachen. There, he reigned among an obeisant circle of advisers including his arch-chaplain, Gunther, archbishop of Cologne; Thietgaud, archbishop of Trier; and his uncle Liutfrid, count of Alsace.

Soon after he became king, the seventeen-year-old Lothar II married Theutberga, the sister of Hubert, lay-abbot of St. Maurice-in-Valais. This notorious bandit ruled the Transjurane region of Burgundy—between the Jura Mountains and the Alps—and the upper Rhône valley. In 864 Hubert was defeated and slain by the Welf Conrad II (see Chart 5), who then inherited his domains and office. For quite different reasons, Hubert's sister also posed immense difficulties for Lothar II. No doubt to the satisfaction of his advisers, Lothar's reign was overshadowed by his struggle to obtain a divorce. This situation distracted him from government and conferred virtual autonomy on his lay and ecclesiastical magnates. Nevertheless, Lothar II was forced to address the mounting threat posed by the Northmen whom his father had permitted to settle in northern Frisia. At his death in 869, the king had failed to secure papal recognition of his second marriage, and his bastard son Hugh remained barred from legitimate succession.

Provence

In 855 Charles of Provence was still a child, and the real master of the realm he inherited was his tutor, Gerard II, count of Vienne. Formerly count of Paris, Gerard chose after 843 to remain in the camp of Lothar I, the brother-in-law of his Etichonid wife, Bertha. Yet he had similar family connections with his enemy Charles the Bald, who had married his niece Ermentrude in 842.

As count of Vienne and "regent" of Provence, Gerard vigorously defended the kingdom against raids by Northmen who ventured up the Rhône as far as Valence. In 860, he ejected the intruders from their bases in the Rhône delta, receiving a congratulatory letter from Abbot Lupus of Ferrières.

Lupus profited from this occasion to recommend his disciple, Archbishop Ado of Vienne (860–875). Ado himself has yet to benefit from a modern scholarly study, but we note in passing that his episcopate amply demonstrates the aims and potential of an educated, reform-minded Carolingian archbishop. Ado worked to restore the prestige of his ancient see. Pope Nicholas I was thus persuaded to reinstate Ado's archepiscopal authority over his suffragans. Meanwhile, Count Gerard of Vienne had already furthered this cause in 858 by negotiating the transfer of the see of Moûtiers-Tarentaise from the realm of Lothar II to the Kingdom of Provence.

Gerard had to mount a determined political struggle to defend Provence from the ambitions of Charles the Bald. Invoking an appeal from the powerful count of Arles, the elder Carolingian attempted to intervene in his nephew's realm in 861. Although he moved to invade, he advanced no further than Mâcon. Gerard had deftly responded to the looming threat with a letter to Hincmar of Reims predicting the devastation of the bishop's lands at Saint-Remi-de-Provence, and Hincmar acted to restrain his king. In 863 the constant menace that Charles the Bald posed to Gerard's Burgundian domains moved the count to place his recent monastic foundation at Vézelay, and perhaps another at Pouthières, under papal protection, in effect instituting a new form of immunity (see below p. 297).

In 858, in attempting to provide for the possibility of his king's death, Gerard had arranged that the Kingdom of Provence should revert to Lothar II should the young Charles die before marriage and the birth of a son. Yet when Charles expired in January 863, Louis II also claimed the inheritance. A compromise was worked out the same year: a northern sector including the bishoprics of Lyon, Vienne, and Grenoble was allotted to Lothar II and placed under the control of count Gerard, while the southern ecclesiastical provinces of Arles, Aix, and Embrun were incorporated into the Kingdom of Italy. Occupied as he was in southern Italy, Louis II had little opportunity to concern himself personally with his new Provençal territories.

THE KINGDOM OF LOUIS THE GERMAN

After 843 Louis of Bavaria acquired title to a much wider kingdom, and this enlarged realm later earned him the epithet "the German." His lands extended from the Rhine east to the Elbe and from the Baltic Sea south to the Bavarian Alps. However vast, his kingdom was thinly settled and counted no important towns outside the Rhine basin, which itself came under increasing threats of Danish and Slavic attack. As king of the eastern Franks, Louis reigned over several quite heterogeneous regions. The real base of his power remained in Bavaria, where he had ruled at Regensburg since 817. His Bavarian subjects were, moreover, conscious of the fact that they differed in history and culture from the other Germanic peoples ruled by their king: the Swabians, Franconians, Thuringians, and Saxons.

Saxony

Although it had been conquered by Charlemagne, Saxony had yet to recover fully from the devastations of the "first Thirty Years War." Louis the Pious had agreed to restore to some chieftains the properties his father had confiscated, and he had also done much to foster the Christian missionary effort by establishing bishoprics and endowing monastic foundations like Korvei. Nevertheless, the Saxons remained a restive people, amply exploiting the infighting among the sons of Louis the Pious. According to Nithard, the Saxons labored under tensions created by their society's division into three major groups: nobles, free persons, and *lazzi*, or slaves. To advance his early struggles against Louis of Bavaria, Lothar I had allied himself with a faction of free Saxons, known as *stellings*, by promising to reinstitute certain ancient Saxon customs. A part of the nobles reacted by supporting Louis of Bavaria, and they crushed the rebel party.

As a consequence of his role in suppressing the revolt, Liudolf of Saxony propelled his family into special eminence (see Chart 3). Absent for a time to combat the Northmen, Duke Liudolf reasserted his authority and presence east of the Weser in 852, when he and his wife, Oda, established a Benedictine convent at Brunhausen, transfered to Gandersheim in 858. Closely tied to the monks of Korvey, the monastery of nuns founded by the ducal couple was ruled by three of their daughters in succession as its first abbesses. Warin, Liudolf's father-in-law, also figured prominently in Saxony as bishop of Hildesheim. After the death of Liudolf in 866, his son Bruno replaced him as duke, and the family's political fortune was guaranteed by the marriage of Liudolf's daughter Liutgard to Louis the Younger, son of Louis the German. Another son, Otto, inaugurated the line of the future Ottonian dynasty.

Other Regions

In other parts of the kingdom of Louis the German, the noble families shared the offices of government among themselves. The descendants of Charlemagne's brother-in-law Gerold became counts in Alemannia and laid the foundations of the future Swabia. To ensure regional stability, Louis married two of his sons into leading South German families. The king's eldest son, Carloman of Bavaria, wed the daughter of Duke Ernst of Bavaria, and the youngest, later known as Charles the Fat, took Richardis, daughter of Count Erchangar of Alemannia. To the north, what would later become Franconia was as yet an assemblage of regions (*Gaue*) and counties under the control of several nobles. Often resident at Frankfurt-am-Main, the king maintained apparently good relations with these men.

Although Louis was able to ensure respect for his authority, he did not always have the means to ensure good government. He reigned over a kingdom made up of often vast counties administered without the benefit of *missi dominici* or general assemblies. Louis the German therefore depended considerably on the church and on a network of great monasteries, each of which constituted an abbatial city-state. Already powerful in the time of Louis the Pious, the abbey of Fulda gained further domains, and in Alemannia, the abbeys of St. Gall and Reichenau were major landowners and important cultural centers. In 852 the abbot of Niederalteich received the privilege of dispensing high justice, including capital sentences.

Moravia

Militarily Louis faced constant challenges from the Northmen and the Slavs. Raids were an abiding concern along the banks of the northern rivers of his kingdom, and east of the Elbe, the Sorbs posed a mounting threat faced by Thachulf, duke of the *limes sorabicus*, or Sorbian March, until his death in 873. Nevertheless the greatest Slavic menace lay in Moravia.

While the Czechs of Bohemia failed to constitute an organized threat, the Moravians farther east set up an embryonic state between 830 and 840 under Mojmir. This pagan duke began by driving out another Moravian leader, the Christian Pribina, who had been baptized at Salzburg in 835 and to whom Louis the German had conceded Slovene Pannonia (east of Lake Balaton). Mojmir also took Nyitra to the north, thereby blocking further Bavarian expansion to the east, although here as elsewhere in Moravia the Frankish church had already struck roots. In 846 Mojmir was overthrown by his Christian nephew Rastislav with the help of Louis the German.

Nevertheless, Rastislav resented royal control as well as the overbearing presence of the Bavarian clergy. With the support of Carloman, eldest son of Louis the German, Rastislav revolted in 861 and turned in 862 to more distant Byzantium for further Christian direction. Embroiled in their own struggle with Pope Nicholas I, Emperor Michael III and Patriarch Photius welcomed the opportunity to step in along the Carolingian frontier. They gladly responded to Rastislav by dispatching Constantine, later known as Cyril, and his brother Methodios. After learning the local Slavonic language, the Greek missionaries proceeded to invent for it a new alphabet—probably the Glagolitic script rather than the simpler Greek-based script known today as Cyrillic. Whichever form of writing they first used, the brothers created for the Slavs a written language into which they translated the Bible and the Roman liturgy. Their use of the vernacular proved a decisive advantage over the Latin of the Frankish clergy, and the new language speeded the success of the Byzantine missionary effort. Yet to clarify the administrative form of the church they were creating the brothers felt obliged to travel to Rome. Thanks to the relics of Saint Clement, which they brought with them as gifts, Constantine and Methodios were received warmly by Hadrian II. Furthermore, the pope agreed to allow the use of Slavonic as a liturgical language. After the unexpected death of Cyril in Rome, Hadrian consecrated Methodios archbishop of Sirmium in 870, and entrusted him with the task of representing the papacy among the Slavs. The Roman church thus hoped to reestablish its influence in former Illyricum. Nevertheless, the creation of a new, independent ecclesiastical jurisdiction directly countered the interests of the Bavarian missionary effort, and it met with predictable resistance.

Partitioning the Kingdom

Despite the relative stability and success of his government, Louis the German faced challenges from within his immediate family (see Chart 2). The king's eldest son, Carloman, twice revolted as an ally of the Moravian duke Rastislav, first in 861 and again in 864. Finally, in 865, Louis the German was obliged to provide for the eventual division of his realm in accord with Frankish custom. To Carloman, he allotted Bavaria and the *Ostmark* along the Danube; to Louis the Younger, Franconia, Thuringia, and Saxony; and to Charles the Fat, a composite realm including Alemannia and Rhaetia—the future duchy of Swabia. The partition took effect on the death of Louis the German on 28 August 876.

THE KINGDOM OF CHARLES THE BALD

In 843 Charles the Bald was a twenty-year-old king, handsome if somewhat balding, courageous, athletic, and cultivated. He had his own circle of followers, even though many nobles preferred to abandon western Francia rather than support him. Those who left included his brother-in-law Eberhard, who settled in Friuli; his wife's uncle Count Gerard, who remained in the service of Lothar I; Matfrid of Orléans, who went to the Rhineland; and Wido, who migrated to Italy. To shore up his power and combat his rival Pippin II of Aquitaine as well as the Northmen, Charles the Bald could count on a few faithful supporters. These included his Welf uncles, Conrad and Rudolph; his cousin Nithard, the historian; his wife's uncle, Adalhard the seneschal; and Count Warin of Mâcon.

Charles and the Nobility

The young king recognized, however, his need to expand this noble backing. Upon his return from an expedition against the Bretons in November 843, Charles convened an assembly at Coulaines, near Le Mans, whose great importance for relations between the king and his nobles has long been recognized. Addressing his lay and clerical followers, the king admitted former misjudgments and "renounced the measures he had taken on account of his inexperience and youth, compelled by necessity or under bad influence." He then promised to safeguard the property of the church and uphold the national law codes: "I agree that, with God's help, I shall respect the laws pertaining to each individual according to the form known to his ancestors in the time of my predecessors, whatever his station in life." In exchange for these commitments, Charles asked that the laity and the clergy provide him with *auxilium* and *concilium*, "help and counsel," so that his royal power should remain unshakeable. This pact of "concord and friendship" which bound the king to his followers constituted a public commitment by the king to adhere to certain principles, and the event marked something new in the Carolingian political order. Charles the Bald had solemnly promised to guarantee peace, justice, and order in return for noble assurances of support and counsel.

The Emancipation of the Nobility

Unfortunately for Charles, the nobility proved less than reliable when it found its interests were better served in other ways. His great lay vassals worked to multiply the functions vested in the public office of count, and then increasingly, they confused these "honors" with the personal benefices they held from the king. Thus, one began to speak of "honors in benefice" (*honneurs bénéficiaires*). Established in a particular region, noble families tended to widen and reinforce their influence; they managed their own groups of followers, whom they also outfitted and dispatched on campaigns; and finally, they conveyed to their heirs whatever rights they possessed or claimed to possess. Their position gained a stability that it had formerly lacked. Thanks in part to its success, the system of vassalage used by Charlemagne to his own advantage could no longer be easily controlled by Charles the Bald. On another plane, the king and his brothers agreed at Meersen in 847 to regulate ties between lords and their vassals more closely. The brothers forbade vassals to swap lords, and one lord to corrupt the vassals of another. Yet these strictures generally meant little if a vassal or a lord found it expedient to violate them.

The Complaints of the Clergy

For their part, the great churchmen ceaselessly worked to recoup whichever sequestered properties had not yet been recovered. They also complained bitterly that Charles continued to assign abbatial offices and revenues to eminent laymen. Thus Lupus, abbot of Ferrières, barraged the king and his closest advisers with pleas for the return of the small but economically important monastic center at St. Josse, near Montreuil. At the assembly of Épernay in 846, the bishops presented Charles with their demands, but the objections of the laity did not permit him to comply. Prudentius, bishop of Troyes, recorded his version of the event in the *Annals of St. Bertin*:

> The pressing admonition by the bishops of the kingdom regarding ecclesiastical affairs was handled so cavalierly that one could scarcely find record of such disrespect for the episcopacy in Christian times.

To maneuver around the shoals of lay and clerical pretensions and cut short the work of insurgents and defectors, Charles the Bald had to make discriminating use of force and diplomacy. He did not hesitate to execute traitors, but he sought as well to rally hesitant supporters by promising to safeguard their rights and privileges. Under the influence of his counselor Hincmar of Reims, Charles the Bald agreed to amplify the commitments he had undertaken at Coulaines in 843 in a new vow pronounced at Quierzy in March 858. Nevertheless, the promises exchanged between Charles and his followers did not avert the invasion launched by Louis the German later that year in August. As we have seen, it was Hincmar's decisive and energetic reaction to this event that helped ensure the survival of Charles the Bald (see above p. 173).

Family Troubles

Although Hincmar played an important role in ejecting Louis the German from western Francia, he was not always a welcome counselor to Charles the Bald. As archbishop of Reims from 845 to 882, Hincmar's relations with Charles grew markedly cooler as time progressed. In his magisterial study of the archbishop, Jean Devisse has shown that the rapport of the two men suffered numerous troubled episodes. In the end, Charles the Bald was a maverick; he could be sure of consistent support from virtually no one among his friends, vassals, or family.

His children, in particular, were a source of great disappointment (see Table 2). Judith, his eldest daughter, inherited both the name and the willful temperament of her grandmother. At first married for political reasons to Ethelwulf of Wessex (d. 858) and then to his short-lived successor Ethelbald (d. 860), Judith finally returned to Francia, where she lived at Senlis "with all honor due to a queen." Yet in 862 she eloped with Count Baldwin of Flanders, and soon married him, to the immense distress of her parents. The king's eldest son, Louis, nicknamed the Stammerer, suffered from both a speech impediment and a nature too easily influenced by others. The king's second son, Charles the Child, was severely brain damaged during a hunt in 864 and died in 866. The fourth son, Lothar, was born crippled, and therefore destined for religious life. The youngest, Carloman, likewise entered the clergy, successively acquiring the abbacies of St. Médard of Soissons, St. Germain of Auxerre, St. Amand, St. Riquier, Lobbes, and St. Arnulf of Metz. Despite his glut of abbatial honors, Carloman revolted against his father in 870 and became a veritable robber baron. In 873 he was captured, blinded, and consigned thereafter to a monastery until his death in 876.

Thanks to his courage, tenacity, intelligence, and ability, Charles the Bald continued to struggle against both his treasonous vassals and the raids of the Northmen. In the wake of the great crisis of 858, he managed to reaffirm his authority, and committed vast regions of his kingdom to the care of a few followers whom he hoped he could trust.

Aquitaine

The most urgent of his problems was to rally the nobles of Aquitaine. The partisans of Pippin II had never embraced the consequences of the Treaty of Verdun, and for nearly twenty years they would resist the West Frankish king. In 844 Bernard of Septimania figured among the most prominent troublemakers. After breaking his alliance with Charles the Bald, Bernard took control of Toulouse. This news immediately prompted Charles to journey south, where he invested the town. Although the siege failed, Bernard himself was captured and decapitated. Faced with continued resistance from Toulouse and the loss of a relief army led by his uncle, Abbot Hugh of St. Quentin, Charles was obliged to come to terms with Pippin II at Fleury in June 845. It was agreed that Charles himself would keep control of Poitou and the western coastal regions of Saintonge and Aunis, while Pippin was credited with lordship over the rest of Aquitaine under the kingship of Charles. The accord was, however, little more than a truce. On 6 June 848, Charles had himself anointed king of Aquitaine at Orléans. When the king continued south to Toulouse, Count Fredelon agreed to turn over the town. The noble and his brother Raymond, who succeeded him as count of Toulouse, inaugurated the Raymondine line which would dominate in the region until the thirteenth century. Meanwhile, the son of Bernard of Septimania, William, seized Barcelona the same year with the help of Count Aledramnus, an ally of the Robertine family. Charles's partisans nevertheless managed to capture the young man, and like his father, William was executed on royal orders in 850. This was the tragic end of the son for whom Dhuoda had written her *Handbook*. As for Pippin II, he was captured, tonsured, and interned at St. Médard of Soissons in 852. He soon escaped, and continued his wanderings and conspiracies until his death in 864.

Charles the Bald now sought to accommodate Aquitainian particularism by restoring the status of the region as a separate kingdom. In 855, he arranged for the royal consecration of his seven-year-old son, Charles the Child, as king of Aquitaine. At first a mere figurehead, the younger Charles moved to exercise real power as he approached his fifteenth year, choosing and marrying a wife without consulting his father. Charles the Bald managed to subdue his son in 863. The young king was accidentally disabled by a sword swipe to his head in 864 and reigned thereafter as a mental cripple until his death in 866. The dead king's elder brother, Louis the Stammerer, inherited the vacant royal office, but Charles the Bald retained effective control.

During this difficult period Aquitaine began to fracture into smaller territorial units. The Raymondine family continued to administer the county of Toulouse and its appendages until 872, when Count Bernard, the son of Count Raymond, was assassinated. His important office was then conferred on Bernard Hairyfoot, a son of Bernard of Septimania, who proceeded to fashion a princedom of his own after the example of his father. His efforts were aided by the connivance and parallel ambition of the marquis of Gothia, another Bernard, who was the son of a Poitevin magnate—also named Bernard—and a scion of the Rorgonid clan. This Bernard of Gothia, whom Charles the Bald had appointed over a district of Septimania in 865, sought to extend his authority over the counties of the Spanish March, largely controlled by the family of Bello, count of Carcassonne. In Auvergne, to the northeast, we find still another important Count Bernard who seems to have been allied to the family of Count Warin of Mâcon. (Some eleven magnates shared the name Bernard in this period, and the historian's task of identifying and tracing individuals is often perplexing.) This Bernard of Auvergne functioned as abbot of Brioude and count of Auvergne and Velay until 868. He was succeeded by a son who was later displaced by Bernard Hairyfoot. Meanwhile in central Aquitaine, scions of the Carolingian house controlled the county of Poitou. Count Ramnulf I (d. 866) of Poitou was born of the marriage of Hildegard, daughter of Louis the Pious, and Count Gerard of Auvergne. Despite intervening difficulties, his son and eventual successor, Ramnulf II, would propel himself and his family into a leading position in Aquitaine.

Burgundy

In Burgundy the political situation was scarcely less complex. After 843, the counties of Autun, Chalon, and Mâcon were controlled by Count Warin, an unbending supporter of Charles the Bald. Bernard Hairyfoot, whose family already possessed lands in the region and who had married Warin's granddaughter, subsequently became count of Autun. Another related family, that of Eccard, a descendant of Childebrand, brother of Charles Martel, also vied to control this and other Burgundian counties. As count of Mâcon and Chalon, Eccard became a leading figure in the region, whose will has survived as a witness to his considerable landed and portable wealth. Although he married twice, taking as his second wife Richildis, mother of Boso of Provence, Eccard died without children of his own. The exceptionally ambitious Boso would, however, succeed in ensconcing himself in the Burgundian counties.

The Northmen

Between the Seine and the Loire, the pattern of a few powerful men controlling vast expanses of territory recurs once again. This policy was the most expedient means of beating off the attacks of the Northmen and the Bretons. Without entering into a detailed account of the "Norman" invasions, it is important to recall that periodic raids by northern pirates began in earnest in the second third of the ninth century. Aquitaine and even Provence were not immune to the assaults, but it was above all between the Loire and the Scheldt that the raiders wrought the greatest havoc. In March 845, the Viking Ragnar sailed up the Seine as far as Paris and threatened the city on Easter Day. Although Paris was not a royal residence, this event had immense repercussions. Pascasius Radbertus interrupted his *Commentary on the Lamentations of Jeremiah* to note his disbelief and dismay:

> Who would had ever believed, pray tell me, that a pack of brigands would ever dare such deeds? Who would have thought that such a glorious kingdom, so strong, so vast, so populous, and so vigorous would be humiliated and smeared with the filth of such people?
> . . . No, I do not think that even a few years ago any ruler on earth would have imagined, or any inhabitant of our world would have consented to hear, that a foreigner would enter Paris.

To rid himself of the invaders, Charles the Bald had to buy them off with seven thousand pounds of silver. In 847, another group moved up the Loire; by 858, things had grown so bad that one band could set up camp on the island of Oscelle in the Seine, while another pillaged the abbey of St. Martin at Tours on the Loire.

The year 856 marks the beginning of what is commonly called the "Great Invasion." In 858 the Northmen managed to capture the abbot of St. Denis, Louis, the arch-chaplain of Charles the Bald and the grandson of Charlemagne by his daughter Rotrude. The monastery and then the kingdom were obliged to pay an enormous ransom. The king then proceeded to lay siege to the raiders based on the island of Oscelle, but had to abandon the effort because of the invasion mounted by his brother Louis the German in August 858. The "Norman" invasions unleashed general panic wherever they struck, prompting whole monastic communities to evacuate, laden with their relics and treasures, and requiring repeated special levies to cover the enormous cost of ransoms. The general population saw in the Northmen an instrument of divine vengeance, and to avert this visitation, men turned to prayer: "O God, deliver us from the cruel nation, from the Northmen who ravage our lands." Only in 860 could Charles the Bald again take the offensive, building fortified bridges over the Seine and a scattering of fortresses, which he entrusted to his leading noble administrators.

Brittany

For their part, the Bretons had never accepted Frankish or Carolingian domination. Louis the Pious had mounted several punitive expeditions against them, and had also appointed the Breton duke Nominoë as his *missus dominicus*. But these measures procured no durable benefits. Nominoë took advantage of the fraternal struggles and the change of rulers to assert his independence. He cast his lot against Charles the Bald in an alliance with the Lambertines who had been set over the Breton March. Charles intervened in the region, but after a defeat at Ballon, north of Redon, on 22 November 845, he was forced to recognize the authority of Nominoë over the counties of Rennes and Nantes. Nominoë, however, also aspired to free the Breton church from the tutelage of the metropolitan of Tours, and he repeatedly petitioned the pope to establish Dol as a Breton archbishopric. It is possible that he also hoped to gain a royal title, perhaps after the fashion of the Carolingian princes who were named subkings to address regional unrest and aspirations. In 851 Nominoë was succeeded by his energetic son Erispoë. The same year at Jengland, near Redon, the new duke inflicted on Charles the Bald what was to date his worst military setback, and the king was again obliged to come to terms. He acknowledged the power of the Breton duke, but sought to temper it by fostering the ambitions of Salomon, Erispoë's cousin and rival. At one point, Charles even schemed to marry his eldest son Louis to a daughter of Erispoë, an unrealized project that may have been favored by the Rorgonids of Maine, themselves allied to the Carolingian house. But such close relations between Erispoë and the Carolingians would have compromised the gains made by Breton and Frankish nobles who profited from a strong and independent Brittany. In 857, Salomon arranged for the assassination of his cousin Erispoë, and replaced him as duke. He thereafter conspired with various nobles and even with Louis the Stammerer against Charles the Bald, and in 868 claimed the title of king.

The Rise of the Robertines

In the wake of the assassination of Erispoë, Charles the Bald gradually transferred his favor from the Rorgonids to the ever more influential Robert the Strong and his family, the Robertines. Although his origins are somewhat obscure, Robert seems to have stemmed from a branch of the family of Chrodegang of Metz. He bolstered his position by marrying Adelaide, the daughter of Hugh of Tours and the widow of the Welf Conrad I, all figures closely tied to the Carolingian house (see Tables 4 and 5). In 852 Robert was a count and lay-abbot of Marmoutier, near Tours, and in 853 he became *missus* for several counties in Maine, Touraine, and Anjou. He was, however, disaffected by the rapprochement between Charles and Erispoë, which threatened his power in the lower Loire region, and he chose to abandon Charles the Bald in the general defection of 858. Robert subsequently returned to grace, and in 861 he received the title of duke of Neustria with the task of defending the lands between the Loire and the Seine against the Bretons. He struggled against the Rorgonids, now allies of Salomon of Brittany, and even against Louis the Stammerer when the prince revolted against his father. In 863 it was now the turn of Salomon to sue for peace. Meanwhile, Robert had to contain the ravages of the Norman mercenaries whom he had hired to assist in his campaign against the Bretons, defending the abbey of St. Martin of Tours as its lay-abbot. In autumn 866 he won a great victory at Brissarthe, north of Angers, but was himself mortally wounded.

Thus ended the short but brilliant career of the "Maccabaeus of our time," as Robert was called in the *Annals of Fulda*. He would later be hailed as the most illustrious ancestor of the Capetian monarchs of France. Because his sons, Odo and Robert, were as yet too young to assume his charge, the Neustrian duchy was entrusted to Hugh the Abbot, a Welf stepson of Robert the Strong and a cousin of Charles the Bald. Hugh retained the office of duke until his death in 883.

Flanders

North of the Seine, Baldwin of Flanders received responsibility for defending this highly exposed region against the Northmen. As Jan Dhondt has shown, Baldwin's family stemmed from the middle Rhine and Alsace, while the count himself had received duties in Flanders and settled there. In 862 Baldwin, later nicknamed Ironarm, eloped with Judith, the daughter of Charles the Bald, with the help of Louis the Stammerer. After taking refuge in the realm of Lothar II, the pair sought help from Pope Nicholas I to obtain the pardon of the West Frankish king. After his fury subsided, Charles received the couple back, and bestowed on Baldwin a series of counties as well as the abbey of St. Bertin. Baldwin proved himself worthy of this great trust. He repulsed every attack mounted by the Northmen until his death in 879.

4. Charles the Bald, the Last Great Carolingian Emperor

The Ambitions of Charles the Bald

THE KING'S SUCCESSES

The decade from 860 to 870 was a period of immense importance for Charles the Bald. By age forty he had managed to overcome the threats of internal intrigue and foreign aggression. His provisions for building fortified bridges and outposts in the early 860s met with such enthusiasm that by 864 he found himself outlawing the construction of unauthorized strongholds in the Edict of Pîtres. The king likewise reminded the counts of their duty of obedience to himself; forbade the maintenance of private citadels; and reaffirmed his special rights over coinage and minting with a body of new monetary regulations. Between 860 and 864 Charles also redrew the jurisdictions of his administrative inspectors, the *missi dominici*. In a word, the king began to rule as a master in his own right.

Nevertheless, the king's personal life was marked by loss. His sons Lothar and Charles the Child died in 865 and 866 respectively. In August 866 Charles the Bald attempted to draw closer to his wife by arranging for Ermentrude to be anointed queen in a special ceremony at St. Médard in Soissons. Yet shortly after this event her brother William revolted against Charles and was beheaded on the king's orders. A year later, the husband and wife of twenty-four years separated and Ermentrude retired to a monastery.

LOTHARINGIA

Throughout this period Charles the Bald was much taken by the affairs of Lotharingia. He devoted special attention to the desperate efforts of his nephew Lothar II to obtain a divorce. During a meeting at Metz in 862, Charles and his brother Louis the German agreed to share Lotharingia between them in the event of Lothar's death. In 869 Lothar died as expected without having secured legitimate status for Hugh, his bastard son by Waldrada. Although Louis II of Italy had the best claim to his younger brother's kingdom, he could not enforce his claim. He had no followers in Lotharingia and was himself embroiled in a distant struggle against the Arabs. The nearest relatives were the dead king's uncles, and they had carefully watched the progress of events. Louis the German was, however, severely ill at Regensburg, and his sons were farther away on a campaign against the Slavs. Hence Charles the Bald took the initiative, confident in the support of several Lotharingian bishops, including Adventius of Metz, Arnulf of Toul, and Franco of Liège, himself also a cousin of the Carolingians. Within a month of his nephew's death, Charles had entered Lotharingia and arranged for his royal coronation at Metz on 9 September 869.

Charles the Bald no doubt chose this town rather than Aachen because he had more partisans in the region and also because of its associations as the cradle of the Carolingian dynasty. It is, in fact, to this period that we can trace the reworking of the life of Saint Arnulf into legend and the emergence of the mythical genealogies linking the Arnulfings to the Merovingian house. Thus Hincmar of Reims, the great impresario of the coronation ceremony, duly evoked the memory of Clovis, the "ancestor" of Charles. He also claimed to have "discovered" a report of the legendary anointing of the first Frankish king by Archbishop Remigius of Reims and even to have found the "heaven-sent" vial of oil used at the event by his illustrious predecessor. Charles was, of course, a man able to appreciate the symbolism of the locale. In early 835 his father had chosen to be re-crowned in Metz after his restoration to the throne, and Louis the Pious had likewise been interred in the town at the church of St. Arnulf. Thus the king of western Francia was "in his element" and could raise reasonable claims to the kingship of Lotharingia.

MARRIAGE TO RICHILDIS

Shortly after his royal anointing, Charles the Bald learned of the death of his wife, Ermentrude, at St. Denis. Almost immediately, he took Richildis as his concubine. She was the daughter of Count Bivin, lay-abbot of Gorze (near Metz), and the niece of Theutberga, the ill-fated bride of Lothar II (see Table 7). On 22 January 870, Charles the Bald solemnly married Richildis at Aachen, counting on the support of her brother Boso to rally the hesitaters who remained in the region. Invigorated by his remarriage, Charles now seemed to be at the summit of his power. In the miniatures of the Bible of St. Paul-outside-the-Walls executed shortly after the *Coronation Sacramentary of Metz*, Charles is depicted in all his glory, flanked by his guards and his wife, his regard lofty, distinctive, and deliberate. The same aspect recurs in the contemporary *Codex aureus* of Regensburg, where the king appears between two personified provinces, his hands laden with horns of plenty.

THE PARTITION OF MEERSEN

As soon as he recovered, Louis the German was quick to remind his brother of their mutual promises, while Pope Hadrian II endorsed the claims to Lotharingia raised by Emperor Louis II. In order to stave off the mounting threat, Charles the Bald came to terms with his brother Louis in the treaty of Meersen of July 870. He ruefully agreed to relinquish a portion of Lotharingia. Although he had to sacrifice Metz and Aachen, Charles retained the valley of the Meuse and the western third of Frisia. Moreover, Louis the German conceded him the regions of Lyon, Vienne, and Viviers, which Lothar II had occupied after the death of Charles of Provence in 863.

Count Gerard of Vienne, the veritable master of these Provençal territories, rejected the Meersen agreement and resisted Charles the Bald. Reinforced by archbishops Remigius of Lyon and Ado of Vienne, Charles besieged Vienne, whose defense was overseen by Bertha, wife of Count Gerard. After its fall, the king permitted the count and his wife to retire to Avignon, a possession of Emperor Louis II, where the count died in 877. Thus ended the political career of a great noble who later came to be celebrated in legend as "Gerard of Roussillon." Charles the Bald established his brother-in-law Boso over the Lyonnais and Viennois, and the new count soon learned to take best advantage of his promotion.

Charles the Bald, Emperor (876)

Once he had become master of northern Provence, the ambitious Charles dreamed of the succession of Louis II of Italy. Because the emperor had no male offspring of his own, Charles and Louis the German became his presumptive heirs. Moreover, their father, Louis the Pious, had implicitly provided for this eventuality in the *Ordinatio imperii* of 817: should his son Lothar I die without a legitimate heir, the empire would revert to one of his brothers. Because Louis II was both king and emperor, his legacy concerned a two-fold dignity. The two uncles of the emperor therefore closely followed events south of the Alps. Although the politically adept Empress Engelberga dangled the hope of her husband's succession before both uncles, Pope Hadrian II had already chosen his imperial candidate. In a letter to Charles the Bald of 872, the pope wrote:

> We confide to you—but let our promise be kept secret and this letter shown to no one save your most trusted followers—that . . . if Your Highness survives the emperor and we are still alive, even though someone should give us piles of gold, we would never consent to, or solicit, or willingly accept anyone other than you as king and emperor of the Romans. Should it happen that you outlive our emperor . . . it is you whom we would choose . . . as leader, king, patrician, and emperor. . . .

Much like his predecessor Nicholas I, Hadrian II meant to confer the imperial crown on a prince of his own choosing, and he aimed at finding a man strong enough to defend the papal state against the aggression of Arab invaders. Hadrian's successor would respect the commitment made to Charles the Bald.

John VIII

Elected to the papacy in 872, John VIII was an elderly man gifted with exceptional energy. Like Nicholas I, he asserted his role as head of "Christendom" (*christianitas*)—an expression that came frequently to his pen— and exalted the grandeur of the Roman church. Upon the death of Emperor Louis II in August 875, John VIII convened a synod at Rome, and then offered the imperial crown to Charles the Bald. As he would later explain, "Charles distinguished himself by his virtue, his struggles in the service of religion, and his care to honor the clergy and foster its education. God chose him for the honor and exaltation of the holy Roman church." The choice was well suited to satisfy the pride and ambition of the West Frankish king.

Nevertheless, few of the king's subjects shared his enthusiasm for the papal proposal. In a treatise entitled *On Keeping Faith with King Charles*, Hincmar of Reims manifested his dismay and foreboding at the new Italian adventure. He could not understand why anyone would dream of an imperial crown when the West Frankish kingdom required defense against the external threat posed by the Northmen and the Bretons. Hincmar also feared greater influence of the papacy over domestic affairs. Finally, the archbishop dreaded a repeat of the invasion of 858 during the king's absence in Italy, as subsequently came to pass. Nonetheless, Hincmar reminded all of their obligation to remain faithful to Charles the Bald, even if his actions were misguided. Charles himself was unswayed by the admonitions of the elderly archbishop, and he left for Italy.

THE IMPERIAL CORONATION

After beating back the troops launched against him by his brother Louis the German, Charles was received by John VIII at St. Peter's on 17 December 875. On Christmas Day, seventy-five years after the famous coronation of his grandfather, Charles the Bald was anointed, crowned, and acclaimed emperor of the Romans. An exchange of gifts followed, during which Charles made over the precious Bible today preserved at St. Paul-outside-the-Walls in Rome and the so-called Throne of St. Peter still ensconced in a reliquary at St. Peter's and recently the object of scientific study. When he arrived back again in northern Italy, Charles quickly disarmed the intrigues of the dowager Empress Engelberga, who had hoped to install Carloman, son of Louis the German, as emperor, and had himself elected king of Italy in Pavia. In an address to the thirty some magnates who came to acclaim him, Charles urged them to honor the Roman church, to aid the pope, and to respect the territories he controlled.

THE ASSEMBLY OF PONTHION

It was now high time for Charles to return to Francia. The very day of his imperial coronation, Louis the German had taken up residence at the palace of Attigny in western Francia. Yet thanks to Richildis and Archbishop Hincmar the great nobles of the kingdom had resisted the invader and forced him to return to his own kingdom. Charles arranged to have his new dignities recognized by his followers at a great assembly convoked at the palace of Ponthion. The gathering included some fifty bishops from across his realm as well as numerous laymen. The written account of the three-week-long proceedings depicts how Charles the Bald related the circumstances of his accession to the empire. He addressed the assembly flanked by papal legates and Ansegisus, the newly appointed archbishop of Sens and papal vicar in France and Germany, whose elevation to the latter status at royal request was viewed by Hincmar as a personal rebuff. On the last day of the ceremonies, Charles the Bald presented himself in Byzantine imperial dress. Although such theatricality impressed the assembly, it was severely criticized across the Rhine. Reflecting the view of Louis the German and his subjects, the annalist of Fulda commented:

> When King Charles had returned to Gaul from Italy, he is said to have begun to wear new and unfamiliar clothing. On Sundays and feasts he took to walk-

ing in procession clothed in an ankle-length dalmatic girded by a heavy belt that draped down to his feet, while his head was swathed in a silk veil topped by a diadem. Despising the customs of Frankish kings, he preferred Greek ceremonial as the best possible; and the better to manifest his puffed up sense of pride, he discarded the name of king, and ordered that he be called august emperor of all kings reigning on this side of the Mediterranean.

Despite the sarcasm of the annalist, it is clear that Charles took his new dignity very seriously. He sought to revive ancient traditions, and henceforth his charters bore an imperial seal proudly inscribed: "The Renewed Empire of the Romans and the Franks" (*Renouatio imperii Romanorum et Francorum*). To consummate his success, a long expected report informed Charles of the death of his brother Louis the German on 28 August 876. Charles now moved quickly to achieve his foiled plans of 870 to expand eastward and make Aachen his capital.

His inordinate ambition squared poorly with the political realities of the moment. It would have been wiser for Charles to settle for the imperial title and administer properly the lands he already possessed in western Francia and Italy. But he believed too much in his own good fortune and was persuaded that God had favored his undertakings. Although Charles hoped to reconstitute the empire of Charlemagne, events proved that this was impossible.

The End of the Reign of Charles the Bald

FAILURE IN LOTHARINGIA

Ignoring the renewed attacks by the Northmen along the Seine and the counsel of his own advisers, Charles the Bald answered the call of a party of Lotharingian nobles. Accompanied by two papal legates, he entered Aachen, and then moved on to Cologne and ensconced himself along the western bank of the Rhine. Faced with this threat Louis the Younger, the third son of Louis the German, moved to defend the eastern kingdom allotted to him by his father. In early October, he crossed the Rhine to Andernach, where he engaged and crushed the forces of Charles the Bald. The emperor, who was ill with pleurisy, had to flee, leaving behind treasures and numerous prisoners. He returned to Richildis only to learn that she had given birth to a still-born son.

THE APPEAL OF JOHN VIII

Scarcely had Charles the Bald recovered from the bout of illness contracted during his eastern adventure when letters of distress began arriving from

Pope John VIII. The pontiff called for help against the Arab raiders who were pillaging Campania and the Sabine Hills south of Rome, ruining churches and threatening the city itself. Although Charles had entrusted counts Lambert and Guido of Spoleto with the defense of the lands of St. Peter, they offered no help, and Boso of Provence, installed as viceroy in Pavia, likewise chose to ignore the pope's appeals. Boso did, however, use his standing to marry the daughter of Empress Engelberga, Ermengard; a few years later, he would exploit this marital connection to further his own royal ambitions in Francia. Meanwhile, John VIII became ever more insistent, exclaiming in one of his many letters to Charles the Bald:

> Come, most excellent of Caesars, assuage our immense misfortune. Relieve the miseries of our people; stretch forth the hand of your power; and deliver this land whose needs we made known to you from the beginning of your imperial vocation, least its loss should defile your empire and bring about the ruination of all Christendom.

Once again, Charles the Bald did not hesitate. His sense of honor obliged him to embark on the defense of Italy, despite his failing health, the Norman raids, growing discontent among his nobles, and the political threat posed by his nephews in Germany. He was driven perhaps by the hope of success, or perhaps by a feeling of resignation before the prospect of this dramatic but suicidal gesture. He levied a special tribute of five thousand pounds of silver to pay off the Northmen and convoked an assembly at Quierzy to make arrangements for his absence.

THE CAPITULARY OF QUIERZY

According to the capitulary promulgated at Quierzy on 14 June 877, Charles the Bald made Louis the Stammerer his regent, but arranged that the sometimes inconstant prince should govern under advice from a circle of trusted bishops, abbots, and counts. Charles also instructed that Louis should be ready to journey to Italy to be crowned emperor after the defeat of the Arab invaders. Meanwhile, detailed provisions were made for the efficient administration of the kingdom, including the upkeep of palaces, the protection of forests, and a tally of the game taken by Louis when hunting. Likewise, the emperor took the occasion to force his nobles to promise to respect his family belongings as well as those of the church.

The most celebrated, and often misinterpreted, articles of this capitulary concerned "honors" and benefices that fell vacant during the absence of the emperor. Were a bishop to die, Charles the Bald ordered that a visitor named by the regional archbishop should administer the vacant diocese along with the local count until his son Louis was informed and returned instructions. But more importantly, were a count to die, Charles instructed that the count's son (or in the case of his absence in Italy, a surrogate appointed by Louis), the county servants, and the local bishop should administer the county until the emperor himself was informed and returned instructions. Charles then separately ordered that the same procedure should be followed for his own vassals and their sons and for the vassals of bishops, abbots, and counts. Finally, were a pledged follower of Charles to decide to renounce the world in the event of the emperor's death, Charles allowed that he might, if he wished, convey his "honors" on a worthy son or relative.

Despite the frequent over-interpretation applied to them, these provisions were not intended to legitimize the hereditary transfer of "honors" and benefices. They were, rather, exceptional instructions issued on the eve of a potentially long and risky expedition. But they do bear witness to the evolution of feudal institutions. The provisional rights of sons as presumptive heirs were recognized, and this feature of the Capitulary of Quierzy was tailored to suit the assembled nobles. It was perhaps necessary compensation. Many were unhappy about the enormous levy used to pay off the Northmen, and still others questioned and criticized the prospect of a new Italian expedition.

The Emperor's Demise

Charles the Bald went forth to Italy with his wife and a huge supply of gold and silver. He was received by the pope at Vercelli, but soon learned of the impending arrival of Carloman, the eldest son of Louis the German, and a huge army by way of the Brenner Pass. Charles withdrew south of the Po River, where he arranged for the coronation of Richildis as empress by the pope and impatiently awaited the arrival of reinforcements from Francia. They were not to come. The news that did arrive reported a revolt among the noble leaders who had not attended the assembly at Quierzy, including Boso of Provence, Hugh the Abbot, and Bernard of Gothia. Louis the Stammerer himself seems to have played a part in the conspiracy. In effect, the nobility responded in kind to their king's "desertion." Faced with these circumstances, Charles the Bald headed back to the north. Along the way, he fell suddenly and violently ill. After traversing the pass at Mont Cenis, the emperor died in a hut at Avrieux, near Saint-Jean-de-Maurienne, on 6 October 877. He was fifty-four years old. Thus ended a reign of thirty-seven years.

Although Charles the Bald has often been judged severely by historians, he was one of the greatest Carolingian kings. Despite inauspicious beginnings, invasions, and repeated noble rebellion, Charles manifested remarkable energy and political skill. He did not lose courage when faced with defeat and sedition. He was prepared to pay tribute to some and negotiate with others, the better to recommence his struggle and strike hard when needed. Like his grandfather, he sought to impart order to every aspect of life in his realm, as witnessed by his numerous charters and capitularies. He drew on the advice and support of churchmen without becoming their servant. His literary and religious interests elevated him above the ebb and flow of passing intrigue. His vision went farther and wider than that of his contemporaries. In blending his memory with that of Charlemagne, later writers of medieval epic did the last great Carolingian emperor the highest honor to which he might have aspired.

Part IV

The Collapse of Carolingian Europe and the Emergence of Regional Princedoms

The death of Charles the Bald did not mark the end of the Carolingian period. His successors remained in power for several decades, his nephew Charles the Fat managed briefly to restore the territorial unity of the empire, and the imperial title was inherited by a succession of various princes until 924. The Carolingians retained some form of political power in western Francia until 987. For the empire, the death of Charles the Bald marked the beginning of a long series of jolts, culminating in de facto collapse at the end of the ninth century. Europe came under the control of great regional nobles, often somehow related to the Carolingian house. These rulers governed their territories independently, but they fondly recalled the prestige of the Carolingian rulers and frequently drew on past achievements for political inspiration.

1. The End of the Imperial Ideal (877–888)

Pope John VIII in Search of an Emperor

LOUIS THE STAMMERER

John VIII had placed his every hope in Charles the Bald, and the emperor's unexpected death was a crippling blow. Although the thirty-one-year-old Louis the Stammerer assumed control of western Francia, he was a sickly ruler of undistinguished character. During his father's lifetime, he had often proved unworthy of the confidence placed in him. Without his father's knowledge or consent, he had chosen in 862 to marry his concubine Ansgard, a daughter of Count Harduin, by whom he had his sons Louis and Carloman. In 878, Louis the Stammerer would repudiate Ansgard to marry Adelaide, daughter of Count Adalhard, who gave birth in 879 to the future Charles the Simple (see Chart 2).

After Charles the Bald died, Louis precipitously moved to confer all manner of "honors" and benefices on the first nobles to appear, and thereby unleashed renewed violence. Those who were delayed by their return from the abortive mission to Italy found themselves unjustly dispossessed. It required all the skill of the aged Hincmar of Reims to avert civil war. In a letter written to Louis, the archbishop advised him to negotiate with his followers and to reread the Capitulary of Quierzy of 877, which had established a sort of contract between the king and his followers. Hincmar recommended six points of action. First, Louis should husband his family wealth for the maintenance of his court and household. Second, he should respect church property and lift from it the new burdens of the past twenty years, which, according to Hincmar, had not existed in the time of Pippin, Charlemagne, or Louis the Pious. Third, the nobles ought not to be deprived of their holdings on baseless pretexts. Fourth, likewise, no more tribute should be levied under the pretense of fighting against the Northmen, since "for many years there has been no defense of the kingdom, but rather only payments of ransom and tribute which have impoverished men and ruined the once rich churches." Fifth, the king should foster concord between the clergy and the laity, accepting counsel from trustworthy men. Sixth and last, Louis must make peace with his cousins, the sons of Louis the German.

Thanks to the help of Hincmar and Empress Richildis, who made over the tokens of royal office, Louis was anointed king at Compiègne on 8 December 877. The bishops, abbots, and great lay nobility commended themselves to the king and pledged their fealty. For his part, Louis, "established as king by the grace of God and the election of the people," promised to respect religion and safeguard the rule of law. He consented to a veritable contract between a king and his subjects destined to influence the future of the Carolingian dynasty.

THE POPE IN FRANCIA

Meanwhile, Pope John VIII was now in desperate straits. He labored under multiple threats: from the Arab raiders who pillaged the Roman countryside; from the clerical partisans of Formosus, cardinal-bishop of Porto; and finally, from the aggression of Lambert of Spoleto and his brother-in-law Adalbert of Tuscany. Compelled to act, John VIII repeated in 878 what Stephen II had done in 754: he journeyed to Francia in search of help. He arrived by sea in Provence, and there he was received by Count Boso and his wife, Ermengard. This daughter of Emperor Louis II dreamed of securing the imperial title for her husband, and pleased by the reception he received, John VIII declared himself ready to "elevate Boso and Ermengard to higher and more considerable circumstances." Yet for the moment, his aim was to convene a great western council attended by all the Carolingian rulers where he might address unsettled business and determine the fate of the empire. The council opened at Troyes on 11 August 878, and gathered together some fifty bishops. In anticipation of the arrival of the princes, the assembly began its work by addressing several ecclesiastical issues and by excommunicating serious political troublemakers: laymen who had seized church property; the Italian enemies of John VIII; Hugh, the frustrated bastard son of Lothar II; and Bernard of Gothia, who was in revolt against Louis the Stammerer. Although King Louis eventually arrived at the synod, his German cousins did not. Carloman of Bavaria was paralyzed by illness and Louis the Younger had gone to him to arrange for the succession. Their younger brother Charles the Fat made no effort to attend the gathering at Troyes. At length the pope ordered a public reading of the promises made to St. Peter by Pippin the Short and Charlemagne and then reanointed Louis the Stammerer as king, in the hope of enticing him back to Italy for an imperial coronation. But Louis was himself laboring against a massive rebellion by Bernard of Gothia, who controlled, "as though he were king," the county of Autun, the Berry region, and Septimania, as well as other counties in the Spanish March. So John VIII ventured back to Italy accompanied by Boso of Provence, with whom he negotiated a secret accord after Louis the Stammerer refused his overtures. The pope sought to convene another assembly at Pavia that would recognize Boso as king of Italy and emperor. But the bishops and the Italian lay nobility failed to appear, and Boso returned empty-handed to Provence.

Although John VIII failed to obtain the help he sought at the Council of Troyes, Louis the Stammerer recognized his own need to come to terms with his eastern cousins. He arranged to meet Louis the Younger in November 878 at Fouron, where the kings recognized the division of Lotharingia established by their fathers and then concluded a treaty that echoed the principles of cooperation articulated at the Meersen conference of 851. The two rulers agreed to help each other in their struggle against the Northmen and to ensure the hereditary rights of each other's sons. Moreover, they hoped to meet with the two other Carolingian princes in February 879 to confirm and widen their accord. There was thus a glimmer of hope that the "rule of brotherhood" might be resurrected. Louis the Stammerer, however, fell gravely ill in the spring of 879 as he prepared to move against Bernard of Gothia, and on 10 April, he died in Compiègne at age thirty-three.

THE SUCCESSION OF LOUIS THE STAMMERER

Despite the assurances exchanged at Fouron, the death of Louis the Stammerer gave rise to a new crisis in western Francia. Gauzlin, abbot of St. Denis and chancellor to the late Louis the Stammerer, persuaded the Welf Conrad, count of Paris, and other nobles to invite Louis the Younger into the kingdom. Himself a member of the Rorgonid clan, Gauzlin also held the abbacies of Jumièges and St. Amand, and was an uncle of the rebellious Bernard of Gothia. The invitation to Louis the Younger was a bid by Gauzlin to maintain his leading political role in western Francia, which had lately been shadowed by the transfer of his abbacy at St. Germain-des-Prés to his rival, Hilduin. Nevertheless, another group of nobles led by the powerful Welf Hugh the Abbot, together with Bernard Hairyfoot and the chamberlain Theuderic, arranged to cede to Louis the Younger the Lotharingian territories acquired by Charles the Bald in 870 in exchange for his renunciation in early 880 of further claims on western Francia. Meanwhile, Hugh the Abbot had seen that the sons of Louis the Stammerer by his first wife, Ansgard, were crowned and anointed in September 879 at Ferrières. Later, in 880, it was decided by the nobles to allot the sixteen-year-old Louis III control over Neustria and the adjoining northern marches, while the thirteen-year-old Carloman received Aquitaine and Burgundy.

THE REBELLION OF BOSO

Shortly after the royal coronation of September 879, news arrived of a stunning move by Boso of Provence. Although the brother-in-law of the late Charles the Bald had failed to obtain a crown in Italy, he managed to arrange for his election to kingship at a gathering at Mantaille, near Vienne, on 15 October 879. Six metropolitans and seven suffragan bishops were persuaded to proclaim him king "by God's consent," because "the bishops, nobles, and common people were without the protection of a royal person." Although allied to the Carolingian house merely by marriage, Boso's claim to be "imperial offspring" (*proles imperialis*) was made to justify his momentous act of usurpation. This was no mere noble rebellion, but the election to royal status of a man who scoffed at the rights of the Carolingian dynasty, and the creation of an independent kingdom. To explain this act, we must look beyond the personal ambition of Boso and his wife to the particularist feelings of the local nobility. This part of the empire had already been set up as a separate kingdom in 855, thereafter administered by Count Gerard of Vienne until his ouster by Charles the Bald. The local nobility thus learned the advantages of having a ruler, or a king, who resided in Vienne, as opposed to a distant and wholly ineffectual sovereign.

The threat implied by the elevation of Boso to kingship helped to close the ranks of the Carolingian rulers. Louis III and Carloman met in June 880 with Charles the Fat and representatives of Louis the Younger at Gondreville on the Mosel. There the parties agreed to form a common front against Boso as well as Hugh, the illegitimate son of Lothar II, who now sought to take over Lotharingia.

Despite the challenges it faced, the Carolingian dynasty retained many decisive advantages. The two kings of western Francia were young and energetic. Despite his age, Hincmar of Reims continued to play the role of political mentor. He held up the ideal of the age when Charlemagne ruled the empire in the circle of his advisers:

Follow this illustrious example if you wish to restore to the kingdom the traditions of justice and the virtues of your ancestors, which alone can save it from disorder and from the pagans.

In 882, the aged Hincmar sent Carloman an idealized portrait of Charlemagne's court in the so-called *De ordine palatii* ("On the Governance of the Palace"). Nevertheless, his admonitions met with little response. Both young kings were under the influence of counselors whose interests lay elsewhere. The immediate concern of Louis III and Carloman was not to pattern their government according to past examples, but rather to withstand a massive Viking onslaught.

THE VIKING INVASIONS

Although the Danes had slackened their attacks after 862 thanks in part to the tribute paid by Charles the Bald, they massively renewed their assaults against Frankish territory in 879. Flanders, Brabant, and northern Saxony suffered especially. From Ghent, the raiders advanced into the interior along the Scheldt and its tributaries. Louis III moved against them, and secured a brilliant victory at Saucourt in 881, which was celebrated in the Old High German poem *Ludwigslied*. The following year Louis continued the effort to secure his kingdom by moving against other bands of Northmen operating along the Loire. But seriously wounded in a riding accident, the king finally died at St. Denis on 5 August 882.

After the death of the capable, lusty twenty-year-old, Carloman assumed control of all western Francia, and prosecuted the defense of the kingdom for another two years. But from their base at Condé-on-the-Scheldt, the Northmen penetrated deeply into the interior. In the entry for 882, the *Annals of St. Bertin* report how the raiders threatened Reims, forcing the elderly Archbishop Hincmar to flee the city with the relics of Saint Remigius and the church treasury:

> After arranging for the canons, monks, and nuns to take refuge in various places, Hincmar had himself carried away in a litter, as his poor health required. Nearly undone by his flight, he reached the *villa* called Épernay across the Marne.

Although undefended by walls, Reims remained unscathed despite the surrounding devastation. Hincmar, however, died in Épernay on 21 December 882. Sometimes victor while other times vanquished, Carloman managed during 883 to quell the marauding Northmen by promising to pay them an enormous tribute of twelve thousand pounds of silver, finally delivered in October 884. A few months later, as he hunted with companions in the forest of Bézu, near Les Andelys, the king suffered an accidental leg wound, and a week later he died at age seventeen on 12 December 884. Fate thus hammered away at the Carolingian dynasty.

Although Louis the Stammerer had produced a third son by his second wife, the future Charles the Simple, the prince was but five years old. Because of the dire circumstances of the kingdom, there could be no question of promoting him to the kingship. Therefore the nobles called on the Carolingian who appeared best able to defend western Francia: Charles the Fat.

The Reign of Charles the Fat, or Illusions Dispelled

THE IMPERIAL CORONATION

King of Alemannia since 876, Charles, the third son of Louis the German, enjoyed a brilliant opening to his career. Although many Italian nobles hoped to see his brother Carloman reign in Pavia, sickness forced the Bavarian ruler to defer to Charles in 879. Still in search of an emperor, Pope John VIII likewise resigned himself to the prospect of negotiating with the new Italian ruler. The two men met in early 880 at Ravenna, where the pope seems to have made the first of many requests for assurances that Charles would "respect the constitution and privileges of the Roman church." John VIII thereby inaugurated a principle destined to last throughout the Middle Ages whereby the king of Italy—later called the "king of the Romans"—would promise to respect the privileges of the papacy before receiving the imperial crown. Charles, however, was reluctant simply to accept the pope's demands, even though he offered expressions and gestures of good will. He did not want to become a servant of the pope. Thus, he waited until February 881 before staging a precipitous arrival at Rome. John VIII was now apparently satisfied with the assurances offered by the king of Italy, and he agreed to crown Charles and his wife, Richardis, as emperor and empress on 12 February 881. The pope ardently hoped the new emperor would aid him against the threat still posed by the Arabs. Charles the Fat, however, soon returned to northern Italy and crossed over the Alps. After the death of his brother Louis the Younger on 20 January 882, the emperor inherited the remaining portion of the German kingdom. In Italy, the unhappy John VIII was left in despair, and before the end of 882 he too was dead, possibly assassinated by one of his clerical entourage.

CHARLES THE FAT IN FRANCIA

Now emperor and king of Italy and Germany, Charles the Fat appeared determined to lead the struggle against the Northmen and to dislodge them from their new base at Elsloo on the lower Meuse River. An army composed of Franks, Alemans, Thuringians, Saxons, and Lombards moved against the camp in mid-882, but to the disappointment of all, Charles broke off the siege after twelve days and concluded a treaty with the Northmen allowing them to settle in Frisia. However, their chieftain, Godofrid, agreed to be baptized, and then married Gisela, a daughter of Lothar II by Waldrada. Although the emperor was not a brilliant soldier, he seems to have been an able diplomat. He managed to earn enough confidence among the nobles of western Francia to receive an invitation to rule the kingdom after the death of Carloman at the end of 884. At Ponthion in June 885, Emperor Charles the Fat received pledges of fealty from the great clerics and laymen of his new kingdom.

The emperor had thus achieved the territorial reintegration of the old Carolingian empire. Charlemagne lived again in Charles the Fat, or so Notker of St. Gall seemed to think when he presented the *Gesta Karoli* to his emperor. Indeed, Regino of Prüm would also fondly remember Charles after his death as a man who gave generously to the needy, prayed, sang Psalms, and placed his trust in God. Yet however admirable in the abstract, these virtues proved inadequate to govern an immense empire and to secure it against ever present threats.

A month after Charles received the homage of the West Frankish nobility at Ponthion, the Danish chieftain Sigifrid began moving up the Seine with a "great army," sacking Rouen at the end of July. With its bridges and fortifications, Paris soon presented an obstacle to the raiders' advance into the interior. By November 885, the Northmen began a lengthy siege of the town, whose history would be vividly chronicled by the monk and eyewitness Abbo of St. Germain-des-Prés in his famous poem *The Siege of Paris (Bella Parisiacae urbis)*.

At this time, Paris—that is, the island in the Seine—comprised some eight hectares secured by a circuit of ancient walls and a number of towers, which had lately been restored. Since 884, the island-citadel had been governed by its bishop, Gauzlin, the Rorgonid abbot of St. Denis who had hoped in 879 to see Louis the Younger reign in western Francia. Bishop

Gauzlin refused to allow Sigifrid's forces to pass upstream, and organized to resist them. He found helpers in the two sons of Robert the Strong, Odo and Robert, who had taken over the administration of Neustria (see Chart 4) after the death of Hugh the Abbot in 883. At age eighteen, Odo was count of Paris, and the townspeople lent him their confidence, although they also counted on the otherworldly protection of their patrons, Saint Germain and Saint Geneviève, whose holy relics were sheltered within the city walls. The tower that defended the approach to the large bridge to the Right Bank was successfully held, but in early 886, the smaller bridge to the Left Bank collapsed from high water. Despite the heroism of the defenders of its now isolated approach tower, the Northmen captured and murdered the twelve men whose names have been preserved in Abbo's poem.

Now in desperate straits, Odo appealed for help to the emperor, who was then in Bavaria. In response, Charles the Fat dispatched Count Henry of Babenberg. As military commander in Austrasia, Henry had lately earned fame by managing to kill the treacherous Danish chieftain Godofrid—whom Charles the Fat had allowed to settle in Frisia—and by capturing and blinding his accomplice, Hugh, the bastard son of Lothar II. This time, however, the count was himself slain by the Viking invaders. On learning this, Charles the Fat journeyed in person to Paris, pitching camp on the hill of Montmartre in October 886. The town's beleaguered inhabitants now hoped for deliverance, but it came rather differently than they expected. The emperor chose to ransom the city with a tribute of seven hundred pounds of silver, and allowed the Northmen to move on to "winter" in Burgundy—that is, to pillage the region. Meanwhile, Charles quickly moved off in order to avoid an encounter with Sigifrid's army.

THE DEPOSITION OF CHARLES THE FAT

Fear of the Northmen was not alone responsible for the precipitous imperial departure. Charles the Fat was gravely ill. He suffered from headaches that made it virtually impossible for him to govern. In early 887, the emperor underwent a surgical skull incision, or trepanation, in the hope that this would relieve his headaches. By summer of the same year, the magnates of Germany had organized a conspiracy aimed at separating Charles from his trusted but widely hated arch-chancellor, Liutward, bishop of Vercelli. Faced with a trumped up charge accusing Liutward of illicit relations with his wife, Richardis, the humiliated emperor was forced in June to dismiss and dispossess his ambitious favorite, thereby losing his chief counselor and aide. Nevertheless, there soon followed a general rebellion in favor of Arnulf, the bastard son of Carloman of Bavaria. Driven from Frankfurt by the approach of forces from all the regions of Germany, Charles withdrew to Tribur, near Mainz, where his attempt to convoke an assembly of his followers failed. Abandoned by all, the sickly emperor agreed to abdicate. By the end of November, Charles the Fat withdrew to Swabia, where he lived out his remaining days on a clutch of estates accorded to him by his nephew Arnulf, the new king of Germany. He died on 13 January 888 at Neidingen on the Danube, southeast of Donaueschingen, and was buried at Reichenau.

Although the dream of restoring the empire still lived on, its territorial unity was definitively broken. Despite numerous setbacks since the beginning of the ninth century, the centrifugal forces of partition now triumphed. Moreover, it was no longer the Carolingian family that presided over the empire in its various parts. Rather, local and regional magnates followed the example set by Boso in 879 and claimed authority through election by the clerical and lay nobility.

The Election of Regional Kings

Commenting on the events that followed the death of Charles the Fat, the chronicler Regino of Prüm wrote:

> After his death, the kingdoms that had obeyed him, as though bereft of a legitimate heir, dissolved from association into separate parts; and they no longer waited for a ruler given by nature, but each chose to create for itself a king from its own innards. This situation sparked tremendous warring. Not that the Franks lacked leaders who could rule the kingdoms with nobility, bravery, and wisdom, but rather because the very equality of birth, honor, and power among them heightened their contention, since no one stood out enough for the others to agree to submit to his authority. Francia would have brought forth many leaders fit to take the reins of the kingdom, had fate not armed them for their mutual destruction through competition for power.

This famous and frequently cited passage vividly evokes the contemporary situation. Leaders with specific qualities had to be chosen by their noble peers, and such choices nurtured rivalries and open conflict. As we have seen, Arnulf of Carinthia was the choice of most leading German nobles. About thirty years old, he had distinguished himself in his wars against the Moravians.

In western Francia, however, there could be no question of conferring the throne on the young Charles the Simple, who was still under the
tutelage of count Ramnulf II of Poitiers. The magnates of the north thus
opted for Count Odo, the hero of the defense of Paris. According to Regino of Prüm, he was "an energetic man who excelled others by his beauty,
great stature and strength, and abundant wisdom." Regino omits to note,
however, that another figure also vied for the royal office in western Francia, Guido (Wido) II of Spoleto. This scion of the Lambertine-Widonid
clan was advanced by archbishop Fulk of Reims (883–900), who was himself somehow related to the Widonids and was no doubt bent on maintaining the leading role played by his predecessor Hincmar. Although
Wido gained a few Burgundian supporters and managed to be crowned at
Langres in early March 888 by Geilo, the local bishop, his relative Fulk
soon abandoned him in favor of Odo, the more viable candidate. Yet it
was Walter, archbishop of Sens and regional metropolitan, who had been
called on to anoint Odo king at Compiègne in February 888, thereby cast-
ing a temporary shadow on the special coronation rights lately claimed for
the archbishop of Reims by Hincmar. Like Louis the Stammerer in 877
and his son Carloman in 882, Odo pronounced a solemn promise at his
coronation to defend the church and to uphold the laws of religion. In
exchange, he received a pledge of fidelity from the lay and ecclesiastical
magnates.

In the Kingdom of Italy there was also no lack of candidates for the
throne. As the bishop of Brescia had lately written to Bishop Salomo II of
Constance: "The people of Italy are by turns prey to this or that faction,
and they impatiently await an agreement about who should possess the
kingdom." In early 888, a gathering of Italian nobles at Pavia led by the
Supponids elected Berengar, marquis of Friuli, as king. This choice, however, was dictated not simply by the personal qualities of the candidate,
but with due regard for his Carolingian descent. Through his mother,
Gisela, Berengar was a grandson of Louis the Pious (see Table 2). Yet
belonging to the Carolingian house was not in itself sufficient to ensure
Berengar's success. Shortly after the election at Pavia, Berengar met with
competition from Guido II of Spoleto, whose candidacy was supported
by Adalbert of Tuscany and a few other Italian nobles, despite the collapse
of his position in Francia. A war commenced that ended with Berengar's
withdrawal to northeastern Italy. Guido used this "judgment of God" to
have himself proclaimed king, and on 21 February 891, he was crowned
emperor by the pope at Pavia. Yet, as we shall see, Berengar did not give

up; until his death in 924 he continued to mount effective resistance to Guido and other rivals.

Likewise in 888 another magnate was voted into kingship by the nobles of the Transjurane region of Burgundy, or Upper Burgundy. Rudolph was a scion of the Welf family: grandson of Conrad the Elder, brother of Empress Judith, and son of Conrad II, the count of Auxerre who had slain the rebellious Abbot Hubert, brother-in-law of Lothar II, and then received the Transjurane duchy along with the abbacy of St. Maurice-in-Valais (see Chart 5). It was at this illustrious abbey that leading churchmen and laymen gathered and elected Rudolph as king of Upper Burgundy. Rudolph, however, aspired to greater things; he was soon scheming to make Lotharingia a part of his own expanded kingdom.

Similar problems of succession also arose in the Provençal kingdom created by Boso in 879. Although the Carolingian rulers had briefly made common cause against the upstart ruler, they never managed to wrest back the southernmost portion of the kingdom. Boso's own brother Richard soon rejoined the Carolingian side, and in 882, he captured Vienne as well as Boso's wife and daughter. Abandoned by his leading supporters, the would-be king slid into obscurity until his death on 11 January 887, whereupon his wife, Ermengard, managed to flee to her cousin Charles the Fat. Of the two children borne to Boso by Ermengard, the daughter, Engelberga, married William the Pious, son of Bernard Hairyfoot, while Charles the Fat adopted the son, Louis, in recognition of the boy's descent from Emperor Louis II (see Tables 2 and 7). In 890 Louis was subsequently elected and crowned king of Provence by a gathering of lay and ecclesiastical magnates in Valence.

Thus, apart from Odo in western Francia, the kings who succeeded Charles the Fat somehow descended from Carolingian stock. Elected by regional leaders, their authority was often incomplete and geographically ill defined, and to shore it up, they often would need to turn to Arnulf of Germany for approval and support. Yet by the end of the ninth century effective power lay in the hands of the rulers of newly formed regional princedoms, and these dominions will require closer attention.

2. The New Kingdoms and Princedoms

Leaving the Carolingians to their fate, or perhaps their ill fortune, let us consider the figures who shaped Europe's future, the new kings and regional princes whose power was now in the ascendant. These rulers descended from nobles who had themselves been allies of the Carolingians, receiving grants of land, offices, privileges, and immunity in exchange for vassalage and pledges of fealty. In the second half of the ninth century, many of these leaders had struck deep roots in the particular regions which they held as administrators. They accumulated local countships, ensconced themselves, and then managed to bequeath the domains they had acquired to their heirs. A number of families thus gathered their own following of clients with whose help they could support or oppose their Carolingian overlords. These new leaders likewise laid hold of abbacies and bishoprics in which they installed their relatives and friends. Hence, their policies closely mirrored those of the early Carolingians of the eighth century.

Moreover, circumstances favored the ambitions of the nobility. In 879, several years before the eclipse of the Carolingians in western Francia, Boso of Provence had seized royal authority, the *bannum* of Frankish kings, and found a ready biblical justification for his actions: "I, Boso, who am what I am by the grace of God" (1 Cor. 15:10). A decade later, others gladly followed suit. Within the kingdoms that emerged, lesser princes also carved out narrower dominions, which they ruled more or less autonomously. By the early tenth century, the bulk of political power had migrated from the Carolingians to other families who lent Europe a new, more differentiated visage.

The Rulers of the Italian Kingdom

NEW PRINCEDOMS

In Italy, the princely dynasties derived for the most part from the Frankish nobles established in the peninsula during the reigns of Charlemagne and

Louis the Pious. In the north, the Unruochings controlled the March of Friuli. Eberhard, the son-in-law of Louis the Pious, had passed on the march to his eldest son, Unruoch, and on the latter's death about 874 Berengar, a younger son of Eberhard, assumed the office of marquis. Like their father, both these sons were well connected by marriage, but to influential Frankish nobles established in Italy rather than in Francia proper. Berengar's wife belonged to the influential Supponid clan, which ruled the counties of Parma, Piacenza, and Brescia. As marquis of Friuli, his duties required him not only to protect northern Italy from the Slavs but also to keep watch over the road that linked Bavaria to the south by way of the Brenner Pass. Farther to the west, Count Ansgar of Ivrea controlled access to and from the other alpine passes leading north; he was the son a Burgundian noble and an ally of Guido II of Spoleto. To the south, a family of Bavarian origin controlled the March of Tuscany, where Marquis Adalbert I formed links to Lambert of Spoleto, the rival of Guido II, by marrying his sister, Rotilda. In central Italy, the Duchy of Spoleto remained under the control of members of the Lambertine-Widonid clan, whose leaders ruled the former Lombard duchy and frequently intervened in the political affairs of Rome, Naples, and Capua. Finally, the patrimony of Saint Peter itself may rightly be considered a princedom. But after the mysterious death of John VIII in 882, a series of mostly short-lived popes were plagued by factionalism and infighting. Hence even Stephen V met with little success at restoring order, despite his comparatively lengthy reign from 885 to 891.

GUIDO II, KING OF ITALY

As we have seen, it was Berengar of Friuli who arranged to have himself proclaimed king by a part of the Italian nobility in early 888. As later recalled by the anonymous poet of the *Gesta Berengarii imperatoris* ("The Deeds of Emperor Berengar"), the new king seemed to possess decisive advantages. He enjoyed the support of the Supponids, and even managed to secure recognition as king from Arnulf of Germany. Yet scarcely had Berengar begun to rule when Guido of Spoleto returned from his disappointment in western Francia and contested the Italian kingship, ultimately with success. Supported by a number of ecclesiastical magnates, Guido II sought to reclaim the Carolingian legacy by arranging for Pope Stephen V to crown him emperor in early 891. Yet this papal gesture was hedged with mistrust and fear of Guido's aggressive interference in the papal territories. Although Stephen V proceeded to make an emperor of his nemesis, the pope had also pleaded in vain with Arnulf in mid-890 to come "rein in the Italian kingdom, which had been seized by evil Christians and pagan ruffians."

As king in Pavia and emperor in Rome, Guido acted to restore order to Italy. In one of his capitularies, he even appropriated the traditional tone of Carolingian rhetoric, speaking of his *Renovatio regni francorum*, or "Renewal of the Kingdom of the Franks." Like Lothar I, Guido had his eldest son Lambert crowned king and even co-emperor by Pope Formosus on 30 April 892. Through his marriage to Agiltrude, whose father Adalgisus of Benevento had imprisoned Emperor Louis II in 871, Guido also hoped to unite the great southern duchy to Spoleto. In early 894, he was challenged by the descent of Arnulf into the peninsula, but he still managed to block the German king's passage to Rome. But this success was cut short when Guido died unexpectedly before the end of 894.

TROUBLES IN ROME

In October 895 Arnulf returned to Italy, where he quashed the maneuvering of Guido's widow, Agiltrude. After storming Rome at the pope's behest, Arnulf was crowned emperor on 22 February 896 by Formosus. Nevertheless, the new emperor fell seriously ill and was forced to withdraw to the north without having entirely subdued the forces loyal to Guido's son Lambert. As had his father, Carloman, Arnulf abandoned Italy in late 896. He returned to Bavaria partially paralyzed, where he died in 899.

The party loyal to Spoleto was now again in the ascendant in Rome. In January 897 the new Pope Stephen VI convened a synod that convicted his pro-imperial predecessor Formosus of usurping the Holy See; exhumed, stripped, and mutilated his body; and declared him deposed. This odious ceremony demonstrates amply enough the sorry state of the Roman clergy. After presiding over this event, Stephen VI was soon himself deposed by a mob, and for many years the "Formosian" and "anti-Formosian" parties continued to battle over the papal throne. There was some hope that Pope John IX (898–900) and Lambert might restore order, but the young emperor died after a hunting accident on 15 October 898. Called a new Constantine and a new Theodosius in his epitaph, Lambert died not long before Italy suffered its first wave of Magyar raiders.

LOUIS THE BLIND

While these somber events were taking place at Rome, Berengar had reestablished himself in Pavia. He was, however, unable to prevent the Magyars from pillaging across the March of Friuli and Lombardy. Modena, Reggio, and Piacenza were all torched, and the abbey of Nonatola was likewise destroyed. Hence the nobles of Italy sought a new king who could protect them and found a willing candidate in Louis of Provence. Through his grandmother Empress Engelberga, Louis could lay as legitimate a claim to the Italian kingdom as Berengar. Moreover, his father, Boso, had for a time been the candidate of Pope John VIII (see Table 7). Once proclaimed king, Louis naturally sought the imperial crown, which he received at Rome from the hands of Pope Benedict IV in February 901. Notwithstanding this success, the new emperor ran afoul of Berengar in northern Italy and only purchased safe passage back to Provence against a promise never to return to the peninsula. In 905, Louis did, however, return at the request of the marquis of Tuscany, Adalbert II, nicknamed "the Rich," the most powerful noble in Italy and the second husband of Bertha, a daughter of Lothar II by Waldrada. Although Berengar momentarily fled from the intruder and his powerful ally, he soon managed to overcome Louis and had his eyes gouged out. The savaged king now returned to Provence, where he ruled for another twenty years as Louis "the Blind."

BERENGAR I, EMPEROR

Now firmly established as king, Berengar maneuvered for many years to gain the imperial title. Finally in November 915, Pope John X, a former archbishop of Ravenna, agreed to crown him emperor in the hope that he would offer assistance against the ever present Arab threat. Writing about this time, the anonymous panegyrist of the *Gesta Berengarii imperatoris* depicted how hopeful crowds acclaimed the new emperor, but like his imperial predecessors, Berengar soon returned to northern Italy—to contain Magyar invaders from the northeast and to face renewed revolt among the nobility. The rebellion was now led by Berengar's son-in-law Adalbert, marquis of Ivrea, with the support and participation of King Rudolph II of Upper Burgundy. Faced with this considerable threat, Berengar retired to Verona to await an opportunity for vengeance, and in the meanwhile, northern Italy came to be partitioned among the opposing forces. Thus riven by internal division, the north of the peninsula was ravaged by repeated Magyar assaults. Finally in 924, Pavia was besieged, captured, and pillaged. Berengar may himself have been scheming to use the Magyar onslaught to his own advantage. Whatever his plans, they were cut short by his assassination on 16 April 924. Although Rudolph II still remained in Italy, he would soon be forced to retire to his own kingdom.

Berengar's tumultuous reign had been little but a lengthy series of failures. As king of Italy, he could master neither external aggression nor internal unrest among the nobility. In fact, the charters issued by Berengar—like those of other royal contenders—make it clear that local counts and bishops managed to secure or usurp a host of formerly kingly prerogatives. Thus at Modena, Cremona, Parma, Piacenza, and Mantua, the bishops ruled with virtual autonomy, enjoying royal revenues granted to them in benefice as well as the public powers of counts. Meanwhile, the lay and ecclesiastical magnates of Italy built castles not only to guard against the Magyars but also to affirm their own power and independence vis-à-vis the king. Indeed, Berengar's unique triumph was to be the last "Carolingian" emperor until Otto I restored the empire in 962.

The Kingdoms of Middle Gaul

PROVENCE

After 888 Provence and the Transjurane region of Burgundy constituted separate kingdoms headed respectively by Louis, son of Boso, and Rudolph I. Yet during the minority of Louis, the dowager Ermengard actually ruled Provence with the help of the archbishops of Lyon and Vienne and Count Teutbert of Avignon. We have already noted the course and outcome of the adventures of Louis in Italy. The anonymous *Visio Karoli III* ("Vision of Charles the Fat"), probably datable to 900, helps to account for the young king's ambitious thrust into Italy this same year. Shortly before his death, Charles the Fat was supposed to have received a vision of the afterworld. In it, he first witnesses bishops and lay magnates suffering torments and learns how his own father, Louis the German, is plunged on alternate days into a vat of boiling water. Then, in Paradise, Charles listens as Lothar I and Louis II fortell the impending demise of the Carolingian line and designate the young Louis, grandson of Louis II, to restore the empire. In October 900 this very descendant of the Carolingians had himself proclaimed king at Pavia, and in February 901 he was crowned emperor at Rome. Although Louis continued to reign in Provence after he was blinded by Berengar in July 905, he could no longer rule effectively. The magnates exploited the king's blindness to obtain a variety of concessions and supporting charters. The archbishop of Arles, for instance, secured the right to strike coinage as well as the benefice of keeping public tolls levied on Rhône shipping.

The leader of the Provençal nobility was Hugh of Arles, who descended by his father from Hubert, lay-abbot of St. Maurice, and by his mother from the illegitimate offspring of Lothar II (see Table 2). After the return of Louis the Blind from Italy, it was the duke of Arles who reigned in the king's name, distributing the choice honors and benefices to his own kith and kin. Hugh was also enticed by the crown of Italy, and further encouraged by the second marriage of his mother, Bertha, to Adalbert II of Tuscany. In 926 he too would answer the call of a group of Italian nobles in search of a king.

Upper Burgundy

From the start of his reign, Rudolph I of Burgundy—that is, of Transjurane or Upper Burgundy—dreamed of adding the lands of former Lotharingia to those he received with his crown at St. Maurice. Thus, Rudolph soon crossed over the Jura Mountains and arranged to be anointed at Toul. Arnulf responded to this expansionism in late 888 with an attack that drove the upstart king back to his own realm. The two rulers came to terms shortly thereafter thanks to a personal appearance by Rudolph in Regensburg and a nominal assurance of his subordination to Arnulf. Despite this adventurism to the north, Rudolph does not seem to have moved to expand southward. Rather, links of cooperation were forged with Louis of Provence, who married Rudolph's daughter Adelaide. Although only distantly connected to the Carolingians through his great-aunt Judith, the Welf bride of Louis the Pious (see Table 5), Rudolph fondly recalled his "glorious ancestors," as he called them, Lothar, Louis, and Charles. His household followed the "Carolingian" model, and included a chancellor and palatine counts. Rudolph also jealously guarded his royal monopoly on the minting of coin, and drew considerable wealth from the domains of his fisc, including the lucrative salt mines at Salins.

In 912 he was succeeded by his son Rudolph II. As we have noted, Rudolph II was later summoned to Italy in 923 by a faction of nobles in revolt against Berengar I. There he reigned for two years counseled by Adalbert (d. 925), marquis of Ivrea, or rather, as some sources report, by Adalbert's wife Ermengard. In 926 Rudolph's fickle Italian subjects revolted and offered his crown to Hugh of Arles. After a struggle that cost the life of Rudolph's father-in-law and supporter Burchard II (d. 926) of Swabia, the disowned ruler had to abandon Italy. He returned to his Burgundian kingdom, where he ruled until his death in 937.

The German Kingdom

THE REGIONAL PRINCEDOMS

In order to describe the regional princedoms of Germany, historians once commonly spoke of national or tribal duchies created by leaders who somehow represented one of the various Germanic peoples (*Stämme*). Today, scholars generally acknowledge that the dukes or marquises (*marchiones*) in question derived from a class of military officers and royal functionaries installed by the Carolingians and often related to them by blood. Carolingian administrative decisions typically determined the shape of Germany's emerging princedoms.

The Duchy of Swabia owes its inception not to the designs of its Alemannic and Swabian populations, but rather to the determination of Louis the Pious to establish a dominion for Charles the Bald composed of three former Merovingian duchies: Alemannia, Rhaetia, and Alsace. In 843, the Treaty of Verdun allotted these regions to Louis the German, who subsequently assigned them to his son Charles the Fat. By the end of the ninth century, the aspiring Hunfriding family, led by Burchard I, count of Rhaetia, came into conflict with the influential Salomo III (890–919), abbot of St. Gall and bishop of Constance. Although the powerful ecclesiastic secured the death of Burchard and banishment of his relations in 911, Salomo soon fell out with Erchanger, the erstwhile opponent of Burchard I and now his replacement. By 917, Erchanger was in turn executed, and succeeded by the son of his Hunfriding predecessor, Burchard II. Meanwhile, the ongoing power struggle had left an opening for the ambitious Rudolph II of Upper Burgundy. After stabilizing his position in Rhaetia and Swabia, Burchard II addressed this challenge, defeating Rudolph near Winterthur in 919. Thereafter, the rulers came to peaceful terms. Rudolph married Bertha, daughter of the Swabian duke, and their marriage produced Adelaide, the future wife of Otto I.

In eastern Francia, later known as Franconia, several leading families vied for supremacy. The Babenberg clan, so named after a family castle, controlled the valley of the upper Main. About 880, the family managed for a time to expand its power eastward when one of its leading members, Poppo, became duke of Thuringia and the Sorbian March. Poppo's brother was the famous Count Henry of Babenberg, hero of campaigns against the Northmen and also their victim during his attempt to relieve the Viking siege of Paris. To the west and north of the lands subject to the Babenbergs, Rhenish Franconia and Hesse lay under the flourishing power of the Conradine family which had helped Arnulf to the throne in 887. As recompense for this support, the new king awarded the bishopric of Würzburg to a member of the family in 892, a certain Rudolph whom one chronicler described as being "as stupid as he was noble." Feeling slighted and threatened by the transfer of this once friendly see to their rivals, the three sons of Henry of Babenberg embarked on a horrible war with the Conradines in 897. Adalbert of Babenberg survived the slaying and decapitation of his two brothers, but he too was finally captured and beheaded in 906. His elimination assured the regional ascendancy of the Conradine family.

In the future duchies of Bavaria and Saxony, two eminent families managed to ensconce themselves more solidly and at less cost. Bavaria, the first and most favored realm of Louis the German, passed to his eldest son, Carloman, and then to Carloman's bastard son Arnulf, duke of Carinthia. When Arnulf assumed the kingship of Germany in 887, he appointed his nephew Liutpold *marchio* of Bavaria in his place. Upon Liutpold's death fighting the Magyars in 907, his "honors" passed to his son Arnulf. As duke of Bavaria, Arnulf proceeded to secularize various monastic properties in order to increase the number of his vassals; he thereby gained the upper hand in his struggle against the Magyars.

Meanwhile in Saxony the sons of Duke Liudolf (d. 866) continued to defend their lands against Viking encroachment. After the eldest son, Bruno, was killed in battle in 880, his brother Otto successfully continued the struggle and even pressed claims in Thuringia. On Otto's death in 912, his son Henry—named after his grandfather—inherited the Saxon duchy before becoming king of Germany in 819.

To the west, Lotharingia formed another great princedom along the fringe of Germany. After the aspirations of Hugh, the bastard son of Lothar II, ended in 885 with blinding and imprisonment in the monastery of Prüm, his supporters eventually chose to rally behind King Arnulf. In an attempt to satisfy particularist sentiment, Arnulf established a new kingdom of Lotharingia in 894, which he entrusted to his own bastard son Zwentibold, keeping for himself the troubled Frisian lands still threatened by the Vikings. Nevertheless, the young king was opposed by powerful local magnates, such as Count Reginar of Hainaut, whose family possessed considerable domains between the Meuse and the Scheldt. Upon the death of Arnulf in 899, these nobles opted to claim his successor Louis the Child as their king and disowned Zwentibold, who was killed in combat the following year. Although reincorporated into the German kingdom, Lotharingia retained a distinct administration led by a clique of lay magnates and the archbishop of Trier. These nobles rejected the intrusion of outside families, and when faced with the enfeoffment of outsiders such as the Conradines, they would not hesitate to call on the king of western Francia for help to safeguard their independence.

Finally, this presentation of the eastern princedoms requires a discussion of Moravia and the Slavic hinterland. After the emergence of the Moravian state, Rastislav (846–869) had managed to establish an independent national church with the help of the papacy. Although Pope John VIII could not keep the Bulgars within the religious orbit of Rome, he hoped to make up for this loss by cultivating Christianity in Moravia. This papal policy was, however, undermined when Svatopulk, Rastislav's nephew and successor, effected a grudging rapprochement with Louis the German in 874. The once independent Moravian church came again under the religious and organizational influence of German bishops. So following the death of Archbishop Methodios in 885 his disciples took refuge in Bulgaria, where they now helped to organize the fledgling Greek-Slavic church. Svatopulk, however, remained master of eastern Pannonia, Slovakia, and Bohemia, perhaps as far north as Krakow. His regime prospered thanks to the traders who journeyed between Regensburg and Kiev. Likewise, recent excavations at Stare-Mesto and Mikulčice have shed light on flourishing new settlements established in this period. In 892 and 893 Arnulf of Carinthia waged two indecisive campaigns against the Moravians. Upon his death in 894, Svatopulk left two sons, Mojmir and Svatopulk II. The new rulers of Bohemia and Moravia came to terms with Arnulf, who received them at Regensburg. Nevertheless, the "empire of Greater Moravia" fell victim to the attacks of the Magyars in the early tenth century. After reaching Pannonia about 895, this new wave of migrants from central Asia commenced a series of raids that devastated the Moravian state and terrorized much of Europe for decades.

KING ARNULF AND LOUIS THE CHILD

Despite these new aggressors and the emergence of new regional princedoms on the fringe of his realm, Arnulf strove to maintain Carolingian traditions. He controlled great estates situated along the Main and in Thuringia and Bavaria; he convened assemblies at Mainz, Frankfurt, Tribur, and Worms; he received visits from his fellow kings, Odo, Louis of Provence, and Rudolph II of Upper Burgundy; and he even had himself crowned emperor. But plagued by illness contracted during his journey to

Rome to claim this honor, Arnulf returned to Bavaria in broken health. After 896 he could do little but allow his dukes to act as they saw fit. On his death in 899, his son Louis the Child was made king at six years of age. The boy's mother, Queen Oda, was removed from power in favor of a collective regency led by archbishops Hatto of Mainz and Adalbero of Augsburg and other magnates.

The personal reign of Louis the Child spanned the years 906 to 911, during which Magyar horsemen invaded the kingdom several times. In 907 Duke Liutpold of Bavaria along with the archbishop of Salzburg and other bishops died in combat. The following year the bishop of Würzburg and Burchard, marcher count of Thuringia, suffered the same fate, while Swabia was also devastated. When Louis the Child died in 911, the magnates of Germany hoped to address their dire needs by electing a king who seemed capable of marshaling an effective defense against the Magyars. They chose the influential Conrad of Franconia, whom some claimed had a link with the Carolingian house through his mother.

CONRAD I
The reign of Conrad I, from 911 to 918, was a series of failures. On the one hand, the nobles of Lotharingia, led by Count Reginar of Hainaut, refused to accept the new German king and switched their allegiance to Charles the Simple, king of western Francia. On the other hand, the dukes of Swabia, Bavaria, and Saxony moved into positions of near independence vis-à-vis their king. Conrad attempted to ally himself to the families in question by marrying Kunigund, mother of Arnulf of Bavaria and sister of Erchanger of Swabia, but this diplomatic marriage did not procure the desired results. Burchard I of Rhaetia and Erchanger defeated the king's forces, while Henry of Saxony crushed Eberhard, Conrad's brother, in 915 and laid a firm foothold in Westphalia. Finally, an expedition by Conrad against Bavaria only managed to galvanize Bavarian hostility against him.

Like the Carolingians of old, Conrad I now sought episcopal support. A synod gathered in 916 at Hohenaltheim (south of Nördlingen near the Swabian frontier with Bavaria and Franconia) in the presence of a legate of Pope John X. In addition to addressing matters of church discipline and the sequestration of property by laymen, the bishops severely upbraided the opponents of royal power. Yet despite the efforts of Heriger, archbishop of Mainz, and Salomo of Constance, canonical sanctions had little more lasting effect than Conrad's military repression. Possessed of their own vassals, assemblies and political programs, the dukes acted as though the king did not exist. Thus Germany seems to have been destined to emerge as a loose association of independent territories, the heirs of regional dominions laid out by the Carolingians.

The Kingdom of Western Francia

THE REGIONAL PRINCEDOMS

In 888, the magnates of western Francia elected Count Odo of Paris to the kingship instead of the available Carolingian heir. This event can be readily explained not only in terms of circumstance—the Viking peril and the minority of Charles the Simple—but in terms of the outlook of the nobility. The followers of Charles the Bald who had served his sons and grandsons had by now faded from the political limelight and had been replaced by younger men with new aspirations and ideas. It would be their work to bring about what Jan Dhondt has called the "constitutional revolution." The king's tenuous links to Aquitaine and Burgundy would soon disappear, and even within the narrow confines of the Île-de-France where he retained vassals and followers, his royal authority would prove frail.

In 877 Louis the Stammerer, king of Aquitaine, succeeded his father, and the southern kingdom thus lost its separate status. Bernard of Gothia, however, was in revolt against Louis, and continued to flaunt royal authority, "behaving as though he in fact were king," according to one chronicler. Long successful, Bernard now foundered; his ambitions were premature. The Carolingian ruler still retained effective authority, and the upstart was stripped of his "honors," which were redistributed among several other families, including those of Bernard Hairyfoot and Bello of Carcassonne. A scion of the eminent Wilhelmine family, Bernard Hairyfoot already possessed considerable property and power in the regions of Berry, Auvergne, Limousin, Rouergue, and Burgundy. Less daring than Bernard of Gothia or Boso of Provence, he died in 886 ostensibly faithful to his legitimate king. His son William the Pious bore the name of his illustrious great-grandfather William of Toulouse and inherited the greater part of his father's legacy except for Gothia and the Toulousain which passed to the Raymondine family. For the next twenty years, William was known as "duke of the Aquitainians" and generally acknowledged as suzerain by the magnates of the region. One of the few who preferred to commend himself to the king was Count Gerald, son of another great noble of the Auvergne and founder of the monastery of Aurillac. Odo of Cluny (d. 942) later reported the situation in his *Life of Saint Gerald*:

> William, by right duke of the Aquitainians, requested and forcefully insisted, but without threatening, that Gerald should withdraw from the king's service and enter his own. But Gerald, who was only recently established in the office of count, refused to consent. He did, however, enroll under the duke's command his nephew Raynaldus together with numerous other faithful armed companions.

Although Ramnulf II of Poitiers, a relative of the Carolingians and a cousin of William, might easily have emerged as a serious rival to William, he died in 890, leaving a young heir, Ebalus Manzer ("the Bastard"). Ramnulf's brother, another Ebalus who was abbot of St. Germain-des-Prés and a hero of the Viking siege of Paris, now worked with William the Pious to defend the interests of his nephew against the interference of King Odo. When William the Pious died childless in 918, he left his domains to his nephew William the Younger, with whom he had signed the foundation charter for the monastery of Cluny in 909.

In the southernmost reaches of Aquitaine, another family benefited from the fall of Bernard of Gothia. The descendants of Bello, count of Carcassonne under Charlemagne, had continued to administer various counties in the Spanish March, although Charles the Bald increasingly opted to confer them on northern followers like Bernard Hairyfoot and Bernard of Gothia. In 878 the failed rebellion of Bernard of Gothia prompted the transfer of many counties in the eastern Spanish March back to the indigenous dynasty of Bello, now represented by Wilfred, nicknamed "the Hairy" (*Pilosus*). As count of Urgel, Cerdanya, Ausona, Gerona, and Barcelona, Wilfred remained faithful to the Carolingian dynasty, and he refused after 888 to recognize the election of Odo as king, from then on dating his charters "during the reign of Christ, in the expectation of a king." However loyalist in appearance, this attitude also proved an expedient means of ensuring political independence and dynastic security. Wilfred the Hairy thus prepared the way for his recognition by later rulers and historians as the veritable founder of Catalonia. Much like the contemporary kings of the Asturias, Wilfred defended his counties against Muslim aggression and also worked to repopulate deserted territory. He founded and endowed the monasteries of Ripoll and San Joan de les Abadesses, where he named his own children as abbot and abbess. In order to renew the church and establish a new bishopric at Vich, Wilfred entered into warmer relations with King Odo and Archbishop Theodard of Narbonne. Nevertheless, the rapprochement with the Robertines did not mark a slackening of the count's firm adherence to the Carolingian cause. After Wilfred the Hairy fell in battle in 897, his sons succeeded him as the rulers of Catalonia: the counties of Barcelona, Gerona, and Vich passed to Wilfred II Borell; Urgel, to Sunifred II; and Cerdanya, to Miro II.

Northwest of the Pyrenees, Gascony was likewise emerging as a distinct duchy, although its history is less well known. Charters from the late ninth and early tenth centuries record the name of the count and marquis Garcia Sanchez, perhaps the son of the Sanchez who had surrendered Pippin II of Aquitaine to Charles the Bald in 852. Garcia Sanchez inaugurated the ducal line that would rule Gascony until 1032. The territory was, however, still quite limited in extent and chronically prey to the Northmen. Bordeaux remained under the separate control of a certain Count Amalvin, who maintained relations with the powerful ruler of the Asturias, King Alfonso III, the Great (868–910).

Upstream on the Garonne River, the Raymondine family was in the ascendant. Upon the death of Count Odo of Toulouse in 919, his sons succeeded him: Raymond II administered the counties of Toulouse, Nîmes, and Albi, while Ermengaud received Gothia and the Rouergue.

To the northeast, the Duchy of Burgundy constituted a region without pronounced natural boundaries, roughly covering the area bounded by the rivers Yonne and Saône and extending south from the middle Seine to the Beaujolais region. From his capital in Vienne, Boso of Provence was unable to defend the rolling Burgundian countryside when Charles the Fat allowed the Northmen to winter there after the siege of Paris of 886. Thus, on the death of the emperor in 888, the Burgundian nobility momentarily supported the effort to elevate Guido II of Spoleto to the kingship before rallying to the cause of Odo of Paris.

Nevertheless, the true sovereign of Burgundy was Richard, nicknamed "the Justiciar," the brother of Boso, who inherited the Burgundian "honors" formerly held by the Provençal king, including the counties of Autun, Sens, and Auxerre. Richard also came to control extensive monastic properties, such as the abbeys of St. Symphorian of Autun, St. Germain of Auxerre, and St. Columba of Sens, as well as numerous bishoprics. He subjected the diocese of Langres and blinded its incumbent; he co-opted the bishop of Autun marrying his daughter to the bishop's son. His family wealth in the region also assured Richard of respect and support from such vassals as the powerful Manasses, who administered eight counties. To the east, the duke enjoyed good relations with Rudolph I of Upper Burgundy, whose sister Adelaide he married. Upon Richard's death in 921, the leadership of the Burgundian duchy he had founded passed to their son Ralph, the future king of western Francia.

The emergence of the Breton princedom predated that of the Duchy of Burgundy. As successor to his murdered cousin Erispoë in 857, Salomon had at first claimed the title "prince by the grace of God of all Brittany and of a large part of Gaul." He was granted the wealthy abbey of St. Aubin at Angers and other lands between the Mayenne and Sarthe rivers. As a consequence of clan feuding, Salomon was assassinated in 874. His relatives Pascwethen and Gurwant arranged an uneasy partition of the peninsula into northern and southern halves. Both men were replaced by another pair of rulers, Alan, count of Vannes, Pascwethen's brother, and Judicaël, Gurwant's son. Judicaël subsequently fell in combat against the Northmen, whereupon Alan the Great became sole ruler of Brittany from 888 to 907. With the help of Berengar of Rennes, the duke managed to organize solid resistance to the Northmen and inflicted several important defeats on them. As the head of Brittany, Alan also titled himself "by the grace of God king of the Bretons." The Breton princedom thus echoed the Carolingian royal formula, and it likewise borrowed other characteristics of the Frankish dynasty. In his residences at Rieux and Seni, near the abbey of Redon, Alan surrounded himself with episcopal advisers, including Fulcher of Nantes (d. 912), as well as the lay *machtierns*, or clan chieftains. Moreover, Brittany had not as yet become culturally and economically isolated, but participated actively in exchange with other regions of the west, as has been amply illustrated by the Rennes hoard uncovered in 1964 and datable to the years 884–924. The 332 denarius coins in question were struck in a variety of centers, some as far off as Metz, Brioude, and Pavia. This interval of independence and prosperity came to an end by 919, when resurgent Viking raiders chose Nantes as their base on the Loire. A large number of lay and ecclesiastical leaders were forced to flee to Francia and even to England.

In the north of western Francia proper, Flanders was likewise exposed to Viking attack. The death of Baldwin I in 879 came at a time of renewed aggression. His successor, Baldwin II, took advantage of this situation to erect wooden citadels at St. Omer, Bruges, Ghent, and Courtrai, and also to seize lands abandoned by royal and ecclesiastical administrators. Although a grandson of Charles the Bald, Baldwin II did not vie for the kingship in 888, but nor did he agree to recognize the election of Odo. His principal aim was to extend the county of Flanders to the south. He thus managed to gain control of Artois along with the wealthy abbey of St. Vaast in Arras, which had been held since 879 by the Unruoching Ralph, son of Eberhard of Friuli. When the abbey was subsequently conferred on Fulk of Reims, Baldwin had the archbishop assassinated. In the upper valley of the Somme, the count faced opposition from Herbert I, count of Vermandois (see Chart 8), himself also of Carolingian descent. Bernard, the king of Italy blinded on orders from Louis the Pious in 818, had fathered a son, Pippin, who came to administer several counties in the Somme region and whose own son Herbert I later controlled both St. Quentin and Péronne. Baldwin II eliminated opposition from Herbert I by arranging for his assassination in 907. As part of another scheme to stabilize maritime relations with Britain, the count of Flanders also strove to dominate the lower valley of the Canche River. To seal his Anglo-Flemish alliance, Baldwin arranged to marry the daughter of the king of Wessex, Alfred the Great. Upon Baldwin's death in 918, his son Arnulf inherited the enlarged and powerful county of Flanders as well as the promise of a brilliant future.

The situation of the Neustrian duchy between the Seine and the Loire differed somewhat from that of other regional princedoms inasmuch as its ruler, Count Odo of Paris, became king of western Francia in 888. After the death of Robert the Strong in 866, the duchy had been administered on behalf of his minor sons by Hugh the Abbot, a Welf cousin of Charles the Bald. In 886, the elder son, Odo, became Neustrian marquis, count of Anjou and Blois, and abbot of St. Martin of Tours and nearby Marmoutier. He likewise served as count of Paris, where he defended the town against the Northmen in 886. When Odo became king, he transferred his Neustrian "honors" to his younger brother Robert, who entrusted the local administration and defense of many counties to other noble families. Thus, Angers came under the control of the viscount, or "lieutenant count," Fulk the Red, an ally of the Lambertine/Widonid family through his wife, Roscella, daughter of Warnar of Loches, himself a descendant of either Lambert III or his brother Warnar (see Table 6). Progenitor of a powerful and often ruthless local dynasty, Fulk became viscount of Angers in 898, and later count. Owing to his marriage, he also came to hold the county of Nantes after 914, and left a son named Wido. Meanwhile, the local Rorgonid family continued to hold a position of eminence in the Maine region. Gauzlin, nephew and namesake of the Rorgonid bishop of Paris who had died during the siege of 886, administered the county of Maine between 905 and 914. Thereafter, his office was bestowed on Count Roger, who had married Rothild, the youngest daughter of Charles the Bald. Roger left the county of Maine to his son Hugh, and one of his daughters married a member of the Robertine clan. At Blois, a certain Warnegald served as viscount between 878 and 906, and was then replaced by Theobald the Elder, whose rise may have resulted from his marriage to Richildis, a cousin of the Rorgonids. Finally, the county of Vendôme was administered by Viscount Burchard I, father of Burchard the Venerable and progenitor of the emerging local dynasty.

King Odo

A member of the great nobility, the Robertine Odo was promoted to the kingship by his peers. As king, he faced the same grinding problems that had dogged the successors of Charles the Bald, without the benefit of the dynastic prestige of the Carolingians. Nevertheless, he followed the best Carolingian traditions. He arranged to be anointed king at Compiègne, and then assumed control of the existing administration. Odo began his reign energetically, and his success against the Northmen permitted him to rally many hesitant supporters, at least in the north of the kingdom. Yet the thirty-five charters known to have been issued by Odo between his accession and 893 authorize for the most part various limitations or alienations of royal prerogatives. They demonstrate that the king's writ was valued as far off as Catalonia, but that his position required him to make numerous concessions. Although he journeyed across his kingdom to garner support, Odo could do little against his powerful opponents south of the Loire. Thus William the Pious barred Odo from installing his brother Robert in Poitou, thereby upholding the interests of the young Ebalus Manzer, son of Ramnulf II. Likewise, Richard the Justiciar obstructed all royal activity in Burgundy. North of the Loire, Odo still possessed numerous supporters, palaces, and royal estates, but he had to contend with the expansionist opportunism of Baldwin of Flanders as well as the constant political scheming of Archbishop Fulk of Reims. In 893, Charles the Simple, the youngest son of Louis the Stammerer, came into his fourteenth year, and while Odo was occupied in Aquitaine, Fulk brazenly seized his chance to anoint and crown the young Carolingian in Reims. War ensued between the rival claimants to the throne. Although Charles the Simple and his partisans gained the support of his Carolingian cousin,

Arnulf of Germany, Odo prevailed militarily. In exchange for renouncing his royal title, Charles was allowed to hold the town of Laon. Nevertheless, Odo recognized the powerful allure of the Carolingian cause and wisely provided that upon his own death Charles the Simple should be elected to the kingship. Thus, in early 898, the Carolingian dynasty returned to the throne of western Francia.

3. Territorial Organization in the First Half of the Tenth Century

Whether or not they descended from the Carolingian family, the kings who came to share control of the former empire did not forget the political aims of their predecessors. Of course, Arnulf of Germany considered his position a privileged one with respect to his fellow rulers. It was he who had recognized the election of Odo, and then supported Charles the Simple. He had likewise thwarted the effort of Rudolph I to become king of Lotharingia, and finally arranged for his own coronation as emperor. Yet the overarching unity of the former empire was broken. Now, regional efforts at integration came into play, and in general they would prove quite successful.

The Restoration of the Italian Kingdom: The Reign of Hugh of Provence (924–947)

After the assassination of Berengar in 924, the Italian nobility refused to recognize Rudolph II of Upper Burgundy as their king. Instead, they opted for Hugh of Arles, the leading figure in Provence and a relative of the Carolingians (see Table 2). At forty years of age, Hugh cut the figure of a brave, educated, and capable ruler, and a noble assembly at Pavia elected him unanimously to the kingship. Over the next two decades, the new ruler would attempt, ultimately unsuccessfully, to restore royal authority in Italy.

KING HUGH

Hugh found the organs of central government disorganized, his treasury empty, and the royal estates and infrastructure dilapidated. Lately ravaged by the Magyars, Pavia still bore the wounds of disaster. Hugh soon arranged to reconstruct and refortify the town, and meanwhile reorganized the royal administration, including its notarial offices and palace tribunal, as well as the royal household and treasury. To curb the prodigality allowed by his predecessors, the new king sought to distinguish his personal lands and belongings from the patrimony of the crown. He likewise departed from recent habit by restricting the transfer of privileges to the bishops and the conferral of domains on the lay nobility. Assemblies and synods became more usual and were convoked, for instance, to coordinate defenses against the Magyars and to recognize the association of Hugh's son Lothar to the royal office. Outside his kingdom, Hugh moved to restore commercial ties with the east, and in 927 an accord was concluded at Venice allowing Pavia to serve as a distribution point for wares imported from the Orient. Hugh also dispatched an embassy to the Byzantine Emperor Romanus I Lecapenus (920–944) led by the colorful memorialist Liutprand of Cremona.

HUGH AND ROME

Hugh's election as king came as welcome news to Pope John X. In February 915, the pope had crowned Berengar emperor in the hope of receiving military aid, but revolt in northern Italy had soon frustrated this prospect. Yet with Byzantine cooperation and help from Adalbert II of Tuscany and Alberic, duke of Spoleto, John X had managed in 916 to dislodge a force of Arab invaders based along the Garigliano River. In Rome, however, John X was dominated by Theophylact, "the Senator," and his powerful family. Theophylact held the offices of *vestiarius* ("keeper of the wardrobe") and *magister militum* (master of soldiers), and as such controlled the treasury and army of the pope. He was seconded by his wife, Theodora, who had played an important role in securing the papal election of John X. After the victory of 916, Theophylact arranged a marriage between his daughter Marozia and Alberic the Elder, duke of Spoleto since 898 and a proven soldier. Until Alberic's death in 925, the couple dominated Rome, but then John X quickly seized his chance to trammel the overbearing Marozia. In 925 he traveled to Mantua to explain his situation to Hugh of Arles. Marozia promptly reacted by contracting a new marriage with Guido of Tuscany, a half-brother of Hugh of Arles by the second marriage of his mother, Bertha, to Adalbert II of Tuscany (see Table 2). For their part, Guido and Marozia soon resolved to eliminate John X. They kidnapped the pope and imprisoned him in the Castel Sant'Angelo, where he was smothered under a cushion in 928. Three years later, after two interim pontificates, Marozia arranged for the election of her own son, a child of her prior liaison with Pope Sergius III (904–911), as Pope John XI.

Marozia now reigned as mistress of the papal palace and aspired to dominate the rest of Italy. Her aims thus coincided with those of Hugh of Arles. The death of Guido of Tuscany in 929 allowed Marozia to negotiate a marriage with the widower Hugh, a prospect no doubt sweetened by the hope of receiving the imperial crown. Pope John XI presided over the marriage in 932, but the celebrations were soon troubled by Alberic the Younger, son and namesake of Marozia's second husband. The eighteen-year-old led a popular uprising against the "foreigners," during which Alberic managed to imprison both Marozia and John XI, while Hugh of Arles fled. This stunning coup opened the reign of Alberic, "glorious prince and senator of all the Romans." Until his death in 954, Rome enjoyed a period of comparative order and decency.

HUGH AND THE NOBILITY OF NORTHERN ITALY
After his disgrace in 932, Hugh of Arles fell prey to ever greater difficulties. He endeavored to combat the Magyar raiders as well as the Arab forces that now partly controlled access to the Alps from a base at Fraxinetum, near Draguignan in Provence. Hugh requested the help of the Byzantine fleet of Romanus Lecapenus. To guarantee his freedom of action in Italy, he concluded a curious treaty with Rudolph II of Upper Burgundy whereby he ceded to Rudolph the Provençal lands belonging to Charles Constantine, the son and successor of Louis the Blind. After a failed conspiracy against him led by northerners, notably Ratherius of Liège, for a time bishop of Verona, Hugh made a wholesale distribution of "honors" and benefices to more trustworthy Provençal followers. His nephew Manasses, formerly archbishop of Arles, became master of the bishoprics of Trent, Verona, and Mantua, thereby creating the "March of Trent." Hugh's own numerous sons and bastards by some nine wives and concubines also figured among the new crop of vassals and administrators. One, for instance, became archbishop of Milan, another, abbot of Nonatola, and still another, marquis of Tuscany. One chronicler was led to remark: "Italians have been deprived of all offices." Nevertheless, Hugh lost all hope of taking control of Rome and the papal domains, even though he managed in 942 to conclude an accord with Alberic, who afterward became his son-in-law.

One of the indigenous aristocrats most threatened by Hugh's regime was the marquis of Ivrea, Berengar, the grandson and namesake of Emperor Berengar I. Although he had married a daughter of King Hugh, Berengar took refuge at the court of the king of Germany in 941, whence he continued to maintain contact with other discontented Italian nobles. In 945 he descended into northern Italy along the valley of the Adige River and managed to rally considerable noble support by promising a redistribution of bishoprics and counties. Faced with this crumbling of his support, Hugh fled back to Provence, abandoning his Italian crown to his son Lothar. Berengar soon took up residence in Pavia, where he commenced his "reign" by ruling in the name of Hugh and his son.

Such was the triumph of the Italian aristocracy. Hugh of Arles had failed to restore royal authority. He had also aroused the bitter hatred of the indigenous nobility by imposing members of his own family across northern Italy. Although this policy had worked in the ninth century, it now foundered because noble power no longer rested exclusively in the hands of the great foreign families. Local clans, like the Supponids and a host of others, had waxed powerful as masters of their own castles, which they now controlled largely free of interference from the great families. Nevertheless, Hugh played the remarkable role of a foreign prince who managed to reign in Italy for twenty years. Without intending to do so, he thus prepared for the coming of Otto I.

The Restoration of the Monarchy in Germany: Henry of Saxony, Heir to the Carolingians

The Accession of Henry I

As he edged toward death in 918 following a campaign against Arnulf of Bavaria, Conrad I of Germany asked his brother Eberhard to make peace with Henry of Saxony and to offer him the insignia of royal power. Henry accepted Eberhard's proposals, and was elected king in his palace at Fritzlar by the nobles of Franconia and Saxony. The strongest of the German princes, Henry controlled numerous estates, palaces, and market centers involved in trade with Scandinavia. He also enjoyed a steady flow of income from the mining of silver in southern Saxony. Only loosely connected with the Carolingians through an aunt who had married Zwentibold of Lotharingia (see Table 3), Henry espoused many principles of Carolingian government. Some historians have emphasized his refusal to be anointed by the archbishop of Mainz, and concluded a conscious effort on Henry's part to avoid the appearance of holding power through an episcopal gesture. Others, however, have accepted the explanation given by the Widukind of Korvei that the king refused out of humility, and they have also noted that royal unction held less importance for the eastern Franks than was the case in western Francia.

HENRY AND THE REGIONAL LEADERS

Once proclaimed king, Henry wielded sufficient power to ensure his recognition as such by the various regional dukes, although he continued to allow them considerable independence. After reluctantly accepting Henry's election at Fritzlar, Eberhard, brother of the deceased Conrad I, had to be subdued by arms before his position in Franconia was reconfirmed. Burchard II of Swabia likewise required military intimidation before submitting. After his death in 826, Burchard's realm was conferred on a relative of Eberhard who married the widowed duchess of Swabia. The population of the duchy nevertheless perceived their new ruler as a foreign tool of the German king. In Bavaria Duke Arnulf seems to have hoped to avoid submitting and aspired to become king himself. He too eventually yielded, and Henry allowed him the privilege of continuing to name the bishops of Bavaria. The troubles of the kings of western Francia soon permitted the German ruler to reclaim control of Lotharingia. Henry considered this region and Saxony as essential to restoring royal power in Germany. Not only was Lotharingia home to the palace at Aachen, but thanks to the commercial axes formed by the Rhine and the Meuse the region supported great towns and ecclesiastical centers of culture. Henry I valued the former kingdom of Lothar II as the richest and most developed in the west.

THE DANES AND THE SLAVS

Having gained the respect of the dukes, Henry could concentrate on defending Germany against its enemies to the north, south, and east. He reoccupied the Danish March once controlled by Charlemagne and forced Knuba, head of the commercial settlement at Haithabu, to recognize his authority in 934. Again like Charlemagne, Henry halted Slavic raids into Saxony from across the Elbe. During the winter of 928/929, his army advanced across frozen marshes along the Havel River and vanquished the Wilzi, the nearest of the Slavic tribes. The German force then proceeded to transform the tribe's fortified camp at Brennabur into a citadel later known as Brandenburg. Henry completed this first episode of Saxony's *Drang nach Osten* (push to the east) by capturing the fortress at Lenzen and building a military outpost farther south on the Elbe at Meissen. Two Saxon counts, Bernard and Thietmar, were made *Grenzgrafen* (frontier counts) charged with administering the new and still restive Slavic inhabitants of the German kingdom.

Still further south, Henry also intervened in Bohemia which had been sheltered from the Magyar invasions by its mountainous terrain. Czech leaders had partitioned and defended the former Moravian state; chief among them was Boris Boj, a forerunner of the Premyslid dynasty who had been converted to Christianity by a disciple of Archbishop Methodios. Meanwhile, Bavarian missionaries had provided for the ecclesiastical organization of Bohemia, dedicating the first church in Prague to Saint Emmeram of Regensburg. In 928 the grandson of Boris Boj, Duke Vaclav, better known as Wenceslaus, was besieged by Henry's army at Prague and forced to submit. Shortly thereafter, the Saxon king presented the duke with relics from the abbey of Korvei, and these were enshrined in Prague's church in the hope that they would ward off Bavarian clerical influence.

VICTORY OVER THE MAGYARS

Although the Magyars spared Bohemia, they had continued to wreak havoc and exact tribute across southern and middle Germany. To counter this threat, Henry fortified abbeys and noble residences, constructing citadels at Merseburg, Quedlinburg, Gandersheim, Korvei, and Goslar. North of Goslar in the Harz Mountains, he also built a palace at Werla ringed by two circular ramparts which withstood the Magyar onslaughts of 924. Moreover, the king organized a new system of defenses based on levies of what Widukind of Korvei calls *milites agrarii* (farmer-soldiers). These were not peasant militiamen, but rather troops drafted from rural estates and used to garrison the new strongholds; they were the ancestors the *ministeriales*, a class of bonded nobles characteristic of medieval German society. Henry also drew his recruits among Saxon peasants accustomed to warfare with the Slavs and even among convicted criminals, who were given the choice of punishment or military service. Finally, Henry encouraged the regional dukes to follow the example of fortress building he set in Saxony and Thuringia.

Once he felt capable of victory, Henry convoked an assembly at Erfurt in 933 where he obliged the lay and ecclesiastical magnates to agree to wage all-out war. According to a largely apocryphal tradition, he is then supposed to have forwarded the Magyars tribute consisting of a dog whose ears and tail had been clipped off. Henry's efforts were crowned with success when the Magyars were defeated in 933 along the Unstrut River at Riade. This event had great repercussions across Germany, and at

Reims in western Francia, the historian Flodoard noted it in his chronicle. Widukind of Korvei reports, moreover, that on the evening of his victory, the army proclaimed Henry "father of his country, supreme lord and emperor." This phrase has prompted much discussion, but it amply reflects the king's prestige. Henry had been acclaimed by his troops after the fashion of a victorious *imperator*.

UPPER BURGUNDY AND ITALY

While Henry reasserted royal power within Germany and led the struggle against the Magyars, he also intervened in the Kingdom of Upper Burgundy. In 926, he profited from the death of Burchard II of Swabia to open contacts with the ex-duke's son-in-law, King Rudolph II of Upper Burgundy. Henry acknowledged the lesser king's dominion over the lands between the Aar and Rhine rivers and in the county of Basel, but in return he required the surrender of the "Holy Lance." This signal relic of the Passion was revered as a symbol of the Burgundian kingship; a copy of it fashioned in the eleventh century is today preserved in Vienna. According to Liutprand of Cremona, "Rudolph surrendered himself to Henry by this act of transfer." Their alliance resembled an act of vassalage, and its effect was to guarantee Rudolph II against the scheming of Ralph, the West Frankish king who was about to gain control of Lyon and Vienne in northern Provence.

The nature of Henry's interest and intentions in Italy remains somewhat unclear. According to Widukind, "when all the neighboring peoples had been conquered, the king wanted to go to Rome." It is difficult to believe that Henry would have considered an expedition against Rome, which was then firmly in the hands of the "senator" Alberic, yet he must at least have envisaged a pilgrimage to the tombs of the Apostles. It is, of course, possible that he intended to intervene in the northern Italian lands ruled by Hugh of Arles, which had once attracted the interest of King Arnulf.

THE CLOSE OF HENRY'S REIGN

Henry still needed to provide for his own succession. He wisely rejected the prospect of partitioning his kingdom among his three sons, and instead he designated Otto for election by the magnates. In 936 Otto thus succeeded his father, elected by "hereditary right" according to the *Annals of Quedlinburg*. The new king's accession marked the end of the ruler whom Widukind called "the greatest of the kings of Europe." Although some nationalist historians have sought to claim Henry as the creator of German nationhood, Germany as a nation or a state did not yet exist. The reign of Henry I should in fact be viewed as a prolongation of the broader Carolingian tradition. Otto I would build on his father's achievements. Regarded by many as a "new Charlemagne," he would also be called Otto "the Great."

The Carolingian Restoration in Western Francia

THE EARLY REIGN OF CHARLES THE SIMPLE (898–911)

In 898, the strength of the pro-Carolingian faction had obliged Odo of Paris to name as his successor Charles III, the youngest son of Louis the Stammerer. Unwittingly, chroniclers have discredited this Charles by giving him the epithet *simplex*, "the Simple," although the term itself is properly understood as meaning "without guile." At twenty years of age, the new king was munificent, pious, educated, and highly conscious of his position as heir to an illustrious dynastic tradition. In the hundred-odd charters that survive from his reign, Charles made ample reference to his forebears, but he also acknowledged the power that now lay with the rulers of Burgundy, Aquitaine and Flanders, who also became royal vassals. Charles wisely chose to confer on Robert, brother of the deceased King Odo, the counties and abbeys that lay between the Seine and the Loire. Without going so far as to call Robert a sort of mayor of the palace, we should note that his power and influence were considerable.

From the start of his reign, Charles aspired to reassert royal authority in Aquitaine, and more especially in its southernmost reaches and in Catalonia. In a charter of 898 issued to a certain Theodosius from the retinue of Count Robert, Charles claimed the title "king of Gothia" and conferred royal estates in the counties of Narbonne, Roussillon, and Besalú. In another charter of 915 issued for the bishop of Elne, he titled himself "king of the Franks and the Goths." On various occasions the king acted to confirm holdings and rights formerly granted by Odo. He also conceded his "vassal" Wilfred Borell rights over taxation and minting in the district of Vich, and even intervened in the nomination of Guido of Gerona as bishop, later delivering royal commands at the churchman's request. Of course these abundant charters often merely served to legitimate the usurpations by the magnates of Catalonia, but by such confirmations the king gained recognition for his authority in this far-off region. In the rest of

Aquitaine, the king usually responded favorably to the requests of church-men who sought to limit the virtual omnipotence of William the Pious, though the duke himself professed loyalty to the Carolingians until his death in 918.

In Burgundy, Richard the Justiciar likewise proved faithful until his death in 921. On several occasions he resided at the court of King Charles, and he obtained several charters in favor of counts under his own control. To be sure, the king was acknowledged as sovereign of Aquitaine and Burgundy more in theory than in fact. But Charles accepted this situation, which guaranteed the political stability of his realm, or rather "empire," to use the term employed by the king.

North of the Loire, Charles possessed effective authority, as is amply demonstrated by his charters. The king controlled counties, royal estates, and the various palaces where he resided. He enjoyed the support of the clergy, above all of Fulk of Reims, who possessed the power and reputa-tion of a veritable prince-bishop. Archbishop Fulk had played a vital role in restoring the Carolingian king, and he proved himself a worthy successor of Hincmar of Reims. He maintained tight control over his metropolitan province, commanded the respect of his suffragans, restored the schools at Reims, and tirelessly defended his ecclesiastical property and possessions. His power was so great that Baldwin II of Flanders resorted to murder to eliminate him in 900. Herveus (900–922) succeeded Fulk as archbishop, and continued his policies. In 909 he convened the Synod of Trosly to initiate a reform of the secular and monastic clergy and, according to Flo-doard of Reims, "to reestablish order in the Kingdom of the Franks." Farther west, Charles the Simple allowed Robert to control the "duchy of Neustria." To assure himself of supporters in other regions, the king had to provide benefices by alienating royal property and abbacies, to the det-riment of his own material strength. Nevertheless, Charles managed to consolidate his position thanks to two daring moves: he allowed Viking colonies to settle along the lower Seine, and he annexed Lotharingia.

Two achievements of Charles the Simple

Charles and the Northmen
Despite occasional defeats, bands of Northmen had continued to ravage areas across Francia with regularity, and for contemporaries, there seemed to be no ready solution to this ongoing catastrophe. In 900 Charles the Simple called together Duke Robert, Richard the Justiciar, and the count

of Vermandois to organize the struggle against the invaders, but no serious moves resulted from this gathering. In 910 the Norman chieftain Rollo was defeated near Auxerre, and retired westward across the kingdom to attack Chartres. The bishop of Chartres appealed urgently for help to Robert, Richard, and Count Ebalus of Poitiers. At this point King Charles, spurred by the archbishops of Reims and Rouen, proposed the idea of settling Rollo and his warriors near Rouen. It was not the first attempt by a Carolingian to fix Vikings in a given district of the empire. Louis the Pious and his successors had also resorted to such a policy near Dorestad, on the island of Walcheren, and along the lower valley of the Weser. Likewise, Charles the Fat had accepted the settlement of Godofrid in Frisia in 882, although the traitorous Danish king was later slain by Count Henry of Babenberg. Finally, Alfred the Great of Wessex had consented to the settlement of Vikings in a region known as the Danelaw, north of a line between the Thames estuary and Chester. These precedents no doubt influenced the decision of Charles the Simple. In the summer of 911, the Carolingian king met with Rollo at St. Clair-sur-Epte, and there in exchange for Baptism and a promise of fealty, the Viking leader received a territory bounded by the English Channel and the rivers Epte, Eure, and Dive—the nucleus of the future Duchy of Normandy. Yet contrary to a common misconception, Rollo did not become a "duke." Contemporary texts refer to him rather as "count of the Normans," which is to say that he became the king's officer and representative across the maritime region of "Normandy."

The establishment of this Norman territory was of immense importance for the history of France and the rest of Europe. It seems that Rollo opted to maintain and develop Carolingian institutions. This is the view espoused by Lucien Musset: "We can readily believe that the Normans reactivated still functional Carolingian machinery in the county of Rouen and other nearby districts (*pagi*), since they later introduced this system—adapted and perfected—in the other regions that they conquered." In the *pagi* entrusted to him, Rollo administered the royal estates, the abbeys, and the bishoprics, and he also controlled the lesser agents of royal power. Later the counts of Rouen endeavored to expand their territory westward so as to include the Bessin region and the Cotentin peninsula, later known as Lower Normandy. These were areas where the Carolingian rulers had exercised little influence and where Scandinavian contributions would be appreciable. The Northmen led by Rollo thus settled down as Normans. With difficulty, they accepted Christianity, thanks to the efforts of the archbishops of Rouen and Reims. Although these new settlers gradually lost their original tongue, it faded only after conferring a host of new placenames on the locales and geography of the region.

Despite its success, the agreement concluded at St. Clair-sur-Epte did not put an end to other Viking raids. Other bands continued to pillage the lower Loire valley, and Brittany was invaded in 918. Yet Charles the Simple secured his prime goal of safeguarding northern "France" from attack. He also acquired new followers in Rollo and his men, and this itself was a source of considerable prestige.

Charles and Lotharingia

It has often been said that Charles the Simple sought to compensate for losses in the west of his kingdom by embarking on a policy of eastern expansion. Yet it is misleading to depend overly on the coincidence of certain dates. Well before 911 Charles dreamed of regaining control of Lotharingia, a territory that he considered his by "hereditary right." In 898, he had entered into negotiations with Reginar I, the leader of the Lotharingian nobility. Through his mother, a daughter of Lothar I, Reginar was himself descended from the Carolingians. Along with the abbacies of Echternach, Stavelot, and St. Servatius of Maastricht, he possessed a vast landed patrimony in the Ardennes, in Hainaut, and in Brabant. Reginar considered himself the leader of Lotharingia, and as such had marshaled resistance to the authoritarian policies of Zwentibold, installed over Lotharingia in 895 by his father, Arnulf of Germany. The indigenous nobility had quickly learned to hate their bastard king for his violence, rapine, and extortions. Himself driven to exile in western Francia, Reginar petitioned the newly elected Charles the Simple to occupy Aachen and Nijmegen. But the death of Arnulf in 899 prompted other Lotharingian nobles to rally behind the dead king's legitimate heir, Louis the Child, in the hope that they could thereby maintain their autonomy. Charles the Simple bent to these circumstances, but continued to monitor events in Lotharingia. In 907 he even chose to marry Frederuna, the daughter of a Lotharingian noble. When Louis the Child died four years later, the nobles of Germany agreed to elect as king Conrad I, a man detested in Lotharingia. Again, Reginar invited Charles to come east, and in 911 the Carolingian became king of Lotharingia. After this date Charles the Simple amplified his title of *rex*, "king," to *rex Francorum*, "king of the Franks," thereby asserting that he was king of all the Franks. Charles frequently resided at Herstal, Aachen, Metz, and Gondreville, near Toul. He issued some twenty charters for his new realm. Upon the death of Reginar I in 915, he confirmed the transfer of the count's "honors" to his son Gilbert and also awarded him the title of marquis. Gilbert, however, aspired to royalty, and he secured support for his enterprise by distributing sequestered church property. In 920 Gilbert's followers proclaimed him "prince" (*princeps*) of Lotharingia.

In nearby Germany the Saxon Henry I had reigned since the preceding year. He too longed to control Lotharingia to reinforce his position and garner additional resources. But he did not dare to challenge openly the position of Charles the Simple. Henry met with the Carolingian king on a barge anchored in the Rhine at Bonn, and there agreed to maintain the status quo. Henry was king of the East Franks; Charles, king of the West Franks.

The Revolt of the Nobility

The Lotharingian policies of Charles the Simple exasperated the nobles of "France" and provoked the king's fall. To protest against his favors to the Lotharingian count Hagano, the nobles led by Duke Robert seized Charles in 920. After Archbishop Herveus of Reims negotiated his release, the king aspired to maintain himself with the help of his Lotharingian followers. In 922 revolt flared up again, and Charles fled across the Meuse to Lotharingia. The rebels then elected Robert to the kingship, and arranged for him to be anointed by Walter, the archbishop of Sens who had also anointed King Odo in 888. The ensuing war turned to the advantage of Charles, and on 15 June 923 Robert was killed in battle at Soissons. Nevertheless, the magnates were unwilling to take back the Carolingian king. After Robert's son Hugh—the future Hugh the Great—refused the crown, the nobles turned to the willing Ralph of Burgundy, Robert's son-in-law. Nevertheless, Charles still hoped to regain his position. He counted on the support of Henry I, and also turned for help to his cousin Herbert II of Vermandois. But his trust was misplaced. Herbert traitorously seized and imprisoned Charles in the citadel at St. Quentin.

Imprisonment

Historians have sought by various means to explain this criminal kidnapping. Herbert II, son of the Herbert assassinated in 900 on the orders of Baldwin II of Flanders, was descended from the blinded King Bernard of Italy (see Table 8), and perhaps the count hoped to avenge his great-grandfather by seizing the Carolingian king? But however strong the notion of *faida*, or "feud," may have been among Germanic peoples, vengeance alone cannot explain the count's behavior. Above all, Herbert was driven by his own immense ambition. Starting from his base in Vermandois, he aspired to carve out a princedom comparable to those of other leaders, as is proved by his subsequent history. By imprisoning Charles, Herbert held a prestigious hostage with whom he could threaten the position of King Ralph at will. Nevertheless, Herbert could not prevent Queen Eadgifu from taking refuge with her father, Edward I, king of Wessex. Married to the widowed Charles about 920, Eadgifu had borne him a son, and this child—the future Louis IV—returned with her to England. Similarly, no threats were made against the king's four daughters by Frederuna or his other illegitimate offspring.

The imprisonment of Charles the Simple had repercussions among the other leaders of the west. In Rome, Pope John X raised protests and threatened Herbert of Vermandois with excommunication. The rulers of southern Gaul refused to recognize King Ralph, and used their adherence to the Carolingian cause as a means to greater autonomy. In the north, the raiders likewise took advantage of the king's captivity. Rognvald, chief of the Vikings established along the lower Loire, mounted expeditions across the kingdom, while Count Rollo of Rouen revolted. Expected to help Charles the Simple, the fickle nobility of Lotharingia rallied instead behind King Ralph, until Henry I finally forced them to acknowledge himself as their sovereign. The marquis of Neustria, Hugh the Great, apparently did nothing to assist Charles, but did help Ralph to combat the various Norman threats. Meanwhile, Herbert of Vermandois exploited his trump magnificently. He gained the support of Seulfus (922–925), the new archbishop of Reims, and prosecuted his expansionist aims. In 927 Herbert brought Charles out of his confinement to negotiate a rapprochement with Count Rollo and to intimidate Ralph. But Charles would nonetheless finish his days in 929 a prisoner of the citadel at Péronne.

Thus ended a reign that had begun brilliantly. Frequently underrated for what he did achieve, Charles the Simple possessed too few resources in land and men to oppose the great feudal magnates. His attachment to past Carolingian policies and his drive to regain the old family heartland that lay within Lotharingia brought Charles the Simple to disaster and failure.

RALPH OF BURGUNDY (923–936)

Ralph of Burgundy, son of Richard the Justiciar, was indirectly connected to the Carolingians through his uncle, Boso of Provence. By defending the interests of his Burgundian domains, Ralph perforce adopted the aggressive policies of his father. Yet it was quite another matter to balance the joint roles of marquis and king. By asserting royal power against regional control, Ralph worked at cross-purposes with himself. Nevertheless, this vital and courageous leader did not hesitate to act on all fronts, sometimes to his own cost. He had to struggle against Herbert of Vermandois, the Normans, and the Magyars, while he sought to impose his authority in the south.

Conflict with Herbert II

It would be tiresome to rehearse all the episodes in the struggle between Ralph and Herbert of Vermandois; it suffices to trace the principal phases of their conflict. Herbert sought by whatever means available to expand his domains and authority, and he aimed specifically to lay hold of the two royal strongholds of Reims and Laon. In 925 he profited from the death of Archbishop Seulfus of Reims to have his own five-year-old son Hugh elected to the post. Thus, he gained control of the immense domains belonging to the see and received homage from the vassals of the archbishop. Three years later, Herbert captured Laon despite a vigorous defense led by Ralph's wife, Queen Emma. The king himself then counterattacked with help from Hugh, the young marquis of Neustria, who rejected Herbert's ambitious dealings and even allowed the king to control his own counties between the Seine and the Loire. In 931, Ralph took back Reims and installed the monk Artoldus as archbishop. With the acquired momentum, the king then captured Laon and the abbey of St. Médard of Soissons. Thanks to the mediation of Henry I of Germany, Ralph was reconciled with Herbert in 935 and allowed him to retain much of what he controlled. Although the king was not able to destroy Herbert's princedom entirely, Ralph managed to retain the two most important centers in northern France: Reims and Laon.

Elsewhere in the Kingdom

Ralph waged a considerable struggle against the Northmen, those of the lower Loire valley led by Rognvald and the Normans of the lower Seine, who had rebelled under Count Rollo in response to the imprisonment of Charles the Simple. After pillaging Burgundy, Rognvald was defeated in 925, while the Normans of the Seine agreed, after suffering setbacks, to halt their raids in exchange for a payment of tribute. Although Rollo himself declined to acknowledge Ralph as king, the count's successor, William I, "Longsword," agreed to do homage in 933 in return for control over the Cotentin peninsula and the region of Avranches, lands already long outside the range of Carolingian power.

The southern rulers still faithful to the Carolingians gradually came to recognize the new king. William II of Auvergne, the nephew and heir of William the Pious, pledged fealty to Ralph in 924. Thus, contemporary charters issued by the lords of Déols, Le Puy, Brioude, and Tulle are dated according to the reign of Ralph. In 932 Raymond Pons, count of Toulouse, and the Gascon leader Lupus Aznar likewise agreed to acknowledge Ralph as king. Only the counts of Catalonia refused, continuing to date their official documents according to the reign of Charles the Simple. Nevertheless, Ralph was so encouraged by the general rally of the southern nobles that his charters sometimes title him as "king of the Franks, Aquitainians, and Burgundians."

In his "kingdom" of Burgundy, Ralph controlled a large patrimony and managed to neutralize lesser nobles with comparative ease. In 924, he convened assemblies at Autun and Chalon, and finally secured the submission of his most powerful feudal rival, the restive Gilbert, count of Chalon.

Farther south, Ralph used his status as a nephew of Boso of Provence to intervene in the kingdom of Louis the Blind. Hugh of Arles, who ruled Provence on behalf of the blind king, did homage to Ralph and married his niece to the northern king's brother. After the death of Louis the Blind in 928, Ralph journeyed to Vienne on three occasions, and received the homage of his cousin Charles Constantine, who succeeded his blind father as count of Vienne. Thus the counties of Vienne, Lyon, and Viviers, which had evaded West Frankish control since the Treaty of Verdun, now came under the authority of King Ralph. Here was a further example of the politics of expansion and consolidation characteristic of the Carolingians and their successors.

In Lotharingia, however, Ralph enjoyed less success owing to the efforts of Henry I. Ralph's brother Boso held the abbacies of Moyenmoutier and Remiremont as well as several castles along the Meuse, and the nobles of Lotharingia had eventually recognized the new king of western Francia and even tolerated his intervention in Alsace. But ever desirous of acquiring Lotharingia, Henry I managed to browbeat its nobles into recognizing him as king, marrying his daughter Gerberga to Count Gilbert, son of Reginar I. Finally, during a conference between Henry and Ralph in 935, Boso himself acknowledged the German king as his sovereign. Lotharingia had once again passed to the king of eastern Francia.

A year later, in 936, both kings died. Historians have amply demonstrated that Henry fared much better than Ralph in his efforts to shore up royal power against local and regional encroachment. Yet with due regard for the differing political circumstances of each kingdom, it is equally clear that Ralph enjoyed appreciable success. He managed to withstand the ambitions of powerful northern rivals, to gain recognition in the south, and to expand his influence into Provence. It has recently been shown that he also minted coins in his own name. His charters also occasionally echo the venerable epithets used by his predecessors: "pious, unconquered and ever august." Like his contemporary Henry, Ralph consciously followed the political example of the Carolingians. Subsequent history would show how potent this inspiration continued to be for the deeds and imaginations of European princes.

4. The Carolingian Restoration (936 to the Close of the Tenth Century)

In 936 a historical chance arranged for both the restoration of the Carolingian house and the accession of Otto the Great, the "new Charlemagne." For a half century longer the old dynasty reigned in "France," while Otto's Saxon dynasty controlled "Germany," annexed Italy, and finally reestablished the empire in 962. This last pivotal event bulks large in the history of the tenth century, for it allowed the coalescence of a new European unity. The princedoms born of the collapse of the Carolingian empire came together under a new common authority, just as Ottonians and Carolingians were joined by family ties. Meanwhile, Christendom gained new lands and believers in the east, and monastic life was reformed in the midst of a cultural and artistic renaissance. The tenth century was not a renewed "dark ages" as some historians once claimed, but rather the final development of Carolingian Europe.

The Return of the Carolingians and the First Years of Otto I

Louis IV
King Ralph died without leaving a direct heir. His brother Hugh the Black laid no claim on the royal succession, content to rule his "kingdom" of Burgundy. North of the Loire there remained a small constellation of other viable candidates: Herbert II of Vermandois and Arnulf of Flanders, both Carolingian scions, as well as William I, count of Rouen since 933, and Hugh the Great, brother-in-law of the deceased king. But it was Hugh the Great who successfully pressed for the restoration of the Carolingians and entered into negotiations with King Ethelstan of Wessex for the return of Louis IV, the exiled son of Charles the Simple. At the time, Ethelstan was the most powerful ruler in the west. After coming to the throne in 924, he had begun the reconquest of the Danelaw that Alfred the Great had conceded to Scandinavian settlers, and soon Ethelstan used the title *rex totius Britanniae*, "king of all Britain," and even *imperator*.

He had also received the Breton chieftains forced to flee the Armorican peninsula by the Vikings, and his sister Edith had married Otto, son of Henry I of Germany. Ethelstan agreed to entrust his nephew to the care of Hugh's emissaries after they solemnly promised to keep faith with the young king.

Many historians have commented on the initiative of Hugh the Great. Although the contemporary Flodoard of Reims merely sets down the facts, Richer (d. 998) later reported that Hugh sought to make amends for the crimes of lèse-majesté suffered by Charles the Simple and that he hoped to restore general concord by reestablishing the legitimate dynasty. Many historians have rejected this interpretation, noting that Hugh himself did not hesitate later to betray the Carolingian king. Because human actions and feelings are prone to fluctuate, it is quite possible that Hugh's initial intentions were upright and sincere. In any case, Hugh surely always intended to guide the young king closely, retaining effective leadership in the kingdom for himself.

Louis IV, nicknamed *ultramarinus* or *d'Outremer* ("from overseas"), landed near Boulogne, and there received the homage of Hugh and nearly all the leading nobles. He was then led to Laon, where Archbishop Artoldus of Reims anointed him king. This return to the hereditary dynasty marked the beginning of a new succession of Carolingian rulers lasting for a half-century. Louis IV reigned from 936 to 954, followed by his son Lothar IV until 986. Although Lothar had his own son anointed in 979, the accidental death of Louis V in 987 marked the definitive end of the Carolingian dynasty.

In general, historians have handled the last Carolingian rulers quite roughly. Nevertheless, they lacked neither courage nor tenacity. Their chancery issued charters—some hundred odd survive today—in the best tradition of their forebears; the seals and monograms of the later Carolingians recall those of the ninth-century rulers. The kings of "France" were conscious of the fact that they were the lone representatives of their illustrious family in the west. In Germany, princes of a more recent dynasty sought in their own way to revive the Carolingian ideals of greatness, unity, and cultural renewal.

THE FIRST YEARS OF OTTO I

Henry I of Germany had three sons by his wife, Matilda: Otto, Henry, and Bruno. Shortly before his death, the king designated Otto as his successor and had him recognized as such by "the Franks and the Saxons."

The Coronation

At the time Otto was 24 years old. He cut an impressive figure with his tall stature, red beard, and athletic build. Shortly after his father had died Otto made a decision that betokened his conviction that he was the "king of the Franks" and successor of Charlemagne. He arranged for his coronation at Aachen, the Lotharingian capital that King Ralph had abandoned to Henry I. Three separate ceremonies were organized. First, in the palace courtyard, the nobles elected the king and pledged their fidelity in accord with ancient custom. Then, inside the chapel, the archbishop of Mainz led the acclamation of the new king by the assembled laity and clergy; he vested Otto by placing the royal insignia over his Frankish garb: the sword, the ceremonial belt and armband, and finally the scepter and crown; then he anointed him and installed him on the marble throne of Charlemagne situated in the upper gallery of the church. Finally, in the palace there followed an official banquet during which the dukes of Lotharingia, Franconia, Swabia, and Bavaria served at the table of the king. This remarkable program was not improvised, but carefully planned by the young king, who no doubt sought to reclaim the Frankish past and perhaps already dreamed of restoring the empire. When the archbishop handed the king his sword, he proclaimed:

> Receive this sword to repulse the adversaries of Christ, the barbarians and evil Christians, as a symbol of the divine authority that is conferred on you and of your power over the empire of the Franks for the abiding peace of Christendom.

The entire program of the Ottonian rulers was encapsulated in this one sentence.

Intervention in Upper Burgundy

A year after his coronation at Aachen, Otto I took another significant action. As a result of the death in 937 of King Rudolph II, his heir, the child Conrad, stood to become ruler of Upper Burgundy. In 932, Hugh of Arles, king of Italy, had concluded a treaty with Rudolph whereby he abandoned his Provençal possessions to the northern king (see p. 241). Now he aspired to exploit the status of Rudolph's successor as a minor to unite Upper Burgundy with his own Italian kingdom, effectively restoring the realm of Lothar I minus Lotharingia to the north. To this end, Hugh married Bertha, the widow of Rudolph II, and betrothed his daughter Adelaide to the six-year-old Conrad.

Otto I appreciated the dangers posed by the creation of a great fold of territories dominating all passage through the Alps. Harking back to the act whereby Rudolph II had commended himself to Henry I and surrendered the "Holy Lance" (see p. 245), Otto intervened decisively. The young Conrad was brought back to Germany, and Hugh of Arles was forced to return to Italy with his wife and daughter. Upper Burgundy now came under the control of the German king, much as the regions of Vienne and Lyon had entered the orbit of the king of "France" in 931.

Magdeburg

In another highly significant gesture, Otto founded an abbey in Magdeburg, already an important commercial center on the Elbe. Otto fortified the town with walls and established a monastery under the patronage of Saint Maurice, patron of the rulers of Burgundy. On the fringe of the Slavic world, Magdeburg became an important outpost for the training of missionaries destined for new pagan lands.

Thus the orientations of Ottonian policy became evident in the first two years of the reign of Otto I. Aachen and Magdeburg together became centers of gravity for the new king's activity.

The Kings, Their Followers, and Their Subjects

The most urgent problem faced by both Otto I and Louis IV was to ensure recognition of their authority among their subjects and to establish a good rapport with the great nobility.

THE SITUATION IN GERMANY

Otto and the Dukes

Because Henry I had accorded the regional leaders of Germany a measure of autonomy, Otto soon faced rebellion among the nobles who were bent on maintaining this situation. In 937, however, the fearsome Arnulf of Bavaria died and was replaced by his son Eberhard. Otto exploited this situation to reclaim his right to nominate bishops in the region. Eberhard's defiance resulted in his own military defeat; he was exiled and replaced by his uncle, Duke Berthold of Carinthia. In order to tighten his rapport with the local ruling house, Otto arranged for his brother Henry to marry Judith of Bavaria (see Chart 3). In Franconia, Duke Eberhard was convicted of "breaking the peace" by taking vengeance on one of his vassals and forced to pay a huge compensation for his misdeeds. In 938, Thankmar, Otto's half-brother, revolted and met death as a consequence. A year later, Henry, the favorite son of the dowager Queen Matilda, also rebelled, leading in train both Eberhard of Franconia and Gilbert of Lotharingia. We shall see later how Otto mastered the nobles of Lotharingia. Suffice it here to record that Otto quashed his brother and used the death of Eberhard in battle as a pretext for annexing Franconia to his Saxon patrimony. Finally, in 940, the king married his son Liudolf to Ida, daughter of Herman of Swabia, and Liudolf thereby inherited the Swabian duchy. Thus by a series of military ventures and marriages Otto reestablished his authority over the regional princedoms. In various places, he set up palatine counts charged with administering his royal estates and monitoring the dukes, and he also revived annual assemblies in Saxony, Franconia, and Thuringia, where he possessed domains of his own.

Surprisingly, these measures did not spare Otto the need to address a further revolt in 953. Not without loss, the king had to quell a rebellious coalition that included his son Liudolf of Swabia; his son-in-law, the Franconian Conrad the Red, lately named duke of Lotharingia; several Bavarian magnates; and even Archbishop Frederick of Mainz. In order to satisfy local sentiment in Swabia, Otto transferred the duchy to the Hunfriding Burchard III, who had married the king's niece. Elsewhere, Otto stepped up surveillance of the dukes, yet he did not go so far as to make them mere royal functionaries, as some have maintained. It would, in fact, be misleading to discount the power of the great noble houses of Germany, which exercised economic and judicial control over immense stretches of territory. Moreover, Germany was still home to numerous allods, or freehold domains, where counts who were neither royal nor ducal vassals ruled with virtual autonomy. The strength of the nobility was such that the deaths of Otto I in 973 and of his son Otto II in 983 would each prompt new waves of noble rebellion.

The German Episcopacy

To counterbalance the power of the great magnates, Otto came to depend heavily on episcopal support. This again was a renewal of Carolingian tradition. At the Magdeburg assembly of 937 that passed judgment on the rebel Eberhard of Franconia, Otto called on advice from two archbishops and eight regular bishops. He later viewed himself as the special protector of the episcopacy and assumed the right to approve new elections or even to choose the new candidates himself. Thus in 937 the king followed the recommendation of his mother, the dowager Queen Matilda, and named his chancellor Adaldag as archbishop of Hamburg. In 941, the king journeyed from Saxony to Franconia to attend the election of the bishops of Würzburg and Speyer, and the following year, he did likewise at Regensburg. Otto chose many bishops from his own family: his son William became archbishop of Mainz; his brother Bruno, of Cologne; and cousins were appointed in Trier, Osnabrück, and elsewhere. The future bishops of Saxony, Bavaria, and Lotharingia were most often picked from the clergy of the court chapel and the chancery. In exchange for their pastoral stave, the king required a pledge of fealty. Yet Otto also granted his churchmen important privileges, including immunity, which allowed them to act free of interference from other royal officers within their territory. Moreover, the king also accorded some bishops royal prerogatives, such as the right to sponsor markets, to collect taxes and tolls, and to strike coinage. Otto even granted them countships, usually lying outside their episcopal town. Such were the origins of the prince-bishops of Germany, the great ecclesiastical vassals of the king who owed their sovereign counsel and military support. Otto followed similar policies for the royal monasteries of Saxony. In exchange for guaranteeing and enlarging their temporal possessions, he secured abbatial pledges of fidelity and support. Thus both bishops and abbots were closely bound up with royal policy and politics. Like Charlemagne, Otto also worked for the reform of the church and presided at religious gatherings. At the Synod of Augsburg in 952, the king pressed for sanctions against clergy found guilty of hunting, carousing, and relations with women, and likewise against laymen who sequestered tithe payments by chasing priests away from their churches. From such cooperation between the king and the bishops there emerged the "state-church system" (*Reichskirchensystem*) typical of Germany up to the Gregorian Reform of the mid-eleventh century.

THE SITUATION IN "FRANCE"

The King and His Vassals

To the west, in "France," the situation was quite different. The heads of the great noble houses ruled over princedoms as feudatories in their own right, that is, as autonomous lords backed by their own independent network of vassal supporters. They enlarged their dominions and passed them on to their children. Unlike the king of Germany, the French kings were unable to suppress these duchies or prohibit their hereditary transmission. They sought instead to secure recognition from the great magnates and to ensure their fealty. Whenever circumstances permitted, the kings also moved to expand their own personal domains. Although acts of homage by the great magnates came "slowly and intermittently," according J. F. Lemarignier, they were nonetheless made. Thus, Louis IV received homage from Hugh the Great and Herbert II of Vermandois in 936; from Hugh the Black in 938; from Duke William I of Normandy in 940; from William Towhead, count of Poitou, and Alan of Brittany in 942; from Count Raymond Pons of Toulouse in 944; and from numerous other counts and bishops.

The Resources of the Carolingians

Although the king had very limited domains compared with those of the regional leaders, his palaces and estates still provided him with considerable income, tax revenue, and other resources. The important estates at Compiègne, Vitry-en-Perthois, Ponthion, Verberie, Quierzy, Ver, and Samoussy still remained in Carolingian control. As Jan Dhondt has noted, the kings of this period reacted against the policies of their predecessors, refusing to grant further concessions to the magnates and bishops. They sought rather to regain lost powers in Normandy, Lotharingia, Flanders, and certain Burgundian counties. A recent study of coinage has established that the Carolingians likewise defended their royal privileges over minting. After an abortive attempt to replace the king's name with his own, Hugh the Great backed down and restored the royal monogram. Hugh's vassal Theobald I, count of Blois, struck a new form of coin, but refrained from applying his own name to it, as Duke Richard I of Normandy would later do. During the reign of Lothar IV, royal coinage was still struck at Chinon, Bourges, Clermont, and Bordeaux, hence in regions where the king no longer enjoyed direct authority. Meanwhile, the Carolingians of the restoration did control some twenty bishoprics in the provinces of Reims and Sens, as well as a number of important abbeys: St. Amand, St. Vaast, Notre Dame of Laon, St. Crispin's in Soissons, and Fleury. A prince and feudatory in his own right, the powerful archbishop of Reims was the king's principal supporter. He anointed kings, thereby conferring on them charismatic aura and power which set them above other leaders. When the archbishop of Reims came to abandon the Carolingian cause in 987, the dynasty's fall became inevitable. Like the contemporary kings of Germany, the last Carolingians conferred immunity as well as counties on certain bishops. Thus, without overestimating the Carolingian position, we can say with Ferdinand Lot: "Without being very powerful or very rich—to claim the contrary would be untrue—the Carolingian kings had a certain material, military, and perhaps even financial wherewithal." How else could we explain the policies pursued by the kings north of the Loire?

Louis IV Versus Hugh and Herbert

In the northernmost regions of the kingdom, the Carolingian kings still retained certain advantages that helped Louis IV to contend with the ambitions of Herbert II of Vermandois and Hugh the Great. Nevertheless, Herbert II controlled a substantial territory between the upper valley of the Somme River and the Marne that he patiently schemed to unify and expand by marriages, ruse, and warfare. Despite the installation of Artoldus at Reims, Herbert continued to press the claims of his son Hugh on the archbishopric. Meanwhile, Hugh the Great—who titled himself "duke of the Franks by the grace of God" and was even called the "prince from beyond the Seine" by the chronicler Flodoard—worked to obtain what he had lacked under King Ralph: unquestioned suzerainty over the lands between the Loire and the Seine. For this, he reckoned on the docility of Louis IV, but, as Flodoard remarked for the year 937, "the king freed himself from Hugh's tutelage." Between the two men there then erupted a long war of pillage and violence punctuated by momentary reconciliations. After the death of his wife, Eadhild of Wessex, in 973, Hugh arranged to ally himself to the Ottonian family by marrying the German king's sister Hadwig. In 942 Hugh met with Otto I in the royal palace at Attigny together with Herbert of Vermandois, and there the men concluded an alliance. The two conspirators were now able to eject Artoldus from Reims and reinstall Herbert's son Hugh as archbishop.

Louis IV in Normandy

Two unforeseen events contrived to reinforce the position of Louis IV: the deaths of Herbert of Vermandois and William I of Normandy. Louis seized this chance to recoup certain advantageous territories, but he could not claim Herbert's succession, which was divided among his numerous sons, even though the king managed to take back several abbeys and the county of Amiens. In Normandy Louis initially enjoyed greater success. Generally faithful to his Carolingian sovereigns, Duke William I had been assassinated by vassals of Arnulf of Flanders, who was fearful of growing

Norman power. The duke's successor was the boy Richard I. Therefore, Louis IV ventured to Rouen, and there received homage from a part of the Norman nobility, installed Richard in his office, and then committed the boy to the care of the count of Ponthieu. The king also defeated a band of pagan Normans who sought to exploit the death of William I to take over the duchy, while further west Hugh the Great captured Évreux and Bayeux from other pagan bands. In 945 Louis could consider himself the master of Normandy, and he accordingly came to reside in Rouen on some five occasions.

The Synod of Ingelheim

Unfortunately, Louis IV was betrayed to a party of Normans who delivered him into the custody of Hugh the Great. Intimidated by threats from the king of Wessex, Otto I, and even the pope, the "duke of the Franks" agreed after several months to release Louis from prison and reestablish him on the throne in exchange for control of the important royal stronghold at Laon. Queen Gerberga, the sister of Otto I, now appealed to the German king to intervene on her husband's behalf. Reims was taken back from the Hugh the Great and Artoldus reestablished as archbishop. To settle the dispute between the two claimants to the see, successive synods were convened at Verdun, Mouzon, and finally, on 7 June 948, at Ingelheim, where a legate of Pope Agapetus II presided over debates that culminated in the deposition of Hugh, the son of Herbert II of Vermandois. In the presence of Otto, Louis IV also used the occasion to inveigh against his erstwhile captor, Hugh the Great, thereby securing the promulgation by the bishops of the following canon:

> In the future no person should violate royal authority nor dishonor it traitorously by perfidious attack. We thereby conclude that Hugh, the invader and ravager of the kingdom of Louis, should be struck by the sword of excommunication unless he makes amends by giving satisfaction for his egregious act of faithlessness.

Thus, in the persons of the bishops of Germany and Lotharingia, the church came once again to the rescue of the Carolingians. Hugh resisted for a time, but after the fall of Laon and a new threat from the pope, he decided to make his peace with the king in 953.

The Power of Hugh the Great

In 954 Louis IV died at age thirty-three as the result of a hunting accident. He left his thirteen-year-old son Lothar IV to inherit the throne. It has often been asked why the powerful "duke of the Franks" did not exploit these circumstances to seize the crown for himself. He possessed the lands between the Seine and the Loire and others in the regions of Berry and Burgundy, and he was likewise lay-abbot of many powerful monastic houses, including St. Martin of Tours, Marmoutier, St. Germain of Auxerre, St. Denis, St. Maur-des-Fossés, Morienval, and St. Riquier.

Nevertheless, the power of Hugh the Great was perhaps less substantial than is commonly thought, for his vassals increasingly looked to the betterment of their own fortunes rather than his. In the county of Angers, the progeny of Fulk the Red, originally attached to the Lambertine/Widonid clan, had successfully ensconced itself. Fulk II, nicknamed the Good, was count of Angers from 941 to 960, and worked successfully to expand his power into Brittany. Farther east, Theobald I, the Trickster, was count of Tours between 942 and 978; he also possessed the county of Blois and, about 960, gained control of the counties of Châteaudun and Chartres. Theobald likewise encroached on the north of the Berry region, where he managed to have his brother named archbishop of Bourges. His influence in the north also grew thanks to his marriage to Liutgard, daughter of Herbert II of Vermandois. Meanwhile, other counts practiced a balancing act to limit the influence of both the king and the "duke of the Franks." To reinforce his own authority, Hugh arranged for the young King Lothar IV to grant him power over Aquitaine and Burgundy. He failed in Aquitaine, however, as a result of opposition from William Towhead, count of Poitou, who came to call himself "duke of Aquitaine." In Burgundy, Hugh succeeded in marrying his second son, Odo, to the heiress of the duchy. He had every hope of profiting from this alliance when he suddenly died in 956.

The death of Hugh the Great delivered Lothar IV from a bothersome protector. The duke's eldest son, Hugh, nicknamed Capet after the capes he wore as tokens of his numerous lay-abbacies, was still quite young. So Lothar was free to embark on his own program to neutralize the regional princes. The king's prestige was such that Arnulf of Flanders consented to relinquish to the king the domains he had annexed up to the Canche River in return for right of use until his own death. When Arnulf actually died in 965, Lothar hoped to seize the Flemish princedom, but the local nobles decided that the count's grandson Arnulf II should receive the succession. Lothar then grabbed Arras, Douai and the land up to the Lys River. Thanks to the help of Bishop Rorgo of Laon, the king's uncle, a compromise was arranged whereby the king allowed the young Arnulf II the bulk of the princedom in return for keeping the land he had captured. Elsewhere, Lothar intervened in Normandy to settle a war between Count Theobald and Richard I. A certain equilibrium thus emerged between the magnates and the king in the north, while other conditions prevailed in the south.

Aquitaine and Provence

A few years after his accession, Louis IV ventured on several occasions into Aquitaine. In 942 he was at Poitiers, where he established good relations with Count William Towhead. Two months later he met with Count Raymond Pons of Toulouse and other Aquitainian magnates at Nevers. A passage from the historian Richer of Reims offers a revealing account of the king's activities:

> The king negotiated with them concerning the governance of the realm. Because he wanted all their possessions to be subject to himself, he required homage from them on behalf of their region and then hastened to name them as his administrators. He delegated rule to them and charged them to govern in his name.

In 982 Lothar IV proved himself more ambitious than his father by arranging a marriage to reestablish his position in Aquitaine. He married his son Louis to the widow of Count Stephen of Gevaudan. Like his ancestors of the ninth century, Lothar had his son crowned king of Aquitaine, but the marriage between the fifteen-year-old and a woman who could be his mother was a failure. Two years later Lothar had to reclaim his son at Brioude, while the boy's wife fled to Provence and there married William, count of Arles.

The only southern region where the French kings retained adherents and intervened directly by issuing charters was again distant Catalonia. Twelve charters of Louis IV and eight more from Lothar IV were issued for Catalonian abbeys. Ever hesitant to recognize the Robertine usurpers, the Catalonian nobility were happy to take up relations with the legitimate Carolingian kings. In 939 the monk Gotmar of Sant Cugat visited the royal court, and he returned to Laon in 944. This future bishop of Gerona also wrote a royal chronicle from Clovis I to Louis IV that he dedicated to the caliph of Cordoba. In 952 the monk Sunyer of Cuxa, perhaps accompanied by the count of Roussillon, journeyed to Reims to request a charter of immunity for his monastery, which the king granted in these terms:

> We place the abbot and his monks entirely under our protection. . . . We prescribe and ordain that no public judge, no judicial power should dare enter the churches. . . . Within the aforementioned counties, we accord the monks all the empty land they might wish to clear, so that they might petition divine mercy for us and for the stability of our kingdom.

The style was still very much Carolingian in tone and purport. These abbots and counts continued to consider themselves subjects of the king of "France," even though the great Catalonian magnates never journeyed to do homage to the king. They remembered the Carolingian king as their natural protector. Thus, when Barcelona was attacked in 985, Count Borell appealed to Lothar IV for reinforcement, quite unaware of the king's very limited resources. Lothar was ill, and the expedition that was to be led by his son Louis V never took place.

Burgundy

The late Carolingians made numerous forays into Burgundy, and they also issued charters for Burgundian monastic houses including the foundation at Cluny. Although Louis IV had helped Hugh the Great to capture Langres in 936, he later chose to support Hugh the Black in his struggle against the "duke of the Franks." In 946 Louis IV went to Autun, where he met with his vassal Hugh the Black and other Burgundian nobles, including Count Gilbert of Chalon. In 951 the king was again in Mâcon, and his visit there was the last by a French king until the return of the Capetians in the twelfth century. The death of Hugh the Black in 952 marked the end of the Bosonid dynasty and the eventual passage of the Burgundian duchy into Robertine hands. Count Gilbert continued to rule with the title "head count of Burgundy" until his death in 956. He left the bulk of his domains to his son-in-law Odo, son of Hugh the Great, while the county of Troyes passed to his other son-in-law, Robert, son of Herbert II of Vermandois. Odo's status as a minor and the convenient demise of his father, also in 956, encouraged King Lothar IV to launch several assaults on Burgundy whereby he reestablished royal control over both the county of Langres and the citadel at Dijon.

Between the Burgundian duchy and the Kingdom of Upper Burgundy there was no clear boundary. Many "western" counts had domains lying east of the Saône and the Rhône. In an attempt to expand on the success of King Ralph, Louis IV ventured into the Rhône valley. In 941, the king traveled to Vienne, where he received the homage of Charles Constantine, the Bosonid who had managed to survive as local count despite both Hugh of Arles and Otto I. It is sometimes thought that Louis IV then agreed to renounce his claims on the regions of Lyon and Vienne at a meeting with Otto I at Visé on the Meuse about the time when the young Conrad returned to claim his kingdom of Upper Burgundy in 942. But it is more likely that the Carolingians gave up their rights in the Rhône valley only after the marriage of Conrad to King Lothar's sister Matilda about 963.

Thus the last Carolingians managed to maintain a certain prestige throughout their realm. Charters and coinage continued to bear their names. Yet for their part, the territorial princes maintained their own independence, organizing their courts and managing their estates according to royal example. The great magnates never wished to break completely with the king as long as memories of the Carolingian past lingered.

The Restoration of the Empire

Since the death of the Italian Berengar I in 924, there had been no emperor in the west. Nevertheless, neither the term nor the idea of empire had disappeared. Every dominion comprising an extended group of territories might be called an empire, without its ruler demanding an imperial crown. Such was the case in England under Ethelstan of Wessex (924–939) and his grandson King Edgar (959–975). Such was also the case in "France," where the terms *regnum* (kingdom) and *imperium* ("empire") were used indifferently. Yet to be recognized as emperor in the west, one required not only exceptional prestige and authority but also the benefit of papal coronation. Otto I of Germany alone could hope to meet these conditions. Anointed king at Aachen in 936, Otto came to rule over Saxony, Bavaria, Franconia, Swabia, and Lotharingia; he engineered the defeat of the pagan Slavs and Magyars; and in 951, he intervened in Italy and became its king. By these achievements Otto proved himself worthy of the imperial coronation conferred on him in 962.

OTTO'S VICTORY OVER THE SLAVS AND THE MAGYARS
Along the Slavic frontier, Otto I continued the work of his father by extending the marcher territories beyond the Elbe and up to the Oder River. The northernmost sector of the march was conferred on Herman Billung, a Saxon count, and for the next seventy years his progeny would control the so-called March of the Billungs along the Baltic coast. Farther south,

the frontier of the Sorbian March was placed under another Saxon count named Gero. To foster the conversion of the Slavs, Otto created three bishoprics: two at Brandenburg and Havelberg in 948, which came under the jurisdiction of the archbishop of Mainz; and later another at Oldenburg, which was made subject to the archbishop of Hamburg. Although the Slavs consistently resisted Saxon Christianity and political domination, Otto crushed and then executed an army of Obodrite warriors along the Recknitz River in October 955, and his brutal victory marked a watershed in the subjugation of the new territories.

Otto I came to intervene in Bohemia as a consequence of the palace revolution of 829 whereby Duke Vaclav—Saint Wenceslaus—was murdered and replaced by his heathen brother Boleslav I. This tragic incident has spawned much commentary. Many scholars have viewed it as a symptom of opposition to German and Christian influence, and suppose accordingly that the dowager Trahomira propelled her younger son Boleslav to the throne as a means of circumventing Saxon control. Whatever the circumstances actually were, Otto had to undertake several expeditions against Boleslav before finally securing his submission in 950.

The Slavic policy pursued by Otto also led the king to open relations with the princedom of Kiev far to the east. Although Olga, widow of Prince Igor, had been baptized into the Byzantine church and actually visited Constantinople in 955, she sent an embassy to Frankfurt in 959 to request priests for the fledgling Kievan church. She hoped perhaps to gain greater religious independence, and surely welcomed the possibility of improved commercial ties with Germany. In 961 Otto commissioned Adalbert, a cleric of the royal chancery, to head the new mission and arranged for his consecration as "bishop of the Russians." Adalbert departed for Russia only to return to Germany with difficulty in 962; he fell victim perhaps to an unwillingness to accept a Latin clergy, perhaps to a heathen reaction. The missionary subsequently became abbot of Wissembourg, and in 968 he was named the first archbishop of Magdeburg.

Between the eastern and western Slavs, the Magyars maintained their hold on the plains of Pannonia and continued to launch devastating raids against the west. Henry I's victory at Riade in 933 had only temporarily quashed the Magyar peril. In 950 Otto's brother Henry of Bavaria led a punitive expedition into Pannonia, but four years later, the Magyars profited from a revolt by the German magnates against Otto to invade once again. They pillaged Bavaria and Lotharingia and even advanced into Champagne and Burgundy. Otto I reacted decisively. He gathered together forces from Bavaria, Swabia, Lotharingia, and a contingent from Bohemia, and achieved a brilliant victory in 955 at the Battle of Lechfeld, near Augsburg. Just as Charlemagne had eliminated the Avar threat, so Otto put an end to the Magyar invasions. To guarantee his victory, he reinforced the March of Carinthia and reorganized the "Eastern March" under the name *Osterriche*, the nucleus of the future Austria.

In the aftermath of his victory, the troops proclaimed Otto "father of his country and emperor," as had happened to Henry I in 933. Yet this time the expression *imperator* had more than a strictly military significance. For some time, royal charters had already spoken of the *imperium* (empire) and of the king's *imperialis auctoritas* (imperial authority). At the Synod of Augsburg of 952, the king and his bishops had even debated the circumstances of the "Christian empire." Otto was preparing to claim the imperial crown, no doubt encouraged by the fact that he had controlled Italy since 951.

THE CONQUEST OF ITALY

In 945 Hugh of Arles fled back to Provence from his crumbling Italian kingdom, leaving behind his son Lothar to reign under the control of the marquis of Ivrea, Berengar II. Hugh of Arles died in 947, as did Lothar in 950, thus leaving the throne of Italy vacant. Berengar II seized the opportunity to have himself crowned at Pavia along with his son Adalbert. To ensure his own position, Berengar imprisoned Adelaide, Lothar's widely favored widow. But partisans of the princess, above all her brother King Conrad of Upper Burgundy, denounced this outrage to Otto I. The German king now had a pretext for acting on his plan to intervene in Italy. But he had to act quickly, since his brother Henry, duke of Bavaria, had already snatched Aquileia and his son Liudolf of Swabia also hoped to gain some part of the peninsula.

Otto gathered his army, crossed over the Brenner Pass and put Berengar II to flight. On 23 September 951, the German ruler followed the example of Charlemagne and had himself elected king of the Franks and the Lombards. A widower since 946, he also married the unfortunate Adelaide, and thereby reconciled the Italian nobility to himself.

Once king of Italy, Otto naturally hoped to travel to Rome, and accordingly dispatched an embassy to Pope Agapetus II to herald his coming. But Alberic the Senator still controlled the city, and had no intention of relinquishing his considerable power. Otto did not press the issue, for he was drawn back to Germany by the revolt of his son Liudolf of Swabia, who balked at his father's marriage to Adelaide. The administration of Italy was entrusted to the king's son-in-law Conrad the Red, duke of Lotharingia. Apparently unattracted by the prospect of remaining in the peninsula, Conrad did not hesitate to make a deal with Berengar. Otto later reluctantly ratified the accord whereby Berengar II became viceroy in exchange for doing homage to the German ruler. Otto, however, detached the strategic marches of Verona and Aquileia from the kingdom of Italy and conferred them on his brother Henry of Bavaria.

Although problems within Germany claimed his immediate attention, Otto I did not lose track of events in Italy. The German king's successes against the heathen Magyars and Slavs increased his prestige across Europe, while Berengar II established himself as a regional tyrant. After 954, Berengar began to dream of seizing central Italy as well. The powerful Alberic lay dead, and Rome now became subject to his bastard son Octavian. Shortly before his death, Alberic had ensured that the boy, already a prince and senator, would emerge as Pope John XII in 955.

The Imperial Coronation

Notorious for his scandalous conduct, the adolescent pontiff wallowed in love affairs and hunting parties, and by 959 Berengar II was poised at Spoleto to launch an assault on Rome. Following the example of his distant papal predecessors, John XII sought help from the powerful king of Germany and Italy, and promised him the imperial crown in return. Otto prepared the expedition meticulously. He arranged for the election of his son Otto II as king, and provided for the administration of Germany by his brother Bruno, archbishop of Cologne, and another son, William, archbishop of Mainz. He also commissioned the monks of St. Alban's in Mainz to elaborate a new ritual for his imperial coronation, and even placed an order for the crown he would receive during the ceremony in Rome. In September 961, he was at Pavia, where he was proclaimed king a second time, and then dispatched Abbo, abbot of Fulda, to organize his journey to Rome. As in the time of Charlemagne, John XII required Otto I to promise solemnly to work for the exaltation of the Roman church, to guarantee the safety of the pope, and to return to the papacy the lands of Saint Peter that had been lost. On 31 January 962, the king camped on the Monte Mario, two kilometers north of the Vatican, and on 2 February John XII crowned him and his wife Adelaide as emperor and empress.

After a lapse of thirty-eight years, Europe again had an emperor.

Having earned his station by virtue of his wide reaching authority and proven military skill, Otto I did not view himself as a Roman emperor or a German emperor, but like Charlemagne he called himself *imperator augustus*. He was simply the "august emperor." Rome was not his capital. In Italy, Otto preferred to reside at Pavia or Ravenna, and the historian Widukind of Korvei even neglected to mention the coronation in Rome, as though to affirm that the reborn empire owed nothing to the pope and everything to Otto's ascendancy in Europe. For his part, John XII, or rather the clerics of his chancery, preferred to view the coronation as papal handiwork. The pope was accordingly supposed to have crowned a defender for the Universal Church over which the bishop of Rome presided. Indeed, by 13 February 962, John XII could proudly point to a new imperial privilege known to history as the *Ottonianum*. This document enlarged on the territorial concessions granted by Louis the Pious in 817, and reconfirmed other commitments to the papacy made by Pippin the Short and Charlemagne. Otto thereby acknowledged that all lands south of a line between La Spezia and Monselice—some three-quarters of Italy—belonged to "Saint Peter." Yet papal ownership remained now as ever more fiction than fact. In his turn, Otto insisted on restoring elements of the Roman Constitution of 824, which had provided for the presence of imperial *missi* in Rome to oversee justice and order within the papal territories. Although Otto considered himself the defender and advocate of the Roman church, he hedged his position against future uncertainties, and events justified his caution.

The Deposition of John XII

Otto I had scarcely advanced into northern Italy to quash Berengar II when John XII began scheming with Byzantine forces worried by the imperial restoration and opened the gates of Rome to Berengar's son Adalbert. Otto returned, and unlike Charlemagne in the case of Leo III, he chose to try the pope before a council. Accused of homicide, perjury, sacrilege, and incest, John XII was deposed and replaced in 963 by the head of the Lateran chancery, Pope Leo VIII. The emperor then required that the Romans should "no longer raise up or consecrate any pope without the consent and decision of Lord Otto or of his son King Otto." Thus, the papal election came, in theory at least, under imperial control. John XII attempted to resist, reinforced by the support of Roman aristocrats traditionally hostile to Frankish interference. He returned to Rome, had his deposition overturned, and resumed his place in the Lateran. Louis

Duchesne has recalled his end in the following terms: "He died as pope on 14 May 964, just as he had lived. The hand of God struck him down in the bed of a married woman." Contemptuous of their promises to the emperor, the Roman clergy named Benedict V as successor to the papal office. Once he had subdued Berengar II, Otto returned to depose the intruder and reinstate Leo VIII. This flux of events clearly illustrates the difficulties Otto faced in dealing with the clergy and people of Rome. He soon realized the intractability of the situation, and when Leo VIII died in 965, he agreed to the election of Pope John XIII, a Roman cousin of Alberic the Senator.

Otto I and Byzantium

Once master of northern and central Italy, Otto advanced into the south of the peninsula with its array of autonomous princedoms and the Byzantine possessions in Calabria, Apulia, and Otrano. Since 944 Byzantium had entertained intermittent relations with the German king. Less hostile than in 800, the easterners agreed in 962 to accept the new "basileus of the Franks." Yet when Nicephorus Phocas became emperor in 963 his instincts as a former general were to mistrust Otto's forays into southern Italy. Hoping to find common ground, Otto proposed the marriage of his son Otto II to a Byzantine princess. Like Charlemagne and other rulers, Otto hoped to unite east and west through a dynastic marriage. But preliminary negotiations collapsed and the German king proceeded to invade Apulia, though he failed to capture Bari. In 968 Otto dispatched Liutprand of Cremona to Byzantium in a renewed bid to arrange a marriage. Despite the utter failure of his mission, Liutprand drafted a remarkable report of his eastern experiences. The assassination of Nicephoros in 969 and the accession of John Zimiskes made it possible to conclude the projected marriage. Already crowned emperor by the pope in 967, Otto II married the Byzantine princess Theophano in Rome. This marriage would have important consequences for the subsequent history of western culture.

The Archbishopric of Magdeburg

The new empire was not a Germanic empire, nor was it the "Holy Roman Empire," a style that first emerged in the time of Emperor Frederick Barbarossa (1152–1190). One may, however, rightly speak of a "holy empire."

With his unction in Aachen and coronation in Rome, Otto I had consciously embraced a mission of immense religious importance. Accordingly, he sought to protect the church, to maintain peace among Christians, to fight off invaders, and to foster the spread of the Gospel among heathen peoples. Only a week after his imperial coronation, Otto obtained special papal endorsement for his plan to erect Magdeburg as a metropolitan see. Perhaps a tactic for securing the *Ottonianum*, the emperor was no less grateful for the politic papal gesture. Otto's project continued to meet with resistance from his son William, archbishop of Mainz, who sought to retain control over the bishoprics of the Saxon frontier, and likewise from Bishop Bernard of Halberstadt, who hoped to stave off the dismemberment of his own diocese. But in 968, after death had silenced both spoilers, Adalbert, sometime missionary to Russia, was consecrated archbishop of Magdeburg, and the bishops of Brandenburg, Havelberg, Zeitz, Meissen, and the new see at Merseburg became his suffragans. Pope John XIII granted Adalbert the pallium, and the new metropolitan came to be seen as a second Boniface.

The Poles

The creation of the new metropolitan jurisdiction soon raised questions about the status of the nascent Polish church, for Christianity was now taking hold among the numerous Slavic bands settled in the valleys of the Warta and Vistula rivers. The Vislanes, based around the stronghold of Krakow, had probably first received missionaries from Greater Moravia during the ninth century. During the tenth century, the Polanes, or "men of the fields," widened their political power from settlements at Gniezno and Posnan. In 960 their chief, Mieszko, of the Piast family, seized a number of strongholds in the vicinity of Warsaw and captured Lubusz on the Oder. Mieszko then came into conflict with Marquis Gero, who bought peace by paying the Poles a tribute. Influenced by his wife, Dobrava, daughter of Boleslav I of Bohemia, and also by the knowledge that Christianity would earn him respect in the west, Mieszko received Baptism in 966, taking Dagobert as his Christian name. Two years later a bishopric was established at Posnan whose first incumbent was Jordan, a missionary who seems to have come from either Lotharingia or Aquitaine. The archbishop of Magdeburg considered this new bishop as his suffragan. But from the start, the bishops of Posnan sought to evade the authority of the metropolitans of Magdeburg, thereby inaugurating the struggle for a separate Polish hierarchy.

The Mission to Hungary

In Hungary, the land of the Magyars, Christianity also made progress. Byzantine missionaries began the work of converting the Magyars settled in Transylvania, and the marriage of Sarolta, daughter of the local Christian chief, promised to favor the passage of their mission into the lands of her husband, count Geza (972–997), a member of the Arpad dynasty who ruled the plains around Lake Balaton. Despite these prospects, Ottonian pressure and a later marriage by Geza to a Polish princess favored German missionary influence. Although Geza fostered the Christian mission, he does not appear himself to have received Baptism; for him it sufficed to conclude a durable peace with Otto I.

At the Quedlinburg assembly of Easter 973, Otto I perhaps relished the success of his eastern policies. Along with emissaries from Byzantium and the Bulgarian princes, Magyar, Czech, and Polish envoys were also present to greet the aged emperor.

Lotharingia: A Crossroads of Ottonians and Carolingians

By attaching Lotharingia to his kingdom, Henry I had made it possible for his son to be anointed at Aachen in 936. Yet restored to power in the same year, the Carolingians continued to lay claim to Lotharingia as their rightful heritage. This was not a conflict between "France" and "Germany" as historians writing near the time of the World War I often portrayed it. Rather, Lotharingia was the ancient Carolingian heartland, and as such it claimed the family's affections. It was home to the supporters of the dynasty and many choice royal estates.

Louis IV, Otto I, and Lotharingia

Louis IV sought to regain the power over Lotharingia that Charles the Simple had exercised for fifteen years. Shortly after his accession, the local nobility invited Louis to claim the territory. Although he was a brother-in-law of Otto I, Gilbert of Lotharingia joined in rebelling against the German king, hoping to rule as duke under the Carolingian as his father Reginar had done in the time of Charles the Simple. Louis IV accepted the homage of the Lotharingian nobles, both the lay magnates and the bishops of Metz, Toul, and Verdun. His acquisition of the territory was nearly realized when Gilbert drowned crossing the Rhine in 939, and all began to unravel. The accident permitted Otto I to redress his situation in the middle kingdom despite desperate maneuvering by Louis, culminating in Louis's marriage to Gilbert's widow Gerberga, a sister of Otto I. To defend his position, the German king proceeded to exploit unrest among the nobles of western Francia, receiving the homage of Hugh the Great and Herbert of Vermandois at Attigny in 942. Although this act has sparked much commentary aimed at indicting Hugh for allying himself with "the enemy," the deed was a political commonplace. Since the ninth century, magnates had moved from one lord to another without great scruple. Now, like the turncoat followers of Charles the Bald, Hugh and Herbert merely acted to further their interests under the other "king of the Franks"—ready from the start to abandon him should that course prove more expedient. Later in 942, Louis IV journeyed to Visé and agreed to acknowledge the German king's suzerainty over Lotharingia. Thereafter, Otto helped his brother-in-law to restore his shaken authority inside western Francia.

Louis IV does not seem to have profited in 953 from the revolt of Conrad the Red, Otto's nominee as duke of Lotharingia. Faced with widespread rebellion among his magnates, Otto charged his brother Bruno, archbishop of Cologne, with the administration of the middle kingdom, and after a difficult and costly victory over local resistance, Bruno eventually partitioned the realm in 959. He entrusted Lower Lotharingia to nobles based around Verdun, and Upper Lotharingia—equivalent to the ecclesiastical province of Trier—to Count Frederick of Bar, a scion of the Carolingians through his mother Kunegund and husband of Beatrix, daughter of Hugh the Great and niece of Archbishop Bruno.

THE REGENCY OF BRUNO OF COLOGNE

After the death of Louis IV in 954, Archbishop Bruno offered his protection to the new king, his nephew Lothar IV, as he also did two years later for his other nephew, Hugh Capet, the son of Hugh the Great. Until his death in 965, the governor of Lotharingia acted as the veritable regent of western Francia, managing to avoid conflict between Lothar and Hugh. He thus came to be called the "archduke" (*archidux*) as well as the "tutor and guide of the west" (*tutor et provisor occidentis*). At once a warrior, diplomat, and cultured churchman, Bruno followed in the Carolingian political tradition. On 2 June 965, he brought together Otto, his sister Gerberga, and her two sons, King Lothar IV and Charles. During this family reunion in Cologne plans were made for the marriage of Lothar to Emma, daughter of Empress Adelaide by Lothar of Italy. In another significant gesture, Bruno did not allow Hugh, the would-be archbishop of Reims, to claim the see after the death of Artoldus in 961; instead Bruno named one of his own friends, Olderic, a canon of Metz who claimed to be a descendant of Saint Arnulf. For the next thirty years the bishops of Reims would stem from Lotharingia. After Olderic's death in 969 there followed Adalbero, a scion of the house of Ardennes. Brought up in the monastery of Gorze under the tutelage of his uncle Adalbero I of Metz, the new archbishop was a nephew of Count Frederick of Bar and the brother of Count Gottfried of Verdun. Yet Adalbero's position in Reims was delicate. While he owed allegiance to both his king and his family, he often favored his relations over his sovereign. He remained a vassal of the king of France, but the province of Reims spread beyond the realm's boundaries to include, for instance, the see of Cambrai inside the empire. Adalbero was a model of the Carolingian prince-bishop; he sought to serve the interests of both the church and the empire.

Lotharingian Politics and the Demise of the Carolingian Rulers

Otto the Great died in 973, and at age eighteen Otto II had to contend with outbreaks of revolt in Swabia, Bavaria, and Lotharingia. The Lotharingian nobility had long chafed at the strong policies of Otto I and his brother Bruno of Cologne (d. 965). For Reginar III, heir to Duke Gilbert I, the result had been an imperial order of exile to Bohemia, while his sons Reginar IV and Lambert had taken refuge at the court of King Lothar. When the sons returned in 973 to claim their property in Hainaut, Otto II attacked and defeated them. In 976 they again ventured back into Lotharingia with the help of Charles, brother of Lothar IV. Otto II reacted to this challenge by moving to co-opt the Carolingian prince, making him duke of Lower Lotharingia in exchange for a pledge of fealty. Charles was pleased with this convenient solution to the troubles he had unleashed between himself and his brother by accusing Queen Emma of illicit relations with the new bishop of Laon, the Lotharingian Adalbero, nephew of the like-named archbishop of Reims.

Lothar in Aachen

Upon the death of Frederick of Bar in 978, Lothar IV secured the support of Hugh Capet for a scheme to reclaim Lotharingia. He foolishly hoped to surprise Otto II at Aachen. Lothar achieved a remarkable but impermanent success in occupying the town. His troops occupied the imperial palace, and as a symbol of their victory, they turned around the bronze eagle fixed to the roof so that it faced eastward. Yet only three days later they withdrew, surely a sign that they were less than welcome in Lotharingia. Otto responded to this incursion with a punitive thrust that reached as far as Paris, with stops at Reims and St. Médard in Soissons, where the emperor made his devotions. But Otto too could not long remain on foreign territory. He was repulsed by Hugh Capet, the duke of Burgundy, and Count Geoffrey Greymantle of Anjou, but it seems that he received help for his retreat from Archbishop Adalbero of Reims. In any event, the two campaigns did not betoken national conflict. Rather, they were large-scale versions of the unseemly raiding common among nobles of the period. Indeed, Otto II earned some measure of discredit among contemporaries who would have preferred to see him fighting pagans instead of further troubling the Christian fraternity that he and Lothar were pledged to safeguard. The two leaders were, however, reconciled in 980 at a meeting in Margut, near Sedan on the Chiers River.

Adalbero of Reims

On 7 December 983, Otto II died in Rome after an extended attack of malaria. His passing unleashed a new series of revolts in Germany. Duke Henry of Bavaria, a cousin of the deceased emperor, seized the three-year-old Otto III, and had himself proclaimed king by his partisans. Yet loyalty to the rightful heir among much of the nobility and above all among the episcopacy caused the usurpation to fail. The most ardent proponents of the young prince were Adalbero of Reims and his relatives in Lotharingia. Greatly influenced by Gerbert of Aurillac, master of his cathedral school and a faithful supporter of the Ottonians, Adalbero imagined a plan whereby Lothar IV would receive custody of the imperial heir. The king hoped to reassert his claims in Lotharingia and willingly accepted. However, by mid-984 the arrangement came to naught since Empress Theophano and Archbishop Willigis of Mainz regained political control and rescued Otto III. Much disappointed, Lothar turned to intriguing with Henry of Bavaria and inflicted his displeasure on the Lotharingian nobility.

Gradually the genuine pro-Ottonian aims of Adalbero of Reims became clear. His relatives possessed choice Lotharingian bishoprics: his first cousin, son of Frederick of Bar, was Bishop Adalbero II of Metz, while two nephews, both also named Adalbero, were bishops in Laon and in Verdun. While the archbishop of Reims increasingly prodded Hugh Capet to draw closer to Otto III and the Lotharingian nobility, Gerbert of Aurillac articulated the view that Lothar only governed France in name, while Hugh was master in fact. Nevertheless, the king managed in 885 to capture Verdun and Gottfried, its count. Thanks to the letters of Gerbert, we know how Adalbero secretly supported his brother and other pro-Ottonian relations against the French king. Lothar finally reacted by summoning the archbishop to an assembly at Compiègne on the pretext that he had granted the see of Verdun to his nephew without royal consent. The king then used the occasion to charge Adalbero with treason. But the approach of Hugh Capet at the head of a small army caused the gathering to disperse, and two weeks later, on 2 March 986, Lothar died.

Lothar's son Louis V, was nineteen years old when he reached the throne in 978. He lacked the political skills of his father, and was encouraged by his mother, Queen Emma, to effect a rapprochement with the Ottonians. Louis, however, chose to keep Verdun, and he dismissed his mother. In a letter drafted by Gerbert, Emma appealed for help to her mother, Empress Adelaide. Although the young king hoped to eliminate Adalbero of Reims by reopening the case against him, the matter was settled by Louis's own accidental death during a hunting party on 22 May 987.

The Election of Hugh Capet

Louis V died without an heir, though his uncle, Duke Charles, remained as a rightful pretender to the throne. Adalbero of Reims, however, seized the opportunity to champion the cause of his own candidate for the kingship of France: Hugh Capet. In his famous address to the assembly at Senlis, Adalbero emphasized that the throne should pass to the ablest leader. He proposed that the throne was not a matter of hereditary right:

> We must place at the head of the kingdom a man who excels not only by his worldly stature, but also by his thoughtfulness, a man whom honor recommends and inner greatness endorses.

Whatever his claims, Duke Charles was hobbled by his scanty means and his unexceptional marriage. Hugh Capet, on the contrary, claimed respect by virtue of his ample "honors," lineage, and military skill:

> You would find in him a protector for both the realm and your private interests. He would be a devoted father. Who has ever gone to him and not received his patronage? What hostage was ever not returned to his fellows?

Moreover, Adalbero scarcely needed to add that Hugh, duke of Neustria, was closely tied to the other greatest nobles: his brother Odo was duke of Burgundy, and he counted Richard I of Normandy as his brother-in-law.

In essence, the arguments at play were those that had brought Pippin the Short to the throne long before. Despite the presence of a Merovingian figurehead, Pippin had actually ruled, and in 987, Hugh Capet could claim to possess real authority and power despite the lingering presence of a Carolingian.

On 1 June 987, Hugh Capet was elected king, and on 3 July he was anointed in Reims by Adalbero and pronounced the ritual promises of the Carolingian rulers. Like his predecessors, he made his fifteen-year-old son Robert a partner in the royal office, having him crowned at Christmas 987. Likewise, Hugh dreamed of securing an illustrious bride for his son, and thus commissioned Gerbert of Aurillac to pen a curious missive to the Byzantine emperor to request a Greek princess. As it happened, Robert II instead married Rozala, the widow of Arnulf II of Flanders, a daughter of Berengar II of Italy, and thereby a scion of the Carolingians. Meanwhile, the new king showed his gratitude to the archbishop of Reims. Gottfried of Verdun was released from custody, and Hugh abandoned the town and further pretensions in Lotharingia.

The Carolingian Pretender

Duke Charles of Lower Lotharingia did not graciously accept his rejection as king. He reacted by seizing Laon and imprisoning Adalbero, its bishop, and the dowager Queen Emma. At the request of Empress Adelaide, he released them, but kept the town. Then in 989 Adalbero of Reims died, and despite Gerbert's expectation to succeed him, Hugh Capet callously bypassed his supporter to nominate Arnulf, a bastard son of Lothar IV and a canon of Laon. The king hoped thereby to conciliate the Carolingian party, but only after taking the precaution of requiring both an oath of fealty and a signed undertaking from Arnulf. Yet the new archbishop was scarcely installed when he joined forces with the invading Duke Charles. Hugh Capet managed, however, to capture Laon and the would-be Carolingian king thanks to help from the wavering Bishop Adalbero. Charles was imprisoned in Orléans, where he died in 991. At home, Charles was succeeded as duke of Lower Lotharingia by his son Otto, who remained thereafter a faithful vassal of Emperor Otto III. Meanwhile, Arnulf of Reims was condemned at the Synod of St. Basle in 991, and then stripped of office and imprisoned. The archbishopric of Reims then briefly passed to Gerbert.

Three centuries after the victory of Pippin II at Tertry in 687, the Carolingian house was removed from power. Although the last Carolingian kings had reigned with dignity, their efforts to reclaim the Austrasian cradle of the dynasty had proved disastrous. They had lost the support of their Ottonian cousins and came into inevitable conflict with a key supporter of the family since the mid-ninth century, the archbishop of Reims. Their policies had been unrealistic. Rooted in the past, the family's claims violated the dynamics of a changed world that was no longer Carolingian.

Part V

Rulers and Civilization in the New Europe

After having sketched the political milestones in the emergence of Europe, we must now consider the legacy of the Carolingians and their successors in the domains of society, economy, culture, and institutions. When the Carolingians first came to political prominence, Europe had scarcely moved beyond the troubled aftermath of the great barbarian invasions. Four centuries later, there existed a new network of institutions and economic structures destined to endure for many centuries. Likewise, the kings, nobility, and clergy of this transformed Europe had brought about a remarkable cultural flowering, distinct from the achievements of both late antiquity and the later Middle Ages.

1. The Carolingian Church

The Christian Church already existed as an established institution by the end of antiquity and before the emergence of the barbarian kingdoms. From the fifth to the seventh century, its leaders "went over to the barbarians" and initiated the Christianization of much of the west. Yet by adapting to the barbarian world the church was in turn "barbarized," so much so that by the end of the seventh century it was suffering a grave internal crisis. The new Carolingian kings acted to foster ecclesiastical reform, and assumed a guiding role in religious affairs. They oversaw a durable renewal of ecclesiastical structures and institutions.

Ecclesiastical Structures

THE SECULAR CLERGY

The Bishops
After a moment of hesitation in the mid-ninth century, the Carolingian kings reestablished the system of metropolitan provinces, each of which was headed by a bishop henceforth known as an archbishop. In 814, Charlemagne's testament included a list of twenty-one provinces: Rome, Ravenna, Milan, Cividale, Grado, Cologne, Mainz, Salzburg, Trier, Sens, Besançon, Lyon, Rouen, Reims, Arles, Vienne, Moûtiers-Tarentaise, Embrun, Bordeaux, Tours, and Bourges. The metropolitans of these sees held authority over the suffragan bishops of their province, and they were often jealous possessors of power. After the mid-ninth century, successive territorial partitions and the gradual acceptance of the *Pseudo-Isidorian Decretals* tended to undermine the broad powers of the archbishops, but most remained nonetheless masters of their provinces. For instance, the influential Hincmar of Reims vigorously upheld his rights in disputes with his suffragans Rothad of Soissons and Hincmar of Laon, the archbishop's own nephew. Some metropolitans expanded their authority over recently

acquired and Christianized territories, as happened with the archbishop of Hamburg in Scandinavia, the archbishop of Salzburg in Slavic territory, and the archbishop of Mainz among the new sees of Middle Germany.

After the mid-eighth century, synods bringing suffragans together with their metropolitans again became regular events, while the king himself often convened larger councils to address moral, disciplinary, doctrinal and even political questions. At its close, each such gathering issued acts and canons, which were collected into compendia that served as a basis for formulating and interpreting church law.

The Diocese

Each bishop governed his diocese with help from his cathedral clergy and especially from his archdeacon, his principal collaborator. The Rule for Canons formulated by Chrodegang of Metz fostered a quasi-monastic regime of communal life among the urban clergy, and together with amplifications promulgated at the Council of Aachen of 816, the Rule was imposed in virtually all bishoprics. Since the fourth century, every bishop was bound in principle to visit each church in his diocese on a regular basis, and the Carolingian kings revived this obligation. Often the arrival of the bishop was a matter of dread for country priests because the visitor came not only to inspect the church but also to exact support payments in money and in kind for himself and his suite. In 844, Charles the Bald had to act to protect the rural clergy by limiting the demands made by the bishop of Narbonne. The *Liber de synodalibus causis* ("Handbook of Synodical Legislation") compiled by Regino of Prüm (d. 915) and dedicated to Archbishop Hatto of Mainz describes how the bishops should conduct visitations and even records the sort of questions they were to ask. For instance, the visitor inquired after the material condition of the buildings, the income of the clergy, the education of the priest, the books that he possessed. Likewise, he looked into the priest's way of life, his morals, his rapport with the faithful. For its part, the clergy was also bound to journey to the bishop to participate at regular diocesan synods. The statutes promulgated at these gatherings shed light on problems of concern at the local level.

The livelihood of the rural clergy in the first millennium was often precarious, and it would remain so throughout the medieval period. Usually of humble origins, the priest shared the life and pleasures of his peasant flock. He was invited to taverns and wedding feasts; his weaknesses were accommodated; despite repeated canonical prohibitions, he kept a woman who tended his house. Of course, many country priests were less the subjects of the bishop than of the local landowner. Often the founder of the manorial church or a descendent thereof, the landlord installed priests who lived under his control, and he also usurped a part of the tithes. Carolingian bishops often sought to uproot such abuse, but neither they nor their medieval successors ever met with complete success.

In order to administer many oversized bishoprics, the Carolingians also established an intra-diocesan hierarchy. Sees came to be divided into archdiaconates and territorial deanships covering a number of villages. The bishops of Reims and Soissons both had archdeacons by the ninth century. The diocese of Langres numbered two archdiaconates in 801, three in 870, five in 889, and six in 903. Such was the emergence of an institution that became generalized in the tenth and eleventh centuries. The rural deanships headed by archpriests were less numerous, though they were common in Italy and in the diocese of Reims. In the words of Joseph Lemarignier, "it was much easier to reorganize twenty provinces than to create several hundred archdiaconates or deanships." It is, however, important to note the birth of these durable institutions, for they betoken the concern for order and hierarchy that was characteristic of all Carolingian reforms.

Organizing the Faithful

By reviving the ancient administrative structure of the church and taking the initiative in creating new ones, the Carolingians sought to organize believers and to ensure their thorough Christianization. The more learned clergy were to oversee the religious instruction of the laity. The kings reiterated this principle to the bishops, as did the bishops to their priests. This policy led to a regime of mandatory religious conformity: baptism of children at birth, the obligation to abstain from work on Sundays, participation at liturgical celebrations, confession and communion three times a year, and the like. To be sure, the instruction imparted to the faithful was usually restricted to a minimum of precepts: what one must do, and above all what one must not do. The respect paid to outward regulation was akin to the "legalism" of the Old Testament. Legal infractions were punished, and individual spiritual growth was sacrificed to the interests of the larger social group. In the emerging "Christian regime," society's leaders sought to impart habits of religious observance. Anything deeper was an incidental benefit.

MONASTICISM

When the Carolingians took power, some three hundred monasteries existed across the west, but not all enjoyed a regular life, and most followed their own rules and observances. Charlemagne was by nature suspicious of men who lived apart and isolated themselves from the world even if their goal was a holy life. On several occasions, he moved to restrict wandering monastic vagabonds—often coming from the British Isles—who were subject to no law but themselves. The emperor wanted stable monastic families living under the direction of a worthy abbot and applying themselves to mental and physical tasks as well as to the liturgy, for he counted on monastic prayers for success in his own endeavors. Capitularies and canonical legislation continually recall the hallmark principles that were to obtain, whatever the rule of an individual monastic house: above all, obedience, chastity, and religious poverty.

At the close of his reign, Charlemagne realized that the best means of reforming the monasteries was to impose everywhere a rule that he believed to be excellent: the Rule of Saint Benedict. In 813, he asked the abbot of Monte Cassino to forward him a copy of the Rule, and he provided for the diffusion of the text from his court. It is also certain that the old emperor was aware of the activity of the man who would soon become the second founder of Benedictine monasticism: Benedict of Aniane.

Benedict, the son of a Visigothic noble, had grown up at the royal court, and in 774 he had withdrawn to a monastery in Burgundy. After having studied various monastic rules, he decided to institute the Benedictine Rule in the monastery that he founded on one of his domains at Aniane. Supported by King Louis of Aquitaine, Alcuin (lately made abbot of St. Martin of Tours), and Theodulf of Orléans, Benedict reformed more than twenty monasteries in Aquitaine. Once emperor in 814, Louis the Pious established a monastery for Benedict near Aachen at Inden, and "placed him at the head of all the monks of his empire so that he could reform Francia by his salutary example just as he had instructed Aquitaine and Gothia in the precepts of salvation." In 817 Louis summoned abbots from across the empire to Aachen, where a synod promulgated the *Capitulare monasticum* ("Monastic Capitulary") prepared by Benedict. This text of 83 articles codified varied monastic usages and customs to agree with the spirit of the Benedictine Rule. Thereafter *missi* were dispatched to apply the reform legislation across the empire.

Without entering into the debates spawned by the capitulary, we should note that, while Benedict remained faithful to the Benedictine spirit, he also introduced a number of innovations that became hallmarks of medieval monasticism. Thus he enlarged the divine office with new prayers and devotions; he guaranteed the assembled monastic community, or chapter, the right to oversee certain abbatial activities; he instituted a uniform monastic discipline, generally stricter than the regimens already in force; he reserved the monastic school exclusively for future members of the community; and he even provided for a prison in each monastery. Benedict has been reproached for a desire to centralize alien in spirit to the independence and autonomy that had formerly characterized monasticism. In this, however, his reforms were in keeping with the efforts of the Carolingian rulers. To renew monastic life, religious leaders sought to standardize observance and to create a sense of spiritual community among the various foundations. The period thus saw the birth of monastic prayer associations whereby the names of deceased monks and benefactors were shared with other monasteries, often preserved in so-called confraternity books. Hence, there arose a nexus of spiritual affiliations among the religious communities of the empire. Indeed, Benedict of Aniane prepared the way for the great medieval monastic order headed by Cluny, the great Burgundian monastery founded by William the Pious in 909. Thus, the biographer of Odo, second abbot of Cluny, asserted that Benedict had been the "institutor of the customs that are still observed in our monasteries." By his reforms, Benedict of Aniane inaugurated a new era in the history of western monasticism.

A Church Subject to Princes

In fostering the reform of the church and restoring ecclesiastical institutions, the Carolingian kings counted on the collaboration and political submission of the clergy. Charlemagne, the "new David," took for granted that the bishops, abbots, other clergy and even the pope were all subject to his control, and his successors believed likewise. Although the kings agreed that the "two swords" of Gelasius I—the temporal and spiritual powers—were to cooperate as one to advance Christendom and secure salvation, they also subscribed to the notion of "sacral kingship" according to which the king decided all important religious and political matters. This notion would remain current until the Gregorian Reform of the eleventh century, when the church took back its autonomy.

THE KING AS MASTER OF BISHOPS AND ABBOTS

The Carolingian king most often named bishops and abbots from his own entourage or from the families of his followers. Since the time of Pippin the Short, the Carolingians controlled many powerful abbeys, some two hundred of them, which they considered as their personal property. They placed over them their legitimate sons and daughters, bastards, and friends. Thus, Alcuin received the monasteries of Ferrières, St. Loup near Troyes, Flavigny, St. Josse, and St. Martin of Tours. Control of the great convent at Chelles was reserved for the sisters and daughters of kings. Wala, a cousin of Charlemagne, was abbot of Corbie and Bobbio, while Adalhard, Wala's brother, had also held numerous abbacies in addition to Corbie. The Carolingians frequently appointed laymen as abbots. Thus, Angilbert, a son-in-law of Charlemagne, was lay-abbot of St. Riquier, and was later succeeded by his son, the historian Nithard. Likewise, Einhard held a number of prestigious monasteries as lay-abbot. Although this situation was clearly at odds with the effort at monastic reform, the kings considered lay-abbacies as exceptions. Moreover, they could ill afford to lose control of the richest and most strategically situated abbeys of the empire if they were to retain effective political control.

The king generally expected his nominees to bishoprics and abbacies to divide their time between pastoral care and service to himself. He often summoned them to his court and charged them with administrative and diplomatic missions. Indeed, some prelates complained that they were so burdened with the king's business that they could not attend to their pastoral obligations. Yet they continued to serve, both because the king commanded it and because they were taken up with the profitable distractions of an active life.

Bishops and abbots also became vassals of the king. In the course of the ninth century, episcopal and abbatial offices gradually came to be viewed as benefices. In return for the pastoral stave of office, ecclesiastical nominees promised fealty to the king like any other vassal. For example, Hincmar of Laon made the following pledge to Charles the Bald:

> I, Hincmar, bishop of Laon, shall now and henceforth be a faithful follower of my lord Charles, as a vassal rightly should be to his lord and as a bishop should be to his king; and I shall be obedient, as a vassal rightly should be obedient to his lord and as a bishop of Christ should, according to his knowledge and power, be obedient to the will of God and to Him who keeps the king safe.

The obligations due to the king from his ecclesiastical vassals were the same as those of any other vassal: the dispatch of a military contingent to the king's host, aid and counsel, presence at the diet, and the like. This was the beginning of a process that would lead the upper clergy into dangerous waters. It required a saint to resist all the temptations of temporal reward, and genuine saints were rare. Unintentionally, the Carolingian kings forced the bishops and abbots to become men of the world and to lose sight of their properly spiritual function.

IMMUNITY

To establish a direct link between ecclesiastical dignitaries and the king, the Carolingians commonly issued charters of immunity to bishops and especially to abbots. While Merovingian immunity barred the intervention of royal agents within the domains of the "immunists" and thus constituted a negative privilege, the Carolingians emphasized the protection that they conferred and the prayers that they expected in return. To free the immunists from administrative responsibilities that might distract them from prayer and religion, the kings appointed lay "advocates" who exercised temporal duties such as collecting taxes, administering justice, and levying troops on the immune domains. The institution of immunity became widespread across the empire, yet it could only function properly if the immunist continued to recognize royal authority. Otherwise, the immunist became a virtual sovereign within his domains, which was in fact what happened throughout western Francia in the tenth century.

Thanks to the king, the western church was strong in material terms. Its bishops and abbots controlled vast domains, often scattered in patches across the empire. Some monasteries were veritable monastic cities with religious buildings as well as other structures for artisans and peasants. The famous Plan of St. Gall traced not long after the reforms of 817 reveals the inner workings of an idealized monastic complex where many different spaces were envisaged for such activities as prayer, study, handicrafts, the reception of visitors, and the care of the sick. In theory at least, this closely planned monastic world was worthy of the example set by the king's attempts to regulate his royal estates.

Charlemagne was, however, also somewhat troubled by the expansion of ecclesiastical property and power. In a capitulary of 811, he reflected: "Is it really the case that a man has abandoned the world who never ceases to enlarge his possessions by whatever means possible?" Like his father and grandfather, Charlemagne did not hesitate to distribute church goods to his lay followers as "precarial holdings by order of the king" (see p. 57). The church remained owner of the lands, but laymen possessed and used them more or less indefinitely. In 779 Charlemagne had moved to compensate the clergy by generalizing the payment of tithes. Destined to survive for a millennium, this form of religious taxation claimed a tenth of all produce or income for the church, and royal agents were charged with ensuring its payment. After the death of the first Carolingian emperor, churchmen sought to profit from the benevolence of Louis the Pious to recoup the lands that they had lost, and menaced their despoilers with divine vengeance. Yet these efforts were in vain. Nobles continued to derive sustenance and power from the church lands they held as lay-abbots or "precarial" tenants.

THE ADMINISTRATION OF CHURCH PROPERTY

Kings commonly intervened to regulate the organization of the ecclesiastical patrimony and the distribution of its revenues. They instructed abbots to draw up inventories of their capital, domain by domain, indicating for each the area, the number of manses, and the adult and child population. The results were documents such as the famous *Polyptych of St. Germain-des-Prés* compiled under Abbot Irmino in 813; it reveals that the abbey possessed more than seventy-five thousand hectares around Paris and farther afield. To avoid the exploitation of monks, nuns, and canons by their superiors, the kings ordered abbots, abbesses, and bishops to apportion their institutional property for the support of specific aims or persons. For instance, revenues from specific domains were designated to supply the *mensa*, or "table," of the bishop and his household, while others went to the *mensa* of the chapter and still others went for alms and building maintenance. Each canon would then receive a prebend (from the Latin *praebere*, "to supply") from the common *mensa* of the chapter. Finally, church resources were assigned by the kings to wider social functions. In 818 Louis the Pious chose to assign the great abbeys of the kingdom to one of three groups: those which were to send armed contingents to the army, those which offered support in cash and in kind, and finally those which would simply pray for the emperor and the well-being of the empire.

It may seem remarkable to us that the clergy did not protest this hefty royal interference and seek to regain autonomy for its religious mission. Yet as partners of the royalty, the clergy benefited materially from the king's strength. Moreover, bishops and abbots themselves could scarcely imagine another system, owing to the confusion of spiritual and temporal activities. If some clerics in the time of Louis the Pious did assert the primacy of spiritual concerns, it was often merely to claim political powers for themselves and to increase their own landed possessions. Far from being a means of liberation, the collapse of the empire and the rise of the great noble families would place the church under far more stringent lay control.

THE CHURCH IN THE TENTH CENTURY

In western Francia the kings and regional princes vied with one another to nominate bishops and abbots, because all political leaders counted on revenues and military contingents levied on church lands to ensure their success. Although the kings retained control of several northern sees, elsewhere the magnates usually made bishops of their own children and followers. Thus, the count of Cerdanya assigned a diocese to each of his four sons, and the counts of Albi held the adjoining bishopric for four generations. The regional princes were also lay-abbots of the greatest monasteries of their respective zones of influence.

The Ottonians, of course, managed to restore their royal authority by relying on episcopal support, and like the early Carolingians, they kept the church under tight control. They installed the bishops by symbolically bestowing on them the crosier of office and exacted an oath of fealty in return. Thanks to their skill in selecting candidates, the results of their policies were excellent. They could depend on the bishops, and therefore moved to confer on them duties formerly discharged by counts: the administration of justice, the collection of market tolls, and the minting of coinage, among other activities. Such were the origins of the ecclesiastical princedoms of the medieval empire. Once master in Italy, Otto I sought to import his German church policies, and in 963, he even subdued the papacy, whose powers and pretensions had been greatly enlarged by the Carolingians.

The Papacy

Between the close of antiquity and the eighth century, the bishops of Rome had managed to secure recognition of their primacy over the western church. Leo the Great, Gregory the Great and other less prestigious popes had affirmed their role as successors of Saint Peter, thereby claiming the spiritual leadership of the Universal Church. Under the authority of the Byzantine emperors, the papacy had suffered a decline in its power and prestige. During the seventh century, however, the missionary work that Rome fostered among the barbarian peoples of the west provided a means of escaping from Byzantine domination. Then, thanks to the Carolingians, the bishops of Rome were able to claim vast new powers and prestige that would nourish the development of the papacy as a European institution.

The Popes and the West

The alliance between the papacy and the Carolingians issued from the papal willingness to accept Pippin the Short as king, from the protection granted by the Franks to the papal state, and finally from the coronation of 800. The effect of this cooperation was to wed the Roman church firmly to the west; the papacy became western in its outlook and concerns. In turn, the Roman ritual and liturgy was slowly adopted across the west, and the veneration of Saint Peter struck firm roots north of the Alps. Rome thus emerged as the spiritual center of Carolingian world, just as it had become the model and focus of the English church. Thanks to the Carolingians, the popes were acknowledged as the temporal sovereigns of central Italy, and would remain as such until 1871. The bishops of Rome sought throughout the Middle Ages to maintain and expand the lands first granted to St. Peter by Pippin the Short. Rome itself became the most important city of the west. The popes repaired ancient buildings, built new ones, and fortified the Vatican palace and basilica. Rome, "the noble city, mistress of the world," attracted pilgrims from across the west to the tombs of Saints Peter and Paul, the true rulers and patrons of the Eternal City.

The Awakening of the Papacy

Papal relations with the kings, who viewed themselves as the masters of the church, were frequently troubled. Charlemagne, king of the Lombards and of Italy, imposed his views easily on Pope Hadrian I and his weak successor Leo III. Louis the Pious granted the papacy its independence in 817, but seven years later reestablished strict controls in the Roman Constitution of 824 and obliged the pope and his subjects to swear oaths to the representatives of the emperor. Nevertheless, the popes were often able to exploit the crises that rocked the empire in the mid-ninth century to reclaim the political initiative and uphold the ideal of western unity. Gregory IV intervened in the conflicts between Louis the Pious and his sons, and Leo IV later dared to arrange his own election as pope without the prior approval of the imperial *missi*. Above all, Nicholas I vigorously affirmed the authority of Rome over all the other churchmen and kings in the service of morality and peace among Christians. Yves Congar has observed:

> If Nicholas heralded the future Gregory VII (1073–1085), it was less by his pretension to be able to depose kings than by his concern to ensure the independence of ecclesiastical institutions, that is their "liberty," as one would say in the eleventh century. Long before the men of the so-called Gregorian reform, Nicholas had reacted against the interference of lay magnates in local churches and among the clergy which served them; he had guarded against lay meddling in elections. . . . Nicholas I surely marks a development in the direction that tended to make submission to the Roman see a criterion and measure of obedience to God and to Christianity.

After Nicholas, John VIII, one of the greatest popes of the early Middle Ages, went further with as much conviction and greater subtlety. At the head of the "priestly and royal city," even calling himself the "governor [*rector*] of Europe," he offered protection and encouragement to the budding church in Moravia; he intervened in virtually every administrative, diplomatic, and military domain, as the ample register of his correspondence indicates. John VIII also advanced and reinforced the notion that the pope alone could choose the emperor and that his nominee had to journey to Rome to claim the imperial crown. The idea of a *translatio imperii* (transfer of the empire) from east to west that vested imperial sovereignty ultimately in the pope first emerged among the papal entourage in this period.

ROME'S PRESTIGE IN THE TENTH CENTURY

The consequences of the failure of the Carolingian empire were devastating for the Roman church. The papacy slipped into the hands of the Roman aristocracy and came under the control of the Ottonian rulers after 962. Yet despite its somber circumstances, Rome still made its voice heard. Even though the popes were personally mediocre or worse, the institution that they represented remained enfeebled but intact. Remarkably, several hundred charters were issued from the Lateran chancery, addressed to all the churches of Christendom. Thus John X (914–928) sent a legate to Germany for the Synod of Hohenaltheim in 916; he rejoiced over the accord of St. Clair-sur-Epte of 911; and he was called upon to intervene in the provinces of Reims and Narbonne. Likewise John XI (931–935) bestowed the pallium on several bishops; Stephen VIII (939–942) threatened to excommunicate those who mounted opposition to Louis IV; Marinus II (942–946) conferred the title of apostolic vicar for Germany and Gaul on the archbishop of Mainz; Agapetus II (946–955) had one of his emissaries preside over the Synod of Ingelheim of 948. Even subject to the Ottonian emperors, the popes intervened in the affairs of Christendom, and in particular in the synods held in western Francia and Burgundy. Benedict VII (974–983) summoned a synod at the Lateran to deal with simony, the buying and selling of church offices. In another vein, John XV (985–996) was the first pope to promulgate a bull of canonization. In 993, a papal writ proclaimed the sainthood of Ulrich, bishop of Augsburg (923–973).

The papacy intervened vigorously when Hugh Capet had Arnulf, the Carolingian archbishop of Reims, convicted of treason at the Synod of St. Basle in 991. Without waiting for the opinion he had requested from Pope John XV, Hugh deposed Arnulf and replaced him with Gerbert of Aurillac, the guiding force behind the synod and the conviction. Drawing on views formerly advanced by Hincmar of Reims, Gerbert espoused a loose relationship between local churches and the church of Rome, sometimes exaggeratedly explained as a "proto-gallican" stance. Like his contemporaries, Gerbert acknowledged certain ties between the church and the state. Yet he believed that the bishops and the pope shared jointly in the direction of the church. Hence, the pope was not entitled to act as an ecclesiastical monarch. These views notwithstanding, John XV recognized neither the degradation of Arnulf nor the election of Gerbert. He dispatched a legate, Leo, who presided over several councils at which Gerbert unsuccessfully attempted to vindicate his point of view. In 997, the new Pope Gregory V went so far as to summon to Rome the bishops who had participated at the 991 Synod of St. Basle. Meanwhile, the marriage of Robert the Pious, son of Hugh Capet, to Bertha, daughter of Conrad III of Burgundy, had met with ecclesiastical opposition on the grounds of consanguinity, and Gregory V threatened the king with excommunication. To be reconciled with the papacy, Robert had to abandon Gerbert and allow Arnulf to resume his duties as archbishop of Reims. To compensate his friend Gerbert, Otto III made him bishop of Ravenna before having him elected pope in 999.

Taking the name Sylvester II, Gerbert followed his predecessor in affirming the "authority of Saint Peter." He began a letter to his former adversary Arnulf of Reims in the following terms:

> It pertains to Apostolic Sovereignty not only to counsel sinners, but also to raise up those who have fallen and to return to those who have been deprived of their office the tokens of their restored dignity, so as to express the power of loosing granted to Peter and so that the glory of Rome shines everywhere.

This formulation and the rest of the letter came from Gerbert, and not from some cleric of the Roman chancery. The seventy-odd charters promulgated by Sylvester II as well as his efforts to foster the nascent churches of Poland and Hungary highlight how much this pope considered himself the spiritual head of Christendom.

MONASTERIES AND PAPAL PROTECTION

The prestige of the papacy in the tenth century is further demonstrated by the fact that monasteries placed themselves under the protection of St. Peter. They sought initially to escape lay encroachment, but soon aspired to exemption from local episcopal control. From the seventh century, the Irish foundation at Bobbio had enjoyed a privilege of papal protection. Other monasteries in England and Germany soon received a similar status from Rome. Despite the certain disapproval of Charles the Bald, Gerard of Vienne successfully secured a grant of papal protection for his Burgundian foundation at Vézelay. In 863 Nicholas I issued the following guarantees:

> By the present decree of Our Apostolic Authority, we undertake, confirm, and establish privileges such that it is allowed to no person, king, bishop, or dignitary of whatever sort, to remove, sequester, apply for his own personal use or to that of any others—even under pretext of some pious cause meant to excuse his greed—the properties granted by you or others to the aforementioned monastery.

At the end of the ninth century the founders of St. Gilles-du-Gard and St. Gerald of Aurillac requested and received similar privileges.

In 909, during the troubled reign of Pope Sergius III, William the Pious of Aquitaine decided to entrust his foundation at Cluny to Saints Peter and Paul. In the founding charter, William stipulated his wish to restore the Benedictine observance, and then enjoined Sergius, the sometime lover of Marozia:

> [As] the pontiff of pontiffs of the Apostolic See . . . by the canonical and apostolic authority that you have received from God, you will bar from the communion of God's holy church and from eternal life any despoilers or invaders of these possessions which I give you, and . . . you will be a guardian and defender of Cluny and of the servants of God who live there.

Odo, second abbot of Cluny (926–942), later secured from John XI an exemption guaranteeing free abbatial elections and the right of the abbot of Cluny to oversee more than one monastery.

When Abbo of Fleury, whose monastery had been reformed with Cluniac help, sought exemption from the bishop of Orléans, he too turned to Rome. Abbo had also argued the papal view at the Synod of St. Basle in 991 and served as the head of the so-called monastic party. In the canonical collection that he compiled, Abbo often tended to exalt the primacy of Rome. After several visits to the pope, the abbot finally received the exemption he sought for his monastery from Gregory V.

It has rightly been observed that the success of Cluny and the exemption of monasteries from outside control and interference played a major role in preparing for the Gregorian reform of the eleventh century. By affirming their prerogatives and authority, the succession of popes from Gregory IV to Sylvester II paved the way for the liberation of the church by their successors in the mid-eleventh century and also laid the foundations of medieval papal monarchy.

The Expansion of Christendom

In order to complete our sketch of the church in the early Middle Ages, we must review how, thanks to royal and papal efforts, Christendom flourished at home and along the expanding frontiers of Europe. When the Carolingians came to power in the mid-eighth century, a great part of the west was still pagan. By the year 1000, Christian communities had grown up along the Vistula and the lower Danube.

GERMANY

The mayors of the palace Charles Martel and his sons encouraged missionaries to evangelize Germany as much for political as for religious reasons. Willibrord in Frisia, Boniface in Germany, and Pirmin in Alemannia, all owed their success to papal encouragement and the material support of the Carolingian princes. It was necessary for Frankish troops to protect the churches and monasteries founded by the Anglo-Saxon missionaries and their disciples. As their work progressed, an ecclesiastical hierarchy was established. New bishops were created and soon made subject to the metropolitans of Cologne and Mainz.

Charlemagne continued this effort, establishing additional bishoprics in Saxony and Frisia and an archbishopric at Salzburg in Bavaria. Although the emperor was not the originator of forcible conversion, his harsh methods of Christianization raised objections from his friends Alcuin and Paulinus of Aquileia. The Gospel had yet to strike deep roots when Charlemagne died, but the foundations of a greatly enlarged German church had been laid.

SCANDINAVIA

Under Louis the Pious missionary efforts turned increasingly toward Scandinavia. In 822 Archbishop Ebbo of Reims was sent by the emperor and Pope Pascal II to Denmark. Three years later the Danish king Harald was solemnly baptized at Ingelheim. He departed home with Ansgar, a monk of Corbie, who established the first church in Denmark and later advanced into Sweden as far as Birka. In 831 Ansgar became the first archbishop of Hamburg and received the pallium from the hands of Pope Gregory IV.

As a consequence of invasions from the north, the young Swedish and Danish churches were destroyed. The missionary effort now came to bear on the invaders of the empire. Amid the struggle to beat back the pagan Vikings, bishops and abbots already dreamed of converting them. The submission of pirate chieftains was generally accompanied by their Baptism and that of their warriors. This pattern recurred when Alfred the Great, king of Wessex, sponsored the Viking king Guthram for Baptism at Aller (near Athelney, Somerset) in 878, and when Charles the Simple negotiated with Rollo at St. Clair-sur-Epte in 911. As much diplomatic as religious, these conversions were superficial, and the Normans frequently reverted to their pagan practices. These circumstances inspired a specially tailored pastoral approach witnessed by an exchange between Archbishop Herveus of Reims and Pope John X and other communications between the metropolitans of Rouen and Reims. Rather than attempting to impose Christianity with thoroughgoing brutality, it was thought better to tolerate some pagan carryovers in accord with the precept of Gregory the Great: "The holy church corrects by charity, tolerates by gentleness, permits and allows by reflection."

The Christianization of Scandinavia resumed in the tenth century from bases in northern England and Germany. Olaf Tryggvesson, the first Christian king of Norway, established bishops and priests from Northumbria on his territory about 995; he also launched Christianity into the Orkney Islands and Iceland. In Denmark and Sweden Archbishop Unni of Hamburg used the victories of Henry I to recommence the work of Ansgar, and advanced again as far as Birka, where he died in 936. Under Otto I three new northern bishoprics were established in Jutland and placed under the authority of the metropolitan of Hamburg. Harald Bluetooth, king of Denmark, converted about 960, and the Jelling Stone, which he erected to commemorate the event, bears the earliest representation of the Crucifixion known in Scandinavia.

THE MISSIONS TO THE SLAVS

As masters of Bavaria and Friuli, the Carolingians worked to extend Christianity into the lands of the South Slavs. Missionaries were dispatched to Carinthia, Slovenia, and the regions acquired from the Avars. In Croatia, the coastal bishopric of Nin was founded about 850. In a letter to Branimir, duke of the Croats, Pope John VIII expressed his joy to see that the Croatian church remained faithful to Rome, as it would throughout its history. In Moravia, Christianization was bedeviled by conflicts between the Bavarian missionaries and the Moravian rulers, who sought to establish a distinct national church. Despite its failure to retain the allegiance of the Bulgars, the papacy supported the efforts of Cyril and Methodios to the point of accepting their Slavonic-language liturgy, but finally the Bavarian clergy prevailed and imported its own brand of Latin Christianity. The triumph proved short-lived owing to the Magyar incursions.

Protected by its southern mountains, Bohemia survived the Magyar onslaught, and gradually emerged as a Christian duchy first under Vaclav (Saint Wenceslaus), and then under Boleslav I. In 976 the archbishop of Mainz consecrated Thietmar the first bishop of Prague. The Saxon monk was, however, poorly received, and after his death the bishopric passed in 983 to Vojtech, a Czech known as Adalbert after his Confirmation in Magdeburg. Adalbert of Prague was a poor administrator and soon came into conflict with local nobles. In 988 he abandoned his immense diocese and took up monastic life in Rome. In 992 Pope John XV forced him to return to his bishopric, which he again fled in 994/995, meeting Otto III in Aachen before returning to Rome. He subsequently became a close friend and counselor to the emperor. Owing to the refusal of Boleslav II to allow Adalbert back into Bohemia, the pope allowed him to work as missionary among the heathen. He preceded first to Hungary in 996, and then into Prussia, where he and his companions were massacred in 997.

The advance of Christianity into the northern Slavic lands was very slow. It was only in the mid-tenth century that the kings of Germany laid the foundations of the church beyond the Elbe. Otto I founded new bishoprics in the frontier zone and attached them to the archdiocese of Magdeburg in 968.

The creation of bishoprics was not, however, enough to ensure the triumph of Christianity. The Slavs did not accept the germanization of their lands. During the revolt that followed the death of Otto II in 983, they completely destroyed the churches established from Saxony. Otto III had to recommence the task begun by his grandfather. He restored the bishoprics and founded new monasteries, such as the one at Poztupimi, the future Potsdam. Fortunately he could count on help from the Christian Poles living farther east.

Christianity had struck firm roots in the Vistula region. Mieszko, the first Christian king of the Poles, had established Jordan as bishop of Posnan about 968. A document known as the *Dagome iudex* ("Dagome" being a deformation of Dagobert, the baptismal name of Mieszko) contains the donation charter commending Polish lands to St. Peter, and it marks the first step toward the creation of an autonomous archbishopric in Poland. Mieszko's son Boleslav the Bold was adopted at age seven by Pope John XIII, and in the year 1000, he received a visit from Emperor Otto III, who came as a pilgrim to the tomb of the martyred Adalbert of Prague in Gniezno. There, in accord with Pope Sylvester II, Otto established a metropolitan see with suffragans at Colobrega (Kolberg) on the Pomeranian coast, Wrocław (Breslau) in Silesia, and Krakow. Meanwhile, the bishop of Posnan remained a suffragan of Magdeburg until 1012. Such were the origins of the national hierarchy of the Polish church.

THE BIRTH OF THE HUNGARIAN CHURCH

During the same period, a national church also emerged among the Magyars of Hungary. The Magyar leader Geza (970–997) had made peace with the Ottonians, and sent envoys to the assembly at Quedlinburg in 973. Thereafter, Bishop Pilgrin of Passau dispatched German missionaries into Hungary, and Geza himself seems to have prosecuted the work of Christianization with some brutality.

Upon his death in 997, the Hungarian leader was succeeded by his

Christian son Vajk. Baptized some years before as Stephen, the new ruler was also married to a Christian princess from Bavaria, and during his long reign (997–1038), he would consolidate both Christianity in Hungary and the foundation of the medieval Hungarian monarchy. Among other notable deeds, Stephen installed Czech monks at Pannonhalma, the supposed birthplace of Martin of Tours, and in 1001 he established an archbishopric at Esztergom with the consent of Otto III and Pope Sylvester II. There, Stephen was also made king on January 1 of the same year with a crown said by a later chronicler to have been sent by the pope. Whatever the value of this report, the crown traditionally associated with Stephen is unfortunately a product of the twelfth century and thus can bear no factual relation with the first Hungarian king. Yet much attuned to the spirit of the Carolingians, themselves formerly raised up by the pope, Stephen chose to call himself the *kral* of Hungary—*kral* being a variant of Karl or Charles.

The Hungarian king, like the leaders of Poland, counted on the support of the church to underpin his power and to ensure the unity of his realm. Although Stephen copied the German kings in his administration, he guarded against the germanization of his domains. Despite some setbacks, Hungary remained Christian. An added benefit of its conversion was the opening of a new route to the east, which came to be used by pilgrims to the Holy Land around the turn of the millennium.

Thus, at the beginning of the eleventh century, the frontiers of western Christendom stretched northward to the coast of the Baltic Sea and westward to the banks of the Vistula and the lower Danube. A line of churches faithful to Rome was now positioned opposite the eastern Christians of Russia and the Balkans who owed their allegiance to Byzantium.

2. Features of Carolingian Kingship

The King's Person and Status

ROYAL UNCTION

After 751 the Frankish kings were distinguished by a ceremony of royal unction, an innovation pregnant with consequences. In the time of the Merovingian rulers, the royal person had traditionally borne an aura of religious mystery also common in many other cultures. According to Germanic belief, his family had received a special charism, and the king himself was the guarantor of cosmic order and earthly harmony. In its turn royal unction came to be viewed as a veritable sacrament of the church, a status it maintained until the thirteenth century. The ritual brought kingship within the church, while the anointed ruler was seen as an "image of God," a "new Christ." He and his family became inviolable under threat of mortal sin.

Harking back to passages of the Old Testament, Charlemagne himself became a "new David " and even a "new Josiah." The latter biblical king had repaired the Temple, restored observance of Mosaic law, renewed the priesthood and reformed the liturgy, and for Charlemagne, he was a model. Accordingly, the Frankish king aspired "to restore to God's service, by inspecting, correcting, and exhorting, the kingdom that God had committed to him." The palace complex at Aachen was thus a new Temple among the Franks. Likewise, Charles the Bald was termed a "new Solomon" who combined in his person both biblical and ancient wisdom. A coronation ritual elaborated in the tenth century included the following prayer:

> Visit him as you visited Moses in the burning bush, Joshua in battle, Gideon in his field, and Samuel in the Temple; fill him with your shinning blessing; imbue him with the dew of your wisdom, which blessed David received in song and which his son Solomon obtained from heaven.

The Old Testament inspired the liturgy of unction and the symbols applied to the royal insignia, as can be seen today on the imperial crown preserved in Vienna.

Moreover, the people guided by the anointed kings was thought to be a chosen one, a new Israel whose resources and talents were placed at the service of religion. The alliance between the Carolingian kings and the Roman church was compared to the covenant between God and the ancient Hebrews. Whatever their trials or afflictions, the Franks believed that God made use of them to test, reprove, and regenerate his elect, just as He had done in the stories of the Old Testament. When the sons of Louis the Pious rebelled, commentators evoked the revolt of Absalom, and conversely, Empress Judith was viewed by her enemies as a new Athaliah or a new Jezebel.

THE "ROYAL MINISTRY"

Much of the king's power and prestige derived from his sacred aura. He named bishops and abbots, oversaw the education of the clergy and the faithful, approved and imposed liturgical norms, guided ecclesiastical reform, presided over synods, and even took the initiative in doctrinal matters. All these activities pertained to his royal function, or his "ministry," to use the term of the period. To fulfill his kingly duties the ruler had to adhere to the moral and ethical standards that some clerics liked to recall in their missives to the king and in the numerous ninth-century "mirrors of princes"—treatises wherein the king was supposed to find a model of rightful royal behavior. Thus Lupus of Ferrières addressed the following lines of exhortation to the young Charles the Bald in a letter:

> Always be mindful of God, your creator and future judge, and give Him thanks. . . . Beseech Him in your daily prayers to help you to begin, continue, and persevere in good deeds. . . .
>
> Do not make yourself so much the servant of anyone that you do everything according to his judgment. Why should you claim the name of king if you don't know how to rule?
>
> Avoid the company of evil men since—as you remember Scripture says—evil conversations corrupt good character [1 Cor. 15:33]. Seek the company of good men because you will be holy with the holy, and innocent with the innocent [Ps. 18:26]. . . .
>
> By diligently keeping these precepts, you will be pleasing to God and to all good men; you will repress and triumph over rebels with—as we believe—God fighting on your side; and at length, after an arduous reign on earth, you will obtain the eternal kingdom of true peace.

Other more substantial "mirrors of princes" were composed by Smaragdus of St. Mihiel for Louis the Pious, by Sedulius Scottus for Lothar II, and by Hincmar of Reims for Charles the Bald and his successors.

When the king ruled badly, when he failed to ensure the peace of the church and of the realm, he was no longer worthy to reign. Thus, in the time of Louis the Pious, some bishops in the camp of Lothar I acted to deprive the elder emperor of his power, temporarily as it turned out. Yet this novel episode in the history of the Carolingians was also heavy with implications. It lay at the root of the notion that kings could be deposed by spiritual authorities.

CORONATION PROMISES

Unlike the prophets of the Old Testament, Carolingian bishops were not content merely to offer counsel to their sovereigns. In the second half of the ninth century, they began to require of their kings, before their anointing, a solemn promise that they would act according to Christian principles. This promise, not yet the oath it would become, first appeared in 869 during the coronation of Charles the Bald as king of Lotharingia. The new king committed himself to maintaining the honor of the church and the worship of God and to rendering justice in accord with the law codes of society and the church. In return, he required that all pay him "due honor" and obedience and offer him help in maintaining and defending the kingdom that he had received from God. The promise thus took on the semblance of a contract, and the skillful jurist Hincmar of Reims was surely its author. Slightly reworked, the same text was used again at the anointing of Louis the Stammerer in 877 and at that of Odo of Paris in 888. It would also serve as a basis for elaborating a true coronation oath in the twelfth century.

Royal Justice

The first duty of the king was to ensure the reign of justice and public peace, to protect the weak and to safeguard the church. These obligations derived from Roman and Germanic tradition, and were later explicitly reinforced by royal promises. Throughout the early Middle Ages there were of course many different codes of law. While written Roman and ecclesiastical law had enjoyed a long prior existence, Germanic legal conventions were at first preserved through custom and oral transmission and later set out in written codes of "barbarian law," some of which were drafted on orders from Charlemagne. In exercising his royal *bannum*—that is, the power to command, forbid, and punish—the king was obliged to apply to each person the code which pertained to his tribe or people. This was the consequence of the so-called personality of law, as distinguished from the universal public law known in modern societies.

In the Germanic world, popular assemblies had the power to judge legal questions. Charlemagne maintained this custom, but determined the makeup of the count's court, or *mallus*, and the intervals at which it was to convene. The count eventually had to hold three judgment sessions per year, and was obliged to call upon the services of qualified legal assessors, probably landowners, called *scabini*—whence the modern German *Schöffe* (lay assessor) and Franco-Belgian term *échevin* (alderman). The Carolingian period also witnessed the emergence of a distinction between a judge's competence to pronounce on "high," or capital, crimes and the handling of misdemeanors. In the event of a contested judgment, royal *missi* could be called upon to rehear a case already tried by a count or his vicar. Finally, all persons were allowed in theory to appeal to the tribunal at the royal court. Thus, in his *De ordine palatii* ("On the Governance of the Palace") of 882, Hincmar of Reims nostalgically recalled how Charlemagne used to consider with care the cases that were submitted to him personally, and also noted how the count of the palace oversaw the court tribunal:

> In accord with justice and reason, he decided all the cases and disputes that had been brought from elsewhere to the court in order to secure an equitable resolution, and it was his task to correct bad judgments so as to be pleasing to everyone, to God by his justice and to men by his respect for the law.

The practice of appealing to the king fostered in the Carolingian period would later do much to increase the popularity of the monarchs of France.

According to immemorial Frankish custom, the burden of proof lay on the accused. He had to establish his innocence either by a "purgatory oath"—that is, the swearing of a solemn oath on holy relics with the help of supporting co-swearers—or by undergoing a "judgment of God," or ordeal. In the latter case, the accused might perhaps plunge his arm into boiling water, and then inspection would prove his innocence if the arm healed within a specified period. Another alternative was to walk barefoot over nine red-hot ploughshares without suffering harm. Likewise, a juridical duel fought by substitutes representing the opposing parties permitted the winning party to claim the justice of its contentions. Although these originally pagan practices were repugnant to clerics like Agobard of Lyon, they would remain current in the west until the thirteenth century.

First among the Carolingian kings, Charlemagne sought to introduce testimony by witnesses and written forms of proof. These enjoyed wide recognition only in the southern parts of the empire where to some extent written culture had survived from antiquity.

The judicial system of the Carolingians was revived by the Ottonian rulers of the tenth century and continued as well in western Francia. In northern "France" justice was pronounced by counts in the name of the king, while in the south it was rendered in the name of the regional ruler. The dates on which the *mallus* convened were fixed by custom, and its gathering included the count, assisted by the *scabini*, increasingly known as *boni homines* (later giving *bonshommes*, or "upstanding citizens," in French). As public power progressively fragmented, the *vicarii*, originally surrogates of the counts, assumed the right to pronounce high justice, and gradually replaced the counts in the exercise of their judicial function. The system of "seigneurial justice" that developed after 1000 thus derived from the remnants of the Carolingian system. Although royal justice could scarcely be exercised outside the immediate domains of the king, it was not forgotten as an ideal. The Capetian kings of France would later restore the Carolingian ideal of the king as quintessentially an agent of justice.

The King as Warrior

The kings of the first millennium were warriors and leaders of warriors. The Frankish king was also in some sense obliged to prove the supernatural origins of his power though armed victories. The various military successes of Charlemagne and the triumph of Otto I over the Magyars constituted a divine endorsement that earned both rulers the imperial dignity. Kings also derived immense wealth from warfare; they enriched their treasury with the spoils of conquest and the tributes paid by vanquished peoples. When the Ring of the Avars fell to Charlemagne, fifteen wagons each drawn by four oxen were brought back laden with gold, silver, garments, and other precious objects. According to Einhard, "no war in human memory had netted comparable booty and a like increase of wealth." These gains allowed the king to be generous to his friends and the church, and to ensure the fidelity of his followers. Moreover, the king risked losing power, affection, and influence in the absence of war, as happened during the reign of Louis the Pious.

THE ROYAL ARMY

The successful king required a large, effective, and well-equipped army. In theory, all freemen were bound to serve in the royal host. Thus, Charles the Bald could declare at the assembly of Meersen in 848:

> If, God forbid, it were necessary to face a wholesale invasion by the barbarians, the men known as *landweri* and the entire population of the kingdom would have to take up arms to repulse it.

Yet the kings were quite aware that they could not demand military service from all, and Charlemagne had therefore instituted a realistic means of levying soldiers whereby groups of freemen were responsible for equipping one of their number to serve. This system of course presupposed that royal officers maintained some sort of roster listing the men obliged to serve from a given county, a fact touched on by Charles the Bald in 864 when he recalled provisions made by his father in 829. Nevertheless, the kings had above all to count on the military support of their lay and ecclesiastical vassals and on the *scarae* made up of elite warriors who lived in the ambit of these vassals. According to the calculations of Karl Ferdinand Werner, the Carolingian kings of the first half of the ninth century could call on a total of some thirty-five thousand heavy cavalry and one hundred thousand foot soldiers.

The Ottonians inherited the Carolingian military system. They mostly depended on the warriors who lived with the royal court (*Heerschild*) and on the heavy cavalry sent to them by their lay and ecclesiastical vassals from across the kingdom. The *Indiculus loricatorum* ("List of Warriors Wearing Coats of Mail") of 981 sheds precious light on the number of horsemen called up by Emperor Otto II for his Italian expedition. The text mentions forty-seven lay nobles, bishops, and abbots from Germany, and it sets down the military resources they had to furnish. This evidence has made it possible to deduce that Otto may have had some six thousand horsemen at his disposal, and even so he was still defeated by Arab forces in southern Italy.

ROYAL CASTLES

The kings also held the right to erect and garrison fortresses. Until the middle of the ninth century, the Carolingians were content to station their men in strongholds seized from the enemy, for example in Aquitaine or in Saxony. Otherwise, they settled for building camps (*castra*) in the frontier regions. However, when enemies later successfully invaded the empire, citadels sprang up everywhere at strategic points, notably in the river valleys menaced by the Northmen. From 862 to 869, Charles the Bald set up a system of fortifications at Pîtres on the lower Seine, and in the capitulary of Quierzy of 877, he ordered the restoration of the ramparts of Paris and of other strongholds along the Seine and the Loire, "especially the fortress of St. Denis." Louis III built a castle along the upper valley of the Scheldt and another at Pontoise.

Nevertheless, the kings were not alone in erecting fortifications. Many local landowners built their own fortresses, and thereby inaugurated a thousand years of contention and rivalry between kings and the proprietors of "illegitimate" castles. In the famous Edict of Pîtres of 864, Charles the Bald ordered the destruction of strongholds built without his authorization. Only those who received specific delegated authority from the king or, in the case of ecclesiastics, a charter of immunity were permitted to build and maintain fortifications. Yet, as the nobles gained ever greater freedom, they did not hesitate to appropriate the royal privilege of fortifying their domains as they thought best. In the course of the tenth century in western Francia, the kings and regional leaders wrangled for control of strongholds that symbolized the king's authority and often guaranteed his military success. The fortified tower of Laon, for example, was a focus of rivalries between the last Carolingians and the Robertines. Through the multiplication of local seigneurial castles—called the *enchâtellement* in France and the *incastellamento* in Italy—the Carolingian period drew to its close. Until the early eleventh century, the traditions of royal power still survived in Germany where the Ottonian kings continued as masters of the citadels that they entrusted to their lay and ecclesiastical vassals.

The Carolingian Warrior

To round out this portrait of the military system, it is appropriate to recall that the Carolingian period gave birth to the rudiments of medieval knighthood. The Carolingian horseman heralded the coming of the medieval knight.

From his early youth, both the noble and the king were destined and prepared for making war. Commenting on Vegetius' *De re militari* ("Handbook on War"), Hrabanus Maurus remarked:

> Today, we see that children and adolescents are brought up in noble households in order to learn to put up with hardship, hunger, cold, and the sun's heat. A well-known proverb has it that "whoever isn't a horseman by adolescence will never be one, or will be one only with difficulty when he is older."

Since he was himself a cleric, Hrabanus conveniently omitted to mention another contemporary proverb: "Whoever stays at school without riding until age twelve is only good for the priesthood." Athletic training through hunting and simulated combat were already part of a knightly education. When a boy reached puberty, his father gave him a sword just as the king did for his own sons. The young man then entered the adult world; he joined his elders at the court of the king or some great noble. He was henceforth ready for the "game of war."

But warfare was more than a profitable diversion. It was also a holy undertaking whenever directed against pagans or enemies of the church, and kings accordingly asked not only their chaplains but also bishops and even the pope to pray for their success. As we have seen, Charlemagne addressed Pope Leo III in the following terms:

> With the help of divine clemency, it is my duty outwardly to defend the holy church of Christ by arms from the various attacks of the pagans and the devastation of the infidels, and inwardly to fortify her by spreading knowledge of the catholic faith. It is your duty, Most Holy Father, with your hands raised to God like Moses to help by prayer in our victory.

Before launching the campaign against the Avars, Charlemagne also ordered his troops to fast and pray for three days. Thus, the Carolingian host tended to resemble an Old Testament army, and its warriors were often viewed as new Maccabeans. In the *Ludwigslied*, one of the few medieval epics to predate the eleventh century, Louis III, victor over the Vikings at Saucourt, was likewise portrayed as a vassal of God. In the poem, God himself calls upon the king to succor the peoples afflicted by the Northmen. Louis accepts, and declares to his men as they prepare to attack: "God has sent me, and given me his command." Not surprisingly, the king's army goes forward to victory singing strains of *Kyrie eleison*. In the tenth century, the troops of Otto III actually did just this when they charged their Slavic adversaries.

The first outline of the "soldier of God" gradually took shape in the Carolingian period. About 930, abbot Odo of Cluny traced a portrait of the perfect lay warrior in his *Life of Saint Gerald*, a warrior who protected the weak and defended the church. Yet although he allowed his hero the right to bear arms and fight, Odo contended that "the holy noble had never been wounded and had never himself wounded another." This was the exceptional case of a layman living the life of a monk—who was thus in reality no layman at all. Yet the lay nobles who were not saints, and the kings who led them, could legitimately make war when they used their swords against the foes of the church. In the tenth century, ritual blessings for arms began to appear in Italy and Germany. Consider for instance the "Prayer over Warriors" found in the *Sacramentary of Fulda*:

> Hear, O Lord, our prayers, and bless with the hand of your Majesty the sword with which your servant wishes to be girded, so that he may defend and protect churches, widows, orphans, and all servants of God against the cruelty of the pagans and so that he may frighten off all who would ensnare him.

Significantly, warriors were also encouraged to view death for a holy cause as a likely means of entering Paradise. When Pope Leo VI appealed for resistance against the Arabs threatening Rome, he wrote: "Whoever dies faithful in this struggle will not see himself refused entry into the heavenly kingdom." Such words presaged the notion of the holy war that fully emerged, along with true medieval cavalry, in the eleventh century.

3. The Carolingians and the Renewal of the Western Economy

The history of economic activity in the early Middle Ages has occasioned a great deal of discussion in recent decades. Some believe that the economic decline and stagnation that set in during the late Roman Empire continued with little reprieve until the eleventh century. Others, however, argue that the west experienced an economic renewal after the seventh century, which the Carolingian rulers exploited and accelerated. It is not our purpose here to examine economic questions for their own sake, but rather to note how the Carolingians fostered an economic turnaround through their initiatives and legislation and later encouraged commerce and production.

The Principles

The leaders of the Carolingian period were not economic thinkers in the modern sense, yet they did formulate a number of religious and moral guidelines that bore on economic life.

The west was still very thinly populated even though the demographic outlook improved after the seventh century. Charlemagne had need of a large and vigorous population. In the famous *Capitulare de villis* meant to regulate the management of royal estates, Charlemagne expressed disquiet over manses that lay unoccupied (*mansi absi*); he ordered his stewards to repopulate them with tenants and bonded laborers. Likewise, in a capitulary issued at Nijmegen in 806, the emperor ordered that domains conferred as benefices should not have their manpower transferred to private allodial estates and thereby fall out of cultivation.

MARRIAGE
Stable families and marital institutions tended to assure the presence of agricultural tenants. Thus Carolingians thinkers occupied themselves with this aspect of social life and the ecclesiastical laws that governed it. Pro-

creation became the end of Christian marriage, and contraceptive practices, abortion, and infanticide were all condemned. Churchmen were
particularly concerned with the prospect of "incestuous" marriages, that
is, unions concluded between near relations. Yet this preoccupation went
contrary to the habits of the Germanic nobility, who were accustomed
to practicing endogamy, and the prohibitions elaborated by the church
could not easily be enforced. A step in this direction was the requirement
that all marriages be conducted in public and only after a public inquiry.
In a capitulary of 802, Charlemagne spoke of laymen "who besmirch
themselves in incestuous nuptials and who contract marriages before the
bishops, priests, and elders of the people can investigate the degree of
consanguinity of the future couple." In a somewhat different vein, the king
and the clergy regularly condemned the high incidence of rapes perpe-
trated by members of the nobility. Charles the Bald even gave special orders that his court tribunal should bring accused rapists to trial. Although
barbarian law allowed divorce, the practice was prohibited among Christians except in cases of adultery and impotence, in which careful inquiries
were still required. While the legislation of Pippin the Short concerning
divorce remained fairly flexible, the policies enforced by Charlemagne and
his successors increasingly reflected the indissolubility of marriage propounded by the church. The divorce attempted by Lothar II further
obliged the church to clarify its views on Christian marriage.

WORK

Refusing to embrace the antique notion of "noble leisure" (*otium*), the
Carolingian rulers looked on manual labor as a worthy and profitable activity. When Charlemagne renamed the months with new Germanic tags,
he often looked to specific agricultural activities. Hence, June became
"Plough-month"; July, "Hay-month"; August, "Ear-month"; September,
"Wood-month"; and October, "Wine-pressing-month." With the king in
the lead, the great landowners encouraged expanding and improving land
cultivation, and they settled new tenants to clear and plant unworked
plots. Thus, to repopulate the territory taken back from the Muslims in
Spain, Charles the Bald granted land to Visigothic refugees and determined the terms of their tenure in the capitulary *Pro hispanis*.

Charlemagne took exception to the vagabonds and beggars who criss-
crossed the kingdom, and in 789 and 806 he gave instructions that they
should be settled down and made to work. His son later established royal
officers charged with keeping watch over the beggars who flocked around

the court. The kings also sought to offer limited protection to laborers against the demands of their masters. For instance, the observance of Sunday as a day of rest was prescribed for all, even for cowherds, the lowliest of all agricultural workers.

The Carolingian rulers also legislated concerning animal husbandry. Contrary to assertions by some scholars, the rearing of livestock did not disappear in the west. Rather, wars of conquest boosted this activity owing to the need for horses and oxen. Warfare in turn offered a ready supply of captured or purchased slaves who swelled the numbers of *manicipia*, or "bondsmen," who worked the great estates. Slaves from the east were also exported across the empire for sale in Muslim Spain. Although the Carolingian rulers did nothing to eradicate slavery, they did intervene to "improve" the circumstances of slaves by forbidding the sale of Christian bondsmen to pagans or Jews.

Fair Prices

Charlemagne was the first of several Carolingian rulers to moralize on commerce and trade. He even offered definitions of fair trade and fair pricing, two concepts that would attract regular attention throughout the Middle Ages. He thought that a transaction was just when supply and demand set prices in the absence of prejudicial circumstances. Hence one of his early capitularies for Italy voided, subject to individual review, any sales of land made under duress at an unjustly low price. In 806 he clarified the definition of just pricing in these terms:

> All those who at harvest time stock up on wheat and wine not out of need but with greedy intentions—for instance buying a *modius* (measure) of wheat for two *denarii* and keeping it until can be sold for six *denarii* or more—make a dishonest profit. If, on the other hand, they buy out of need, to keep a supply for themselves or to sell it after a normal period, we call this an act of commerce (*negotium*).

Thus Charlemagne forbade the hoarding and speculation common in periods of famine. In 794, perhaps recalling Diocletian's *Edict on Prices*, Charlemagne fixed the maximum price of grain, and to set an example, he made known the price charged for wheat coming from his own estates. To ensure the intended effect, he soon had to define a common standard of weights and measures for use across the realm. Citing Proverbs 20:10, "Diverse weights and diverse measures are an abomination to God," Charlemagne declared: "All should use equal and exact measures as well as just and equal weights for buying and selling, whether in the towns or at a monastery or on a country estate." In 854 Charles the Bald would reiterate this principle and order his counts to verify weights and measures to prevent sellers from cheating purchasers.

USURY

The Carolingian rulers likewise struggled against the rampant evil of usury, which Charlemagne had occasion to define in 806: "Usury exists when one claims back more than one has given, for example, if you have given six *solidi* and ask for more back, or if you have given one *modius* of wheat and then demand an extra one back." In another capitulary, Charlemagne also forbade claiming interest on loans under a penalty of sixty *solidi*, that is, the fine for violating the *bannum* of the king. His successors continued to support the church's attempts to eliminate interest-bearing loans. Thus, Charles the Bald intervened to mitigate the effects of "mortgages." Originally, these loans bore a veiled form of interest. The borrower promised his creditor income or services from a possession (the *gage*, in French) that secured the loan, and the possession was often the borrower's person. When the loan came due, the original sum had to be repaid, or ownership of the security was forfeit (*mort*) to the lender. In the Edict of Pîtres of 864, Charles limited to seven years the period for which a mortgagor might be indentured, and he also stipulated that the children of a woman entangled in a mortgage remained free.

Royal power thus came to affect economic life significantly. Religious as well as practical concerns spurred the Carolingian rulers to act in ways that contributed to new economic and material progress.

Economic Developments

THE MANAGEMENT OF ROYAL DOMAINS

The Carolingian kings were great landowners. Thanks to inheritance and conquests, they possessed some six hundred domains from the Loire valley to the Rhine basin, and from these they drew the better part of their income. The kings thus sought to stay abreast of circumstances on their *villae*, and required their stewards to compile inventories of the available resources. Some such inventories have survived for five royal estates, but it is difficult to date them precisely. It seems likely, however, that those in question were compiled at the time Louis the Pious put together a dowry for his daughter Gisela in consideration of her marriage to Eberhard, the future marquis of Friuli. Known to scholarship as the *Brevium exempla* ("Examples of Manorial Accounts"), these inventories describe farm buildings, their furnishings and agricultural implements; they provide lists of livestock; and they indicate the produce harvested in the year that the inventory was compiled. As we have seen from an extract of the *Capitulare de villis* (see p. 137), Charlemagne also took great care to describe how his royal estates should be managed. The steward (*iudex*) of a domain resided in a manor house; assisted by overseers (*maiores*), he was responsible for assigning field work and domestic tasks to the laborers of the *villa*, which was understood to include both a farm and adjoining workshops. This steward fixed the date for sowing and harvesting the crop and managed the breeding of horses and the upkeep of mills, cider presses, and the forest, which in this period provided all manner of goods in addition to serving as a hunting ground for the king.

Charlemagne set an example for both his successors and for other great lay and ecclesiastical landowners who sought to regulate their own domains along similar lines. As we have seen, Abbot Irmino of St. Germain-des-Prés ordered the compilation of the famous *Polyptych* in which he listed his abbey's widespread domains (see p. 292), and there exist other similar testimonies from St. Père of Chartres, St. Remi of Reims, St. Amand, St. Bertin, Lobbes, Prüm, and even from St. Victor of Marseilles. Likewise, Adalhard of Corbie, a cousin of Charlemagne, drafted precise guidelines for the artisans and peasants working on the domains of his monastery. Himself a great landowner, Einhard used letters to direct his stewards and to offer advice on such things as breeding livestock, collecting honey, and brewing bear. A certain Swabian bishop about to visit an estate dispatched the following directives his steward:

> Mind that you have excellent wheat on hand, and arrange for bread. Ask twelve tenants for the sheep they owe, and give the animals salt and good fodder every day so that they will be ready upon my arrival. . . . Have wine brought from Constance, and bring in firewood.

Similarly, to accommodate their own travels from palace to palace, the Carolingian rulers elaborated a system of provisioning whereby leading vassals were obliged to furnish royal armies and the court with fodder and victuals (*fodrum*) as well as lodging (*gistum*). The Ottonians also lived from their own resources, moving from domain to domain, and they applied the same Carolingian system in Germany and Italy.

One of the goals of efficiently managing the estates was the sale of surplus produce. Although men dreaded the lean period that preceded the annual harvest, barring famine, some crops were sold at local markets. Despite its limitations, the Carolingian economy was not entirely closed. Commercial exchanges existed, and the rulers often acted innovatively to encourage them.

TRADE AND MERCHANTS

Markets

While still mayor of the palace, Pippin the Short ordered the introduction of designated market days in those episcopal towns that did not already have them. His aim was to fix a time and place where commercial transactions could be monitored, thereby enriching the treasury with the various imposts and tolls levied on cartage and sales. Markets grew into regular events, attracting ever larger numbers of buyers and sellers. Thus in his *Capitulare de villis*, Charlemagne instructed that his agricultural tenants should not go "waste their time in the marketplaces." In 802 the emperor also forbade the sale of precious articles, slaves, horses, and other animals during nighttime, and commanded that such transactions be carried out in public. In 820 Louis the Pious addressed warnings to those who sold their wares secretly to evade paying taxes. The markets in different goods were generally held once a week, often on Saturday. To accommodate Jewish merchants in Lyon, Louis also agreed to reschedule the markets that were held on the Sabbath, a gesture that provoked virulent protest from Archbishop Agobard, one of the rare anti-Semites of the period.

The development of commerce was such that in 864 Charles the Bald ordered the counts to draw up a list of the various markets, distinguishing centers according to the period of their establishment: in the time of Charlemagne, in the time of Louis the Pious, or since his own accession. The useful public markets were to be maintained, the clandestine gatherings were to be suppressed; and those that had shifted locales were to be returned to their original site.

Markets were so profitable that bishops and abbots regularly requested charters allowing them to collect and keep part or all of the duties levied on commercial exchanges. They also asked for permission to establish new markets under their own auspices, and such matters prompted royal interest and intervention in town affairs.

Towns and Emporiums

The kings spent little time in urban centers, and generally preferred to live at their country residences. Nonetheless, some rulers occasionally resided for extended periods in towns like Frankfurt, Pavia, Regensburg, and Reims, where they built new churches and monasteries and also commissioned work from craftsmen and artists. By virtue of his royal prerogatives over fortifications, the king had to authorize any plans to tear down or rebuild city ramparts. Finally, he also had occasion to intervene when a bishop or abbot founded an "emporium," or *portus*, outside the walls of a town, thereby establishing a new trading-place. Major emporiums of this type were situated along the Scheldt at Valenciennes, Tournai and Ghent, and on the Rhine at Mainz, but above all they were to be found in Austrasia on the Meuse. Newer commercial settlements were also founded at such locales as Piacenza on the Po and Regensburg on the Danube.

The largest trading centers attracted the professional merchants who engaged in long-range trade among the various regions of the west. Their activities were also subject to royal control. English merchants arrived on the continent by the seaports of Quentovic and Dorestad, and from there they continued on to sojourn at either St. Denis or Mainz. Thus, Charlemagne had a chance to complain to King Offa that the sections of woolen cloth he purchased varied too much in length. To the east, Charlemagne moved to stop sales of highly prized Frankish weapons to Slavic tribesmen. In the capitulary of Thionville of 806, he listed towns through which merchants going east had to travel in order to have their wares inspected: Bardovick and Scheessel in Saxony, as well as Magdeburg, Erfurt, Forchheim, Pfreimd, Regensburg, and Lorch, and he added: "They are not to take arms and coats of mail to sell; and if they are discovered carrying them, all their stock is to be confiscated." In a similar vein, passes through the Alps were guarded by officers of the fisc who collected duties.

In 828 Louis the Pious promulgated a capitulary in favor of the merchants who journeyed to trade at the court. The emperor forbade his officers to seize their goods and barges:

> They, as well as Jews, should be allowed to serve us freely at our palace. And should they wish, with God's help, to improve their means of transport within the kingdom so as to trade with greater profit for themselves and for us, let them do so. No seizures of goods should be tolerated or inflicted upon them at passes in the Alps or anywhere else. Let no one anywhere claim any duty except for the one reserved for our count at Quentovic and Dorestad

and at the alpine passes where a duty of ten percent is required. Should any case come up against them that they could not settle in their home region without unfair and excessive cost, let the trial be suspended until it is brought before us or before the officers whom we have set over such matters and over other merchants, and let the judgment be reserved until they receive a definitive sentence according to the king's command.

This text has been variously interpreted as a sign of long-distance commercial activity or as a means of attracting purveyors to the royal court through special privileges. In fact, the capitulary was a component of a wider program to encourage trade and traders. A commercial treaty concluded between Lothar I and Venice in 840 that allowed the free circulation of merchants throughout northern Italy was conceived in the same spirit.

Roads

As much to facilitate commerce as to expedite the movement of armies, Carolingian kings worked to maintain bridges and ancient Roman roadways (*via regia, via publica*). Over the Seine they restored fixed bridges, while elsewhere they set up removable bridges of tethered pontoons. As much as they could, the rulers sought to keep up the decaying system of ancient roads. For military reasons, Charlemagne even sought in 793 to excavate a canal to connect the Rhine and the Danube rivers. In the second half of the ninth century, the troubles provoked by invasions and political uncertainty encouraged ever greater use of river transport. An early tenth-century inquiry made at Raffelstetten, near Linz on the Danube, revealed, for instance, that boats with three-man crews regularly moved salt from Bavaria into Moravia.

MONETARY POLICY

A genuine commercial policy presupposed the existence of a medium of exchange, that is, coinage. Aware of this fact, the Carolingian kings promulgated several capitularies regulating money and minting.

Under Pippin the Short

Gold coinage had largely disappeared by the end of the seventh century. No longer minted, it was replaced in circulation by silver coinage struck in a variety of lay and ecclesiastical workshops, while silver *sceattae* from Anglo-Saxon and Frisian lands also filtered into the Frankish kingdom. In

755, four years after his coronation, Pippin promulgated the earliest surviving act of Frankish monetary legislation at the assembly of Ver:

> With regard to coinage, we order that no more than twenty-two *solidi* [worth of *denarius* coins] should be made from a pound-weight [of silver] and that the minter should keep one [*solidus* of coins] and turn over twenty-one *solidi* to whoever brought the metal.

These silver denarii, of which some 150 still exist, bore the name of the king, not that of the minter, as well as the name of the place where they were struck. As Jean Lafaurie has written:

> Pippin the Short wrought a monetary revolution. He was the first king to legislate on coinage. He managed to impose his coinage and to reaffirm the royal monopoly on minting. This achievement, brought to fullest effect under Charlemagne, would endure for a century and a half, that is, as long as the kings had the strength to protect it.

Under Charlemagne

About 781, Charlemagne introduced silver *denarii* into Italy, where a highly debased gold coinage still continued to circulate. Later, Charlemagne resolved to strike a heavier *denarius* weighing 1.69 grams to replace the *denarii* minted under Pippin, which weighed only 1.35 grams. This increase in weight has usually been tied to successful mining operations pursued in places like Melle, near Niort in western France, a locale whose name in the Carolingian period was *Metalia*. More daringly, some specialists have also sought of explain the low value of silver by a rise in the price of gold in Byzantium even though this solution presupposes a high, no doubt unrealistic degree of economic interdependence between east and west. At the Council of Frankfurt in 794, Charlemagne imposed his new standard:

> As regards *denarii*, know that we have decreed that everywhere, in every town and every trading-place, the new *denarii* are also to be legal tender and to be accepted by everybody. And if they bear the monogram of our name and are of pure silver, should anyone reject them . . . he is to pay fifteen *solidi*.

The study of *denarii* issued after this date has demonstrated that Charlemagne also adopted a new heavier pound to replace the ancient Roman pound, which had remained unchanged for centuries. The weight of Charlemagne's *denarius* was keyed to the new standard weight: twenty *solidi* made a pound, and twelve *denarii* equaled one *solidus*. While pounds and *solidi* existed merely as units of reckoning, Charlemagne's *denarius* became the new medium of exchange. The emperor would act on three further occasions to limit the number of workshops entitled to strike coins and to privilege the status of the court's own mint, no doubt as part of the fight against counterfeiting. Thanks to the discovery of a number of important coin hoards, numismatists have been able to study the evolution of *denarii* marked on one side with Charlemagne's monogram and on the other with a cross or a stylized temple. They have also been able to distinguish contemporary coins struck in the local mints operated by Louis of Aquitaine and Pippin of Italy.

Under Louis the Pious

In his turn, Louis the Pious took measures in 819, 823, and 829 to regulate activities in royal mints and the quality of their coinage. To frustrate the efforts of counterfeiters, he introduced a new type of *denarii*. Although he commissioned the minting of a limited number of gold *solidi* in Frisia, northern Italy, and at Aachen, this effort was largely an attempt to create a prestige coinage, or perhaps medallions that were not intended for use in commerce. We should note, however, that gold had not disappeared from the west even though it was virtually never used as legal tender. Employed in the creation of jewelry, reliquaries, and luxury items, the metal arrived in the west from Byzantium and the Arab world. Moreover, it was still an object of trade since Charles the Bald ordered that a pound of pure gold should not be sold for more that twelve pounds of silver.

Under Charles the Bald

The grandson and namesake of Charlemagne remained true to the example set by his predecessors. In 854 and 856, he issued new sanctions aimed at counterfeiters and those who attempted to pass counterfeit tender. In 864, the Edict of Pîtres included eight articles devoted to coinage and minting. The king designated workshops entitled to strike coinage, including those at the court, Quentovic, Rouen, Reims, Sens, Paris, Orléans, Chalon-sur-Saône, Melle, and Narbonne. He ordered the minting of new coins, and instructed that after July 1 everyone should exchange his silver bullion for the new coins. These were to be accepted everywhere. This capitulary is the last known to have addressed monetary concerns.

Revival of Local Economies

The spread of the *denarius*, or penny, across the west had an enormous impact. To begin, these coins, bearing the monogram of the Carolingian rulers, served to enhance royal prestige and authority. Their proliferation along with that of the half-penny, or *obolus*, certainly contributed to the renewal of local and regional trade. Deals were made in quantities of produce estimated in *denarii* (whence the French word *denrée*, meaning "foodstuffs"). Moreover, controls on minting and trade could be more easily enforced thanks to the uniform standards of coinage. In the Edict of Pîtres of 864, Charles the Bald instructed his officers to inspect the coinage in use in the marketplaces and to prosecute those who refused legitimate *denarii*. The officers were, however, instructed to be lenient with women, for they were "accustomed to haggle" (*barcagnare*, whence the English "to bargain") before settling on an agreeable price.

With some exaggeration, Jan Dhondt says that *denarii* circulated "by the millions." Ample scope still remained for barter, but coinage was used for trade and wages, to redeem obligations in kind, to collect taxes from merchants, and notably, to levy the tribute paid to the Northmen. A number of coin hoards witness how Carolingian *denarii* passed to Scandinavia and England. Moreover, King Offa of Mercia copied the Carolingian monetary system by fixing the value of the shilling at twelve pennies, and the "duodecimal" system he inaugurated survived in Britain until 1971. Carolingian monetary reforms resulted in a vast monometallic "silver zone" that prevailed across Europe until the reemergence of gold coinage in the thirteenth century.

The Successors of the Carolingians

The kings of the tenth century benefited from the economic renewal of the west, and when their authority permitted, they maintained the economic policies introduced by the Carolingians. They endeavored to open up new lands to agriculture, to foster trade, to create marketplaces and human settlements. They appreciated, as Alfred the Great said in a celebrated passage, that "the king's raw materials and the tools by which he governs are a well-populated country: he needs men for prayer, men for war, and men for work."

Coinage and minting differed, however, according to the kingdom in question. In western Francia, the kings gradually lost their monopoly on striking coins. Although they increasingly awarded minting privileges to abbeys and bishoprics, the sovereigns sought to ensure the presence of their own name on the coins produced. Charles the Simple issued a reminder to this effect to the abbot of Tournus in 915. Although Hugh the Great placed his own name on some coins, his son reversed this move. The hoard of Fécamp buried about 980 has revealed more than 1,500 *denarii* and *oboli*. Its coins have made it possible to gauge the diffusion of the right to mint, but they have equally demonstrated the hesitation of regional leaders to appropriate this royal privilege. Thus Françoise Dumas has observed:

> The overarching authority of the last Carolingians was recognized in the immediate vicinity of the royal domain and in the more distant regions where these kings somehow made their presence felt. The majority of local lords who had their own mints did not struggle to assert their independence. Perhaps their power was not sufficient; perhaps they did not attach enough importance to that form of sovereignty. Although royal power petered out, no other authority came to replace it over the entirety of the kingdom.

In Germany the Ottonian kings, like their Anglo-Saxon contemporaries, retained control of all minting centers. Otto I worked new silver mines at Rammelsberg, near Goslar in the Harz Mountains, and he had *denarii* struck at Magdeburg, Halle, Mainz, Verdun, and above all at Cologne. The Cologne *denarius* was based on Carolingian models, and it came to be used far and wide. The ties established between Germany and the Slavic and Scandinavian territories served to introduce *denarii* into these regions. The Polish rulers also began to strike silver coinage.

As in the time of the great Carolingian rulers, the opening of a minting workshop was accompanied by the founding of a market. According to Otto III in a privilege for Selz, "coinage and a marketplace are necessary for the multitude of people who come together here, but also for the monks and people who live here." The Ottonians thus provided places for changing money in fortified castles or at monasteries. In 936 Otto I established in Magdeburg the so-called *Wick*, where Jews and other merchants from beyond the Elbe met. Of the twenty-nine locales that were home to fortified marketplaces, twelve soon became full-fledged towns joining the ranks of other urban settlements based at episcopal centers or around royal palaces. The king also profited from the new settlements by collecting imposts, which he shared with local nobles, and merchants also placed themselves under royal protection. Hence in 946 Otto I conceded a public market to the abbey of Korvei and instructed his agents "to ensure a stable peace for those who come and go and for those who reside there;" in 965, merchants traveling to the market at Bremen received protection, and in return, they had to deliver goods to the court; and in 996 Otto III authorized the bishop of Freising to found a daily market, and placed visitors to it under the *bannum* of imperial peace. These were survivals of policies initiated by the Carolingian rulers.

Continuations were also evident in the realm of long-distance trade. The kings encouraged merchants who transported wares from the Rhine or the Danube to the Elbe, and from the Elbe on to Prague and Krakow. Political alliances with the Slavic princes also favored these lines of trade. As masters of Italy, the Ottonians practiced the same policies. They did not lose sight of the resources that the court at Pavia could gain from long-distance trade. Since the Lombard period, Pavia was Italy's largest urban center and would long remain so. The famous *Honoranciae civitatis Papiae* ("High Offices of Pavia") offers a portrait of the profits from commerce taken in by the royal treasury at the end of the tenth century. According to the author of the report, the merchants who entered into the kingdom at the various customs posts in the Alps paid a duty of 10 percent on horses, slaves, textiles, tin, and swords. English merchants were, however, dispensed from these charges in exchange for sending the palace fifty pounds worth of silver and weapons every three years. The Venetians who had long traded with Pavia were obliged yearly to pay out some 12,000 *denarii* worth of silver. Traders from Salerno, Gaeta, or Amalfi had to turn over fixed amounts of silver and products in kind. The text adds:

> The great, noble, or rich merchants will always receive from the hand of the emperor in Pavia a privilege valid everywhere they are doing business in order that no one should importune them in any fashion on land or sea.

In the face of such a document, it appears difficult to advance the notion of economic lethargy in the west.

4. The First Flowering of European Culture

Whenever the cultural achievements of the Carolingian period come under consideration, the phrase "Carolingian renaissance," first coined by Jean-Jacques Ampère in 1839, immediately comes to mind. Yet this expression should not be taken to imply that the west had wallowed in barbarism and darkness before the accession of the Carolingian kings. Remnants of late antique Roman culture survived down to the seventh century and provided foundations for a new Christian culture in Spain, Italy, and the British Isles. These were the forerunners of the "renaissance" in the Carolingian period. Gothic and Lombard rulers as well as Irish and Anglo-Saxon monks also fostered learning and left their own valuable legacy.

It was the merit of the Carolingian rulers to take advantage of the first stirrings of cultural awakening in the west, to have restored centers of learning, and to have patronized and encouraged their own circle of artists and men of letters. Contemporaries were conscious of the impetus to learning given by the Carolingian kings, and if they did not use the term "renaissance," they did use the word *renovatio*, or "renewal." Very often they ascribed the entire credit for the flowering of letters to Charlemagne personally. In the words of Heiric of Auxerre, the emperor was the man who had "made flames arise from ashes." Lupus of Ferrières went further: "Literature is so obliged to him that it will ensure his perpetual remembrance." Finally, the learned Walafrid Strabo offered the following assessment in his preface to Einhard's *Life of Charlemagne*:

> Of all kings, Charles was the most avid in seeking out learned men and in according them patronage so that they could philosophize at their ease. Indeed, through a new burst of light virtually unknown to the barbarians before his time, he restored brilliance and (thanks to God's own radiance) sight to the murky and (I dare say) blind vastness of the kingdom committed to him by God.

Nevertheless, Charlemagne was not the only king responsible for this renewal. His father, Pippin, had begun the renaissance before him, and his successors would continue it after him. Despite the crisis of the empire and the political turmoil of late ninth century, the Carolingian *renovatio* continued into the tenth century across much of the west. Without considering every aspect of the Carolingian renaissance, it is important to show how the new dynasty was able to create the conditions necessary for the first great flowering of European culture.

Educational Policies

The birth of ecclesiastical schools in the west dated from their appearance at cathedrals, monasteries, and even rural parishes in the sixth century. The clergy and monks had organized a program of study centered on Holy Scripture that contrasted markedly with the curriculum of the schools of late antiquity. Nevertheless, such Christian schools as continued to exist suffered from the general crisis that had overtaken the church by the beginning of the eight century.

Pippin the Short

By focusing his reform effort on the clergy, Pippin III had already prepared the terrain for a restoration of learning and culture. His court was open to men of letters, and his episcopal appointees were educated. Thus, Pope Stephen III knew that he would be understood when he asked the king in 769 to send him "learned bishops versed in the Holy Scriptures and in the teachings of the holy canons." At the Synod of Gentilly of 767, the Frankish bishops had been able to face Byzantine experts in discussions on the veneration of holy images and the nature of the Trinity.

The Restoration of Schools

Charlemagne built on the achievements of his father by restoring schools. In this, he followed an example already set by his cousin Tassilo III, who had asked the bishops of Bavaria in 772 to organize schools attached to their churches, but in so doing, Charlemagne also restored an ancient tradition of the Roman emperors. It is certain that the early sojourns in Italy and the influence of Lombard scholars who later settled at the Frankish court, such as Paul the Deacon, Peter of Pisa, and Paulinus, later archbishop of Aquileia, helped to shape Charlemagne's policies. But in 871 the king met the Anglo-Saxon scholar Alcuin in Parma, and this master of the cathedral school at York came to play a decisive role in the emerging cultural renewal.

Charlemagne's interest in schooling had a particular goal. He wanted the clergy to be educated well enough to teach in turn the people entrusted to its care. With the reform of the liturgy launched by Pippin, the reorganization of the church would only succeed if the clergy knew Latin and could read and meditate on the Scriptures. Moreover, Charlemagne appreciated the vital importance of literacy for improving the administration of his kingdom. For quite practical reasons, he needed to restore to the written word the role that it had played in the Roman empire. The counts and the *missi dominici* had to be educated, or at least have men with them who could read the orders dispatched by the king and then draft replies, reports, and inventories. Writing became an instrument of government.

In these circumstances, Charlemagne decided in 789, some twenty years after his accession as king, that in each monastery and each bishopric instruction should be given to boys in reading, writing, stenography, singing, reckoning, and grammar. The program outlined in the *Admonitio generalis*, or "General Exhortation," of 789 was thus scarcely original; it merely restated the traditional program of studies taught in ecclesiastical schools since the sixth century. What was important was the aim to set up schools in every monastery and bishopric in the realm. Later Charlemagne even encouraged the bishops to establish rural schools in villages and hamlets, thus harking back to a decision of the Synod of Vaison of 529. Little is known of this later effort of reform except for what can be gleaned from a collection of the statutes promulgated at the diocesan synods of Theodulf of Orléans. The bishop had great hopes:

> In villages and hamlets, the priests should hold school. If some of the faithful entrust them with their children to teach them to read, they should not refuse to receive them and to instruct them, doing so in complete charity.
> When the priests discharge this function, they should require no payment, and if they receive anything, it should only be some small kindness offered by the parents.

In a questionnaire of 803 Charlemagne recalled that parents were supposed to send their children to school. About 813 a synod at Mainz hoped that when children returned home they would teach the prayers they had learned in school to their relatives and neighbors.

Charlemagne was painfully aware of the difficulty of applying his educational reforms across the kingdom. Throughout his reign, in capitularies, instructions to the *missi*, and interventions at church councils, he repeated that clerics and monks should be well educated and that laymen should at least know the rudiments of their faith. The bishops also hammered at these instructions at the diocesan level. About 813, Archbishop Leidrad of Lyon proudly reported to the emperor the circumstances in his episcopal school:

> I have groups (*scolae*) of cantors, most of whom are so learned that they could also teach others. Moreover, I have groups (*scolae*) of lectors who are able not only to read the lessons of the offices but also to derive the fruits of spiritual understanding from their meditation on holy books.

The archbishop also thanked Charlemagne for having sent him a cleric from Metz who had helped to introduce in Lyon the liturgy celebrated at the court.

It was long thought that Charlemagne had established a school at his own court. To support this thesis, scholars turned to an anecdote reported by Notker the Stammerer: the king one day went to inspect the school and ended up reproving the lazy sons of nobles and praising the diligent commoners. It is likely that Charlemagne monitored the clerics at his court, but those who formed the *schola*—in reality a band of scribes, notaries, cantors—were simply young men who were learning their trade in the offices and the chapel of the court.

LOUIS THE PIOUS

Assisted by the bishops, Louis the Pious continued the educational policies of his father. Under the guidance of Louis and Benedict of Aniane, the reform council of Aachen in 817 decreed that henceforth monastic schools should be strictly reserved for boy oblates preparing to become monks. Consequently the great abbeys like St. Gall had to open external schools where secular clerics and laymen could receive instruction. Thus, in the famous Plan of St. Gall, the school, its twelve small classrooms, and the master's house were situated north of the church, while the precinct reserved for the boy oblates and novices lay east of it. Of course most monasteries did not have the means to operate a double school, and the decision of 817 went largely unheeded.

At Attigny in 822 the bishops expressed regret that they could not organize schools as they should and resolved to establish the needed facilities as means became available. Three years later the emperor reminded them of their commitment:

Do not neglect to organize well-functioning schools for the education of the sons and ministers of the church. They should be set up in adequate places wherever this has yet been done.

In 829 bishops who had attended the Synod of Paris issued a report wherein they suggested that the emperor follow the example of his father and establish "public schools" at three locales in the empire. The term *publicus* does not, however, imply that the school would be open to both clergy and laymen, but rather that they would be under the control of the civil authorities.

This proposal had in fact already been advanced in northern Italy four years earlier. At the assembly of Corte Olona, near Pavia, King Lothar had decided to establish nine schools where "student teachers" sent from different bishoprics could perfect their skills. These school were located at Pavia, Ivrea, Turin, Cremona, Vicenza, Verona, Cividale, Florence, and Fermo. A year later Pope Eugenius II followed the king's example and opened schools in the bishoprics and important towns of the lands of St. Peter, where instruction would be given in the liberal arts and sacred doctrine.

After the partition of 843, legislative texts concerning schools are more rare. However, Pope Leo IV repeated the instructions of his predecessor in 853, emphasizing the importance of religious instruction, and he requested that schoolmasters submit reports on their activities. Bishops at the Synod of Savonnières in 859 also recalled how the Carolingian rulers had brought light and learning to the church thanks to the schools they had fostered. The churchmen now hoped that Lothar II and Charles the Bald would take measures to establish public schools everywhere men could be found to teach.

THE RESULTS

Although it is difficult to determine how educational directives were applied, qualitative and quantitative advances in literary activity demonstrate that the kings' efforts bore fruit. The results were still modest in the "first Carolingian renaissance," that of Charlemagne's reign, but cultural centers flourished in Francia, Italy, and even Brittany, though none can be documented for Aquitaine and Provence.

Some schools were directed by eminent masters, and some are known especially for the interest devoted to the rediscovery of classical authors. Students applied themselves with enthusiasm to such subjects as grammar, rhetoric, astronomy, and medicine. As Alcuin put it, the study of such liberal arts permitted one "not only to attain the summit of Holy Scripture, but also the true wisdom that is the knowledge of God." In a famous letter to Charlemagne, the Anglo-Saxon deacon described the ideal:

> If most men were to embrace your outstanding intentions, perhaps a new Athens would be brought to perfection in Francia, indeed a far more excellent Athens. For ennobled by teaching of Christ the Lord, our Athens would surpass the wisdom of the Academy. Educated only in the disciplines of Plato, the old Athens glimmered thanks to the seven liberal arts. But enriched by the sevenfold plenitude of the Holy Spirit, the new Athens would surpass every glory of worldly wisdom.

Whatever the success of the ideal, students did rediscover a taste for correct Latin, and this was not the least considerable achievement of the Carolingian renaissance.

CAROLINGIAN LATIN

To grasp the enormous linguistic improvement that marked Carolingian Latinity, it is enough to compare a text written at the beginning of the eighth century with one written at its end. This transformation was due in part to royal complaints and exhortations. In a circular letter to the abbots of his kingdom, Charlemagne complained that the monks who prayed for him often knew little grammar and were thus incapable of correctly understanding the scriptural texts they read and copied. For the king, piety began in a sense with the quality of one's Latin, and improving it was a duty. Thus one poet praised Charlemagne for applying as much effort to removing mistakes from books as to defeating his enemies on the battlefield. Of course some modern scholars have also noted that by arresting the evolution of Latin into a written vernacular language Carolingian scholars helped to create a gulf between high and low culture. Nevertheless, the success of liturgical and educational reform as then conceived as well as an effective imperial administration presupposed a well-disciplined common tongue. Thanks to the Carolingians, the west acquired a shared means of communication: a Latin lingua franca.

VERNACULAR LITERATURE

The Carolingian rulers were also mindful of the fact that most nobles did not have access to Latin culture. Faithful to his own Austrasian origins, Charlemagne ordered transcriptions of the "ancient barbarian poems that recounted the history and wars of the kings of old." Einhard, who reports this detail, also adds that the emperor sketched out a grammar of his mother tongue and assigned Germanic names to the months. Although nothing remains of these barbarian epic poems (except perhaps the fragments of the *Hildebrandslied*, written in Fulda around 800), several sources report that Frankish aristocrats knew of them. Louis the Pious likewise commissioned a poem in the Saxon language: an epic based on the Gospels called *Heliand*, or "Savior." Somewhat later, Louis the German also received the dedication of a poetic evocation of the Last Judgment, the *Muspilli*. This Christian vernacular poetry was an outgrowth of the general effort to ensure that the common people understood their faith and their prayers in their own language. At a synod held in Tours in 813, the bishops were thus enjoined to deliver their sermons in either the Romance vernacular (*lingua romana rustica*) or the Germanic tongue (*lingua theotisca*). In most regions, local priests probably did this already.

The Court as a Center of Learning

Restoring schools and training men in the rudiments of reading and writing were the indispensable preconditions for renewal of learning, but they did not make for a renaissance in themselves. The kings had to offer the good example of commissioning new works as patrons of literary learning.

THE PALACE AT AACHEN

In one of his capitularies Charlemagne declared his aim to restore the study of literature that the negligence of his predecessors had allowed to decline and likewise his intent to foster the liberal arts. From the beginning of his reign, he received writers at his court, and as Einhard reports, he himself became a student first of the elderly Peter of Pisa and then of Alcuin. The king had enormous curiosity for all things touching on grammar, rhetoric, astronomy, and theology. His sons, daughters, and the other young nobles who lived at the court enjoyed lessons from masters chosen by the king. According to Alcuin, all took part in the intellectual debates held at moments of leisure, over dinner, or even in the baths at Aachen. Such was the visage of the "palace academy" where religious, scientific, and philosophical questions were discussed. For example, at Charlemagne's behest and for the general enlightenment of the court, the Anglo-Saxon Fridugisus, a disciple of Alcuin, composed a discourse on the nature of nothingness and shadows. Yet the tenor of discussions was often less serious, as when Charlemagne and his friends engaged in literary games.

The king knew as well how to encourage his learned associates to further his religious policies. Thus, to defeat the Adoptionist heresy from Spain, Charlemagne enlisted help from Alcuin and Paulinus of Aquileia, and he called on Theodulf of Orléans to respond to Byzantine arguments concerning the procession of the Holy Spirit and the proper use of icons. From Paul the Deacon he requested a *History of the Bishops of Metz*, which gave pride of place to his illustrious forebear Saint Arnulf. All writers, whatever their origins or domicile, might be called upon to serve the king.

Under Louis the Pious, the reputation and influence of the court was just as great, at least at the beginning of his reign. The Irishman Dicuil dedicated a geographic treatise to the emperor, and other learned men like Einhard, Walafrid Strabo, and the prolific Hrabanus Maurus also resided at the court. Louis the Pious commissioned his arch-chaplain, Abbot Hilduin of St. Denis, to translate the Pseudo-Dionysian corpus that the Byzantine emperor Michael II sent as a gift in 827.

A year earlier, a Venetian priest had offered to build a hydraulic organ for the royal chapel. It was the second such organ to be enjoyed by the Carolingians; the first had arrived in 755 as a gift to Pippin the Short. Although the impact of these organs was limited, scholars have long recognized that the royal court played a leading role in the development of western religious chant. Pippin the Short and Charlemagne both had worked to introduce *cantilena romana*, or "Roman-style chant," into the Frankish church. Singers from the royal *schola cantorum* were dispatched to various local churches to pass on their vocal technique and melodies. About 800, the abbey of St. Riquier produced the first *tonarium*, or "singing manual," known to indicate the musical modes in which its antiphons were to be sung. Significantly, the abbot of the day was Angilbert, Charlemagne's son-in-law. In the time of Louis the Pious, the imperial chancellor Helisachar and archbishop Agobard of Lyon worked to expand and perfect the so-called Gregorian Antiphonary. These efforts were encouraged by the Carolingian rulers, and the impetus they gave to musical studies continued to bear fruit. In the tenth century, a rudimentary system of musical notation based on neumes—accent-like marks traced above the sung text—developed. This century also witnessed the emergence of the earliest liturgical tropes and the first medieval treatises on music and harmony.

CULTURAL ENDEAVORS AFTER 843

The demise of imperial political unity had consequences for the renaissance of learning and culture. Each king attempted to keep scholars of his own and even vied with others to patronize certain men. Hrabanus Maurus, Angelomus of Luxeuil, and Sedulius Scottus addressed poems and exegetical treatises on the Bible to Lothar I and his wife, Ermengard. Encyclopedic in his learning, the Irishman Sedulius came to settle at Liège in the circle of Bishop Franco, a relative of the emperor. After 855, Sedulius remained a follower of Lothar II, for whom he composed a "mirror of princes" entitled *Liber de rectoribus christianis* ("On Christian Rulers"). The episcopal court of Drogo of Metz, a half-brother of Louis the Pious, also welcomed the Irishman Murethach, the author of an important commentary on Donatus. Meanwhile, Louis the German found his own circle of scholarly adherents. Hrabanus Maurus offered him several exegetical works as well as his great encyclopedia *De universo*. Ermenric of Ellwangen, a student of Hrabanus, also proposed to write the king a treatise on the liberal arts. As successor to Louis, Charles the Fat continued to cultivate close relations with the monks of St. Gall, then home to the most famous school in Germany. It was Charles who asked Notker the Stammerer to write his famous *Gesta Karoli* ("The Deeds of Charlemagne").

CHARLES THE BALD, THE LEARNED KING

Of the Carolingian rulers, Charles the Bald was surely the most cultivated. Carefully educated by his mother, Judith, and his tutor, Walafrid Strabo, Charles was interested in all manner of subjects. Frechulf of Lisieux addressed his *Universal History* to the seven-year-old prince, and Lupus of Ferrières later compiled a brief résumé of the history of the Roman emperors intended to provide Charles with models for emulation. Charles himself commissioned a poem on his ancestors and asked his cousin Nithard to "write down for posterity the story of the events of his time." Desirous to pray along with the church, the king requested Usuardus of St. Germain-des-Prés to compile a martyrology. The king's interest in hagiography likewise prompted Milo of St. Amand to offer Charles a metrical reworking of the *Life of Saint Amandus*, while Heiric of Auxerre offered his own verse *Life of Saint Germain* to the king. In addition to these local religious heroes, Charles was also interested in the saints of the east. For example, Paul, a deacon in Naples, dedicated his translation of the *Life of Saint Mary the Egyptian* to the Frankish ruler, thereby acquainting the west with the first elements of the Faust legend. In 876 Anastasius Bibliothecarius also offered Charles his Latin renderings of the *Passion of Saint Demetrios* and the *Passion of Saint Denis*.

As lay-abbot of the monastery of St. Denis, Charles was particularly interested in the story of its illustrious patron saint. He shared in the general belief of the time that the first bishop of Paris was both the Dionysius converted by Saint Paul on the Areopagus at Athens (cf. Acts 17:34) and the author of the eastern mystical treatise *On the Celestial Hierarchy*. This and other works by Pseudo-Dionysius (fl. 500 A.D.) were preserved at St. Denis in the treasured Greek codex sent to Louis the Pious by Michael II in 827. The texts also existed in a rather poor Latin translation by Abbot Hilduin. Aware that the Irish scholar John the Scot was competent in Greek, Charles the Bald commissioned him to provide a new translation of the Dionysian corpus. The results came to exercise a significant influence on the subsequent course of European speculative thinking. In the short term, Carolingian clerics gained access to the rich theological mysticism of Pseudo-Dionysius, and first among the beneficiaries was John the Scot himself. In his own speculative work entitled *Periphyseon* ("On the Division of Nature"), he propounded the first great mystical synthesis written in the west.

Yet this was not the first occasion on which Charles the Bald called on the learning of John the Scot. A few years earlier he had asked him to clarify some theological questions troubling the church. Charles was also very much taken by various theological questions. In 842 the king asked Ratramnus of Corbie to respond to a treatise on the Eucharist that he had lately received from Pascasius Radbertus, himself abbot of Corbie. Later, Charles also sought answers from Ratramnus and Lupus of Ferrières concerning the notion of predestination espoused by the monk Gottschalk and condemned by Hincmar of Reims, whereby God was said to have foreordained that some men would be damned and others would be saved regardless of their earthly deeds. Hincmar of Reims himself seems to have consulted John the Scot, but was bitterly disappointed when the Irishman drew conclusions quite different from those of all other players in the dispute.

Despite his importance among the circle of royal protégés, John the Scot was only one of many learned clerics and monks to frequent the court. According to Heiric of Auxerre, "all men were attracted to wisdom by the example" of King Charles himself, whose "palace could rightly be called a school, since every day effort was applied as much to scholarly as to military exercises." Indeed, Charles aspired to be not only a new Solomon but also a philosopher king after the fashion of the ancient emperors. These aims made for one reason among many others that led John VIII to crown Charles emperor in 875.

Kings and Books

The Carolingian kings were not satisfied merely to establish schools and patronize learning. They also attached considerable importance to books, the instruments of learning.

THE CAROLINGIAN SCRIPT

After reviewing the recommended scholastic program in his *Admonitio generalis*, or "General Exhortation," of 789, Charlemagne went on to request that "catholic" books be carefully corrected, "for often, although some desire to worship God rightly, they fail to do so because of the imperfection and errors of their books." Furthermore, "should there be need to copy the Gospels, the Psalter, or Mass books, this should be the task of mature men who write them out with great care." Charlemagne was aware that in the *scriptoria*, or "copying rooms," of the great monasteries, a new script had come into use. First perfected about 780, perhaps at Corbie, the new form of writing has since been called Caroline, or Carolingian, minuscule in honor of Charlemagne. This delicate minuscule, or lower case, script was regular in appearance and characterized by careful efforts to provide proper spacing between words. It was gradually adopted across Europe and finally displaced all other regional varieties of script. Indeed, the printers of the Renaissance so much admired the clarity of Carolingian script, actually mistaking it for ancient Roman writing, that they adopted it for their italic fonts and lower cased "roman" typography, and as such the Caroline letter-forms survive today.

It is impossible to overstate the enormous importance of the Carolingian *scriptoria*. Their work began in earnest during the reign of Charlemagne and continued throughout the ninth century. While some eight thousand hand-written books of the period have survived, they represent but a fraction of the total output of the workshops of the period. Scholarship owes a great debt to Carolingian scribes, since some important classical works were saved for posterity thanks to a single copy prepared in the eighth or ninth century. Collectively, the labors of scribes preserved a whole range of texts written by the Fathers of the Church and classical Latin grammarians, rhetoricians, poets, and prose authors.

ROYAL LIBRARIES

The books copied out by scribes were collected and safeguarded in libraries, and here as elsewhere the kings offered an example to others. The Carolingian rulers assembled great libraries not only to read and admire but also to satisfy specific religious needs. Books that offered training in the liberal arts were of course stepping stones to the study and understanding of the Bible, and the Bible was *the* book par excellence, as regards its contents and usually its appearance. Biblical volumes were often prepared on the finest skins, illuminated and decoratively bound. The copying and decorating skills involved might represent the work of a whole team of artisans or of one highly gifted and practiced individual. Whatever the origins of these most impressive books, the Carolingian rulers wanted to possess them as much as any bishop, abbot, or church might have hoped to do so. The highly public liturgical ceremonies celebrated at the royal court required a set of the finest and most sumptuous volumes containing the various scriptural and Gospel readings, prayers of the Mass, and texts of the sung office. By commissioning books for their chapel or court library, the Carolingian kings initiated a policy adopted by virtually all subsequent rulers in the west.

According to Einhard, "Charlemagne possessed great numbers of books." A partial catalogue of the library at Aachen lately discovered in Berlin lists some of its impressive holdings, including works by Lucan, Statius, Juvenal, Tibullus, Bede, and Isidore of Seville. To add to his library, Charlemagne commissioned Paul the Deacon to compile a new collection of homilies to be read at the night office of Matins, and he also prompted Alcuin to prepare a corrected version of the Latin Bible that became the standard text in the Middle Ages. In 810 the emperor also asked for a condensed handbook of astronomy and date-reckoning (*computus*) which would be widely recopied. In 783, Charlemagne brought back a certain scribe named Godescalc from Italy whom he commissioned to created an evangelary, or set of Gospels, written on purple parchment decorated with miniatures. Somewhat later, Dagulf headed a team of scribes ordered to prepare a psalter subsequently presented to Pope Hadrian I. About 800, the workshops at Aachen also produced a set of luxury manuscripts represented by the richly decorated *Ada Gospels*, apparently commissioned by a nun or abbess connected with the court or family of

Charlemagne, and an evangelary given to the abbey of St. Riquier which is today preserved in Abbeville. Scholars have also dated to this period the Evangelary that Otto III is supposed to have found when he opened Charlemagne's tomb in 1000 and which later served in the coronation ritual of the kings of Germany.

In his will, Charlemagne instructed that his books should be sold and the proceeds given to the poor. As it happened, Louis the Pious kept a number of his father's books, as Professor Bernhard Bischoff has proved. Ebbo, Louis's foster son, served as the new emperor's librarian until his nomination to the archbishopric of Reims in 816. Thereafter, Ebbo patronized a group of scribes and miniaturists residing at the nearby monastery of Hautvilliers. These artisans produced a magnificent evangelary today preserved in nearby Épernay as well as the famous Utrecht Psalter whose pen sketches bear witness to rare technical and artistic mastery.

After 843 the scribes and artists formerly gathered at the imperial court were dispersed into the several royal workshops and associated abbeys. Drogo of Metz, half-brother of Louis the Pious, used the talent of scribes formerly based at Reims to execute the *Drogo Sacramentary*, still preserved in Paris. The recipient of books from many scholar friends, Lothar I commissioned an evangelary produced at Tours whose first page was a novel portrait of the emperor himself seated in majesty. A great lover of books and luxury manuscripts, Charles the Bald received some fifty works from the scholars who frequented his court and from book production centers like the abbeys of St. Martin of Tours and St. Denis. In 846, the lay-abbot of Tours offered the king the magnificently illustrated *Vivian Bible*, wherein Vivian himself is depicted presenting the book to Charles. The so-called *Second Bible of Charles the Bald* is stylistically akin to the Anglo-Saxon tradition of geometric decoration, and appears to have been executed for the king at St. Amand where the royal offspring were also sent for their education. Finally, the *Third Bible of Charles the Bald* (also known as the *Bible of St. Paul-outside-the-Walls*) was commissioned in 869 on the occasion of the king's marriage to Richildis. The contemporary *Coronation Sacramentary* seems to have been prepared in connection with Charles's accession as king of Lotharingia in September 869. A group of miniaturists who signed their work also executed a psalter for the king as well as an evangelary known as the *Codex aureus* ("Golden Book"), today conserved in Munich. With so many treasures, Charles took great care of his library. In 874 he entrusted it to Hilduin, abbot of St. Omer, and when he decided to return to Italy in 877 he arranged for his books to be distributed between the abbey of St. Denis, his own royal foundation of St. Mary at Compiègne, and his successor, Louis the Stammerer.

NOBLE LIBRARIES

Members of the nobility also shared the king's taste for books. Although the contents of the impressive library amassed by Einhard are unknown, extant records do report, for instance, that Charlemagne's son-in-law Angilbert bequeathed two hundred odd volumes to his abbey of St. Riquier. Likewise, the sources used by Dhuoda, wife of Bernard of Septimania, in the *Handbook* she wrote for her son allow us to reconstruct the library at her disposal. It contained works on grammar and date-reckoning (*computus*); extracts from Augustine, Gregory the Great, and Isidore of Seville; Christian poetry and hagiography; and other writings. The wills of Eberhard of Friuli, a son-in-law of Louis the Pious, and of Eccard of Mâcon, a scion of the Nibelungens, also give an idea of the value and size of the libraries owned by some nobles. Eberhard was a friend of learned men such as Anastasius Bibliothecarius, Lupus of Ferrières, and Hrabanus Maurus, and even unwittingly befriended the renegade monk Gottschalk before returning him to the custody of Hincmar of Reims. In 864, Eberhard provided for the posthumous dispersal of his library among his four sons and four daughters, taking care to ensure an equitable division. Eccard of Mâcon likewise shared out a library of some twenty books among his wife, his nephews, and a few bishops and abbesses. In each case, the books were of a similar sort; they included liturgical volumes for the chapel, biblical texts, hagiography, and a variety of works on ethics, law, history, medicine, and agriculture. In a word, both men owned well-rounded libraries of useful, instructive, and edifying books. Their wills also reveal that these nobles had acquired a number of art works.

Artistic Treasures

In the Carolingian period as in all others, both kings and nobles loved to collect art and to surround themselves with valuables. It was a matter of both taste and necessity. They had to show their attachment to friends by offering gifts, and many a vassal was confirmed in his allegiance through gifts of precious gems, weapons, and textiles. Moreover, the Carolingians considered that beauty was an important aspect of their service to God. Thus they lavishly decorated their own chapels while other churches benefited from their gifts of golden altars, reliquaries, lampstands, and precious cloths and imports from the east. In their capitularies, the kings instructed the bishops to guard such treasures carefully, and in 806 Charlemagne expressed alarm that merchants boasted of being able to buy anything they wanted from the clergy. Lothar I later ordered an inquiry into the losses suffered by some churches in Italy. Indeed, churchmen were obligated to protect their treasures and were to remove none except in cases of extreme necessity, as when marauding Northmen approached. Churches were also compelled to take periodic inventories, thanks to which we can occasionally form an idea of the precious objects they once possessed.

Kings as Patrons and Collectors

The Carolingian kings do not appear themselves to have compiled such inventories. But evidence remains of the artistic treasures they acquired as gifts or booty. The kings also commissioned artisans to create new pieces of art at workshops located at various palaces and abbeys.

According to Einhard, three years before his death Charlemagne partitioned his riches, clothing, and furniture in the presence of his friends and royal officers. A protocol outlining this distribution follows Einhard's account of the event. It speaks of gold, silver, precious stones, vases, weapons, coverlets, cloth, and many other articles. The most impressive royal chattels appear to have been a series of tables wrought in silver, one embossed with a map of Constantinople and another with a map of Rome. The third silver table, "the greatest in size and artistry," was decorated with a map of the world "in the form of concentric rings." This Louis the Pious kept for himself, only for it to be broken up in 842 by Lothar I.

To decorate and bind his luxury manuscripts, Charlemagne called on groups of goldsmiths and ivory-carvers. These artisans drew inspiration from antique models but arrived at their own distinctive style. The covers of the Dagulf Psalter probably included an entire series of ivory carvings produced in the workshops at Aachen. Bishop Drogo of Metz later arranged for his famous sacramentary to be covered with a series of six ivories depicting a celebration of Mass by a bishop. One of these panels even includes a delicate representation of the so-called *Throne of Saint Clement* still preserved in the cathedral of Metz.

Louis the Pious kept many of the precious objects owned by his father, and they subsequently passed from the imperial court to the treasuries of various churches. An inventory from the abbey of Prüm lists, for instance, works in precious metal donated by Lothar I. Some of these may have been created during the reign of Louis of Pious, for among others, his arch-chaplain, Hilduin of St. Denis, is known to have supported a workshop of goldsmiths at his abbey which produced articles whose excellence was noted by Lupus of Ferrières. After 843 royal workshops in the Middle Kingdom continued to turn out precious metalwork and carved ivory. An additional contemporary masterpiece stemming from this region is "Lothar's Crystal," today preserved in the British Museum. Etched in rock crystal, this magnificent pendant depicts the story of Susannah recounted in the Vulgate Bible (Daniel 13), and is traditionally associated with the marriage difficulties of Lothar II, whose name it bears.

For his part, Charles the Bald was as much a lover of art as a connoisseur of books. From the start of his reign, the young king passed as an expert of sorts, so much so that Lupus of Ferrières sent gems cut by his jeweler for appraisal by Charles. The king would continue to foster work in gold and ivory, and even addressed such matters in one of his capitularies. He commissioned extraordinary bindings for his luxury manuscripts, in particular his psalter, today preserved at the Bibliothèque Nationale in Paris, and the *Codex aureus*, so named for its cover in gold repoussé. Lay-abbot of St. Denis, the king encouraged the monastery's artisans to produce such masterpieces as the famous jewel-covered Screen of Charlemagne (*Écrin de Charlemagne*) melted down in 1794 by treasury officers of the French Revolution. Contemporary West Frankish artisans probably also produced the Talisman of Charlemagne (found today in Reims), the portable altar later given by King Arnulf to St. Emmeram's in Regensburg, and the so-called Throne of St. Peter (*Cathedra Petri*) preserved at St. Peter's in Rome.

Art and the Nobility

The noble contemporaries of Charles the Bald also enjoyed collecting works of art. When he established a monastic community in his palace at Plélan, Duke Salomon of Brittany compiled a list of exceptional, foreign-made treasures: a gold chalice studded with 313 pearls weighing ten pounds; a gold paten studded with 145 pearls weighing seven-and-a-half pounds; a gold case containing Gospel books; a small chest in beautifully sculpted Indian ivory and, according to the source, "what is more important, full of holy relics"; a priest's chasuble covered in gold given by Charles the Bald; and so on. Boso of Provence likewise presented the church of St. Maurice in Vienne with seven gold crosses and—a novelty for its time—a bust-shaped reliquary. The treasury of Berengar I of Italy is also known from an early tenth-century inventory preserved at Monza. As a son of Eberhard of Friuli, Berengar inherited books, as we have seen, yet his father's will also mentioned such treasures as gold chalices, silver thuribles, precious brooches, crystal pendants, and reliquaries. The contemporary will of Eccard of Mâcon sheds light on another noble of no less considerable wealth.

The Carolingians Kings as Builders

The Carolingian renaissance also manifested itself as a remarkable flowering of architecture and building. Some one hundred royal residences were erected or refurbished, twenty-seven cathedrals were constructed, and hundreds of monasteries raised new buildings. The kings were not alone responsible for this construction activity, but they contributed to it by supplying architects and funds. The rediscovery of ancient treatises on building such as that of Vitruvius prompted a renewal of construction in stone, a hitherto uncommon medium north of the Loire. Moreover, the journeys of the kings to Italy impressed on them the beauty of Roman basilicas, triumphal arches, and Italian palace chapels. Yet the evidence that remains proves that the Carolingians did more than slavishly copy what they found elsewhere. Architects elaborated new plans and programs to accommodate the needs of Carolingian ceremony and ritual.

Royal Palaces

The Carolingian kings traveled with their court from palace to palace. Many country residences were not "palaces" in the accepted sense of the term, but rather manors usually inhabited by a representative of the king who managed activities on the domain in question. The buildings themselves were generally of wood. True palaces meant to house the king were generally substantial complexes. Unfortunately, nothing at all remains of these royal centers except for a few outlines amid cultivated fields at Quierzy-sur-Oise, the foundation of the royal throne at Paderborn in Saxony, and a few vestiges unearthed at Ingelheim, near Mainz. Thanks to ongoing archaeological investigations and descriptions found in contemporary sources, it is possible to imagine the grandeur of the royal complexes. Of the palace at Aachen important elements remain in the current town hall and, above all, in the miraculously preserved Royal Chapel, whose construction commenced about 792. On a square-shaped area of some twenty hectares—reminiscent in fact of ancient Roman military encampments—four groups of buildings were constructed. To the north lay the *aula regia* ("royal audience hall") measuring forty-seven by twenty meters, an echo of the late antique *aula palatina* in Trier; it adjoined the royal residence, situated just to the south. From here, a long covered walkway continued south. It connected the palace to a group of religious buildings arranged as a Latin cross whose focus was the octagonal Royal Chapel designed by Odo of Metz. At the apex of a triangle of land stretching east lay the bath house that gave access to the famous hot springs of Aachen. The entire palace compound was girded by walls pierced by gateways at four points. Outside came the dwellings of merchants, a marketplace, and the houses of bishops, abbots, and other dignitaries. Nearby lay a hunting park bounded by a palisade and a menagerie where Charlemagne kept Abul-Abaz, the elephant that he received in 802 from the Abbasid caliph Harun al-Rashid.

In arranging his palace complex at Aachen, Charlemagne hoped to construct something worthy of a great king. From Ravenna, he brought marble columns retrieved from older structures and a statue of Theodoric, king of the Ostrogoths, which may have inspired the creator of the equestrian Statuette of Charlemagne found today in the Louvre. In Aachen, Charlemagne also opened a foundry that created the impressive wrought grills and bronze doors still preserved in the Royal Chapel. As in Byzantium, the Carolingian palace was a holy space, in some sense a center of the religious world; the palace and its church formed a unity. The audience hall was a great chamber with a rounded apse, a "basilica" in the ancient Roman sense. Meanwhile, the gilt and decorated octagon of the Royal Chapel also served as a throne hall not unlike the *Chrysotriklinios* (golden audience hall) at Byzantium. Yet while the throne of the *basileus* stood in the east in place of an altar, Charlemagne installed his throne to the west in the upper gallery of the chapel. From there, surrounded by his courtiers, he could look upon the altar of the Savior below and the altar of the Virgin situated directly above it in the opposite gallery. Raising his eyes further upward, he beheld the mosaic of the dome that depicted the elders of the Apocalypse acclaiming Christ seated in majesty.

The Aachen chapel enjoyed such great prestige in the west that it was repeatedly imitated from the ninth to the eleventh centuries. A source reports, for instance, that when Theodulf of Orléans raised his oratory at Germigny-des-Prés he hoped to vie with the grandeur of Charlemagne's

Royal Chapel. Yet however rich in conception and design, it is clear that Theodulf's square church was based on models from the east or from Visigothic Spain, the bishop's own homeland. Genuine affinities with the Royal Chapel are more in evidence in Lotharingia. Built at the beginning of the eleventh century, the church at Ottmarsheim in Alsace embodies perhaps the clearest echo of Aachen.

Charlemagne passed the last decades of his life at Aachen. When he died, he was buried in his chapel, perhaps in a surviving antique sarcophagus depicting the kidnaping of Proserpina. His son Louis the Pious divided his time between Aachen, Thionville (where he built a chapel modeled on that of Aachen), Compiègne, and Ingelheim. In his poem "In Honor of Louis," Ermold Nigellus evoked the palace at Ingelheim: "immense, born up by a hundred columns, overflowing with intricacies and features of all sorts, doors, alcoves, innumerable dwellings." He described the paintings of its chapel, which depicted scenes from the Old and New Testaments, and those of the royal audience hall, which portrayed the exploits of the kings of antiquity and of the Carolingian past.

After the partition of 843, Lothar I and Lothar II remained at Aachen. Meanwhile, Louis the German wintered at Regensburg and spent summers at Frankfurt, where he built a chapel in 852 served by twelve clergy. As for Charles the Bald, he sojourned happily at the great abbeys of his kingdom, and when the Treaty of Meersen of 870 ended his hope of regaining Aachen, he resolved to build a chapel equal to that of his grandfather. While the chapel of his monastic foundation of St. Mary's at Compiègne has disappeared, a description survives in a poem of John the Scot:

. . .

Great Mother of God, thrice blessed Saint Mary,
Be a near protector, a high rampart to Charles,
Who has fashioned for you this wondrously excellent home;
A house built varied with columns of marble,
Made beauteous in accord with the hundred-length norm!
Behold the curving angles and the rounded vaults,
The regular articulation of the walls, the capitals, the footings,
The towers, the parapets, the coffered ceiling, and skillful roof;
The tapered windows, the breaths of light beglassed;
Within, the stone-wrought pictures, the paving, and the steps;
All about, arcades, chests, chambers for the priests;
Above, below, people around the altars,

> High circular crowns and lampstands full of lights!
> All glimmers with gems and glistens with gold.
> Hangings and frontals encircle the Temple all around.
>   . . .

CATHEDRAL COMPLEXES

With the help of the Carolingian kings, the bishops undertook to renew and build up the physical fabric of their towns. Religious reforms and particularly the new obligation for canons to live as a community around their bishop required the construction of new buildings forming a cathedral complex. In the mid-eighth century, Chrodegang had established a cloister adjacent to his cathedral of St. Stephen in Metz, which he then enlarged. This cloister corresponded to the Place des Armes in modern Metz; it was one hundred meters long and seventy meters wide. Its walkway connected the chapter house, refectory, dormitory, infirmary, and several oratories. Upon his accession as archbishop of Lyon in 798, the Bavarian Leidrad proceeded to copy Chrodegang's complex, and two years later he reported his achievements to Charlemagne. He even noted that he had prepared an apartment for the king should he someday visit the region, which he never did. Meanwhile, the bishop of Vienne expanded his own cathedral complex, made up of three chapels, with a new church whose considerable size has been revealed through modern excavations. Such building efforts continued during the ninth century. In 817, Louis the Pious granted the cathedral at Tournai portions of one of his estates in the region so that the bishop could afford to enlarge the canons' cloister. Louis also helped Bishop Aldric of Le Mans—a former canon of Metz, a relative, and an ever faithful ally—to build a cathedral close with both individual houses and communal buildings. Aldric also refurbished the town's aqueduct, built two hospices (one for paupers near the close and the other across the Sarthe River), and restored the cathedral and several monasteries.

Numerous new cathedrals were build during the Carolingian period. Although none remain, excavations have often uncovered foundations, which allow scholars to conjecture about the floor plans and elevations of the buildings they supported. In Cologne. Bishop Hildebold (787–818) began construction of a new cathedral about 800; the church was completed some 70 years later. According to excavations undertaken after World War II, the building was built in several stages. The result took the form of a Latin cross with two apses, one in the east and the other in the west over a crypt. This western apse and crypt recalled the layout of the great basilicas in Rome. Although churches were normally "oriented"— that is, their altars were situated in the east (*oriens* meaning the "quadrant of the rising sun")—the cathedral of Reims erected by Hincmar had its principal altar in the west. It thus followed the arrangement of liturgical space incorporated in the Cologne design, practiced at Fulda, and no doubt based on St. Peter's in Rome.

The bishops, as magnates in their own right, were also fond of ample and comfortable palaces. At Auxerre a pair of dining rooms was built to accommodate the need for warmth in winter and the desire for fresh air in summer. According to Sedulius Scottus, Bishop Hartgar of Liège constructed a large hall whose walls were painted in brilliant colors and that received light—an often scarce indoor luxury in this period—from vaulted and glazed windows.

Monasteries

The great monasteries were veritable cities unto themselves. Their buildings reflected the same architectural patterns and techniques applied in episcopal complexes. Monastic building programs were often the object of special royal favor, since royal children and vassals governed the greatest abbeys, where the king himself occasionally resided.

One of the first abbeys to benefit from Carolingian interest was St. Denis, the burial place of the Merovingians and of Charles Martel. Pippin the Short had, moreover, been a student in this monastery, and its monks figured among his closest collaborators. It was Pippin who arranged for the first stone of the new abbey church to be laid by Pope Stephen II during his stay in 754. The church building today identified with Abbot Fulrad was completed in 775. It had a vast nave some 22 meters in width and 36 meters in length with a large sanctuary, of which sections survive in the crypt of the present church. The monastic complex that arose thanks to royal generosity made St. Denis virtually a town in its own right.

The Carolingian buildings at Centula, today known as St. Riquier, were due in large part to financial support from Charlemagne. The emperor's son-in-law Angilbert was lay-abbot of this monastery. Particularly devoted to the symbolism of the Trinity, Angilbert had three hundred monks and three churches linked by a covered gallery in the shape of a triangle. The west end of the principal church was situated above a large crypt housing holy relics brought from Jerusalem. Like the cathedrals in

Cologne and Reims, the church of St. Riquier was dominated by a *Westwerk* (*opus occidentale*) featuring a fortress-like apse and flanking towers, typical of much Carolingian and Romanesque architecture. For the canonical offices, groups of monks gathered in the apses at either end of the church, and their alternating singing washed across the space in between. Angilbert provided for processions by erecting twelve secondary altars within his church. For great feasts, he organized long routes for his chanting monks to follow that included the two chapels situated at the far corners of the cloister. On such occasions, seven crosses and seven reliquaries preceded the monks, and the clergy followed in groups of seven, symbolizing the seven-fold gifts of the Paraclete. Thus, with a few original twists, Angilbert elaborated a stational liturgy that reflected the Roman custom of using different chapels and churches for different occasions. The complex of buildings at St. Riquier made for a "Rome in microcosm" with a western crypt, like that of St. Peter's, and a variety of chapels used for rotating liturgical celebrations.

Rome also served as the example for the abbots of Fulda, who enlarged their church by introducing a western transept, apse, and atrium *more romano* (after the Roman fashion). Their church came to have two crypts, the larger of which, in the west, housed the earthly remains of Saint Boniface. The novel practice of constructing large western crypts was an invention of Carolingian architects. It was related to the cult of relics, and may represent an attempt to reproduce the western-facing crypts of Rome, from which some relics had been acquired. Indeed, every church sought to possess relics of the most illustrious saints possible, and theft was a common and accepted means of laying hold of them. For instance, Einhard acknowledges without regret that one of his agents had actually stolen the relics of the Roman martyrs Marcellinus and Peter. When they arrived in Francia, he placed them in his church at Steinbach, and later removed them to another at Seligenstadt, both of which remain standing today. In theory, no translation of relics could be undertaken without royal approval, for the kings wanted some control over the sometimes shady dealings that accompanied these important religious occasions. Because all newly converted lands needed churches whose altars required relics, a great scarcity of these holy objects arose in the Carolingian period. Thus in 836 the church of Paderborn in Saxony obtained permission from Louis the Pious to acquire relics of Saint Liborius (d. 397) from Le Mans. The decision naturally dismayed the residents of Le Mans, but they were obliged to bend to the emperor's instructions.

Both to safeguard relics and to permit the faithful to venerate them, a crypt was generally built under the sanctuaries of larger churches. This vaulted space housed side chapels, reliquaries, and the tombs of dignitaries who wished to be buried near the holy relics. Generally, such crypts were somewhat lower than the main floor of the church and lit by narrow windows penetrating the thick foundation walls. Carolingian examples are still visible at St. Médard in Soissons and also at St. Germain in Auxerre.

The rebuilding of the abbey church of St. Germain was completed between 841 and 865 with help from the Welf relations of Charles the Bald, namely Conrad I, his wife Adelaide, and their sons Conrad, count of Auxerre, and Hugh the Abbot. The architects who designed the building fashioned a wax model before construction began. The masters in charge of constructing the edifice had antique columns transported from Provence up the Rhône and Saône rivers as far as Chalon and from there overland to Auxerre. On 6 January 859, Charles the Bald himself presided over the solemn translation of Saint Germain to his new resting place. In the crypt, the corridor and chapels flanking the stone repository (*confessio*) that contained the saint's relics were then decorated with frescoes. Among the oldest existing in France, these fine murals were rediscovered by René Louis in 1927 under a covering of plaster.

In each abbey founded or controlled by the Frankish kings, the ruler had a reserved place in the monastery church as well as special apartments in the monastic complex. Of the abbey church built at Corbie under Wala, Charlemagne's cousin, and later enlarged in 867, the *Westwerk* still survives. From its upper gallery, the king participated at liturgical events much as he might have done from the elevated throne of the Royal Chapel at Aachen. The magnificent Carolingian gatehouse that survives at Lorsch is itself an innovative variation on the Roman triumphal archway. The stately structure included a hall in its upper story measuring some ten meters in length and seven meters in breadth. Its fresco decoration in Roman-style trompe l'oeil suggests that it may have served as an audience hall during royal visits. In the *Plan of St. Gall*, an apartment for the emperor was also included, as was a guest house for distinguished visitors.

This remarkable architectural study consists of five sheets of parchment sewn together and measuring 112 x 77 cm. The drawing seems to have been prepared in connection with a project to rebuild the monastery of St. Gall in the 820s. Commissioned by Haito, bishop of Basel, the highly detailed plan in red ink with brown captions was probably copied at the nearby monastery of Reichenau, where Haito was also abbot. It was then offered to Abbot Gozbert of St. Gall as an object of consideration and reflection. As such, the plan is a unique artifact for the study of Carolingian monastic realities and concerns. Its 341 captions indicate the purpose of each building in the tightly ordered complex, even distinguishing any separate use to be made of upper stories. To note just one feature of the *Plan*, its great church includes two apses, one east and the other west. The drawing thus reflects what we know of new intentions and details of architectural and monastic planning in the Carolingian period, yet it seems no less clear that the *Plan* was conceived to visualize an ideal of organization and symbolic arrangement. Although this ideal never fully materialized at any one time or in any one place, it was not arbitrary or imaginary.

DECORATION AND IMAGES

The finest Carolingian churches were richly decorated with walls faced in marble and plaster and adorned with sculpted columns, capitals and panels. Because the marble quarries of the Pyrenees had fallen out of production in the mid-eighth century because of instability and warfare in Aquitaine, builders resorted to the reuse of architectural spoils, for instance columns and capitals removed from standing or ruinous buildings in Italy and Provence. A few new efforts were also made to create stone capitals, for instance at St. Denis, as well as stone panels for the screens separating the choir area from the nave in some churches. Such is the case for the chancel screen recovered from St. Pierre-aux-Nonnains at Metz. The work appears to date from about 750 and may be contemporary with a similar artifact found at nearby Cheminot in the ruins of a monastery founded by Charlemagne. In northern Italy, Switzerland, and Austria, hundreds of cut paving stones dating from the end of the eighth century have likewise been recovered. They seem, in fact, to betoken a massive effort to restore dilapidated churches and chapels. As noted by Jean Hubert, "the introduction of new chancel screens was surely a part of the great work of renovating churches prescribed by the royal power."

In addition to restoring the churches' physical fabric, the Carolingian kings were also interested in the painted decoration commonly applied to churches. This was a consequence of the position they took in the Iconoclastic Controversy. In 787 the Second Council of Nicea had restored the veneration of holy images in Byzantium. Ever more inclined to think of himself as an equal of the eastern emperor, Charlemagne had Theodulf of Orléans prepare a theological compendium known to history as the *Libri carolini* ("The Books by Charles") under the pretense that Charlemagne himself was the author. Among other matters, this set of writings presented the Frankish position on icons and their place in religious worship. Unfortunately, the Franks had been wrongly convinced by the miserable Latin translation of the Nicea proceedings prepared in Rome that Byzantium now proposed to *adore* images as though they were divine. For Theodulf, an image had a purely esthetic and pedagogical value; in no sense was it to be revered with the adoration due to God alone. It was a sacrilege to call an image sacred or to burn incense before it. For, as Theodulf wryly inquired, if one censed a portrait of the Flight into Egypt, would one be censing the Virgin or the ass that carried her? The beauty of the image was not to lead to its adoration:

> If a person venerates one image with greater piety than he venerates another simply because it is more beautiful, he judges its sacred character as a function of the talent of the artist. Those who believe that they venerate something sacred because they are moved by beauty deceive themselves, as it were, without knowing it. But those who adore a picture whose ugliness masks any artistic merit are as inexcusable as if their error were conscious and willful.

Speaking very much as a man of letters, Theodulf thought the text superior to the image:

> A man can save himself without possessing icons, but he cannot save himself without the knowledge of God. Moreover, unfortunate is the soul who, to remember Christ's life, has need of pictures and paint and cannot derive strength from its own powers.

The Council of Frankfurt of 794 officially condemned the Second Council of Nicea, though it had, alas, been grossly misunderstood. Charlemagne thereupon dispatched Angilbert to Rome to report this bold move to a flabbergasted Hadrian I.

Though quite resolved in the eyes of the Byzantines, the Iconoclastic Controversy continued to impassion Carolingian leaders and churchmen of the early ninth century. Claudius, the intransigent Visigothic bishop of Turin, even demanded the complete destruction of all religious images. He drew searing attacks from the Irishman Dungal, a hermit at St. Denis, and still others from Bishop Jonas of Orléans, whom Louis the Pious commissioned to study the question further. The emperor also used the arrival of a Byzantine embassy in 825 as a pretext for having the problem of images debated once again at the Synod of Paris of the same year. The views expressed in the *Libri carolini* were reaffirmed. Echoing a teaching propounded by the Roman church since the time of Gregory the Great, the Frankish bishops noted the special pedagogic value of images for the illiterate and the unlearned. Shortly after the gathering, Walafrid Strabo offered his own telling comments:

> We often see how simple and unlearned souls, who could scarcely be brought to faith by words, are so touched by a painting of the Passion of Our Lord, or of other miracles, that they avow by their tears that these images are deeply engraved in their hearts.

Indeed, Carolingian churches were commonly painted with frescoes based on the Bible and on the lives of the saints. Built with a grant from Charlemagne, the Church of St. John at Münster, Switzerland, still retains its rich painted decor: twenty scenes from the Old Testament and sixty-two from the Gospels. At nearby Malles-Venosta, in South Tirol, the oratory of St. Benedict likewise houses original portraits of saints and of the Carolingian nobleman who commissioned the chapel. However scant, these rare survivals give some idea of the pictorial splendor of the Carolingian past.

The Heirs of the Carolingian Kings

Despite the empire's failure and the devastation of libraries, art works and architectural monuments by invaders, the Carolingian renaissance continued into the tenth century. After a period of crisis, there was again a renewal of intellectual and artistic life at various monastic centers. Some of these were part of new tenth-century reform movements. For instance, the abbey of Cluny, founded in 909, gradually expanded its reformed observance across Burgundy, southern France, and Italy. To the north, the counts of Flanders and the dukes of Normandy also encouraged monastic renewal, while in Lotharingia bishops and kings restored the discipline of the Rule of Saint Benedict. These reforms of monastic life went in tandem with liturgical renewal, the expansion of libraries, and a blossoming of monastic learning.

CULTURE AND LEARNING IN FRANCE

The kings of western Francia scarcely contributed to cultural renewal in the tenth century. Even though Charles the Simple was an educated ruler, his son Louis IV derived profit neither from his instruction at the court of

King Ethelstan of Wessex nor from his marriage to Gerberga, sister of Otto I. According to one chronicler, his vassal Fulk II of Angers is supposed to have mocked the king with the proverb: "An illiterate king is a crowned ass." The only man of letters known to have frequented the royal court was the king's half-brother Rorgo, bishop of Laon. On the other hand, learned authors were associated with some great nobles. For instance, Richard I of Normandy asked Dudo of St. Quentin to set down a history of his ancestors, and Arnulf of Flanders had the priest Vitger compile a genealogy of his family back to its link with the Carolingians through Judith, daughter of Charles the Bald. While nothing is known of the education of the Robertines, King Odo had taken an interest in the valuable art works preserved at St. Denis: as lay-abbot of the monastery, he had some of them melted down for their precious metal. It was probably Odo as well who gave Arnulf of Germany the *Codex aureus* and the golden altar that Arnulf later bequeathed to St. Emmeram in Regensburg. Although Hugh Capet himself knew no Latin, he ensured that his son received the very best education. In 972, he entrusted the boy to Gerbert of Aurillac, the schoolmaster of Reims.

At a very tender age Gerbert himself had been given as an oblate to the abbey of St. Gerald of Aurillac. He had been able to advance his studies thanks to the sponsorship of Count Borell II of Barcelona. In this period, thanks to the proximity to Muslim Spain, Catalonia boasted a number of excellent monastic and episcopal schools that offered scientific training unknown elsewhere. Thus, it was at Vich and Ripoll that Gerbert acquired his exceptional knowledge of astronomy, arithmetic, and music. In 970, he accompanied Borell II to Rome, and there he met Otto I and the future Otto II. He struck up a friendship with these Ottonians destined to grow closer over time.

THE OTTONIAN RENAISSANCE

The Learned Emperors

Much like the Carolingian kings, the Ottonians attracted, befriended and supported men of letters both for personal and for political reasons. Otto I possessed a lively and curious intelligence, and he appreciated the role that secular and religious learning had jointly played in the consolidation of his power. Like Charlemagne, Otto sought to surround himself with learned bishops capable of teaching and training the clerics who would later serve in the royal chancery. The king's brother Bruno became arch-chaplain before his subsequent nomination as archbishop of Cologne. In many regards, Bruno was to Otto what Alcuin had been to Charlemagne. For instance, he wrote a poem to congratulate his brother on having restored the kingdom's schools. The great monasteries of St. Gall and Reichenau were now the foremost institutions of higher learning, turning out a long line of fine teachers and scholars. In addition, Otto profited from his conquest of Italy, much as Charlemagne did, to recruit new masters for the schools of Germany, such as Stephen of Novara and Gunzo, an Irish scholar also based in Novara who came north with his personal library of some one hundred manuscripts. The Ottonian queens and princesses were likewise mindful to ensure the education of the daughters of the nobility in the monastery-palaces of Nordhausen, Magdeburg, Gandersheim and Quedlinburg (where two tenth-century crypts still survive). Gandersheim was also home to the learned nun Hrotsvitha. Brought up by Otto's niece, Abbess Gerberga, Hrotsvitha wrote a history of her monastery as well as a chronicle celebrating the deeds of Otto the Great. It was for the king's daughter Matilda that Widukind of Korvei composed his *History of the Saxons*.

Otto II was also an educated ruler who enjoyed study and books. In 972, he took advantage of a sojourn at St. Gall to requisition several manuscripts from the abbey's celebrated library. Otto also knew the famous Gerbert of Aurillac, from whom he had received several lessons in Rome. Thus in 980, he organized a debate in Ravenna between the schoolmaster of Reims and Otric, the master in Magdeburg. The encounter was later described by Richer of Reims:

> I believe, said the emperor, that reflection and frequent exchanges advance human knowledge provided that appropriate subjects are chosen and discussed in language mutually agreed upon by all learned men. Since we too often languish in idleness, it is very useful for others to press us with questions so as to prod us to think. By this means the wisest scholars caused knowledge to increase, and by this means also they transmitted their knowledge by divulging it to others and setting it down in books so that we could pride ourselves on making good use of it. So let us occupy ourselves with several questions. This inquiry will uplift our spirit and lead it to greater intellectual certainty. Let us review the table of philosophical parties which was shown to us last year. All of you examine it, and let each one say what he thinks of it or what he reproves in it.

The marriage of Otto II to Theophano was hailed by all chroniclers as a high point of his reign. This very learned Byzantine princess arrived with a suite of Greek clerics that apparently included several craftsmen, since the chapel of St. Bartholomew at Paderborn was built by Greek workmen. Without overstating eastern influence on Ottonian art, it is quite clear that the luxury textiles, ivories, and manuscripts executed for Otto II were inspired by Byzantine models and techniques. Elements of Greek culture still had survived in southern Italy and at Rome and were still present at some centers in Lotharingia. They were now powerfully reinforced by the personal links established between east and west.

Born of a Saxon father and a Byzantine mother, Otto III received a solid education from his first masters: Willigis, archbishop of Mainz; Bernward, the future bishop of Hildesheim; and John Philagathos of Rossano, who taught him a few rudiments of Greek. Yet when the boy reached adolescence he felt that his education was still inadequate. In 996 he wrote a letter to Gerbert of Aurillac, rather forced in its eloquence:

> We would like to attach to ourselves your universally revered excellency as well as your most charitable amity. We hope unceasingly to have with us such a great master, for the eminence of your knowledge and your teaching have always been recognized as authoritative next to our own ignorance. We desire that you should not abide our Saxon roughness and that you awaken our Greek subtlety. Thus, please desire to bring the powerful flame of your vast knowledge nearer to the minuscule fire which is found within us. We ask you this humbly.

Contested as the archbishop of Reims by the papacy and other clergy, Gerbert was pleased to place himself in the service of Otto III. He accompanied the emperor on his journeys and on his expeditions against the Slavs. He introduced his master to arithmetic, music, and philosophy. Like his great model Boethius, Gerbert hoped as imperial counselor to introduce philosophical principles to the realm of politics. He naturally believed that philosophy and the use of reason taught moderation and the mastery of the passions. Thus Gerbert composed a treatise for Otto III "on the reasonable and the use of reason," which opens with a manifesto hailing the "renewal of the Roman empire":

> Ours is the Roman empire! Italy rich in fruits and Gaul and Germany fertile in warriors make for the empire's strength, and the powerful kingdoms of the Scythians [i.e., the Slavs] are also behind us. Caesar, you are our august emperor of the Romans. Born of the most prestigious Greek blood, you surpass the Greeks in empire, you command the Romans by virtue of hereditary right, and you outshine everyone in genius and eloquence.

Like his father, Otto III loved books. He amassed a library of which part survives today. After passing to Henry II, the bulk of the library was then bequeathed to Henry's episcopal foundation at Bamberg. The numerous manuscripts still preserved there include a *De arithmetica* of Boethius, a volume of Livy originally from Piacenza, the *Institutes* of Justinian, the *De natura rerum* of Isidore of Seville, the *Institutes* of Cassiodorus, and an autograph copy of the *History* of Richer of Reims once owned by Gerbert of Aurillac.

Imperial Patronage of the Arts

Conscious of their role as masters and protectors of the church, the Ottonian emperors sought to visualize God's majesty through luxurious manuscripts commissioned for their court chapel. The Ottonians do not appear to have kept their own book artists as the Carolingians sometimes did. Nevertheless, they must have had capable scribes and illuminators attached to their court who were responsible for the sumptuous *Ottonianum* presented to Pope John XII in 862: a document written in gold lettering on purple parchment. The charter prepared for the marriage of Otto II to Theophano (today preserved in the Herzog-August Library in Wolfenbüttel, Germany) was similarly executed and also includes decoration based on the pattern of fine Byzantine textiles.

When the Ottonians wished to procure new luxury manuscripts, they turned to the workshops of monasteries that held Carolingian books, and these then provided inspiration for the commission. Thus Korvei produced the *Evangelary of Quedlinburg* as well as other fine examples of Franco-Saxon art. The scriptorium at Fulda executed the *Codex Wittekindeus* for Otto I in a style reminiscent of the manuscripts produced for Charles the Bald. Likewise about 1000, Reichenau filled an imperial commission for an evangelary. The resulting book included a portrait of the emperor amid his lay and ecclesiastical followers as he symbolically received the four provinces of the empire and their offerings. Another Reichenau evangelary preserved today in Aachen contains the "Apotheosis of Otto III," a painting on gold leaf that seems to represent Otto I flanked by his two successors.

The Patronage of Bishops and Abbots

The abbatial and episcopal collaborators of the emperors also patronized scholars and artists. Ruled for a time by a relative of Otto I, St. Gall was the empire's foremost center of learning. Its school was headed in the tenth century by a series of remarkable scholar-teachers: Ekkehard I (d. 973), who composed the verse epic *Waltarius*, a work steeped in Germanic legend, then Notker the Physician, and finally Ekkehard II (d. 990), a friend of Otto II. Contemporary Reichenau was subject to Abbot Witigowo (985–997)—nicknamed "the golden abbot" (*abbas aureus*), or sometimes "the royal mouthpiece" owing to his constant presence at the court. Witigowo is also remembered for commissioning the nave of St. Mary's church at the Mittelzell (the monastic complex midway along the island), as well as the famous frescos at St. George's at the Oberzell (near the island's eastern tip). Meanwhile Abbot Gozpert of Tegernsee enriched his abbey library and thereby helped to advance the studies of the scholar monk Fromund. At St. Emmeram in Regensburg, Abbot Ramwold (975–1001) commissioned the restoration of the Carolingian *Codex aureus*.

The great archbishops of the empire also fostered learning and culture in their towns. After 977 Archbishop Egbert of Trier sought to restore his episcopal city to its late antique splendor. He brought an artist from Italy known as the Master of the St. George Register who painted a portrait of Otto II now preserved at Chantilly. This Italian master, who knew late antique illuminations as well as Carolingian products located in Trier, also decorated the evangelary given to the Sainte Chapelle in 1379 by Charles V, now in the Bibliothèque Nationale, Paris. In addition to commissioning portraits of himself and his predecessors in the *Codex Egberti*, a Reichenau product, Egbert also encouraged local monks from the abbeys of St. Maximinus, St. Eucher, and St. Martin to compose hagiographic texts on the saints of Trier.

Cologne was the immemorial rival of Trier. Named archbishop in 953, Bruno of Cologne proceeded to make his town a center of learning and culture. Despite his political duties, he always continued to study, and according to his biographer, he never journeyed without books. He was acquainted with the Latin poets and philosophers and enjoyed debating with Greek visitors to the court. Bruno's successors continued his policy of sponsoring culture. First Archbishop Gero (d. 976) and later Heribert of Cologne (d. 1021), a former chancellor of Otto III, enlarged the monastery of St. Pantaleon originally founded by Bruno. Here as well, Empress Theophano was buried in 991. The *Westwerk* of this structure still survives, and it is much indebted to that found at Korvei. Cologne was also an established artistic center throughout this period. Illuminators inspired by a Carolingian model decorated the *Gero Codex* (today in Darmstadt), goldsmiths executed the *Gero Cross* (Cologne) as well as other treasures, and ivory-carvers continued to ply their craft based on Byzantine and Carolingian originals. Byzantine style also influenced the illuminations found in the *Lectionary of Everger*, archbishop of Cologne (985–999), as well as those of the *St. Gereon Sacramentary*.

Liège, a suffragan bishopric of Cologne, was particularly favored by the Ottonian rulers. In 953 Ratherius, the monk from Lobbes who had for a time been bishop of Verona, was installed at Liège by Otto I. He came to a bishopric whose school had already been active in the domains of music and literature. Bishop Stephen of Liège (903–920), a former canon of Metz and a relative of Charles the Simple, had acclaimed the glory of Saint Lambert in his poems and liturgical compositions. The antiphon *Vox magna* sung with the *Magnificat* already constituted the regional anthem of Liège, as it would until the advent of the French Revolution in 1789. Himself one of the more interesting authors of the period, Ratherius placed his own student Heraclius in charge of the cathedral school. The bishop, however, soon alienated his flock with his bizarre and combative temperament and was for a second time driven from his see. Heraclius succeeded him, and thereafter shared his time between his work as schoolmaster and service at the court. In 972, Notker was nominated to the bishopric from his position in the imperial chancery. He did much for the town, building a rampart and several new churches in addition to restoring the cathedral and its close. At the same time, he oversaw the development of the abbey of Lobbes which his friends Folcuin and Heriger successively ruled as abbots. Notker also employed ivory-carvers from Metz and Cologne, as well as illuminators, including the Master of the St. George Register, who moved to Liège after the death of Egbert of Trier in 993.

In 954 William, son of the Otto I, became the archbishop of Mainz, and he soon enlisted the talents of the cathedral clergy and the monks of St. Alban's in the cause of the royal dynasty. During this period the so-called *Romano-Germanic Pontifical of the Tenth Century*—a liturgical book stipulating the ceremonial for the rites celebrated by bishops—was compiled. Introduced from Ottonian Germany into Italy, this set of texts and rubrics was adopted by the Roman church by the mid-eleventh century. In addition to liturgical learning, Mainz may also have been the home of the workshop that created the famous imperial crown preserved today in Vienna. Upon his death in 975, William was succeeded by Archbishop Willigis (d. 1011). A remarkable statesman, Willigis also built a new cathedral in Mainz modeled on the church of Fulda and commissioned a number of manuscripts produced by the monks of St. Alban's. After the death of Otto II, it was Willigis who managed to safeguard his young heir from the intrigues of Duke Henry of Bavaria. In 983, he crowned Otto III in Aachen, and then entrusted the prince to one of his own followers, the cleric Bernward.

A firm friendship soon developed between Otto III and Bernward, and in 993 the emperor named his former tutor bishop of Hildesheim. As such, Bernward filled the ideal of the active and learned imperial bishop. He journeyed to across France to St. Riquier, St. Denis, and Tours. After several visits to Rome, where he had occasion to admire Trajan's Column, Bernward commissioned a smaller-sized column in cast bronze to adorn his own episcopal town. His smiths and sculptors also executed a set of impressive bronze doors for the abbey of St. Michael, which he founded in Hildesheim at the turn of the eleventh century.

The church of St. Michael's was without doubt the greatest masterpiece of Ottonian architecture. To be sure, Saxony already possessed a number of great imperial monuments. Otto I had built a vast cathedral at Magdeburg, importing antique columns and capitals to decorate it from Rome and Ravenna. Gero, duke of the Sorbian March, had also erected the church of St. Cyriakus at Gernrode, which still stands today. Yet the undertaking of Bernward far exceeded these earlier efforts by its size and graceful proportions.

Among the beautiful manuscripts executed for Bernward, the cathedral treasury at Hildesheim still possesses a *Liber mathematicus* copied from the Bamberg *De arithmetica* of Boethius. A Carolingian copy of Vitruvius' treatise on architecture has also been found that bears the signature of Gauderamnus, the first abbot of St. Michael's. Significantly, the elevation of the transepts of the abbey church and the proportions of its paired east and west apses demonstrate a precise application of the geometrical principles outlined in such works. Thus, this magnificent building was scarcely the product of the "darkness" that some suppose to have overtaken Europe at the turn of the millennium.

ITALY AND ENGLAND

As in the past, Italy contributed to the intellectual and artistic renewal of the west. Novara, Verona, and Cremona still had active schools, and Otto I tapped them as a source of scholars and teachers for the north. Bishops Ratherius of Verona and Liutprand of Cremona were close friends of the emperor. Meanwhile, Italian abbeys with especially rich libraries were entrusted to choice scholars from the north. Thus Gerbert received Bobbio from Otto II in 982, and John Philagathos, teacher of Greek to Otto III, later received Nonantola. Similarly, Reichenau maintained artistic connections with active Italian centers such as Milan, where ivory carvings were produced akin to those executed in the north.

The city of Rome also experienced a renewal. Quarters of the city which had lain abandoned were reclaimed, and new mills were built along the Tiber. Both phenomena betoken a rise in the city's population. The Vatican quarter, compassed by the *Civitas leonina* of Pope Leo IV, welcomed numerous travelers and pilgrims, who found accommodation in special national hostels, or *scholae*, founded to receive pilgrims from the various lands of the north. Sigeric, an archbishop of Canterbury who visited Rome in 990, compiled a list of the twenty-two churches he visited during his Roman sojourn. The monasteries at St. Paul-outside-the-Walls and on the Aventine Hill were restored and reformed by monks whom Alberic the Younger summoned from Cluny. At the end of the tenth century, the monastery of St. Boniface and Alexis was also founded on the Aventine and placed under the direction of Leo, papal legate to France in 991, and was later headed by John Canaparius. When in Rome, Adalbert of Prague stayed in this monastery, and it was there that he met Otto III. This emperor also provided for the construction of a church on the Tiber Island after his death. Of this church, subsequently St. Bartholomew-on-the-Island, there remain today several reused antique columns and the sculpted footing of a well on which Otto III is portrayed in the company of bishops. It was long believed that Otto had also built a palace for himself on the Aventine, but it was in fact the Palatine Hill that he chose for his residence and there reconstructed the palace of Augustus. Nearby stood St. Sebastian's, a church founded by a certain Peter the Physician about 977 and also chosen as the locale of a synod convened by Otto III and Pope Sylvester II in 1001; fragments of its painted decoration still remain. Though Otto III aspired to make Rome his capital, the plan was thwarted by his death in 1002.

To conclude this overview of the renaissance of the tenth century, England demands brief attention. Although it lay outside the Carolingian world, its religious and cultural history were closely linked to that of the continent. At the end of the ninth century, Alfred the Great, once a visitor at the court of Charles the Bald, worked to make his own court a focus of culture after the Carolingian example he had admired. He attracted young nobles and insisted that they receive at least a rudimentary education. Conscious of the decline of Latin culture, Alfred himself translated and also commissioned others to translate a number of classic works of literature into Anglo-Saxon: the *Dialogues* and *Rule of Pastoral Care* of Gregory the Great; the great historical works of Orosius and Bede; excerpts from Augustine; and above all the *Consolation of Philosophy* of Boethius. Alfred's grandson Ethelstan, king of Wessex (924–939), was in his time the most prestigious ruler in the west. He was connected by marriage to the kings of both western Francia and Germany. A collector of relics and manuscripts, Ethelstan also distributed books to various churches and inaugurated a movement of monastic reform in England. This reform was prosecuted by Edgar the Pacific, the "august emperor of all Albany," as he styled himself. Edgar enlisted support for this effort from three great reformers: Dunstan of Canterbury, Oswald of Worcester, and Ethelwold of Winchester. After spending time at Ghent on the continent, Dunstan encouraged religious and musical studies and sponsored the work of insular scribes and illuminators. Oswald lived for a time at the abbey of Fleury, and after his return home, he retained schoolmen from France to help renew life in monasteries across England. According to Oswald's biographer, "the liberal arts, which had wallowed in oblivion, flowered everywhere." Ethelwold also took inspiration from the monastic usages of Fleury, and he arranged for monks from Corbie to come teach chant. In 963, he was named bishop of Winchester, the seat of the royal court. Anglo-Saxon kings and bishops also encouraged the educated lay nobility to protect the monastic centers. In 970, Edgar presided over the synod that promulgated Dunstan's *Concordance of Monastic Rules* as a guide for observance in all monasteries. Further testimony of the cultural flowering in England comes from the richly illuminated manuscripts executed by the so-called Winchester school. While some recall the style of Ottonian productions, many others were based on Carolingian models. Brought to southern England at the end of the tenth century, the artful sketches of the *Utrecht Psalter* prompted a number of faithful imitators.

Conclusion

About the year 1000, Europe took on a new visage. A large part of the west including France, Italy, and Burgundy underwent what has been called a "feudal transformation." The great princedoms of the late Carolingian period disintegrated into local dominions. Alongside the old nobility whose credentials, according to Adalbero of Laon, "came from their royal blood," there arose a new aristocracy of counts and viscounts who took over political power. These men installed their own vassals in citadels and came to exercise the formerly royal *bannum* within the territories they controlled. The court of the count became a feudal court, and the *pagi* established by the Carolingians were subdivided into smaller political units. On immunist abbatial lands, the lay advocates who formerly helped to run the monastic government gradually assumed full control. Meanwhile, bishops commonly assumed the public powers formerly exercised by the local count. The system of vassalage known in the Carolingian period also developed from a nexus of personal ties and alliances into a system of benefice-holding in return for "advice and support." Receiving land or a castle became the hallmark of becoming a lord's man. Finally, along with new local dynasties there began to appear a class of "knights"; these were the warriors and robbers who opposed the "peace of God" that the bishops of southern France sought to introduce at the end of the first millennium.

Of course, the disintegration of public authority occurred differently in different locales. In Flanders, Normandy, and Catalonia, the traditional nobility kept the reins of public power. In the German kingdom, the Carolingian order largely resisted "feudalization." Yet there as well new groups of aristocrats emerged alongside the old nobility. The Carolingian world thus evolved into the Europe of the first period of feudalism.

It was, however, *Europe* that was developing: a fold of territories whose people had become conscious of their common attributes and aspirations, not merely the geographic area formerly distinguished from Africa and Asia. Charlemagne had been called the "father of Europe" and the "beacon of Europe"; his grandson Charles the Bald, the "prince of

Europe"; and Pope John VIII, the "governor (*rector*) of Europe." Such expressions and many others like them betokened a change in understanding. Thus, Otto I was the "emperor of all Europe," and his grandson Otto III was a ruler "called king not only by the people of Rome, but also by all the peoples of Europe." It was "Europe severed of its head" that lamented the death of Henry II at the beginning of the eleventh century. This was a Europe not yet subdivided into regional blocks, each coming to possess a distinct national consciousness. There was no France, no Germany, no Italy in our sense, but rather a common fold of peoples. To be sure, each population had its language, its "character," its sympathies and antipathies, but these had been marshaled into the service of common goals and thereby overridden thanks to the leadership of kings and the influence of the church. The Carolingian kings and their successors had cooperated with the church to invent a new idea of the state founded on the binding power of the Christian religion.

The Europe that emerged was the Europe of the Latin Church, or as contemporaries called it, the Europe of "Christendom" (*christianitas*). All the lands that the Carolingians converted by choice or by force to Christianity became part of this Christendom, but it also included the Kingdom of the Asturias, England, and Ireland. These lands lay outside the political orbit of the Frankish rulers. Yet the quarrel over the Adoptionist heresy born at Toledo drew together the rulers of Oviedo and Aachen. Alfonso III, the Great (866–910), also resembled the Carolingian kings in his love of learning and by his taste for beautiful manuscripts. After his victories over the Muslims, he even adopted the title of "emperor" and commissioned a golden crown executed in the monastic workshops at St. Martin of Tours. The Christian communities in Muslim Spain remained in regular contact with the Christians of the Carolingian world until the tenth century. It was, in fact, to the Spaniard Recemund, bishop of Elvira (Granada), that Liutprand of Cremona dedicated his *Deeds of the Kings and Princes of Europe*, better known as the *Antapodosis*. Likewise, the learned Irish monks who settled on the Continent in the ninth and tenth centuries created links between their island home, northern France, and Lotharingia. There was of course an ongoing relationship with the rulers of England from the time of Charlemagne. During the tenth-century renewal of the English church, ties to the Continent played an important role. Finally, the new peoples converted in the tenth century thanks to the efforts of the Ottonians and the papacy also became part of Christendom: the Danes, the Magyars, and the Poles.

The religious map of Europe had taken on more or less definitive shape. While Byzantine influence penetrated into the Balkans and Kievan Russia, the Latin Church blocked its progress to the west. Byzantium itself responded to the challenges posed by Islam on the one hand and the "barbarians" of the west on the other with increasingly inflexible Greek patriotism. The old empire chafed at the emergence of a new one in the west. Moreover, these new emperors posed an additional threat to the remaining Byzantine outposts in southern Italy.

Though defined by religion, Europe was also a community of scholars who read and wrote the same Latin language and who also rescued a great part of the legacy of antiquity from irretrievable loss. In the ninth and tenth centuries, schoolmasters devised a new curriculum of studies based in part on the classics that they had rediscovered. In doing so, they laid the foundations of educational practices for centuries. Whatever its benefits or disadvantages, western education would long remain dominated by grammar, rhetoric and a taste for poetry. From Alcuin to Gerbert, scholars sponsored by political leaders also composed a host of new works that actually built on the achievements of antiquity.

Europe was also an assemblage of monuments and artworks that would continue to inspire the imaginations of the second millennium. After the year 1000, illuminated manuscripts continued to amaze and influence artists. The new canon of architectural forms was maintained, for instance the *Westwerke* recurring in Norman architecture and carried over into the west fronts of later medieval cathedrals as well, as the doubled east/west apses still seen on many later churches in the lands of Lotharingia and the Rhine basin.

The heritage of the Carolingian period was institutional as well. The hierarchical structure of the church had emerged restored and reinforced. The papacy itself had received new temporal power from the Carolingians, and also gained a reserve of new principles that it could later apply to free itself from lay tutelage. The exemption that the popes accorded to monasteries facilitated the monastic reform that began in the time of Benedict of Aniane and was continued by Cluny. For their part, the kings and emperors did not easily relinquish the authority that Charlemagne had gained over the church. Here lay the root of the great struggles between popes and emperors in the eleventh and twelfth centuries. The Carolingians and Ottonians had provided many useful precedents for emperors who aspired to dominate the pope. The canonization of Charlemagne ordered by Frederick Barbarossa in 1165 was accordingly both a pious gesture and a calculated political move.

The first Capetian kings erected their royal office on the foundations of the Carolingians. They organized their court on the now traditional model. They requested that the archbishop of Reims anoint them as kings, and they turned to clerics in their royal chancery for guidance and support. Their coronation oath derived directly from the promises made by Frankish kings since the end of the ninth century. The Carolingian notion of the "royal ministry" also remained intact. The king worthy of his office had a duty to ensure the reign of justice and peace. He had to accept the aid and counsel of the bishops and the great laymen of the kingdom. As ultimate suzerains, the Capetians would ably use their judicial prerogatives to recapture genuine royal authority and power.

Throughout the Middle Ages, secular leaders across the west constantly sought to associate their persons and their achievements to the Carolingians. Moreover, this illustrious family had produced so many descendants spread across Europe that the claim to be their offspring could well be true. But pretense far outweighed genuine connections. Every leader was proud to trace his descent from some great Carolingian hero lauded in epic poetry. In this, fantasy and mythology were equally part of the Carolingian legacy.

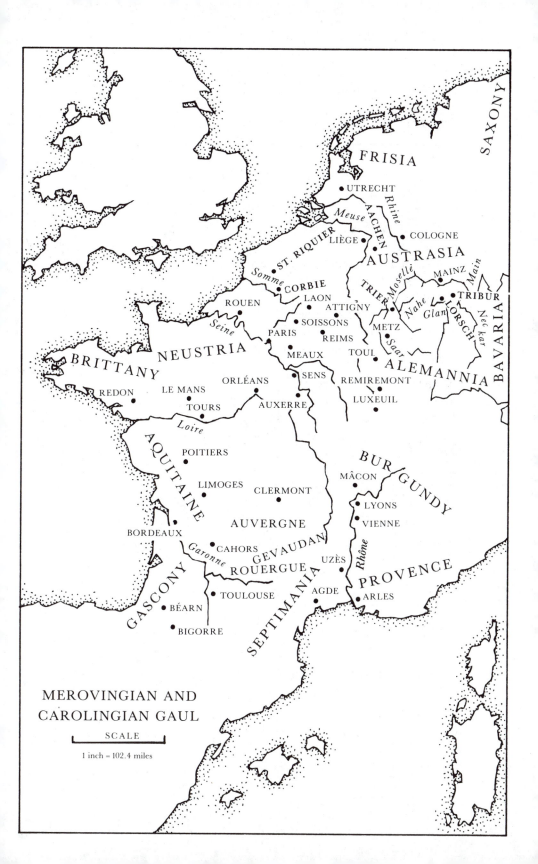

MEROVINGIAN AND
CAROLINGIAN GAUL

SCALE

1 inch = 102.4 miles

Genealogical Tables

Abbreviations used in the tables:

a. after	d. died in
archbp. archbishop	dau. daughter
b. before	emp. emperor
bp. bishop	k. king
c. count	m. married to
c. circa	marq. marquis
cf. compare with	T. Table
cont. continued in	

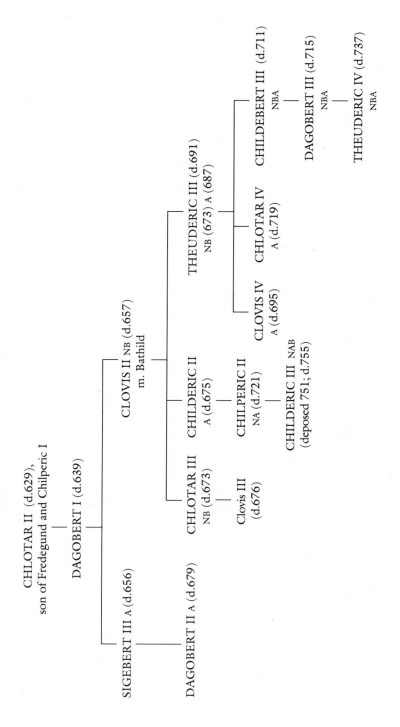

Table 1. The late Merovingians. Key: A = Austrasia; B = Burgundy; N = Neustria.

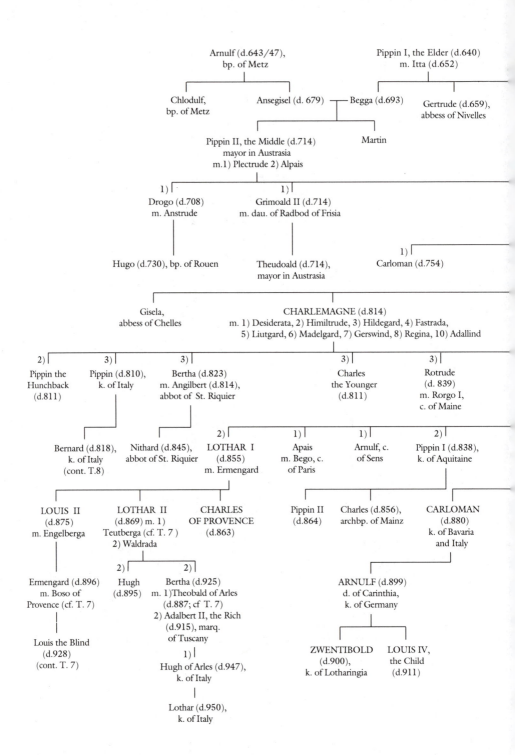

Table 2. The Carolingians. Compiled by Michael Idomir Allen

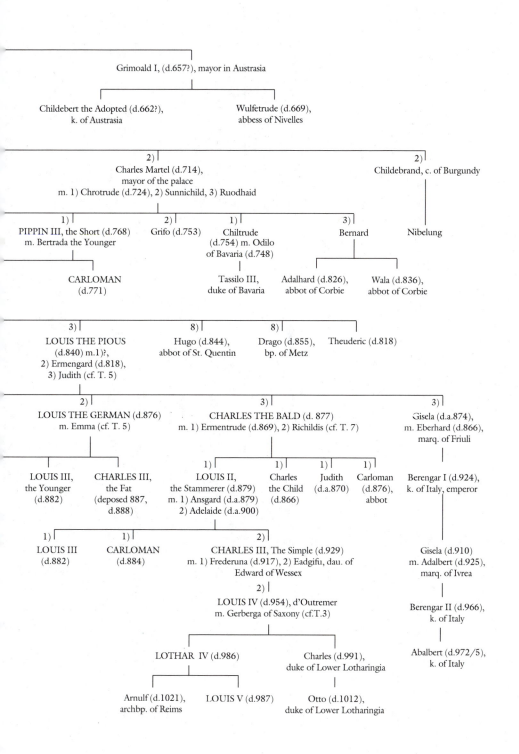

Grimoald I, (d.657?), mayor in Austrasia

Childebert the Adopted (d.662?),
k. of Austrasia

Wulfetrude (d.669),
abbess of Nivelles

2)
Charles Martel (d.714),
mayor of the palace
m. 1) Chrotrude (d.724), 2) Sunnichild, 3) Ruodhaid

2)
Childebrand, c. of Burgundy

1)
PIPPIN III, the Short (d.768)
m. Bertrada the Younger

2) Grifo (d.753)

1)
Chiltrude
(d.754) m. Odilo
of Bavaria (d.748)

3)
Bernard

Nibelung

CARLOMAN
(d.771)

Tassilo III,
duke of Bavaria

Adalhard (d.826),
abbot of Corbie

Wala (d.836),
abbot of Corbie

3)
LOUIS THE PIOUS
(d.840) m.1)?,
2) Ermengard (d.818),
3) Judith (cf. T. 5)

8)
Hugo (d.844),
abbot of St. Quentin

8)
Drago (d.855),
bp. of Metz

Theuderic (d.818)

2)
LOUIS THE GERMAN (d.876)
m. Emma (cf. T. 5)

3)
CHARLES THE BALD (d. 877)
m. 1) Ermentrude (d.869), 2) Richildis (cf. T. 7)

3)
Gisela (d.a.874),
m. Eberhard (d.866),
marq. of Friuli

LOUIS III,
the Younger
(d.882)

CHARLES III,
the Fat
(deposed 887,
d.888)

1)
LOUIS II,
the Stammerer (d.879)
m. 1) Ansgard (d.a.879)
2) Adelaide (d.a.900)

1)
Charles
the Child
(d.866)

1)
Judith
(d.a.870)

1)
Carloman
(d.876),
abbot

Berengar I (d.924),
k. of Italy, emperor

1)
LOUIS III
(d.882)

1)
CARLOMAN
(d.884)

2)
CHARLES III, The Simple (d.929)
m. 1) Frederuna (d.917), 2) Eadgifu, dau. of
Edward of Wessex

Gisela (d.910)
m. Adalbert (d.925),
marq. of Ivrea

2)
LOUIS IV (d.954), d'Outremer
m. Gerberga of Saxony (cf.T.3)

Berengar II (d.966),
k. of Italy

LOTHAR IV (d.986)

Charles (d.991),
duke of Lower Lotharingia

Abalbert (d.972/5),
k. of Italy

Arnulf (d.1021),
archbp. of Reims

LOUIS V (d.987)

Otto (d.1012),
duke of Lower Lotharingia

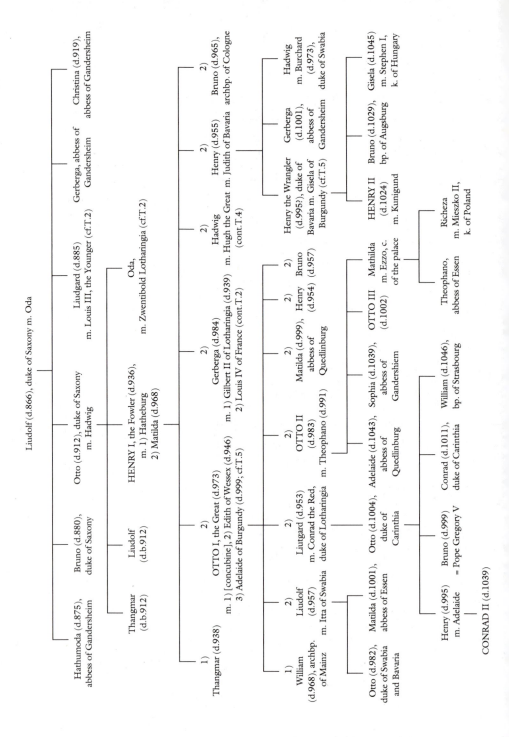

Table 3. The Liudolfings and the Ottonians. Compiled by Michael Idomir Allen.

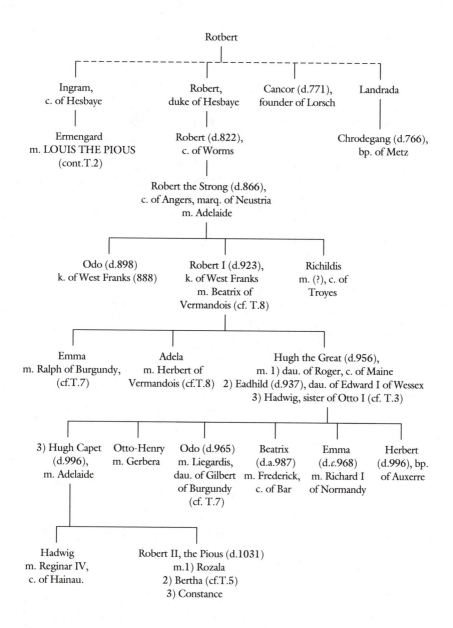

Table 4. The Robertines

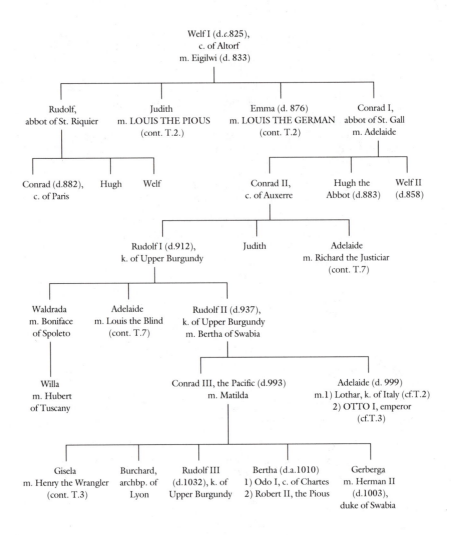

Welf I (d.*c*.825),
c. of Altorf
m. Eigilwi (d. 833)

Rudolf,
abbot of St. Riquier

Judith
m. LOUIS THE PIOUS
(cont. T.2.)

Emma (d. 876)
m. LOUIS THE GERMAN
(cont. T.2)

Conrad I,
abbot of St. Gall
m. Adelaide

Conrad (d.882),
c. of Paris

Hugh

Welf

Conrad II,
c. of Auxerre

Hugh the
Abbot (d.883)

Welf II
(d.858)

Rudolf I (d.912),
k. of Upper Burgundy

Judith

Adelaide
m. Richard the Justiciar
(cont. T.7)

Waldrada
m. Boniface
of Spoleto

Adelaide
m. Louis the Blind
(cont. T.7)

Rudolf II (d.937),
k. of Upper Burgundy
m. Bertha of Swabia

Willa
m. Hubert
of Tuscany

Conrad III, the Pacific (d.993)
m. Matilda

Adelaide (d. 999)
m.1) Lothar, k. of Italy (cf.T.2)
2) OTTO I, emperor
(cf.T.3)

Gisela
m. Henry the Wrangler
(cont. T.3)

Burchard,
archbp. of
Lyon

Rudolf III
(d.1032), k. of
Upper Burgundy

Bertha (d.a.1010)
1) Odo I, c. of Chartres
2) Robert II, the Pious

Gerberga
m. Herman II
(d.1003),
duke of Swabia

Table 5. The Welfs

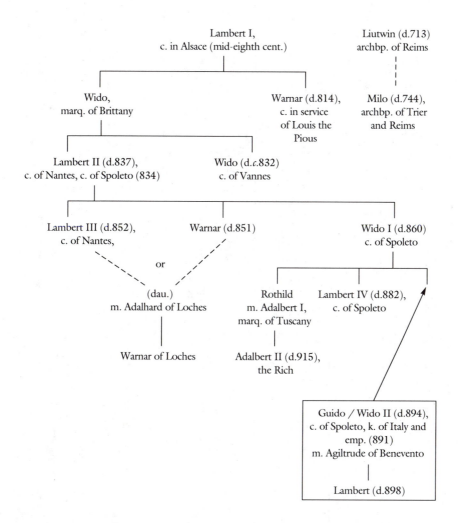

Table 6. The Lambertines/Widonids

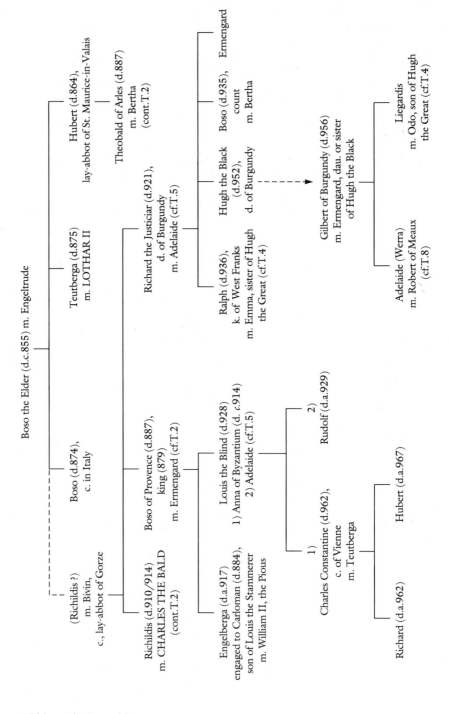

Table 7. The Bosonids

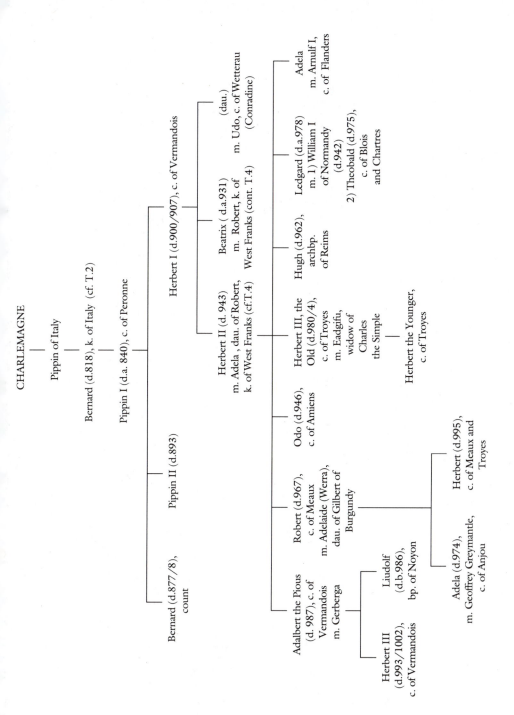

CHARLEMAGNE
|
Pippin of Italy
|
Bernard (d.818), k. of Italy (cf. T.2)
|
Pippin I (d.a. 840), c. of Peronne

Bernard (d.877/8), count

Pippin II (d.893)

Herbert I (d.900/907), c. of Vermandois

Herbert II (d. 943)
m. Adela, dau. of Robert,
k. of West Franks (cf.T.4)

Beatrix (d.a.931)
m. Robert, k. of
West Franks (cont. T.4)

(dau.)
m. Udo, c. of Wetterau
(Conradine)

Odo (d.946),
c. of Amiens

Robert (d.967),
c. of Meaux
m. Adelaide (Werra),
dau. of Gilbert of
Burgundy

Herbert III, the
Old (d.980/4),
c. of Troyes
m. Eadgifu,
widow of
Charles
the Simple

Hugh (d.962),
archbp.
of Reims

Ledgard (d.a.978)
m. 1) William I
of Normandy
(d.942)
2) Theobald (d.975),
c. of Blois
and Chartres

Adela
m. Arnulf I,
c. of Flanders

Herbert the Younger,
c. of Troyes

Adalbert the Pious
(d. 987), c. of
Vermandois
m. Gerberga

Liudolf
(d.b.986),
bp. of Noyon

Herbert III
(d.993/1002),
c. of Vermandois

Adela (d.974),
m. Geoffrey Greymantle,
c. of Anjou

Herbert (d.995),
c. of Meaux and
Troyes

Table 8. The House of Vermandois (Herbertines)

Suggested Works for Further Reading

Boussard, Jacques. *The Civilization of Charlemagne*. Translated by Frances Partridge. New York: McGraw-Hill, 1968.

Bullough, Donald. *The Age of Charlemagne*. 1965. 2d ed. London: Elek Books, 1973.

———. *Carolingian Renewal: Sources and Heritage*. Manchester and New York: Manchester University Press, 1991.

———. *"Europae Pater*: Charlemagne and His Achievement in the Light of Recent Scholarship." *English Historical Review* 75 (1970):59–105.

Campbell, Joseph. *The Anglo-Saxons*. Ithaca, NY: Cornell University Press, 1982.

Collins, Roger. *Early Medieval Spain: Unity in Diversity, 400–1000*. New York: St. Martin's Press, 1983.

Conant, Kenneth John. *Carolingian and Romanesque Architecture: 800 to 1200*. 4th ed. Harmondsworth and New York: Penguin, 1978.

Contreni, John Joseph. *The Cathedral School of Laon from 850 to 930: Its Manuscripts and Masters*. Munich: Bei der Arbeo-Gesellschaft, 1978.

Dawson, Christopher Henry. *The Making of Europe: An Introduction to the History of European Unity*. 1932. Reprint. New York: World Publishers, 1956.

Duby, Georges. *The Early Growth of the European Economy: Warriors and Peasants from the Seventh to to the Twelfth Century*. Translated by Howard B. Clarke. London: Weidenfeld and Nicholson, 1974.

Duckett, Eleanor Shipley. *Alcuin, Friend of Charlemagne: His World and His Work*. 1951. Reprint, with additional preface and bibliography. Hamden, CT: Archon Books, 1965.

———. *Carolingian Portraits: A Study in the Ninth Century*. 1962. Reprint. Ann Arbor: University of Michigan Press, 1988.

Dvornik, Francis. *The Slavs in European History and Civilization*. New Brunswick, NJ: Rutgers University Press, 1962.

Fichtenau, Heinrich. *The Carolingian Empire*. Translated by Peter Munz. 1957. Reprint. Medieval Academy Reprints for Teaching. Toronto: University of Toronto Press, 1979.

———. *Living in the Tenth Century: Mentalities and Social Orders*. Chicago: University of Chicago Press, 1991.

Fleckenstein, Josef. *Early Medieval Germany*. Translated by Bernard S. Smith. Amsterdam and New York: North-Holland, 1978.

Folz, Robert. *The Coronation of Charlemagne, 25 December 800*. Translated by J. E. Anderson. London: Routledge and Kegan Paul, 1974.

Ganshof, François Louis. *The Carolingians and the Frankish Monarchy: Studies in Carolingian History*. Translated by Janet Sondheimer. Ithaca, NY: Cornell University Press, 1971.

———. *Frankish Institutions Under Charlemagne*. Translated by Bryce and Mary Lyon. 1968. Reprint. Ann Arbor, MI: UMI Books, 1991.

Gibson, Margaret T., and Janet L. Nelson, eds. *Charles the Bald: Court and Kingdom*. 2d ed. Aldershot, Hampshire: Variorum, 1990.

Godman, Peter. *Poetry of the Carolingian Renaissance*. Norman: University of Oklahoma Press, 1985.

Godman, Peter, and Roger Collins, eds. *Charlemagne's Heir: New Perspectives on the Reign of Louis the Pious (814–840)*. Oxford: Clarendon Press, 1990.

Grierson, Philip, and Mark Blackburn. *The Early Middles Ages*. Vol. 1 of *Medieval European Coinage: With a Catalogue of the Coins in the Fitzwilliam Museum, Cambridge*. Cambridge: Cambridge University Press, 1986.

Halphen, Louis. *Charlemagne and the Carolingian Empire*. Translated by Giselle de Nie. Amsterdam and New York: North-Holland, 1977.

Herlihy, David, ed. *The History of Feudalism*. 1970. Reprint. Englewood Cliffs, NJ: Prentice-Hall, 1979.

Herrin, Judith. *The Formation of Christendom*. Princeton, NJ: Princeton University Press, 1987.

Hildebrandt, M. M. *The External School in Carolingian Society*. Leiden and New York: E. J. Brill, 1992.

Hinks, Roger P. *Carolingian Art: A Study of Early Medieval Painting and Sculpture in Western Europe*. 1935. Reprint. Ann Arbor: University of Michigan Press, 1962.

Hodges, Richard. *Dark Age Economics: the Origins of Towns and Trade, A.D. 600–1000*. New York: St. Martin's Press, 1982.

Hubert, Jean, Jean Porcher, and Wolfgang Friedrich Volbach. *The Carolingian Renaissance*. Translated by James Enamons, Stuart Gilbert, and Robert Allen. New York: Braziller, 1970.

James, Edward. *The Franks*. Oxford: B. Blackwell, 1988.

———. *The Origins of France: From Clovis to the Capetians, 500–1000*. New York: St. Martin's Press, 1982.

King, P. D. *Charlemagne: Translated Sources*. Lambrigg, Kendal, Cumbria: P. D. King, 1987. (In the present edition, this excellent set of translated sources is published and distributed privately by Dr. P. D. King, Moresdale Hall, Lambrigg, Kendal, Cumbria LA8 0DH, England.)

———. *Charlemagne*. Lancaster Pamphlets. London: Methuen, 1986.

Krautheimer, Richard. *Rome: Profile of a City, 312–1308*. Princeton, NJ: Princeton University Press, 1980.

———. *Three Christian Capitals: Topography and Politics*. Berkeley: University of California Press, 1983.

Laistner, Max Ludwig Wolfram. *Thought and Letters in Western Europe, A.D. 500 to 900*. Revised ed. Ithaca, NY: Cornell University Press, 1957.

Latouche, Robert. *The Birth of Western Economy: Economic Aspects of the Dark Ages*. 1961. 2d ed. 1967. Reprint. London: Methuen, 1981.

Levison, Wilhelm. *England and the Continent in the Eighth Century*. Oxford, 1946. 2d ed. Oxford: Clarendon Press, 1950.

Leyser, Karl. *Medieval Germany and Its Neighbours, 900–1250*. London: Hambledon, 1982.

Lot, Ferdinand. *The End of the Ancient World and the Beginnings of the Middle Ages*. Translated by Philip and Marion Leon. 1931. Reprint. New York; Harper, 1961.

Loyn, Henry Royston, and John Percival, trans. *The Reign of Charlemagne: Documents on Carolingian Government and Administration*. 1975. New York: St. Martin's Press, 1976.

Marenbon, John. *From the Circle of Alcuin to the School of Auxerre: Logic, Theology and Philosophy in the Early Middle Ages*. Cambridge: Cambridge University Press, 1981.

McKitterick, Rosamond. *The Carolingians and the Written Word*. Cambridge: Cambridge University Press, 1989.

———. *The Frankish Church and the Carolingian Reforms, 789–895*. London: Royal Historical Society, 1977.

———. *The Frankish Kingdoms Under the Carolingians, 751–987*. London: Longman, 1983.

Nees, Lawrence. *A Tainted Mantle: Hercules and the Classical Tradition at the Carolingian Court*. Philadelphia: University of Pennsylvania Press, 1991.

Nelson, Janet L. *Politics and Ritual in Early Medieval Europe*. London: Hambledon, 1986.

Noble, Thomas F. X. *The Republic of St. Peter: The Birth of the Papal State, 680–825*. Philadelphia: University of Pennsylvania Press, 1984.

Partner, Peter. *The Lands of St. Peter: The Papal State in the Middles Ages and the Early Renaissance*. Berkley: University of California Press, 1972.

Pirenne, Henri. *From the End of the Roman World in the West to the Beginnings of Western States*. Vol. 1 of *A History of Europe*. 1939. Reprint, with an introduction by Jan-Albert Goris. Garden City, NY: Doubleday, 1958.

Reuter, Timothy, ed. *The Medieval Nobility: Studies on the Ruling Classes of France and Germany from the Sixth to the Twelfth Century*. Amsterdam and New York: North-Holland, 1978.

Riché, Pierre. *Daily Life in the World of Charlemagne*. 1973. Translated by Jo Ann McNamara. Philadelphia: University of Pennsylvania Press, 1978, revised 1989.

———. *Education and Culture in the Barbarian West, Sixth Through Eighth Centuries*. Translated by John J. Contreni. Columbia: University of South Carolina Press, 1975.

Scholz, Bernhard Walter, with Barbara Rogers, trans. *Carolingian Chronicles:* Royal Frankish Annals and Nithard's Histories. Ann Arbor: University of Michigan Press, 1970.

Smith, Julia M. H. *Province and Empire: Brittany and the Carolingians*. Cambridge: Cambridge University Press, 1992.

Sullivan, Richard E. "The Carolingian Age: Reflections on Its Place in the History of the Middle Ages." *Speculum* 64 (1989):257–306.

———, ed. *The Coronation of Charlemagne: What Did It Signify?* 1959. Reprint. Boston: Heath, 1965.

Thorpe, Lewis G. M. *Two Lives of Charlemagne: Einhard and Notker the Stammerer.* Baltimore: Penguin, 1969.

Ullmann, Walter. *The Carolingian Renaissance and the Idea of Kingship.* London: Methuen, 1969.

Wallace-Hadrill, J. M. *A Carolingian Renaissance Prince: The Emperor Charles the Bald.* Raleigh Lecture on History, 1978. London: Longwood, 1980.

———. *Early Germanic Kingship in England and on the Continent.* The Ford Lectures, 1970. 1971. Reprint. London: Oxford University Press, 1980.

———. *Early Medieval History.* Oxford and New York: B. Blackwell, 1975.

———. *The Frankish Church.* Oxford: Clarendon Press, 1983.

Wemple, Suzanne Fonay. *Women in Frankish Society: Marriage and the Cloister, 500–900.* Philadelphia: University of Pennsylvania Press, 1985.

Wickham, Chris. *Early Medieval Italy: Central Power and Local Society, 400–1000.* London: Macmillan, 1981.

Index